The Ideology
of Genre

Also by Thomas O. Beebee
Clarissa on the Continent: Translation and Seduction

The Ideology
of Genre

A Comparative Study of Generic Instability

Thomas O. Beebee

The Pennsylvania State University Press
University Park, Pennsylvania

Excerpts from *Tristes tropiques* by Claude Lévi-Strauss. Copyright © 1955 by Librairie Plon. English translation copyright © 1974. Reprinted by permission of Georges Borchardt, Inc.

Excerpts from *Empire of Signs* by Roland Barthes, translated by Richard Howard. Translation copyright © 1982 by Farrar, Straus & Giroux, Inc. Reprinted by permission of Hill & Wang, a division of Farrar, Straus & Giroux, Inc.

Excerpts from *Mythologies* by Roland Barthes, copyright © 1957 by Editions du Seuil. Reprinted by permission. English translation by Annette Lavers copyright © 1972 by Jonathan Cape Ltd. Reprinted by permission of Hill & Wang, a division of Farrar, Straus & Giroux, Inc.

Excerpts from the following songs by Bob Dylan gratefully acknowledged: "All Along the Watchtower," copyright © 1968 by Dwarf Music; "Dark Eyes," copyright © 1985 by Special Rider Music; "A Hard Rain's A-Gonna Fall," copyright © 1963 by Warner Bros. Inc.; "John Wesley Harding," copyright © 1968 by Dwarf Music; "My Back Pages," copyright © 1964 by Warner Bros. Inc.; "Restless Farewell," copyright © 1964, 1966 by Warner Bros. Music; "Song to Woody," copyright © 1962, 1965 by Duchess Music Corporation; "The Times They Are A-Changin'," copyright © 1963, 1964 by Warner Bros. Inc.; "When He Returns," copyright © 1979 by Special Rider Music. Reprinted by permission.

Excerpts and translations from *Kommt an den Tisch unter Pflaumenbäumen. Alle Lieder von Franz Josef Degenhardt*, copyright © 1979 C. Bertelsmann Verlag GmbH, Munich. Reprinted by permission. All rights to musical performance remain with the author.

Excerpts from *The Name of the Rose* by Umberto Eco, translated by William Weaver, copyright © 1980 by Gruppo editoriale Fabbri-Bompiani, Sonzagno, Etas S.p.A., English translation copyright © 1983 by Harcourt Brace & Company and Martin Secker & Warburg, Ltd., reprinted by permission of Harcourt Brace & Company.

Library of Congress Cataloging-in-Publication Data

Beebee, Thomas O.
      The ideology of genre : a comparative study of generic instability
  / Thomas O. Beebee.
          p.   cm.
      Includes bibliographical references (p.) and index.
      ISBN 0-271-01022-3 (cloth : acid-free paper).
      ISBN 0-271-01023-1 (pbk. : acid-free paper)
      1. Literary form.   2. Literature — Philosophy.   3. Discourse
  analysis.   I. Title.
  PN45.5.B38   1994
  801'.95 — dc20   93-8462   CIP

It is the policy of The Pennsylvania State University Press to use acid-free paper for the first printing of all clothbound books. Publications on uncoated stock satisfy the minimum requirements of American National Standard for Information Sciences — Permanence of Paper for Printed Library Materials, ANSI Z39.48–1984.

Contents

Às tres meninas da minha vida:
Jizelda, Palavina,
Chavaya

Preface

The work that appears in this book was written over a fifteen-year period, from my undergraduate days, when I completed my first comparative paper on Bob Dylan and Franz-Josef Degenhardt, to the writing on Walter Benjamin done at Penn State after I had grown too stubborn, truculent, tenured, and published-and-perishable to be corrected by anyone. Over such a long period, many people have read parts of this work, and have undoubtedly since forgotten them; they may be slightly shocked at coming across their names in these pages, especially grouped as they are with the names of people they have never met. I thank Patsy Baudoin, Lincoln Faller, Christian Wolf, Charles Hamm, Konrad Kenkel, Louis Renza, and Nathaniel Wing for these very early readings of my work and for their encouragement in the discipline of comparative literature.

The book as a whole has had three very sharp-eyed and learned critics: Douglas J. Canfield, Ross Chambers, and James Jellison. It has also had an excellent proofreader, Michelle Meilly, and copyeditor, Andrew Lewis, and a generous sponsor, Philip Winsor. Without the support of a fund created by Melvin and Rosalind Jacobs, I would not have had the time to polish the manuscript. To all of these people I owe a debt of thanks. And a very special thanks to Lisa Ruch, who went out of her way to track down the most puzzling scholarly problem in the book, the source of the mysterious Lonnie Mack quotation that begins Chapter 8, and to Paul Oorts, who helped unravel the mysteries of crabbed Renaissance Latin. To Stuart McDougal and Caroline Eckhardt goes, as always, my gratitude for their sound advice and unwavering support.

Thanks are also due to the editors of journals who have given me permission to reproduce my own earlier material. The embryo of Chapter 4 was first published in the *Rackham Journal of the Arts and Humanities* 2 (1980): 47–71. An earlier version of Chapter 5 appeared in *The International Journal for the Semiotics of Law* 2, no. 5 (1989): 159–82, published by Deborah Charles Publications, and is reprinted here with permission. For the Dylan material in Chapter 6, the Speech Communication Association has kindly allowed me to reuse parts of my article published in *Text and Performance Quarterly* 11 (1991): 18–34. Again, the dates of these articles show what a long-term project this was.

On the other end of the spectrum, I should apologize to my reader both for the somewhat artificial length of this book and for a certain confusion, both caused by my use of original languages; I believe very strongly in quoting all primary material in the original. To shorten the book somewhat and to make things easier on the reader, I have provided only English for all "secondary" material. I am not completely satisfied with this procedure, resting as it does on a generic distinction. Sure enough, the distinction is unstable; the line between primary and secondary was in many cases an arbitrary decision. Where not otherwise acknowledged, translations are my own.

1

Introduction:
Why Genre?

"Ohne Absonderung findet keine Bildung statt, und Bildung ist das Wesen der Kunst. . . . Das Wesentlichste sind die bestimmten Zwecke, die Absonderung, wodurch allein das Kunstwerk Umriß erhält und in sich selbst vollendet wird. Die Phantasie des Dichters soll sich nicht in eine chaotische Überhauptpoesie ergießen, sondern jedes Werk soll der Form und der Gattung nach einen durchaus bestimmten Charakter haben.

(Without division, creation does not take place; and creation is the quintessence of art. . . . Of most importance are the definite purpose and the separation through which alone the work of art receives form and becomes complete in itself. The imagination of the poet should not spend itself in a chaotic generalization of poetry, but each work should have a thoroughly definite character according to form and genre.)
    —Friedrich Schlegel, *Gespräch über die Poesie*

IN HIS *GESPRÄCH ÜBER DIE POESIE* ("Dialogue on Poetry"), the German romantic critic and philosopher Friedrich Schlegel allows a certain

Markus to defend the concept of literary genre and the legitimacy of its
study against one Amalia, who feels that categorization in whatever form
kills the spirit and the imagination: "Mich schaudert's immer, wenn ich
ein Buch aufschlage, wo die Phantasie und ihre Werke rubrikenweise
klassifiziert werden" ("I shudder whenever I open a book where the
imagination and its works are classified under rubrics").[1] But this is after
all a dialogue, a fragment. No one has the last word. And like the ghosts
of Paolo and Francesca, whirled around by the noxious gases of critical
discourse, the spirits of Markus and Amalia have haunted every debate on
genre theory down to the present day; representing the two poles of
necessity and freedom, they struggle for mastery in every work and in
every act of reading.

Their dialogue is situated on the divide between ancient and modern
approaches to genre. Like Markus, the ancients saw generic boundaries as
necessary for poetic production. A good example is Horace, who wrote his
Ars poetica in the form of a letter of advice to a literary family. Genre in
Horace is a subtopic of *to prepon* or *decorum,* of the ability to find what is
fitting:

> Descriptas servare vices operumque colores
> cur ego si nequeo ignoroque, poeta salutor?
> Cur nescire pudens prave quam discere malo?
> Versibus exponi tragicis res comica non vult;
> indignatur item privatis ac prope socco
> dignis carminibus narrari cena Thyestae.

> (If in producing my work I cannot observe [and don't know] the
> required genres and styles, why am I hailed as "Poet?" Why prefer
> wanton ignorance to learning? Comic material resists presentation
> in tragic verse. Likewise the "Feast of Thyestes" resents poetry
> that is conversation and worthy almost of the comic sock.)[2]

This production-oriented view of genre continued through the Renaissance, during which "literary invention . . . was largely generic, and [the]

---

1. Friedrich Schlegel, "Gespräch über die Poesie," 304; translated by Ernst Behler and
Roman Struč, under the title "Dialogue on Poetry," 76. The epigraph to this chapter is taken
from Schlegel, "Gespräch," 305–6; Behler and Struč, trans., "Dialogue," 77. [Works of general
theoretical interest in the field of genre studies are cited in full in the Bibliography—AUTHOR.]

2. Horace, "Epistula ad Pisones," lines 86–91; translated by Ross S. Kilpatrick, in *The Poetry
of Criticism* (Calgary: University of Alberta Press, 1990), 74.

transfer of ancient values was largely in generic terms, accomplished by generic instruments and helps."³

Amalia, however, is a modern. She sees all attempts at defining genre as coming from *outside*. Later thinkers such as Ferdinand Brunetière constructed a phylogeny of genres, hoping to trace and classify the growth and hybridization of texts.⁴ In reaction, the formalists of the early twentieth century became intent on isolating specific textual features that determine the genre of a work containing them. By contrast, the postwar theoretical discourses of structuralism and reader-response criticism declare that readers and their conventions assign genres to texts, which makes it impossible for adherents of these schools to speak of genre as any kind of permanent or transcendental construct. These four stages of generic criticism—genre as rules, genre as species, genre as patterns of textual features, and genre as reader conventions—correspond to the four positions in the great debate about the location of textual meaning: in authorial intention, in the work's historical or literary context, in the text itself, or in the reader.⁵ But how does the law of genre operate today? Let us look at some examples.

I

The ideology of genre is all around us. On a recent research trip to the local supermarket I paused in front of the "Reading Center." There stood all the garishly multicolored books, hundreds of titles, in a handful of categories. There were of course the romances, with names like *Cajun Kiss, Tame the Fury, Sweet Savage Love, Sweet Texas Promise,* and so on. Like "sweet," the word or concept of fire appears quite often, as in *Forbidden Fires, Fires of Surrender, The Flame and the Flower,* and *Embers of the Heart.* Need I describe the covers? A half-naked man and a half-naked woman in some sort of embrace, with a castle or cypress tree or clipper ship or mountain range in the background, perhaps a sword covering the pudenda, everything in pastels and earth tones. The genre of modern romance can actually be subdivided, because the Harlequins are a bit different. Whereas

3. Rosalie L. Colie, *The Resources of Kind: Genre-Theory in the Renaissance,* 17.
4. The title of J. M. Manly's 1904 article, "Literary Form and the Origin of Species," is an almost absurd evocation of this approach. Manly applies evolutionary thought in a very direct way when he characterizes medieval drama as a "mutation" from another species of literature. See also Charles Letourneau's "Origins of Literary Forms," which relates the evolution of genres to the evolution of human societies.
5. As a supplement to this telescoped history of genre theory I recommend Heather Dubrow's *Genre* and Klaus Hempfer's *Gattungstheorie: Information und Synthese.*

the romances just described are basically for married or older women
trying to escape humdrum reality, Harlequins target younger women
trying to learn where they can locate their desires within that reality.
Younger, more fully clothed men and women, who are not always embrac-
ing, grace these covers. They are depicted in undeniably middle-class,
unexotic surroundings—golf courses, shopping malls—and under titles
that do not evoke passion as much as they attempt to invoke rules of
conduct: *A Matter of Principle, Jester's Girl, Scout's Honor, Capture the Rainbow,*
each a proverb and guide to behavior.[6]

Many students of the modern popular romance insist that the genre
reinforces patriarchy by showing women as living in order to be desired
by men. Janice Radway took a different tack by actually asking women to
explain why in fact they read romances and to identify features they like
and don't like. She discovered a defining feature of the genre: The romance
is *"compensatory literature.* It supplies [its female readers] with an important
emotional release that is proscribed in daily life because the social role
with which they identify themselves leaves little room for guiltless, self-
interested pursuit of individual pleasure. Indeed, the search for emotional
gratification was the one theme common to all of the women's observations
about the function of romance reading."[7] In other words, the contemporary
genre of romance may be a response to the fact that American women are
not provided with nurturers the way men are. Men and children, emotion-
ally pampered beings that they are, develop different desires, and hence
they enjoy different genres.

Radway's genre analysis proceeds from this point. After noting the
particular use-value that romance has for its readers, she identifies those
romances which best provide that use-value and from them constructs an
ideal plotline:

> Instead of attempting to assemble an "objective," "representative"
> sample of the romance, I have relied on [my interviewees'] tenden-
> cies to separate their books into the categories of the "good" and
> the "bad." I have therefore departed from the usual procedure of
> focusing attention on a particular publisher's line or on a narrative
> subgenre, because virtually all of the . . . women read more than

6. Nowadays even Harlequin is further reticulated into several different series, with "Temptation" and "Silhouette" offering more explicit sex and featuring women characters who work after
marriage. For an analysis specifically of the Harlequins, see Tania Modleski, *Loving with a
Vengeance: Mass-Produced Fantasies for Women* (Hamden, Conn.: Archon, 1982).

7. Janice Radway, *Reading the Romance: Women, Patriarchy, and Popular Literature,* 95–96.

one kind of romance. . . . [A]n analysis of these twenty quintessentially romantic books would reveal the crucial generative matrix of the genre *as the readers understand it*.[8]

On its surface, Radway's final list of thirteen essential plot elements, moving from the destruction of the heroine's social identity through the development of the emotional ties between heroine and hero to the restoration of the heroine's identity, looks analogous to the results of generic analyses Vladimir Propp carried out on the fairy tale.[9] Propp, however, does not identify the use-value of the texts of his genre, whereas Radway's structural analysis of the genre of romance makes sense only when framed by the use-value that defines it.

To find and (in particular) to express the exact use-value of a genre is not always such an easy matter. Which (presumably) male needs are fulfilled in combat books, for example, with those predictable titles apparently designed to cause physical unease? *To Hell and Back, Helmet for My Pillow, The Old Corps* (the old corpse?). The titles of the romances are evocative, those of the Harlequins are proverbial, but these titles show that this genre is dedicated to Dostoyevsky's proposition that "Suffering is the sole cause of consciousness."[10] There is no nudity on these covers; in fact, there are no women at all, just soldiers and planes and guns. The colors are surprisingly subdued, lots of green, dark brown, black. Interestingly, a combat book's cover and title rarely reflect whether the work is fact or fiction. Romance must be fictional because history has not fulfilled the needs of women, but combat books can be either. War exists, whereas we must imagine love. However, these covers and titles do clearly differentiate between combat past and combat future. The covers of the future are bright red and yellow, the titles emphasize abstract action rather than personal experience: *Night Launch, Red Star, Hostile Fire, Black Sky*.

Westerns tend to be named after places or persons: *The Burning Hills, Milo Talon, Cimarron, The Texans, The Californios, Hanging Woman Creek*. Like romances, they nearly always depict humans, but unlike romances the number of people depicted can vary greatly, and the mode of depiction is always realistic rather than stylized. Like combat books, the western is a male-oriented genre, and one whose compensatory message is generally clear enough: it poses individualism as a primary and necessary attribute.

8. Ibid., 120.

9. See Vladimir Propp, *Morphology of the Folktale*.

10. Fyodor Dostoevsky, *Notes from Underground*, translated by Michael R. Katz (New York: W. W. Norton, 1989), 24.

A man acting alone can solve a collective problem, a *sententia* that noted scholar Henry A. Kissinger took from the western into his office as secretary of state. When Oriana Fallaci asked him about the image he was cultivating as a "shuttle diplomat," Kissinger replied, "Americans like the cowboy who leads the wagon train by riding ahead alone on his horse, the cowboy who rides all alone into the town, the village, with his horse and nothing else. Maybe even without a pistol, since he doesn't shoot. He acts, that's all, by being in the right place at the right time. In short, a Western."[11] It is fascinating to watch Dr. Kissinger betray his German origins with the solecism of "village," which of course does not exist in the American West. His slip hints that perhaps his relative newness to American culture allowed him to grasp both the ideological core and the use-value of the western more quickly than most of us.

To name a place and depict the people who inhabit it is to conjure up a visible, imaginable, and hence attainable utopia, a new race, a sphere in which individual action can have a meaning—in other words, American market capitalism. So at least concludes Will Wright in his study *Six-Guns and Society*.[12] Wright argues that westerns essentially reflect, through their narrative sequence, the structure of American free-market capitalism. Like Radway, he supplies a Proppian sequence of sixteen "events" whose ordering is invariable, even if not all elements are present in every western. In the first complex of events, according to Wright, the hero enters a social group in which he is unknown, but to which he reveals that he has an exceptional ability. In the final complex, the hero saves that society, which then finally accepts him.[13] Wright goes on to link changes in the genre (for example, its disappearance from television) to the transition from free-market entrepreneurship to a "corporate," postindustrial capitalism that has de-emphasized the individual. Thus, if romances supply women with the understanding partner they lack in real life, westerns remove the unwanted partners whose presence brings about the male double-bind: "Be a hero, but don't rock the boat."

The covers of thrillers differ radically from any described so far in their use of a visual "alienation effect." Often photographed rather than painted as the other covers always are, they depict a few, apparently unrelated

---

11. Oriana Fallaci, *Interview with History* (Boston: Houghton Mifflin, 1976), 41; cited in J. Fred MacDonald, *Who Shot the Sheriff? The Rise and Fall of the Television Western* (New York: Praeger, 1987), 3. MacDonald labels Kissinger's idea "heroic activism."

12. Will Wright, *Six-Guns and Society: A Structural Study of the Western* (Berkeley and Los Angeles: University of California Press, 1975).

13. Ibid., 142–43.

objects (a doll, a knife, and a drop of blood, for example). Here photographic realism combines with compositional stylization to produce a fetishistic image appropriate for the worship of violence. The covers of thrillers are visual zeugmas—a nail through a hand, a hammer beside a statue of Buddha, drops of blood on a map. These are also the only covers that dare to place their objects on the diagonal, thus further disorienting the viewer. Their titles are similarly opaque, metaphorical, and suggestive (*Size, Dark Room, Hard Candy*) rather than deictic as in the westerns or evocative as in the romances. All these features reflect the nature of this genre's plots, which ask the reader to put the pieces together. The disorientation at the heart of this genre provides a kind of "alienation effect" and an alternative to the familiar patterns of behavior. Apparently, this disorientation is a use-value, which makes thrillers the roller coasters and funhouses of reading.

So far, I have described a particular generic system within the American culture industry. I have hinted at both how these genres carefully differentiate themselves from their neighbors in terms of their titles, their covers, and how they are to be used by their readers. I have defined and subdivided the genres according to what I call their use-values. I propose, accordingly, that generic differences are grounded in the "use-value" of a discourse rather than in its content, formal features, or its rules of production. I have chosen to begin with popular literature for several reasons, one of which being that my colleagues are more likely to hear me out when I discuss these works than if I were to make similar statements about Shakespeare's plays, for example. The reason for that, however, is even more significant, and brings us back to Schlegel and the conflict between Markus and Amalia. It is, if I am correct, that most readers of this book concur that popular culture is indeed "genre-driven," that the sorts of formal similarities and differences I have been describing here are not artifacts of my critical fantasy—though the details of my analysis may be debated—but deliberate creations of an industry (not of "individuals," to concede Amalia's point) according to preconceived formulas that have created well-defined markets for exploitation; hence the emphasis on the cover art, so crucial at the point of sale of these books in the context I have described.[14]

Still, my subjective treatment of how these texts seek to seduce their

14. Ross Chambers has developed the idea of "narrative seduction" and links it explicitly to the increasing commodification of literature. The promise of encountering an identifiable genre would be one such means of seduction. See his *Story and Situation: Narrative Seduction and the Power of Fiction* (Minneapolis: University of Minnesota Press, 1984).

readers may seem to have precious little to do with "Literature" (books that get taught). Indeed, the academic reaction against the marketability of genre is typified by formulations such as this one by Fredric Jameson:

> With the elimination of an institutionalized social status for the cultural producer and the opening of the work of art itself to commodification, the older generic specifications are transformed into a brand-name system against which any authentic artistic expression must necessarily struggle. The older generic categories do not, for all that, die out, but persist in the half-life of the subliterary genres of mass culture, transformed into the drugstore and airport paperback lines of gothics, mysteries, romances, best-sellers, and popular biographies, where they await the resurrection of their immemorial, archetypal resonance at the hands of a [Northrop] Frye or a[n Ernst] Bloch.[15]

Though one wonders about the logic of making "bestseller" a generic category, Jameson has created, with his usual magisterial compression, a little fable of a Golden Age, in which artistic genius and the adherence to generic rules of production harmoniously coincided, and of a subsequent Fall, in which true creativity, exiled from a genre system that both creates and limits its readers' appetites (Amalia's shudder) rather than writers' invention (Markus's defense), takes up its lodging *outside* or *between* genres. In other words, a literary work's adherence to generic rules becomes inversely proportional to its aesthetic quality. The problem, as with Marxist criticism's great shibboleth, the ubiquitous "rise of the bourgeoisie," is one of specifying just when and where this Fall took place. But one need not be a Marxist or believe in the difference between "true" and "popular" cultures to explain genre away. In their own ways, Benedetto Croce, Jacques Derrida, Adena Rosmarin, and Tzvetan Todorov all denigrate genre as an aporia, a critical phantasm, or an imposition on literature.[16] One could make a little anthology of declarations of "resistance to genre," such as the following by R. K. Hack: "The doctrine of literary forms has always turned our eyes from . . . reality, has caused us to rest content with a futile label."[17] "Literature with a Capital L" is now

---

15. Fredric Jameson, *The Political Unconscious: Narrative as a Socially Symbolic Act*, 107.

16. For the works of these theorists, see the Bibliography. In Chapter 8 I discuss their ideas at length. For now I only wish to emphasize that they write *against* the possibility of genre as something real and inherent in texts.

17. R. K. Hack, "The Doctrine of the Literary Forms," 64. How odd that the subject of Hack's article is Horace's *Ars poetica*, in which Horace argues that the generic production of literature is ineluctable.

consistently characterized by "generic instability," that is, by its ability to confound our generic expectations—including those for "Literature with a Capital L."

The effect that many identify as postmodern is produced by defeating the generic expectations of the reader. One example, and a parable of this process, is Jorge Luis Borges's short story "Tlön, Uqbar, Orbis Tertius," which can be read as an antidote against any belief in generic stability. Borges's story masquerades as a report on the narrator's gradual discovery of a centuries-old conspiracy to create an artificial world through the production of, among other items, a fictional encyclopedia. Clearly, the use-value of an encyclopedia, the applicability of its contents to the reader's world-at-hand, should be annihilated by its assignment to the realm of fiction. But there is a twist; at the end of the story, the narrator reports that Tlönian discourse is remaking the world, that is, turning the traditional "true discourses" into fictional ones, encyclopedias into novels:

> El contacto y el hábito de Tlön han desintegrado este mundo. . . .
> Ya ha penetrado en las escuelas el (conjetural) «idioma primitivo»
> de Tlön; ya la enseñanza de su historia armoniosa (y llena de
> episodios conmovedores) ha obliterado a la que presidió mi niñez;
> ya en las memorias un pasado ficticio ocupa el sitio de otro, del
> que nada sabemos con certidumbre—ni siquiera que es falso—.
> Han sido reformadas la numismática, la farmacología y la arqueo-
> logía. Entiendo que la biología y las matemáticas aguardan tam-
> bién su avatar.

> (The contact and the habit of Tlön have disintegrated this world.
> . . . Already the schools have been invaded by the conjectural
> "primitive language" of Tlön; already the teaching of its harmoni-
> ous history [filled with moving episodes] has wiped out the one
> which governed in my childhood; already a fictitious past occupies
> in our memories the place of another, a past of which we know
> nothing with certainty—not even that it is false. Numismatics,
> pharmacology and archaeology have been reformed. I understand
> that biology and mathematics also await their avatars.)[18]

18. J. L. Borges, "Tlön, Uqbar, Orbis Tertius," in *Ficciones* (Madrid and Buenos Aires: Alianza & Emece, 1971), 35–36; translated by James E. Irby, under the title "Tlön, Uqbar, Orbis Tertius," in *Labyrinths* (New York: New Directions, 1964), 18. Further citations in text.

Like the Tlönists with their encyclopedia, Borges the narrator also sets up a dialectic between fact and fiction. His text opens not with the third-person preterite verb so common to fictional narration, but rather with the first-person present and a long, dry, bibliographic rambling of the sort one expects to find not in a short story but in that other brief genre at which Borges excelled, the *nota* (a cross between an essay and a critical article):

> Debo a la conjunción de un espejo y de una enciclopedia el descubrimiento de Uqbar. El espejo inquietaba el fondo de un corredor en una quinta de la calle Gaona, en Ramos Mejía; la enciclopedia falazmente se llama *The Anglo-American Cyclopædia* (Nueva York, 1917) y es una reimpresión literal, pero también morosa de la *Encyclopædia Britannica* de 1902. (13)

> (I owe the discovery of Uqbar to the conjunction of a mirror and an encyclopedia. The mirror troubled the depths of a corridor in a country house on Gaona Street in Ramos Mejía; the encyclopedia is fallaciously called The Anglo-American Cyclopædia [New York, 1917] and is a literal but delinquent reprint of the Encyclopædia Britannica of 1902. [3])

Two sentences later Borges provides another false lead that this is a *nota* by mentioning the real person Alfredo Bioy Casares, while at the same time revealing—in a veiled fashion—the very genesis of his "novel":

> Bioy Casares había cenado conmigo esa noche y nos demoró una vasta polémica sobre la ejecución de una novela en primera persona, cuyo narrador omitiera o desfigurara los hechos e incurriera en diversas contradicciones, que permitieran a unos pocos lectores—a muy pocos lectores—la adivinación de una realidad atroz o banal. (13)

> (Bioy Casares had had dinner with me that evening and we became lengthily engaged in a vast polemic concerning the composition of a novel in the first person, whose narrator would omit or disfigure the facts and indulge in various contradictions which would permit a few readers—very few readers—to perceive an atrocious or banal reality. [3])

The first-person narrative here—a marker of another genre entirely—along with the overlap in subject matter, allows us to suspect that this *nota* is really the novel. Indeed, the contradictions start here, for in what sense can a novelist write down *hechos* (facts)—much less omit them!—and how can contradiction lead to a deeper view of (alternately atrocious or banal) reality? Borges, then, is the master Tlönista; like the encyclopedia of Tlön, the text "Tlön, Uqbar, and Orbis Tertius" is a "reference" work that reveals itself to be a fiction that in turn creates its own facts: among them, the fact of generic instability.

Generic instability is so prevalent a feature of the postmodern that Ralph Cohen sees fit to ask the question, "Do Postmodern Genres Exist?" (I propose, obliquely in the form of a fiction in Chapter 7, that theory itself is *the* postmodern genre.) However, this and the other Borgesian games of generic hide-and-seek with which contemporary literature abounds are not unique to postmodernism. In Chapter 3 I examine how the readily definable *ars dictaminis* or letter-writing manual—originally a sort of reference work or textbook—has repeatedly been turned into a work of fiction in its thousand-year history. Furthermore, postmodernism's dissolution of the boundaries between certain genres has created not an *Überhauptpoesie*, but rather a new genre: critical theory, an interdisciplinary discourse that never contents itself with a single defined object, but finds its use-value in the practice of social criticism, taking up the same position at the center of moral debate that Homer had for the Greeks, or which the novel came to have for the eighteenth century. Because theory has taken over roughly the same use-value that the novel once had, I am able in Chapter 4 to compare eighteenth-century novelist Samuel Richardson with twentieth-century theorist Roland Barthes as critics of legal discourse. Perhaps the generic instability of Lévi-Strauss's *Tristes tropiques*, discussed in Chapter 2, derives from the fact that it is one of the first works in this theoretical line, and not quite sure of what to do with itself. But even theory, seemingly all-powerful and protean as it is, can become unstable and collapse back into the form of fiction. This is what happens in Walter Höllerer's long poem *Die Elephantenuhr* and Umberto Eco's detective novel *Il nome della rosa*, a history of and a practical guide to semiotics which alludes to everyone from Borges to Conan Doyle.

In moving from the supermarket to Borges we seem to have reversed course entirely, and to be moving away from the seduction of generic certainty into the chaos of generic fluidity. But it is really our perspective that has changed, from being "outside" the system (as potential buyers) to being "inside" Borges's text (as actual readers). Though the system appears to us to function differently in the two cases, its effects are equally powerful in both. And although many critics might respond to the prolif-

eration of such unclassifiable works by proclaiming the attenuation or
futility of generic classification, I perversely insist on seeing Borges's
calling attention to his text's generic instability as merely the negative
image of my supermarket display. Both phenomena confront us with
choice: the supermarket with that of which text will best fulfill our needs;
the "literary" text with that of what exactly to do with it or how to read it.
Genre is just as much present in the latter case as in the former. The force
of postmodernism depends profoundly on there being readers sufficiently
familiar with the system of genre to appreciate the deliberate confounding
of that system. Thus, my undergraduate students consistently find "Tlön"
unreadable and uninteresting because they are unfamiliar with the various
features and use-values of the genres that collide in it. The story has no
point for them—and no power. No genre, no power. But as Adena
Rosmarin has asked, whence derives this "power of genre"?

II

Why genre? If philosophers can ask the question, "Why is there *something*,
instead of *nothing?*" then this book can ask, "Why are there (always) genres
and not just *language* (or music, or pictures)?" One popular response to
this question has been to ground generic distinctions in logical necessity:
Northrop Frye, for example, distinguishes genres on the basis of their
"radical of presentation," of the link established between narrator and
spectator or reader.[19] Käthe Hamburger and Emil Staiger, however, distinguish genres by their orientation toward past, present, or future, that is,
by the different ideas of time they embody.[20] This basic disagreement over
where to locate the markers of generic difference certainly weakens the
claim that genre is an essential feature of literature. An alternative approach would be pragmatic: we simply do not know what to do with texts
without the "user's guide" that genre provides. Artificial-intelligence expert Douglas Hofstadter has remarked that all messages are really composed of three "layers." These are (1) the message itself, (2) a message
about how to decode the message, and (3) a message that tells us "This is
a message."[21] Now the statement "this is a message" can be taken both as

19. Northrop Frye, "Rhetorical Criticism: Theory of Genres," 243–337.
20. See Käthe Hamburger, *Die Logik der Dichtung*, and Emil Staiger, *Grundbegriffe der Poetik*, 5th
ed. (Zurich: Atlantis, 1961).
21. Douglas R. Hofstadter, *Gödel, Escher, Bach*, 2d ed. (New York: Vintage, 1989), 166–67.

an act of generic classification and as a statement about the purpose a particular object should serve. Thus, one may read Hofstadter's analysis as an extension, beyond purely linguistic sign systems, of E. D. Hirsch's dictum: "All understanding of verbal meaning is necessarily genre-bound."[22] In looking at genre from the point of view of information theory, Jan Tryznadlowski has similarly described genres as "various types of programmes. . . . The programme is goal-directed. Whereas individual and synthesized instructions within a literary work are a literal code for the information contained in the work, the programme, outlined by the directives and criteria of the given literary genre, is the central directional information with considerable interpretive values." Furthermore, those values adhere not to the abstract and the private, but to the "artistic and ideological sphere of operation of a given literary work."[23] Faced with the question of just how an authentic legal text, when reproduced verbatim in Pushkin's novel *Dubrovsky*, can lose its legal character and gain a literary one, Jurij Lotman is forced to conclude: "A change in the function of a text gives it a new semantics and new syntax. Thus, in the example [of Pushkin's novel], the construction of a document according to the formal laws of a legal text is perceived as construction according to the laws of artistic composition. . . . The social function of a text determines its typological classification."[24] If the text's *mode d'emploi* is not somehow marked, reading—in the sense of that word which transcends merely translating black marks on white paper into sounds—becomes impossible.

So far I have talked about such markers as garish cover art, titles, and even the ambience of presentation—certain genres, however, cannot be sold in the supermarket. But as a counterpart to my supermarket experience, I could cite my participation in an informal reading group where I saw learned philosophers vexed at the impossibility of getting a handle on Ernst Bloch's three-volume utopian essay, *Das Prinzip Hoffnung* (*The Principle of Hope*). Why couldn't they? Because Bloch's style, subject matter, and tone change so drastically—one chapter being an intensely private memoir and the next blatant political invective, with some philosophy in between— that his book does not fit into any particular textual category. To count as philosophy, at least for other philosophers, a text must be (literally, Socratically) questionable, and Bloch's book is too personal and slippery to be interrogated. Philosophical analysis of a text can only begin once the

22. E. D. Hirsch, *Validity in Interpretation*, 76.

23. Jan Tryznadlowski, "Information Theory and Literary Genres," 44–45.

24. Jurij M. Lotman, "Problems in the Typology of Texts," 120. I consider the appearance of legal language within literature (and vice versa) in Chapter 4.

text has been generically classified as philosophy. Martin Heidegger, Jacques Derrida, and a number of other philosophers infringe on this law of genre by interrogating literary texts as though they belonged to the genre of philosophy. Predictably, others have come to insist that the texts of Heidegger and Derrida cannot be philosophy since they interrogate texts that are not philosophy, and so on. Our group's evaluation of Bloch's ideas had to be postponed until we could determine how to "handle" his writing, a determination that seemed to depend on what I call Bloch's "style." (This particular hermeneutic circle became a vicious one, ending in our decision to postpone the reading of Bloch indefinitely.) In "Exkurs zur Einebnung des Gattungsunterschiedes zwischen Philosophie und Literatur" (Digression on the leveling of the generic difference between philosophy and literature), Jürgen Habermas argues for differentiating the genres of philosophy and literature on the basis of their different use-values, namely *Problemlösung* (problem solving) and *Welterschließung* (revelation of the world).[25] Habermas's response to the attempts of Derrida and others to treat all forms of discourse as subject to the same methods of interpretation is in the end circular. He maintains that there is a distinction between philosophy and literature beyond their shared rhetorical and figural strategies, but he does not explain how we can make this distinction. He treats "problem solving" and "revelation of the world" as transcendental essences of texts which remain invisible—and yet understandable—to their readers. Nevertheless, like Habermas, I began to see genre as a set of "handles" on texts, and to realize that a text's genre is its *use-value*.[26] Genre gives us not understanding in the abstract and passive sense but use in the pragmatic and active sense. Use-value is what Radway and Wright and Habermas feel perfectly free to talk about, but which has been virtually absent from genre theory per se. And since the use-values that Radway and Kissinger and Wright and Habermas find lying at the heart of the romance, the western, and philosophy are social rather than private

25. Jürgen Habermas, "Exkurs zur Einebnung des Gattungsunterschiedes zwischen Philosophie und Literatur."

26. This idea can, of course, readily be identified with pragmatism or neopragmatism. On pragmatism's relation to literary theory, see Anthony J. Cascardi, "The Genealogy of Pragmatism," *Philosophy and Literature* 10 (October 1986): 295–302; Ludwig Grünberg, "La Littérature et la tentation d'une 'culture postphilosophique,'" *Cahiers Roumains d'Études Littéraires* 1 (1987): 35–47; and Rosmarin, *Power of Genre*. Paul Hernadi's definition of pragmatic genre theory is the differentiation of genres by the varying effects they have on readers' minds. My approach could almost be described as the reverse of this. See his *Beyond Genre: New Directions in Literary Classification*, 37–53.

(reading as a hidden, imaginary form of social action), genre theory in their works inevitably becomes a form of ideology.

The ideological nature of genre explains not only its necessity but also its instability. Ross Chambers has demonstrated that in order to function, an ideology cannot be identical with itself, a phenomenon he calls ideological split:

> An ideology is not a doctrine to be accepted or not accepted but a discursive proposition that positions subjects in relations of power (power being itself a differential phenomenon, existing only through being unevenly distributed). Ideology necessarily produces these subjects relationally, and it is in the difference between them that the potential for ideological split resides, these subjects being differently positioned regarding the system that produces them. They "perceive" it, "understand" it, from different angles, so to speak, and in differing perspectives.[27]

Chambers's view of ideology as a positioning of subjects is derived from the work of the French Marxist Louis Althusser, who in turn was influenced by the structuralist views of society in the work of Claude Lévi-Strauss and Jacques Lacan. While maintaining the received Marxist notion of ideology, which opposes "ideology" to "knowledge,"[28] Althusser locates the workings of ideology in the realm of the unconscious and makes it a pragmatic matter, the possibility of carrying on lived relations between people:

> Ideology is a matter of the *lived* relation between men and their world. . . . In ideology men do indeed express, not the relation between them and their conditions of existence, but *the way* they live the relation between them and their conditions of existence: this presupposes both a real relation and an *"imaginary," lived*

27. Ross Chambers, "Irony and the Canon," *Profession* 90 (1990): 19. Terry Eagleton posits the non-self-identity of ideology in a more overtly political way: "A dominant ideology has continually to negotiate with the ideologies of its subordinates, and this essential open-endedness will prevent it from achieving any kind of pure self-identity. . . . A successful ruling ideology . . . must engage significantly with genuine wants, needs, and desires; but this is also its Achilles heel, forcing it to recognize an 'other' to itself and inscribing this otherness as a potentially disruptive force within its own forms." *Ideology* (New York: Verso, 1991), 45.

28. For a good brief discussion of the development of the concept of ideology and of its "classic" Marxist formulation, see Raymond Williams, *Keywords*, 2d ed. (New York: Oxford, 1983), 153–56.

> relation. Ideology . . . is the expression of the relation between men and their "world," that is, the (overdetermined) unity of the real relation and the imaginary relation between them and their real conditions of existence. In ideology the real relation is inevitably invested in the imaginary relation, a relation that *expresses will* (conservative, conformist, reformist or revolutionary), a hope or a nostalgia, rather than describing a reality.[29]

Though Althusser rejects the notion of ideology as a belief system open to choice (his rejection is echoed in the first sentence of the quotation from Chambers), he nevertheless still identifies ideology as false, as can be seen from his use of the term "imaginary" as contrasted to "describing a reality." Rather than contrast imagination to reality, contemporary cultural critics tend to contrast the imaginary order against the symbolic and to identify ideology with the eccentric subject created by their correlation—reality being that which is unavailable to either realm. The imaginary operates on a metaphysics of wholeness, on the illusory identification of the subject with a unified body, whereas the symbolic implies culture's creation of subjects as products of its discursive systems.[30] Thus, for John Frow, who draws heavily on Michel Foucault's concept of "discursive practices," Althusser's "lived relation" of ideology has become a discursive relation, "the production and the conditions of production of categories and entities

---

29. Louis Althusser, *For Marx*, trans. Ben Brewster (New York: Random House, 1970), 233–34.

30. This terminology is drawn from Jacques Lacan's theory of the constitution of the subject. One possible source (among many) for approaching the topic of "ideological split" in Lacan would be the following passages from the *Discours de Rome*: "The subject goes a long way beyond what is experienced 'subjectively' by the individual, exactly as far as the Truth he is able to attain. . . . [T]his Truth of his history is not all of it contained in his script, and yet the place is marked there by the painful shocks he feels from knowing only his own lines, and not simply there, but also in pages whose disorder gives him little by way of comfort. . . . The Symbolic function [thus] presents itself as a double movement within the subject: man makes an object of his action, but only in order to restore to this action in due time its place as a grounding. In this equivocation, operating at every instant, lies the whole process of a function in which action and knowledge alternate." *Speech and Language in Psychoanalysis*, translated by Jonathan Wilden (Baltimore: Johns Hopkins University Press, 1981), 26–27, 48. Lacan goes on to relate two examples of the workings of the Symbolic: the abstract use of number (to add together two discrete collections), and a worker participating in a strike because he considers himself a member of the "proletariat." Lacan's concept of psychic disturbances as *products* of the very structures that create subjects is a good example of the dialectic between systems and noise which grounds my idea of generic instability.

within the field of discourse," including the category of the subject on which ideology is supposed to act.[31]

To this conception of ideology Chambers adds two additional nuances. One, derived from the Foucauldian view of power, is that ideology, which creates power by repositioning subjects, must then necessarily appear differently to those different subjects. At this point, a term that Marx had made the instrument of falsity shatters into a controlled perspectivism—ideology, like interpretation, varies infinitely but not randomly according to the perspective of those who participate in it. Chambers's second twist involves naming this perspectivist element of a totalizing system "noise." The concept of "noise," adapted from communication theory by social and cultural theorists,[32] tells us that categories and entities can only be developed against a background of non-entities and non-categories; systems, in other words, can function only by means of the non-systemic they necessarily produce. Thus, the non-systemic is simultaneously inside and outside the system. Chambers then applies this concept of "noise" directly to sites of literary conflict such as canonicity: "As the mediation that produces power, then, the system of ideology necessarily produces 'noise,' a degree of play without which it would not be a system and consequently could not function to produce power. Canonicity is the site of such noise, a place of play within the system."[33] Now, beside the fact that they are both acts of sorting, canonicity and genre are also related in the sense that the recognition of an artifact as belonging to a certain genre can automatically exclude it from even potential canonizing—as is the case with rock music videos, for example, at least for the present. To put it another way, the act of canonizing is one of the potential use-values associated with certain genres. I contend that, aside from canonicity, whose institutional power is quite obvious, genre is also a site of such noise, the cusp between different use-values of texts and between discursive entity and non-entity. Hence, not only are genre systems ideological, but their cusps provide a most advantageous place from which to observe the workings of ideology in literature.

31. John Frow, "Discourse and Power," in *Ideological Representation and Power in Social Relations,* ed. Mike Gane (New York: Routledge, 1989), 207.

32. See, for example, Michel Serres, *Le Parasite* (Paris: Grasset, 1980); translated by Lawrence R. Schehr (Baltimore: Johns Hopkins University Press, 1982); and Jacques Attali, *Bruits* (Paris: PUF, 1981); translated by Brian Massumi, under the title *Noise* (Minneapolis: University of Minnesota Press, 1985).

33. Chambers, "Irony and the Canon," 19.

The conception of ideology one finds in Chambers and Frow solves old problems and creates new ones. For literary studies, this revised conception resolves the question of literature's relation to ideology. It was clear to even the most hard-line sociopolitical critic that literature is almost never simply an embodiment of ideology (the "system" in Chambers's description), that it is also equally its negation (the "noise" in that system). Literary texts take up a differential position to ideology, shaking up its "ideologemes," so to speak.[34] We are now saying that these "-emes" are only differences, and that literature can be considered fully ideological, because ideology is never fully identical with itself anyway.

The greatest problem associated with this way of talking about ideology is that it quickly forces us to *stop* talking about it, since we have difficulty describing something that is not a set of beliefs to be accepted or denied. To "know" ideology is no longer to know the summary of a number of ideas. Ideology is no longer something that can be represented or paraphrased. Instead, it becomes something like the magnetic field that arranges a chaotic mass of iron filings into intriguing, ordered curves on a piece of paper. Ideology itself is usually invisible; it is noticeable and perhaps existent only in its interactions with the material world (which includes thought). Ideology is the magnetic force that simultaneously holds a society together by allowing it to communicate with itself in shorthand and pushes society apart by conflicting with people's realities. It is only in the deformations and contradictions of writing and thinking that we can recognize ideology; genre is one of those observable deformations, a pattern in the iron filings of cultural products that reveals the force of ideology.

In particular, what makes genre ideological is our practice of speaking of it as a "thing" rather than as the expression of a relationship between user and a text, a practice similar to that identified by Marx as "commodity fetishism." As Lacanian Marxist Slavoj Žižek explains, "When we are victims of commodity fetishism it appears as if the concrete content of a commodity (its use-value) is an expression of its abstract universality (its exchange-value)—the abstract Universal, the Value, appears as a real

---

34. The idea of literature's relating given ideologemes in novel and unexpected ways is advanced in Mikhail Bakhtin and Pavel M. Medvedev, *The Formal Method in Literary Scholarship*, translated by Albert J. Wehrle (Baltimore: Johns Hopkins University Press, 1978), 16–30. Terry Eagleton has succinctly stated the dilemma of situating literature in relation to ideology in *Marxism and Literary Criticism* (Berkeley and Los Angeles: University of California Press, 1976), 16–19. Eagleton cites Althusser as a way out of the dilemma, in that literature reports experience (the lived relation) in such a way that readers can take up a critical position toward it.

Substance which successively incarnates itself in a series of concrete objects."[35] Schemes identifying different genres with different universal values have been erected in most historical periods; perhaps the most elaborate and explicit are those of the French neoclassical period for painting (genre painting was ranked above portraiture, which was ranked above still-life) and literature (tragedy ranks above satire, as Boileau points out). My treatment of genre as use-value is thus an attempt at penetrating one veil of an aesthetic ideology that continues to posit genre as universal.

As a form of ideology, genre is also never fully identical with itself, nor are texts fully identical with their genres. Furthermore, if genre is a form of ideology, then the struggle against or the deviations from genre are ideological struggles. Jameson locates literature outside the constraints of genre; I locate it in those texts where the battle is most intense, where the generic classification of a text determines its meaning(s) and exposes its ideology.

III

Herman Melville's *Moby-Dick* is just such a text. Not only does it seem to evade generic classification, it also discusses and theorizes its own generic instability. I read *Moby-Dick* the way I read Borges's short story, as metafiction, looking for connections between what happens in the story and what the story tells us about itself. The political message in Borges remains on a rather abstract level, but Ishmael gives us plenty of the lived experience, which is, according to Althusser, the basis of ideology. Among other things, Ishmael gives us a particularly dramatic depiction of the

35. Slavoj Žižek, *The Sublime Object of Ideology* (New York: Verso, 1989), 31. In Marx's writings, use-value is related to the material reality of commodities: "A commodity, such as iron, corn, or a diamond, is therefore, so far as it is a material thing, a use-value, something useful," whereas exchange-value "appears to be something accidental and purely relative, and consequently an intrinsic value, i.e., an exchange-value that is inseparably connected with, inherent in commodities, seems a contradiction in terms." Karl Marx, *Capital, Volume One*, in *The Marx-Engels Reader*, ed. Robert C. Tucker (New York: W. W. Norton, 1978), 303, 304. However, it should be noted first of all that though language and discourse are material, it is difficult to treat them fully as commodities and in particular to differentiate clearly between their use-value and their exchange-value. Second, my adoption of the term "use-value" owes as much to twentieth-century language theory (e.g., Saussure, Wittgenstein, Bakhtin, and Halliday) as it does to Marxist thought. I develop the linguistic side of use-value in Chapter 8.

workings of ideology in the transformation of a whale hunt begun for economic gain into a personal religious quest, and in the analogous anthropomorphizing of an animal into a malicious adversary.

The ideological transformation of the *Pequod*'s crew is carried out by Ahab literally before the reader's eyes: the title of the relevant chapter, "The Quarter Deck: Enter Ahab: Then all," is that of a scene in a play. The captain's first act of suasive magic is to offer a gold doubloon for the first masthead who raises the white whale: " 'Look ye! d'ye see this Spanish ounce of gold?'—holding up a broad bright coin to the sun—'it is a sixteen dollar piece, men,—a doubloon. D'ye see it? . . . Whosoever of ye raises me that same white whale, he shall have this gold ounce, my boys!' "[36] Ahab's repeated invocations from various perspectives of the bounty's value—it is Spanish, it is a doubloon, it is or was worth sixteen dollars, it is an ounce of gold—emphasize its "Quito glow," its exotic antiquity, its belonging to another time and economic system. The doubloon's primitiveness seems to determine its value and its suasiveness. Sailors and readers are made to notice how the doubloon contrasts strongly with the normal system of paying whalers: in its form; in its extraordinary materiality and *visibility;* and in its singular and unitary source in Ahab, the captain of the ship, rather than in the ship's owners or sailors, who normally divide the profits of the voyage. For it had been pointed out much earlier, in chapter 16 when Ishmael first signed on board the *Pequod,* that a whaling ship is a kind of joint-stock company. The capitalist nature of whaling is rendered here unambiguously: "People in Nantucket invest their money in whaling vessels, the same way that you do yours in approved state stocks bringing in good interest" (73). The sailors and harpooners perform all their work and risk life and limb for shares of the net profits of the voyage, called lays. The concept of the lay is emphasized twice, once in chapter 16, in which Ishmael, expecting to be given the 275th lay (that is, one out of every 275 cents of the net profits) is shocked when Bildad offers him the 777th, and again in chapter 18, in which Queequeg, after showing his prowess with the harpoon, is given the unusually high 90th lay.

The contrast between Ishmael's share of the profits and Queequeg's serves to explain and justify the "joint-stock" nature of the whaling ship, aboard which there are no differences in *kind,* only differences in skill and experience. The *Pequod* is thus the translation into economic terms of the

36. Herman Melville, *Moby-Dick, or The Whale* (Evanston and Chicago: Northwestern University Press, 1988), 161–62. Further citations in text.

Lockean/American political philosophy that all men are created equal, and that the cause for existing inequalities lies in the variations in individual ability and desire. Ishmael himself makes the connection between the economic order and that of lived relations, telling us that "the community of interest prevailing among a company, all of whom, high or low, depend for their profits, not upon fixed wages, but upon their common luck, together with their common vigilance, intrepidity, and hard work . . . tend to beget a less rigorous discipline [in whalers] than in merchantmen generally" (147). In contrast, the present offer of bounty from Ahab tends to make him a master hiring his vassals directly, thus creating an entirely different economic relation from that which should obtain for the voyage in general. This different, archaic relationship between Ahab and his crew had been alluded to most clearly in chapter 34, "The Dinner-Table," in which feudal-monarchical references to Ahab abound: his is a "sultan's step" (149); he is the "Grand Turk" (150); he enjoys over his messmates a "social czarship" (150); and his meals are compared with the German kaiser's "Coronation banquet at Frankfort" (151). The clearest example of the lived relations corresponding to the doubloon is revealed later, when Fedallah and his crew emerge from belowdecks to man Ahab's boat (although present through the entire voyage, they are first mentioned only in chapter 48). Whereas the crew remain ideologically split between the whaling system they are used to and Ahab's new order, Fedallah and his four companions are loyal only to Ahab, speak only to Ahab, and remain hidden from the crew except at the lowerings for whales, particularly for Moby-Dick. What *their* compensation will be we never find out, but clearly they are motivated by Ahab's direct bounty rather than by the profits of the voyage.

But for now, by nailing the gold doubloon to the mast, Ahab has transformed the (relatively) egalitarian, capitalist shipboard into a feudal hierarchy, in a covenant to be reinforced by the sacrament of the drinking ceremony in which he assigns the role of "knights" to his harpooneers, whose harpoons are now described as lances, and that of "cupbearer" (the medieval *Mundschenk*) to Pip. Whereas all others seem ready to act in Ahab's drama, only Starbuck attempts to break the spell and bring Ahab back to the present. He begins his attack at the other end of the production cycle, at the level of the economic object: the whale itself. Ahab has had to abolish the whale as an economic resource in order to transform the shipboard society. There is a tendency, in reading *Moby-Dick*, to focus on Ahab's relation to the whale and perceive all other relationships as deriving from that one. However, one could equally see the whale as the reification of and justification for Ahab's real objective, the transformation of the social relations aboard the *Pequod*. Ahab has anthropomorphized and mythologized the white whale, invested him with a mind capable of malice. Only Starbuck points out the falsity of this. Moby-Dick has, after all, acted merely out of instinct: " 'Vengeance on a dumb brute!' cried Starbuck, 'that simply smote thee from blindest instinct! Madness!' " (163–64). And with that piece of zoological common sense comes also a reminder of the true economic relations under which the crew had supposed they were voyaging: " 'I came here to hunt whales, not my commander's vengeance. How many barrels will thy vengeance yield thee even if thou gettest it, Captain Ahab? it will not fetch thee much in our Nantucket market" (163).

But Ahab persists. Starbuck's protest against the economic absurdity of the quest is silenced by Ahab's drama—a defeat read by one critic as "the defeat of American democracy."[37] Rather than respond directly to the logic of Starbuck's arguments, Ahab continues to use literature as his weapon, and in particular to metaphorize the relation between them. There are repeated references to extralinguistic signs taken from medicine, theater, and physics. Starbuck first falls prey to the metaphor of a passed contagion: "Something shot from my dilated nostrils, he has inhaled it in his lungs. Starbuck now is mine" (164). Then the ceremony of the crossed lances, by inserting the actors into Ahab's medieval drama, invests them with an energy, metaphorized here as electricity:

> "Advance, ye mates! Cross your lances full before me. Well done! Let me touch the axis." So saying, with extended arm, he grasped the three level, radiating lances at their crossed centre; while so doing, suddenly and nervously twitched them; meanwhile, glancing intently from Starbuck to Stubb; from Stubb to Flask. It seemed as though, by some nameless, interior volition, he would fain have shocked into them the same fiery emotion accumulated within the Leyden jar of his own magnetic life. (165)

Ahab has not offered his crew a set of beliefs to be accepted or rejected; rather he has given them new roles to play, a new imaginary lived relationship with each other, with their captain, and with the whale. It is

37. Wai-chee Dimock, *Empire for Liberty: Melville and the Poetics of Individualism* (Princeton University Press, 1989), 122. Although she does not treat the question of genre at length, Dimock's argument, like my own, concerns the ideology of authorship: "Textual governance, I believe, cannot be divorced from the social governance of antebellum America" (7).

the sensuous form of these relations and of the gold coin which is ideological. The scene connects social relations ("joint-stock" versus feudal), productive activity (profitable versus unprofitable killing of animals), and ecology (man's relation to the physical and animal world), yet Ahab can win his game only if no one present at the scene can fully grasp the interrelations among these three areas. A change in any of these three realms necessitates an analogous shifting in the others. Ahab uses a fourth domain of culture and language, altering the crew's position vis-à-vis the other three realms through his act of theater, through his rhetorical prowess, through his knowledge, in short, of literature.

Ahab's use of ritual drama to indoctrinate the crew parallels Ishmael's turning to dramatic form in order to relate the indoctrination. Just as Ahab changes the nature of the *Pequod*'s mission from profit-making venture to mythic monster-killing quest, so too at this point Ishmael changes the genre of *Moby-Dick* into ritual drama. This is necessary, as Robert Milder points out, because the novelistic genre cannot be used to involve its reader in a quest that goes beyond the phenomenal realm: "Novels may have . . . mythic elements, but these usually take the form of archetypal patterns enacted by the characters with reference to their fictional world, not rituals that involve the audience in a symbolic action. This communal function of myth has traditionally been served by the drama."[38] Or, as John Miles Foley has pointed out, "From point of view and characterization to the illusion of sequence and the power of dénouement, the novel *Moby-Dick*—to the extent that it is encoded with the reading signals familiar to us from experiencing other novels—directs its own reformulation, oversees its own creation as a work of art."[39] In other words, we witness in *Moby-Dick* a narrator using certain generic markers in order to forge a novel from a variegated patchwork of different genres: "Ishmael is the self-ironizing writer seeking, and finally achieving, realization through self-effacement in the work of art; following him in the process, we see the poetry arise from its (cetological) materials, and the discontinuities acquire the meaning of imaginative gestures within the context of a work in progress."[40] Ishmael's constant reformulation of his narrative requires not just the patience but also the complicity of the

38. Robert Milder, "Moby-Dick: The Rationale of Narrative Form," in *Approaches to Teaching Melville's Moby-Dick*, ed. Martin Bickman (New York: Modern Language Association, 1985), 43.
39. John Miles Foley, "The Price of Narrative Fiction: Genre, Myth, and Meaning in *Moby-Dick* and the *Odyssey*," *Thought* 59 (December 1984): 437.
40. Glauco Cambon, "Ishmael and the Problem of Formal Discontinuities in *Moby-Dick*," *MLN* 76 (June 1961): 523.

reader—a complicity not always forthcoming, as most of us who have taught the book to undergraduates can confirm. And genre provides the link between the reformulation of the book and the reformulation of the reader.

This double dramatization (Ahab's and Ishmael's) in a central scene of *Moby-Dick* depicts ideology at work. If Ahab transforms the whale and the crew, it is Ishmael who constantly transforms *Moby-Dick* from one genre into another. Ishmael forces on the readers of *Moby-Dick* a contract remarkably similar to the one that Ahab forces on his crew; his readers must agree to follow Ishmael through the bewildering tangle of the many genres his narrative will assume. There are similarities between Ahab and Ishmael on precisely the level of lived relationships. For example, the joint-stock company against which Ahab rebels is mentioned in chapter 26, the aptly titled "Knights and Squires." There, in language reminiscent of Hamlet's meditation on the splendor and misery of man, Ishmael contrasts the nobility of the individual with his degradation within organizations of anonymity (*société anonyme*, the French term for corporation): "Men may seem detestable as joint-stock companies and nations; knaves, fools, and murderers there may be; men may have mean and meagre faces; but man, in the ideal, is so noble and so sparkling, such a grand and glowing creature, that over any ignominious blemish in him all his fellows should run to throw their costliest robes" (117). *Moby-Dick* becomes by turns "sermon; short story; occasional, scientific, political, and moral essay; satire; dictionary; encyclopedia; drama; dramatic monologue; manual; travelogue; character; tall tale; and prophecy."[41] In giving this list Nina Baym does not mention epic; and yet surely there is some truth to John Foley's claim that the use-value of *Moby-Dick* corresponds closely to that of the traditional epic.[42] Moreover, perhaps drama can be further differentiated into Ahabian tragedy and Ishmaelian comedy, as William H. Shurr suggests.[43] Edward Ahearn's list of genres in *Moby-Dick* corresponds to none of those already listed; like Baym, however, he includes nonliterary genres. According to Ahearn, *Moby-Dick*, "as representative of the Schle-

---

41. Nina Baym, "Melville's Quarrel with Fiction," *PMLA* 94 (October 1979): 918.

42. "In performing for the rapidly evolving American consciousness what the *Iliad* and *Odyssey* did for pan-Hellenic Greece or what the Gilgamesh epitomized for the ancient Sumerians or even what Elias Lonnrot intended the *Kalevala* to do for Finland, the novel *Moby-Dick* serves American literary history as an epic." Foley, "Price of Narrative Fiction," 436. Note the generic contradiction of the main clause.

43. William H. Shurr, "*Moby-Dick* as Tragedy and Comedy," in Bickman, ed., *Approaches*, 32–49. As Shurr points out, Ishmael gives a (non-Aristotelian) theory of tragedy in chapter 47.

gelian total romantic art form . . . include[s] at least: first person narrative, proto-Conradian framing, pictorial art, philosophy-theology, science, history, lyric, song, myth, etymology, legal affidavit, sermon, melodrama, and dream."[44]

Even these extended lists are not complete. The genre of bibliography provides for a metafictional reading of Melville's book. Ishmael invites such a reading plainly enough in the remarkable "Cetology" chapter, in which he spends pages engaged in quasi-scientific discourse classifying whales as types of printed books ("folio," "octavo," and "duodecimo"). Ishmael's catachresis in the following passage, which begins with a pun on the word "volume," compares whales to books and thus turns cetology into bibliography. Both sciences, like generic classification, are acts of sorting: "And if you descend into the bowels of the various leviathans, why there you will not find distinctions a fiftieth part as available to the systematizer as those external ones already enumerated. What then remains? Nothing but to take hold of the whales bodily, in their entire liberal volume, and boldly sort them that way. And this is the Bibliographical system here adopted."[45] The sorting Ishmael carries out is itself a kind of generic classification as much in the etymological as in the literary-metaphorical sense of the word. That is, Ishmael identifies the *gens* or clan of each whale according to its physical differentia.

Several critics have argued that the cetological material in *Moby-Dick* represents Melville's *aesthetics of heterogeneity*, itself a corollary of a world fraught with "epistemological fragmentation and disarray."[46] If, as Howard P. Vincent has argued, the " 'Cetology' is a parody of the efforts of limited men to pigeonhole the phenomena of Nature,"[47] it is equally a parody of the efforts of limited men to pigeonhole the phenomena of writing, an implicit question of "why genre?" In using metaphors of "book" and "bibliography," Ishmael plays with his readers' generic expectations the way Ahab plays with his crew's perception of the "real" purpose of their voyage. For example, Ishmael refers to his encyclopedic description of whales as a "bibliography" rather than a "zoology." We may describe the catachresis of "bibliography" for "zoology" as a point of dehiscence between types of writing, as a point where genres collide. Ishmael's

44. Edward J. Ahearn, "A Mutual, Joint-Stock World," in *Marx and Modern Fiction* (New Haven: Yale University Press, 1989), 191–92.

45. Ibid., 140.

46. Robert M. Greenberg, "Cetology: Center of Multiplicity and Discord in *Moby-Dick*," *ESQ*, n.s., 27, no. 1 (1981): 9, 11.

47. Howard P. Vincent, *The Trying-Out of "Moby-Dick"* (Boston: Houghton-Mifflin, 1949), 141.

exasperation with the inadequacy of his bibliographic system itself becomes the subject for representation. It is, like Ahab's quest for Moby-
Dick, an attempt to create an essence that explains what simply *is*.

As has been pointed out more than once, the search for Moby-Dick is
an allegory of reading. Thus we come to see, in Edgar A. Dryden's words,
that "surrounding and structuring Ishmael's encyclopedic treatment of
whaling is the metaphor of the whale as a book." Dryden's formulation,
along with the dialectical struggle invoked by the title of his book, *Melville's
Thematics of Form: The Great Art of Telling the Truth*, together show how
much *Moby-Dick* depends for its meaning not on its genre, but upon its
generic instability.[48] *Moby-Dick* rests on—or takes flight from—the foundations laid by Melville's previous attempts at fiction, which John Samson
has argued to be transformations or parodies of established genres, particularly of an American genre he calls the "narrative of facts."[49] Samson
argues that Melville wrote what he calls antifactual narratives, where the
anti indicates an important parodistic relationship to what is being written
against. In converting these narratives into "antinarratives," Melville was
combating the dominant ideology, which invested such narratives with
ideological content concerning the superiority of the white race, the truth
of Christianity, the effectiveness of Western science, and the like. As
Samson puts it:

> The white culture's generic-ideological security—the self-assured
> sense that the historical tale has been told and understood—can
> be maintained only if its narratives accept unquestioningly the
> generic claim to factuality; to move beyond that point and examine
> the ideological assumptions—as Melville does—is to break down
> that claim. . . . Melville calls attention to the unstated generic,
> ideological, and narratological premises and thus writes a defla
> tionary but corrective antihistory.[50]

There are several complicating factors that Samson disregards in this
analysis of the ideology of genre. First, he has had to "invent" a genre for
Melville to write against. Although Samson specifies a "genre *then* commonly called narrative of facts" (emphasis added), he unfortunately gives
no citations from nineteenth-century sources to show that this term was in

48. Edgar A. Dryden, *Melville's Thematics of Form: The Great Art of Telling the Truth* (Baltimore:
Johns Hopkins University Press, 1968), 84.
49. John Samson, *White Lies: Melville's Narratives of Facts*, 2.
50. Ibid., 14–15.

use then. It would seem that he has identified a group of texts according to their use-value, and then given them a name.

Second, Samson goes on to treat this genre, the "narrative of facts"—not to mention "white culture" itself—as somehow homogeneous, as more "self-assured" than it really was—particularly if it had no name and no set of prescriptive rules (the earliest kind of genre "theory"). He thus depicts genres in general as more stable and coercive than they really are. Of course, certain genres—legal discourse (see Chapter 5, "What Is Legal Discourse Made Of?"), some kinds of philosophical writing—suppress their heterogeneity and their ultimate dependence upon other genres. It seems more accurate to say that Melville discovered the heterogeneity that was already *in* the "narrative of facts" to begin with. For example, Baym concludes that "because of its continual references to so many familiar literary genres both fictional and nonfictional, *Moby-Dick* manages to be interpretable even while submitting itself to no single genre."[51] Note that Baym implicitly assumes that only genre makes works interpretable. Our relation to the book before us changes with its generic transformations, the way the crew's relationship to Moby-Dick is changed through their altered relationship to Ahab. But what if all literature achieves its meaning the way *Moby-Dick* does? What if all literature makes itself interpretable by referring to what it is not, by cordoning itself off from the contamination of other genres, to carve out a space for itself in the inhospitable universe of discourse? What if "every text participates in one or several genres, there is no genreless text; there is always a genre and genres, yet such participation never amounts to belonging"?[52] I contend that a text's generic status is rarely what it seems to be, that it is always already unstable, and thus that *Moby-Dick* is merely an extreme and extremely self-conscious example of the positioning and marginalization that every work takes toward its place "within" a generic system.

IV

Without denying Jameson's historicist account of the appearance of generic differentiation within today's commodified mass-cultural production, I argue that this particular visibility is a material difference that

51. Baym, "Melville's Quarrel with Fiction," 918.
52. Jacques Derrida, "The Law of Genre," 65.

disguises an essential struggle between genres—and *within* individual
works—that has been at the heart of our reading and writing process for a
long, long time. I argue that, since a "single" genre is only recognizable as
difference, as a foregrounding against the background of its neighboring
genres, every work involves more than one genre, even if only implicitly.
The position I argue, then, is double-edged, both asserting the inescapability of genre as a kind of Kantian faculty of reading, and at the same time
detailing genre's volatility and flux as a system of cultural values and as
the only partly realizable possibility of "using" any particular text. Stephen
Greenblatt has formulated the issue succinctly, though he limits it to the
ideological differentiations between the literary and the nonliterary: "It is
important to expose the theoretical untenability of the conventional boundaries between facts and artifacts, but the particular terms of this boundary
at a specific time and place cannot simply be discarded. . . . These impure
terms that mark the difference between the literary and the nonliterary are
the currency in crucial institutional negotiations and exchange."[53] The
concept of generic instability mediates between previous attempts at
theorizing genre, which have either looked at genre as something that *is*,
which must then be classified, systematized, and renamed (Brunetière,
Fowler, Frye, Hamburger), or else have attempted to prove that genre
really doesn't exist, that each work is its own genre, that we must get
"beyond genre" by accepting multiple criteria for generic categorization
(Hernadi), or that genres are critical tools for interpretation rather than
static categories (Rosmarin). The "flashings" I have pointed out in *Moby-
Dick* do not only occur in "great" literature. They have also been produced
by a nineteenth-century Parisian hack polygraph who sneaks literature
into his textbooks. Some are carried out by pop singers very much aware
of and ill at ease with audience expectations. Some are carried out by
anthropologists, others by theorists testing the limits of their dialogic
language.

The theory of ideology and of its relation to genre adumbrated above
can be described, metaphorically, as "refractive" or "anaclastic." The
critical readings appropriate to such a theory would approach their objects
from the side, as it were, using the comparative method to bring together
texts from different periods (such as Lévi-Strauss and Aphra Behn in the
next chapter, or Roland Barthes and Julián del Casal in Chapter 4) and
from different cultures (Dylan and Degenhardt, Richardson and Barthes).

---

53. Stephen Greenblatt, "Shakespeare and the Exorcists," in *After Strange Texts*, ed. Gregory
S. Jay and David L. Miller (Tuscaloosa: University of Alabama Press, 1985), 103.

The refracted meanings that result from such comparisons are similar to what is "said" through metaphor—metaphor is precisely the "unsaid." A further aspect of such refraction is that the texts are necessarily treated as decentered, torn apart by the various genres for which the most accessible record is the critical readings and listenings they have received. Therefore, in those chapters where I do not treat texts as reading each other (as I do in my study of the *ars dictaminis*, or in the chapter on Degenhardt's "reading" of Dylan), criticism takes on the same importance and uses the same strategies as the primary texts. The resulting "thick descriptions," in which texts fade not so much into their historical background as into their transhistorical critical contexts, is my way of bringing to light the unsayable of generic systems.

2

The Genres of Ethnography:
Oroonoko in the *Tristes Tropiques*

> If the discourse of manners and customs aspires to a stable
> fixing of subjects and systems of difference . . . its project is
> not and never can be complete. . . . In the case of travel
> writing, manners and customs description is always in play
> with other sorts of representation that also bespeak difference
> and position subjects in their own ways.
>
> — Mary Louise Pratt, "Scratches on the Face of the Country"

MARY LOUISE PRATT SUGGESTS that the writing of cultural confrontation will inevitably exhibit generic instability. The unstable genre of
what she calls the "discourse of manners and customs" continually oscil-
lates between the poles of anthropology (description and analysis of the
manners and customs of others) and autobiography (description and
analysis of the observing self). While trying to describe this play of genres,
Pratt begins to lose control of her own prose. She allows an indeterminacy
in the term "subjects," which, like a carelessly used pronoun, becomes a
sign containing totally opposite concepts and positions (the anthropological
"subject at hand" versus the autobiographical "writing subject"), thus
creating a subject that stands simultaneously in front of *and* behind the
camera, as it were.[1] The analysis of ideological split made in Chapter 1

1. Mary Louise Pratt, "Scratches on the Face of the Country; or, What Mr. Barrow Saw in
the Land of the Bushmen," *Critical Inquiry* 12, no. 2 (1985): 121.

would suggest that this doubleness constitutes the subject as a creation of ideology. In this chapter I note this shifting between subjects and between genres, in two rather different discourses of manners and customs, Aphra Behn's *Oroonoko* (1688) and Claude Lévi-Strauss's *Tristes tropiques* (1955).

I

In 1663 Aphra Behn, then twenty-three years old, made the long and perilous voyage with her family to the tropics of South America and the English colony of Surinam, of which her father had been appointed governor. *Or then again, maybe he never was governor; maybe she never made the voyage at all.* While in Surinam, Behn met a remarkable African prince named Oroonoko, who had been brought to Surinam as a slave and renamed "Caesar," with whom she visited the indigenous people of the area. *Or then again, perhaps no such man ever existed; perhaps Oroonoko is just another literary character stitched together out of the generic conventions of "Romance" and of the "True Relations," which acquainted Europeans with the New World; and what are we to think of the resemblance between his supposedly African name and that of the well-known South American river?* Behn was forced to witness—*or to imagine*—the ill-treatment of this noble prince, his subsequent revolt, and his horrible mutilation and execution by the whites of Surinam. Aphra Behn told the story many times to her friends as if it was her own story, but for some reason (*guilt, horror?*) did not write it down until 1687. It was published the following year—a year before Behn's death—under the title *Oroonoko; Or, a History of the Royal Slave*.

The twenty-six-year-old lycée teacher Claude Lévi-Strauss made *his* voyage to the tropics on the promise of a telephone call, received one autumn morning in 1934 from Célestin Bouglé, head of the École Normale Supérieure. Bouglé offered Lévi-Strauss a post as a visiting professor of sociology at the University of São Paulo. During their four-year stay in Brazil, Lévi-Strauss and his wife, Dina Dreyfus, made several expeditions into the *sertão* (backlands), gathering data on the rapidly disappearing cultures of the Caduveo, Nambikwara, Bororo, and other indigenous peoples of the tropics. But the narrative of those expeditions, *Tristes tropiques*, would probably not have been written had not Lévi-Strauss made a second, more sinister voyage in 1941 from France to the island of Martinique. Europe had fallen to the Nazis, and the Jewish Lévi-Strauss, awaiting word on whether he would be admitted to the United States or sent back to France and almost certain death, undoubtedly saw his life passing before his eyes—perhaps in much the same way Aphra Behn saw her life passing before her eyes in her last year—as he contemplated the enormous mass of index cards, maps, and other field data yet to be turned into a finished work. Many years later, in 1955, *Tristes tropiques* was published. It quickly became a classic not so much of anthropology, as of literature.

One of our books, then, was written by a Frenchman, the other by an Englishwoman; the former is an exalted member of the Académie Française, the latter was a commercial playwright despised for her alleged obscenities; one book is usually classed as anthropological nonfiction, the other as novel and romance; one book was published a year after Bien Dien Phu had signaled the collapse of the French colonial empire, the other was an early modern work, "with the one exception of *Pilgrim's Progress*, the most considerable work of fiction produced in English up to the end of the seventeenth century."[2] *Oroonoko* appeared when the English colonial period was still in its infancy, when Barbados was still the empire's most important mercantile outpost and the North American colonies insignificant. However, there is already in this novel an implicit reference to former colonies as well: the English had lost Surinam, the scene of the story, a few years before its publication.

At first glance it seems that only contrasts would be possible between these two works. Indeed, in his dream of being transported back to the crucial period of European exploration and colonization, Lévi-Strauss seems to conjure up early visitors to South America such as Behn:

> Je voudrais avoir vécu au temps des *vrais* voyages, quand s'offrait dans toute sa plendeur [*sic*] un spectacle non encore gâché, contaminé et maudit. . . . Eût-il mieux valu arriver à Rio au XVIII⁢e siècle avec Bougainville, ou au XVIᵉ, avec Léry et Thevet? Chaque lustre en arrière me permet de sauver une coûtume, de gagner une fête, de partager une croyance supplémentaire.

> (I wished I had lived in the days of *real* journeys, when it was still possible to see the full splendour of a spectacle that had not yet been blighted, polluted and spoilt. . . . Would it have been better to arrive in Rio in the eighteenth century with Bougainville, or in the sixteenth with Léry and Thevet? For every five years I move

2. George Woodcock, *The Incomparable Aphra* (London: T. V. Boardman, 1948), 205.

back in time, I am able to save a custom, gain a ceremony or share in another belief.)[3]

Yet, despite having preceded Lévi-Strauss by two and a half centuries, Behn shares Lévi-Strauss's elegaic tone, while taking the opposite stance from his praise of the power of historical imagination. Thus, both works document a voyage to the New World and the horrific discovery by the narrator of what the Old World has wrought there. Lévi-Strauss's genre dictates that he observe and record his observations; instead, he chooses to imagine and to present *Tristes tropiques* as a work of his subjectivity. Aphra Behn's genre dictates that she arrange and present a construction supposedly derived from her imagination; instead, she stubbornly insists that *Oroonoko* is a plain record of fact. Indeed, most critics have been more concerned with whether or not she was ever in Surinam than with what *Oroonoko* achieves as a narrative. The twin providers of information, imagination and experience, serve these two authors only inasmuch as they work to undermine the norms of their respective genres. These works therefore pose the same interrelated questions about writing: what is the relationship between writing and domination, and what genre is appropriate to the capture in writing of the non-Europeans of the New World? What sort of act would this writing be, and what are the motives behind it? In "La Leçon d'écriture," in *Tristes tropiques* Lévi-Strauss answers all three questions with the daringly simple equation: "La fonction primaire de la communication écrite est de faciliter l'asservissement" (344; "The primary function of written communication is to facilitate slavery" [299]). But if writing facilitates slavery, is a writing of liberation possible, and what would it look like?[4] Rather than taking the "La Leçon d'écriture" out of context, it is necessary to relate its message to the generic instability and thematization of writing found in the book as a whole. A comparison of these two works reveals a common dialectical interplay—rather than a simple equation—between writing and ruling, an interplay in which subject

3. Claude Lévi-Strauss, *Tristes tropiques* (Paris: Plon, 1955), 44; translated by John Weightman and Doreen Weightman, under the title *Tristes tropiques* (New York: Atheneum, 1974), 43. Further citations in text.

4. Jeffrey Mehlman has pointed to Lévi-Strauss's dilemma between "the temptation to objectify the other, or to emphathize abusively with him," and to its solution in the concept of structuralism as the elaboration of the unconscious, "mediating between self and other, unknown to either . . . the condition of possibility for communication between the two." "Punctuation in *Tristes tropiques*," in *A Structural Study of Autobiography: Proust, Leiris, Sartre, Lévi-Strauss* (Ithaca: Cornell University Press, 1974), 209. Mehlman, however, sees the difficulties posed by the writing process as psychological rather than social.

and object of writing are constructed and deconstructed in the flux of genre. I compare *Tristes tropiques* with *Oroonoko* not on the basis of shared genres, but on the basis of a shared generic instability arising from their depictions of cultural confrontation.

II

No reader of *Tristes tropiques* would doubt that it was, as Lévi-Strauss himself has admitted or boasted, constructed from the ashes of an unfinished novel which he had attempted to write on his return home from Brazil.[5] After its publication, Roger Bastide reported, "I had the same pleasure, I mean, the same *genre* of pleasure, in reading Lévi-Strauss as in reading Proust."[6] Bastide risks identifying the genre of *Tristes tropiques* through its effect on the reader. The experience of pleasure first of all isolates certain types of writing from others (literature from anthropology, for example). However, Bastide's statement is clearly meant not to categorize *Tristes tropiques* as a novel and hence dismiss it as a work of ethnography, but rather to unfold what is hidden in the work. Bastide finds the value of Lévi-Strauss's anthropology to lie in its replacement of the empirical by the *caché* or hidden, a movement that problematizes the genre of (cultural) anthropology. Lévi-Strauss's Proustian attitude is meaningful precisely because this is not a novel, but a work of ethnography haunted by the novel's shadow.

If Bastide reduces the generic instability of *Tristes tropiques* to a single opposition between novel and anthropology, Edmund Leach has been more expansive in designating it an "autobiographical ethnographic travel book."[7] (It is not clear whether Leach intends this statement to be paradoxical or redundant.) Every travel book is autobiographical and every ethnography implies travel, but the intersection of these three genres in a single book resembles one of those trick drawings in which one can see either a woman or a death's head, just not both at the same time. Carl A. Rubino, who like Bastide believes that Lévi-Strauss's project in *Tristes tropiques* is to bring science and literature back into the single discourse

5. James Boon, *From Symbolism to Structuralism: Lévi-Strauss in a Literary Tradition* (New York: Harper & Row, 1972), 32.
6. Roger Bastide, "Aphra Behn ou l'ethnographe «A la recherche du temps perdu»," *Présence Africaine 7* (April–May 1956): 150. Emphasis added.
7. Edmund Leach, *Claude Lévi-Strauss* (New York: Viking, 1970), 4.

they had shared in early times (in Empedocles, for example), adds a few more genres to our list. It is, "besides being a work of anthropology, intellectual history, literature, and philosophy, both personal and intellectual; in this sense it qualifies as 'exile literature,' for it is the story of a European Jew compelled to seek the new world both south and north as the Nazis gained control of the great centers of European civilization."[8] Anthropologist Clifford Geertz adds yet another possibility, classifying *Tristes tropiques* as a *Mischgattung* of "theoretical treatises set out as travelogues."[9] The only thing common to all these views is a recognition of the work's generic instability. The reactions of all of Lévi-Strauss's readers show them at a loss to place *Tristes tropiques* generically, or rather, sure of the fact that it cannot be placed in any single generic category. They see field data, literature, autobiography, and philosophy woven together into the fabric of a travel narrative. This generic instability is synonymous with the controversial status of Lévi-Strauss's findings both here and elsewhere, which I formulate in the following question: given the compelling nature of this writing, to what *uses* can it be put? The "problem" of Lévi-Strauss, which is basically the controversy over whether his structural method of anthropology can be used to produce scientifically valid results, is as much a problem of writing and its generic classifications as it is a problem of content, methodology, or the reliability of data. I have gone to the trouble of analyzing these various generic readings—and shall do the same for *Oroonoko*—because the inconclusiveness of such readings, coupled with the effort critics feel (and should continue to feel) compelled to spend over them, become an essential theme of both Lévi-Strauss's book and Aphra Behn's.

For example, we might ask why both works devote their first sentences to questioning their generic status. Lévi-Strauss begins with the following disclaimer: "Je hais les voyages et les explorateurs. Et voici que je m'apprête à raconter mes expéditions" (13; "I hate travelling and explorers. Yet here I am proposing to tell the story of my expeditions" [17]). A work generally places clues to its genre rather early, so that readers will not be confused, will know how to use what is being said. Instead, this first sentence proclaims generic instability, announces that, as Jeffrey

8. Carl A. Rubino, "Winged Chariots and Black Holes: Some Reflections on Science and Literature," *Genre* 16 (Winter 1983): 342.

9. Clifford Geertz, "Blurred Genres: The Refiguration of Social Thought," 165. [Works of general theoretical interest in the field of genre studies are cited in full in the Bibliography—AUTHOR.]

Mehlman has put it, "this travel journal will be other than a travel journal if it is to succeed."[10] It places the work *en abîme*, makes it what it is not, invokes the other genres against which it will struggle.

The opening of *Oroonoko*, on the other hand, is striking for how it works against the conventions of writing, as Behn repeatedly inserts her own person and a sense of the tactile into the act of storytelling. Her insistence on the corporeal is due at least in part to the fact that she locates the use-value of her story in its literal "re-membering" of the protagonist. Body parts appear constantly in her account, as though their fleshly weight were to be placed in the scales against her readers' incredulity: "I was myself an Eye-witness to a great Part of what you will find here set down; and what I cou'd not be Witness of, I receiv'd from the Mouth of the chief Actor in this History."[11] So far, this is a standard phrase for opening a story; Behn uses it in other texts as well. But Behn lays bare this narrative device by continuing to insist on presence and vision. Throughout this written account, Behn insists on its oral nature and on its basis in experience; she establishes herself as storyteller rather than *romancière*, as Walter Benjamin would put it.[12] For example, in the very next passage, she is led to her own corporeality by way of the idea that she lives in the same London neighborhood as her readers, a place where specimens of the fauna of Surinam which she has brought back with her can be seen: "For Skins of prodigious Snakes, of which there are some three-score Yards in length; as is the Skin of one that may be seen at his Majesty's *Antiquary*'s; where are also some rare Flies, of amazing Forms and Colours, presented to 'em by myself; some as big as my Fist, some less" (130). The same juxtaposition of corporeality and the exotic recurs later in the narrative, where Behn describes herself, with her "Hair . . . cut short" and dressed in a "Taffety Cap, with black Feathers on my Head," going with Oroonoko and her

---

10. Mehlman, "Punctuation in *Tristes tropiques*," 187.

11. Aphra Behn, *Oroonoko; or, The Royal Slave. A True History*, in *The Works of Aphra Behn*, ed. Montague Summers, vol. 5 (New York: W. W. Norton, 1973), 129. Further citations in text.

12. "Es hebt den Roman gegen alle übrigen Formen der Prosadichtung—Märchen, Sage, ja selbst Novelle—ab, daß er aus mündlicher Tradition weder kommt noch in sie eingeht. Vor allem aber gegen das Erzählen" ("What differentiates the novel from all other forms of prose literature— fairytale, saga, even novella—is that it neither originates from nor becomes part of oral tradition. And this differentiates it especially from storytelling"). Walter Benjamin, "Der Erzähler. Betrachtungen zum Werk Nikolai Lesskows," 37. Benjamin, writing in the 1920s, was convinced that storytelling, based on experience and travel, as in *Oroonoko*, was coming to an end. Both the complicated textuality of the eighteenth-century novel (as in Laurence Sterne) and the narrative control of the nineteenth-century novel (as in George Eliot) are very different from what Behn is up to.

brother to visit the Indians, who "touch'd us, laying their Hands upon all the Features of our Faces, feeling our Breasts, and Arms, taking up one Petticoat, then wondering to see another; admiring our Shoes and Stockings, but more our Garters, which we gave 'em. . . . In fine, we suffer'd 'em to survey us as they pleas'd, and we thought they would never have done admiring us" (185). This description differs from the usual explorer's account, which spends all its time dwelling on the native bodies. It also contrasts with the process of production that slave and Indian are meant to further. Behn never describes the work that slaves perform in the New World, and never describes any products of the Surinam plantation.

Behn's invocations of her own fleshly existence take on the aspect of a nervous self-assurance when read against the gradual dismemberment of her title figure. Brought to America as a slave, Oroonoko chafes at his owner's incessant, unfulfilled promises of freedom and leads a slave revolt. Betrayed by his fainthearted followers, Oroonoko is captured and severely whipped, and his wounds are rubbed with Cayenne pepper. Driven to despair by the shame of being whipped, Oroonoko then runs away with his wife Imoinda; and when they are surrounded, he kills her to prevent her capture and pulls out his own entrails in an abortive suicide. The whites carefully sew him back together so as not to deprive themselves of the pleasure of burning him alive. The final disintegration of Oroonoko's body is described as follows:

> The Executioner came, and first cut off his Members, and threw them into the Fire; after that, with an ill-favour'd Knife, they cut off his Ears and his Nose, and burn'd them; he still smoak'd on, as if nothing had touch'd him; then they hack'd off one of his Arms, and still he bore up and held his Pipe; but at the cutting off the other Arm, his Head sunk, and his Pipe dropt, and he gave up the Ghost, without a Groan, or a Reproach. . . . They cut *Cæsar* into Quarters, and sent them to several of the chief Plantations. (208)

By the end of the story, then, only Oroonoko's mouth (and perhaps, as we shall see, his name) remains, the mouth that composedly smokes the pipe and out of which Behn had received the story. But Behn's presence as storyteller—we must be able to see her fist—is contradicted both by the marvels of the African romance in the first half of her book, and by her crucial absences from the side of Oroonoko in its second half.

There is also a genetic reason for Behn's emphasis on physical presence and with it on the genre of storytelling. Behn wrote *Oroonoko* in the context of oral interchange, and it was the written version of what had previously been an oral narrative: "[Behn wrote] very quickly and, according to her editor, Charles Gildon, often in a room full of company and taking part in the conversation, as he had observed her. But Southerne, who turned the novel into a very successful play, claimed that she told the story even better than she wrote it. No doubt over the years it had acquired embellishments of various kinds."[13] The transition from spoken to written is reflected in the other curious dichotomies of this work: in the generic conflict between novel and romance; in the alternate domination and powerlessness in it of the written word; and in Behn's shifting between two roles—narrator and actor—in the tragedy of Oroonoko.

From its beginning, *Tristes tropiques* explores the subversive possibilities of language and links them to the work's generic instability. One signal, warning the reader that the main subject of *Tristes tropiques* will be its own genesis and reception, is the title of the first part of the book: "La Fin des voyages." John and Doreen Weightman have translated this as "An End to Voyaging"; but "fin" here could also indicate "goal" or "object." The goal and end of the voyage is the beginning of the book. Although the core of the book is a presentation of the findings from Lévi-Strauss's anthropological fieldwork in Brazil, the author puts the objectivity of his findings in doubt from the beginning by subordinating them to the more important self-reflexive definition of the anthropologist's task. He informs the reader, for example, that his fascination for Brazil was stimulated by the paronomasia between the proper name "Brésil" and the French verb *grésiller*, "to sizzle" (50). He was attracted by the aroma of Brazil, so to speak. Lévi-Strauss will practice not an objective anthropology modeled on the natural sciences, but rather a literary science that springs from the bodily appetites of its practitioner. Similarly, the data gathered in Brazil took twenty years to coalesce into *Tristes tropiques*, at which point it had been reshaped by the author's memories and lapses of memory.

Years after gathering his data, while emigrating to the United States during World War II, Lévi-Strauss worries that the "malle remplie de mes documents d'expédition: fichiers linguistiques et technologiques, journal de route, notes prises sur le terrain, cartes, plans et négatifs photographiques—des milliers de feuillets, de fiches et de clichés" ("trunk full of documents relating to my fieldwork . . . linguistic and technological card-indexes, a travel-diary, anthropological notes, maps, diagrams and photo-

13. Maureen Duffy, *The Passionate Shepherdess* (London: Jonathan Cape, 1977), 38.

graphic negatives—in short, thousands of items") would be seen by the
tropical arm of the Vichy police on Martinique as different genres, as
"instructions en code (en ce qui concerne les vocabulaires indigènes) et
des relevés de dispositifs stratégiques ou des plans d'invasion pour les
cartes, les schémas et les photos" (33; "instructions in code [the notes on
native dialects], or diagrams of fortifications, or invasion plans [the maps,
sketches and photos]" [33]). What makes Lévi-Strauss (in his own mind
at least) the object of fear and respect by the police is also what gives him
a hold over his reader, for although the police thought those materials,
whose heterogeneity is lingered over at such length by the *bricoleur* Lévi-
Strauss, might be "intelligence" information, in fact they became the book
we are holding in our hands. I use the term *bricoleur* (handy-man, jack-of-
all-trades) here, because Lévi-Strauss himself made it an important critical
term. Lévi-Strauss opposes the *bricoleur,* whose trial-and-error, untrained
approach to problem solving uses whatever materials are at hand, to the
engineer, whose formal approach from first principles requires specified
parts. This *bricolage* makes *Tristes tropiques* similar to myth, since "mythical
thought is . . . a kind of intellectual 'bricolage' " which "can reach brilliant
unforeseen results."[14] The contrast between field data, spy material, and
Tristes tropiques shows the same kind of structural mastery that Lévi-Strauss
will find in mythology and in Caduveo face and body painting. That is, he
will find that myth serves the same function for a culture as face painting,
whose symmetrical designs are "hiéroglyphes décrivant un inaccessible âge
d'or qu'à défaut de code elles célèbrent dans leur parure" (224; "hiero-
glyphics describing an inaccessible golden age, which they extol in their
ornamentation, since they have no code in which to express it" [197]). The
scene on Martinique reminds us that *Tristes tropiques* is composed of this
mythical *bricolage,* which Lévi-Strauss prefers to an "engineered" ethnography, which would allow the reader to "see" the Brazilian Indians as they
"really are" without the anthropologist stepping in front of the lens to
comment or to remove the tin cans from the picture in order to make it
more "primitive." Hence, one set of materials that this *bricolage* works over
are the various genres that find their way into it. An "engineer" would
have tried to write his account within the restrictions of a single genre; the
bricoleur Lévi-Strauss continually and self-consciously jumps between one
genre and another.

　　Three hundred pages later, we read the counterpart of this opening
scene in Martinique, another "Birth of Structuralism from the Spirit of

14. Claude Lévi-Strauss, *The Savage Mind* (Chicago: University of Chicago Press, 1966), 17.

Generic Miscegenation," another loving description of the generic incest between ethnography and literature, as Lévi-Strauss begins to write a play, "L'Apothéose d'Auguste," a new version of the neoclassical drama *Cinna* (1640) by the French playwright Pierre Corneille. The choice of *Cinna* is exact. This monument of neoclassicism is an overtly ideological exploration of the problems of empire and of the qualities of a good ruler. Corneille chose Augustus as an example of the latter; Lévi-Strauss rewrites him as an anthropologist. Lévi-Strauss's literary inspiration springs from a crisis in his work. He carefully draws a bleak, almost Dantesque picture of his situation in the Brazilian backlands: people are dying of malaria all around him; he is cut off from his (civilized?) companions; he can do no fieldwork because the two groups of Indians present are hostile toward each other and toward him. A dramatic enough situation, then, and tones of dramatic self-pity enter his description as he once again places himself in front of the camera and confronts the limits and ironies of anthropology:

> A pratiquer ce métier, l'enquêteur se ronge: a-t-il vraiment abandonné son milieu, ses amis, ses habitudes, dépensé des sommes et des efforts si considérables, compromis sa santé, pour ce seul résultat: faire pardonner sa présence à quelques douzaines de malheureux condamnés à une extinction prochaine? (434)

> (As he practises his profession, the anthropologist is consumed by doubts: has he really abandoned his native setting, his friends, and his way of life, spent such considerable amounts of money and energy, and endangered his health, for the sole purpose of making his presence acceptable to a score or two of miserable creatures doomed to early extinction? [375])

Those familiar with *Cinna* will have already recognized in this harangue a parody of the speech of the Emperor Augustus at the beginning of the second act, in which he questions why he gave up so much for the very unsatisfying job of running the Roman Empire. Auguste expresses his *ennui* in the following couplets:

> J'ai souhaité l'empire, et j'y suis parvenu;
> Mais, en le souhaitant, je ne l'ai pas connu:
> Dans sa possession, j'ai trouvé pour tous charmes
> D'effroyables soucis, d'éternelles alarmes,

Milles ennemis secrets, la mort à tous propos,
Point de plaisir sans trouble, et jamais de repos.
> (II, lines 371–76)

(I wished for empire, and I have achieved it;
But wishing for it, I knew not what it was.
In its possession I have found no charms,
But fearful cares, endless anxieties,
A thousand secret foes, death everywhere,
No pleasures unalloyed, and never peace.)[15]

Auguste's anguish is that of a man who has compromised himself morally in order to arrive at a position that having reached it, he recognizes as empty and unsatisfying. Similarly, Lévi-Strauss, having undergone considerable hardships himself and imposed them on others in order to mount the river of time and return to the origins of man, has found only the place "où manque pourtant l'empreinte de Vendredi" (384; "from which, however, Man Friday's footprint is missing" [334]). The occasion for this remark is Lévi-Strauss's inability to fathom the substance of his newly discovered tribe of Indians. He recognizes his scientific game of the discovery of man's true self as a fantasmagoria, as the myth of Robinson discovering Friday. His solution is to write the significance of his encounter in personal terms and as absence. And if one can read the chapter "Robinson" as dramatic *anagnorisis* (the scene of recognition), in which Lévi-Strauss recognizes ethnography's inability to escape the prison-house of "language as *empreinte* or *écriture*,"[16] then the chapter "L'Apothéose d'Auguste" is the dénouement, as the hero turns to positive action, to beginning a kind of writing that will always remind itself of its status as sign, as the union of what is present with what is inevitably missing. Lévi-Strauss's empire, of course, is that which his reading and writing lessons—including Corneille—have given him, an empire of signs. Again and again in his writings, Lévi-Strauss invokes the sign as the only level at which the conflict between empiricism and idealism can be sublated, as the only means by which disparate cultures can be compared.

The invocation of neoclassical drama as one antigenre against which *Tristes tropiques* works involves the play of presence and absence that haunts

15. Pierre Corneille, *Cinna, in Théatre II* (Paris: Garnier-Flammarion, 1980), 377; translated by Lacy Lockert, under the title *Cinna, The Chief Plays of Corneille*, 2d ed. (Princeton: Princeton University Press, 1957), 175.
16. Mehlmann, "Punctuation in *Tristes tropiques*," 198.

"L'Apothéose d'Auguste" as it haunts Behn's *Oroonoko*. Seventeenth-century verse is rewritten as prose, and the language of action is halted by memory in this bizarre juxtaposition of different historical epochs, ideologies, and genres. Anthropology here reduces itself to this game of *fort/da*, a game that continues into the actual genesis of the drama:

> Il me sembla que les problèmes qui me tourmentaient fournissaient la matière d'une pièce de théâtre. Je la concevais aussi précise que si elle eût été déjà écrite. Les Indiens avaient disparu: pendant six jours, j'écrivis du matin au soir, au verso de feuilles couvertes de vocabulaires, de croquis et de généalogies. (436)

> (I had the idea that the problems bothering me could provide the subject-matter of a play. It was as clear in my mind as if it had already been written. The Indians had disappeared: for six days, I wrote from morning till night on the backs of sheets of paper covered with word lists, sketches, and genealogical tables. [378])

The situation of generic instability first seen on Martinique has returned (for the reader; chronologically, this is its anticipation), as Lévi-Strauss creates literature out of his data. And as the drama enters into this work, its conflict with anthropology is suggested: "The Indians had disappeared"—physically, so that the author would have the time and peace needed to write; generically, so that literature could replace anthropology. Lévi-Strauss's remark should be read in the context of another, made in the preceding chapter "Robinson," in which he finally finds his natives untouched by civilization, and discovers that he cannot "read" them: "Au terme d'un exaltant parcours, je tenais mes sauvages. Hélas, ils ne l'étaient que trop" (383; "After an enchanting trip up-river, I had certainly found my savages. Alas! they were only too savage" [333]). And so the Indians must disappear, just as anthropology, which Lévi-Strauss had imagined as a trip to origins, as the discovery and description of a pure and uncontaminated other that could act as a mirror for examining the self, must give way to another genre of self-discovery, literature.

The result, single sheets of paper with drama on one side and anthropology on the other, united as signifier and signified in Saussure's famous analogy for the sign, stands as an affirmation of structuralist *bricolage*. As Josué Harari has noted, "The Saussurian image of the sheet of paper uniting two independent entities [signifier and signified] back to back applies here *literally:* The imaginary scenario constituted by the play grafting itself on the obverse of the ethnological material (reality)."[17] If the two parts of the sign are drama and anthropology, the sign itself as greater than the sum of its parts is yet another genre, myth. Of course, myths have been with us from the first page of *Tristes tropiques*: the myth of the Golden Age, the myth of El Dorado, the myth (encountered on Martinique) of the Turkish (or Persian) spy writing down his observations on Europe in code, the myth of the wandering Jew, the myth of Robinson Crusoe. By theorizing that myth is a kind of binary thinking machine whose operands are signifiers, Lévi-Strauss tried to close the gap between "savage" and "civilized" thinking. And if it was only in his later *Raw and the Cooked* that Lévi-Strauss felt able to claim proudly that "this book on myths is itself a kind of myth," it is possible to show that *Tristes tropiques* begins to mythologize itself as well.[18] And one set of signifiers it brings into opposition are genres. The definition of a "supergenre" by its composition out of several other, "smaller" genres, or by what I call genre's recursive aspect, is common enough. Schlegel and Bakhtin both feel that the novel is just such a "supergenre"; so too is contemporary theory. What makes *Tristes tropiques* unique is the way its genres oppose and negate each other.

Hence, it is not only the Indians who must disappear; like Robinson's footprint, Corneille, the central representative of French classicism and hence of French "high" culture, must also be repressed in being rewritten. Let us not forget the significance of the two-sided sheets, covered with anthropological data and with *nouveau* Corneille. One can read either side of the sheet, but not both. We will be allowed to read only the "symptoms" of Corneille in the writer; we can read only the myth of anthropology. Concretely, we as readers are never given the *Apotheosis*, but only its mythical rewriting in *Tristes tropiques*.

In what has so far been the longest piece of criticism devoted to the "*Apotheosis*" chapter, Josué Harari argues that in it "the cornerstone of the structuralist operation is put into place at the very moment that Lévi-Strauss grants total license to the imaginary signifier." Harari concludes that the unfinished *Apotheosis* play "clearly illustrates that professional and methodological preoccupations play, for Lévi-Strauss, a central role in activating a powerful theoretical production that excludes ethnographic reality. For even while *The Apotheosis* founds in a systematic and complete manner the theory of structural anthropology, the play 'deconstructs' and

17. Josué V. Harari, *Scenarios of the Imaginary* (Ithaca: Cornell University Press, 1987), 210 n. 15. Harari credits Pierre St Amand.

18. Claude Lévi-Strauss, *The Raw and the Cooked*, translated by John Weightman and Doreen Weightman (New York: Harper & Row, 1969), 6.

exceeds the limits of meaning and structure that are produced by structuralist knowledge. This paradox is evident from the play's own structuration."[19] The paradox, I would argue, lies at a deeper level than is presented in Harari's argument, for in order to question the play's structuration one must agree that it is a play, which Harari accepts without question. I contend, however, that in the *Apotheosis* we find ourselves, like the police on Martinique, faced with the task of identifying genre. For we have here a play that can be considered neither in terms of (since it is not presented in dramatic form) nor apart from (since the French reader will inevitably think of Corneille when reading it) the features of drama.

The genre of the *Apotheosis* thus draws attention to itself through its absence: it is presented not as a play, but as a myth in the sense that Lévi-Strauss later formulates the use-value of myth in the endless playing out and successive mediation of binary oppositions. In his famous analysis of the Oedipus myth, Lévi-Strauss argues that the meaning of Oedipus does not lie in its plot, as millennia of Western culture have told us it does, but rather in the achronic ordering of oppositional elements within a story that has no definable beginning or end.[20] Just as his later essay shifts the significance of Oedipus's infraction and punishment to a logical space *between* those acts and other elements of the legend, here too Lévi-Strauss ignores the plot and dramatic structure of Corneille's *Cinna*—and jettisons the women characters who exert such a profound influence on the men—for the purpose of investing the remaining oppositions between the play's two heroes with a deeper "message."

Lévi-Strauss's rewrite tackles one of the central issues in the interpretation of *Cinna:* who is the hero? Both the Emperor Augustus and the conspirator Cinna appear in the play's full title. The nineteenth century tended to favor Augustus, who forgives his friend for conspiring against him, and to denigrate Cinna as a coward and sneak, whereas the twentieth century has returned to a view of Cinna as the play's real hero.[21] In a sense, the conflict in Corneille's play is never between the two title figures, but between them and the pressures that other characters place on them. Cinna would rather have the love of both Auguste and Émilie, but finds he must choose one or the other; Auguste, as we have seen above, is torn between an inner disgust for the horrible actions he has committed as

19. Harari, *Scenarios*, 209, 219.

20. See Claude Lévi-Strauss, "The Structural Study of Myth," *Journal of American Folklore* 78 (October–December 1955): 428–44.

21. Cf. Herbert Fogel, *The Criticism of Cornelian Tragedy* (New York: Exposition Press, 1967), 119–22.

emperor, and the necessity to condone them as justified by his position. Gone from Lévi-Strauss's version are the supporting characters, Émilie and Livie, who pull Cinna and Auguste in two directions. Lévi-Strauss's version not only locates conflicts within the contradictory desires of individual characters, but also eliminates the very difference between Cinna and Auguste, as each is allowed to turn into the other. Eugenio Donato notes that *L'Apothéose* is another example of the doppelgänger motif around which *Tristes tropiques* is structured: "Augustus and Cinna, in spite of their apparent differences, are really identical to each other, since both of their beings stem from the same desire for recognition."[22] Thus, both protagonists become equally heroic and equally cowardly, and agree to cooperate in Auguste's murder. This death, besides adding an obvious "hanged god" motif to the play, doubly reverses Corneille, who had seen cooperation as the result of both main characters seeking to preserve their lives.

In the following passage, we can see how the two heroes now both represent and subvert the Nature versus Culture dichotomy with which Lévi-Strauss occupies himself:

> [La pièce] mettait en scène deux hommes, amis d'enfance et qui se retrouvaient au moment, crucial pour chacun d'eux, de leurs carrières divergentes. L'un, qui avait pensé opter contre la civilis- ation, découvre qu'il a employé un moyen compliqué d'y rentrer, mais par une méthode abolissant le sens et la valeur de l'alternative devant laquelle il s'était jadis cru placé. L'autre, marqué dès la naissance pour la vie sociale et ses honneurs, comprend que tous ses efforts ont tendu vers un terme qui les voue à l'anéantissement. (437)

> (There were two main characters, who had been childhood friends and had met again at a crucial moment for both of them in their divergent careers. One, who thought he had opted out of civiliza- tion, discovers that he has used a complicated means of returning to it, but by a method destructive of the meaning and value of the choice with which he had originally believed himself to be faced. The other, who has been singled out from birth for social life and its attendant honours, realizes that all his efforts have been strained towards an end which dooms them to oblivion. [378])

22. Eugenio Donato, "*Tristes tropiques:* The Endless Journey," *MLN* 81 (1966): 280.

To introduce his plot summary Lévi-Strauss uses theatrical verbs of vision and physical presence, similar to those which Behn uses to open *Oroonoko*. They reverse the first sentence of *Tristes tropiques*, which invoked travel books by rejecting them. "Se présenter" and "mettre en scène" (both ignored by the English translators) only alert the reader even more to the absent stage of this drama, and thus to the replacement of the metaphysics of presence by a theory of the sign.

Another indication of Lévi-Strauss's mythologizing of Cornellian tragedy lies in his eschewing climax and dénouement for his play. It comes as a shock when Lévi-Strauss tells us, "Je ne sais plus au juste de quelle façon tout cela se terminait, les dernières scènes étant inachevées" (441; "I cannot quite remember how it was all supposed to end, as the last scenes remained unfinished" [381]), but I take this as a clue that Lévi-Strauss was not really writing drama at all and hence did not need to provide closure. His version of myth needs neither beginning nor ending because its meaning lies not in its plot in the Aristotelian sense, but rather in the events' repeated statement and mediation of symbolic oppositions. In his later work, he repeats over and over again that myths have neither beginnings, nor endings, nor generic boundaries—in "The Structural Study of Myth," he claims that Freud's "reading" of the Oedipus story in fact becomes a part of that myth, and I have already quoted from *The Raw and the Cooked*, which he finds has come to resemble the myths it analyzes.

The women figures must also disappear. A few pages earlier, Lévi-Strauss's wife made her only appearance in the book, already formulated as a dismissal: "La maladie s'étendit à notre groupe: d'abord ma femme, qui avait participé à toutes les expéditions antérieures avec en partage l'étude de la culture matérielle; elle se trouva si gravement atteinte qu'il fallut l'évacuer définitivement" (345; "The disease [putrid opthalmia] spread to our group: the first person to catch it was my wife who had taken part in my expeditions so far, her specialty being the study of material culture and skills; the infection was so serious that she had to be evacuated" [301]). Astoundingly, this is the only sentence which Lévi-Strauss devotes to the woman whose work was undoubtedly indispensable to the writing of *Tristes tropiques*. (He has, on the other hand, devoted many to the indigenous women, particularly to their sexual charms.) Cleo McNelly writes of this passage that its "slightly formal tone, the elaborate compliment, are themselves indications of precisely the attributes of 'home,' of civilization. . . . It is not insignificant, either, that the disease affects the eyes, the organ of sight, that it spreads from the natives to the narrator's camp, and that it threatens to bring the white woman into the same ambivalent relationship to the narrator that the Indians have."[23] In other words, Mrs. Lévi-Strauss threatens to step in front of the camera and must be evacuated. The writing of liberation, the anthropology that mythologizes itself, has located its own blind spot—how appropriate, as McNelly points out, that a malady of vision carries off the unsung heroine of this book. Madame's "appearance" is also her disappearance; her gender simply does not fit into any of the various genres of *Tristes tropiques*: certainly not into *Cinna*, in which a woman is the nearest thing to a villain; nor into those romantic or Rousseauvian passages where we marvel at the lone white man in the midst of primeval nature; nor into those essays that, since the days of Pascal and Montaigne, have fostered the illusion of a solitary subject casting light on a problem from the force of his inner reflection. Had Mrs. Lévi-Strauss been as important in this book as she was in the author's life during this period, she would have moved its genre in the direction of the family romance, one of the few genres that *Tristes tropiques* does not use in its structuralist enterprise. Romance, on the other hand, is one of *Oroonoko*'s main genres.

III

The readings of *Oroonoko* revolve around the exact positioning of its narrator in history and space. The positionings then can become evidence in the debate over the exact mixture of romance, ethnography, and (auto)biography in this work. If Behn really lived in Surinam—*voilà*, an autobiographical anecdote. If not, then we are dealing with the "earliest American novel," as William Spengemann puts it.[24] Choice of a genre would determine the use-value of Behn's text, but that text itself will not help us make the choice. Its subtitle, "History of the Royal Slave," is ambiguous, denoting with equal facility a true or fictional account. Nor does Behn's introduction help much, though it seems to be trying:

> I do not pretend, in giving you the History of this ROYAL SLAVE, to entertain my reader with the adventures of a feign'd Hero,

23. Cleo McNelly, "Natives, Women, and Claude Lévi-Strauss: A Reading of *Tristes tropiques* as Myth," *Massachusetts Review* 16 (Winter 1975): 23.

24. William C. Spengemann, "The Earliest American Novel: Aphra Behn's *Oroonoko*," *Nineteenth-Century Fiction* 30 (1984): 384–414.

whose Life and Fortunes Fancy may manage at the Poet's Pleasure; nor in relating the Truth, design to adorn it with any accidents but such as arrived in earnest to him. (129)

Such an introduction immediately calls forth suspicion, for there is no more popular preface to a work of fiction in this era than the one claiming truth. Indeed Behn's *Fair Jilt*, which scholars consider pure romance, begins with very similar protestations:

> For however it may be imagin'd that Poetry (my Talent) has so greatly the Ascendant over me, that all I write must pass for Fiction, I now desire to have it understood that this is Reality, and Matter of Fact, and acted in this our later Age: And that in the person of Tarquin, I bring a Prince to kiss your Hands, who own'd himself, and was receiv'd, as the last of the Race of the Roman Kings; whom I have often seen, and you have heard of; and whose Story is so well known to your self, and many Hundreds more: Part of which I had from the Mouth of this unhappy great Man, and was an Eye-Witness to the rest.[25]

Again, we see Behn's interest in physically positioning herself between the origins of the story (in mouth, ear, and eye) and the audience who have already heard it.

As pointed out above, the occurrence of corporeality as a theme in *Oroonoko* seems to make Behn's opening statement there more credible. There is now general agreement that there was a factual basis to Behn's story, something which she experienced as a young woman in Surinam and only much later put into writing. As with *Tristes tropiques*, the great length of time between experience and text is significant. The text of *Oroonoko* appeared beside Behn's other stories, novels, and plays, which made no particular claims to verisimilitude. If *Tristes tropiques* seeks to undermine both the authority and the disrepute that its standing outside established genres might lend it, whatever truth *Oroonoko* speaks about Aphra Behn and about the slave trade in Surinam is undermined by our inability to determine its genre.

If Lévi-Strauss's theoretical musings in *Tristes tropiques* make the criterion of facticity seem oddly irrelevant to his brand of anthropology, the

---

25. Aphra Behn, *The Fair Jilt*, in *The Works of Aphra Behn*, ed. Montague Summers, vol. 15 (New York: Benjamin Blom, 1967), 70.

generic struggles around Behn's *Oroonoko* have always been waged on the basis of "what really happened." In contradistinction to most works of fiction, in which verisimilitude is praised because of its falseness (simply relating the facts requires much less skill than making them up), Behn's work has been treated as autobiography and condemned for its untruths. For example, we might ask why Ernest Bernbaum felt that he was passing a judgment on its literary worth when he declared in 1913 that "Mrs. Behn, in *Oroonoko*, deliberately and circumstantially lied."[26] Bernbaum justifies his statement through a generic misprision of Behn's text: his article is titled "Mrs. Behn's Biography, a Fiction." Nowhere does Behn use the designation "biography"; the term was not in general use in 1688. Thus Bernbaum uses genre to make a powerful move in "the politics of naming," of which we shall hear more later. Other critics followed his lead. The struggle over *Oroonoko* became a struggle not to interpret the text itself, which contains traps as deep and cunning as any laid by Lévi-Strauss, but rather to determine the correct "program" through which it should be run in order to provide the right answers, to place it in relation to facts, lives, and other texts. Indeed, the extensive bibliography surrounding it reveals not so much the "facts of the matter" as the underlying assumptions that make critics believe that the biographic relevance of Behn's tale affects it as a work of art.[27] In essence, we may say that critics are arguing—perhaps without realizing it or even wondering what they are doing—about the use-value of Behn's text. Can it be used as biography? Can it be used as history or ethnography? Can it be used as an antislavery tract?

Robert Chibka has suggested that the power of *Oroonoko* rests not with its location within a genre, but with its playing off of several genres against each other: "This narrative, by continually suggesting correlations between truth-claims and manipulative power and by implicitly contrasting the

26. Ernest Bernbaum, "Mrs. Behn's Biography, a Fiction," *PMLA* 28 (1913): 433.

27. I will not be reviewing this debate, part of which has been summarized by Frederick M. Link in *Aphra Behn* (New York: Twayne, 1968), 139–42, nn. 10–13. The bibliography mentioned includes H. A. Hargreaves, "New Evidence of the Realism of Mrs. Behn's *Oroonoko*," *Bulletin of the New York Public Library* 74 (1970): 437–44; Harrison Gray Platt, Jr., "Astraea and Celadon: An Untouched Portrait of Aphra Behn," *PMLA* 49 (1934): 544–59; J. A. Ramsaran, "*Oroonoko*: A Study of the Factual Elements," *Notes and Queries* 7 (1960): 142–45; Katherine M. Rogers, "Fact and Fiction in Aphra Behn's *Oroonoko*," *Studies in the Novel* 20 (Spring 1988): 1–15; and Wiley Sypher, "A Note on the Realism of Mrs. Behn's *Oroonoko*," *Modern Language Quarterly* 3 (1942): 401–5. Rogers's study is especially noteworthy in that it argues for the realism of certain details of the African part of *Oroonoko* in a way that does not damage the story's romantic aspects.

narrator's relations with her reader and those with her hero, problematizes readers' 'simple and receptive faith.' "[28] One such thematization of the text's claim to truth, discussed above, hinges on the genesis of the story and on Behn's role in its transmission. But there are other interlocking aspects of the text which problematize its use-value: the division of the text into "romance" and "novel"; the enslavement of orality by literacy; Behn's alternating inscription and erasure of both herself and the title figure; and the gender of her pen. Though the discussion of these aspects of *Oroonoko* might seem to take us far from the question of its genre(s), it relates to that question through the concept of use-value.

Behn's text is (ideologically) split by the conflict in English fiction between romance and novel, that is, between typological and "realistic" representation, between what Michael McKeon would term "overarching pattern" and "individual life."[29] The first part, which tells of Oroonoko's days as a prince in Africa and of his wooing of Imoinda, has all the generic features of romance, complete with battle scenes, an impotent king (that favorite theme of the Restoration), and a damsel in distress. Oroonoko, a grandson of the king, whose father has been killed in battle, is raised to be a great warrior and ruler by his uncle. The conflict in this romance revolves around a grandfather-grandson love triangle, since the former made the latter's intended, Imoinda, part of his *otan* (harem). Various intrigues (complete with the secondary couple of Aboan and Onahal) finally allowed Oroonoko to enter the *otan* where he "ravished in a Moment what his old Grandfather had been endeavouring for so many Months" (152). The African romance ends when the grandfather-king, suspecting the worst, sells Imoinda into slavery. In the second half of her story, which recounts Oroonoko's being tricked into captivity by the English merchant to whom he formerly sold slaves, his journey to Surinam, and his leading of a revolt, Behn turns to a hard-nosed realism culminating, as we have seen, in the horrific depiction of Oroonoko's mutilation and murder at the hands of the English. Though I use the term "novel" as a description of Behn's writing of "factual fictions" in the second half of *Oroonoko*, William Spengemann has less anachronistically classified these two readily distinguishable narrative genres as "Romance" and the "Brief True Relation,"

28. Robert L. Chibka, " 'Oh! Do not fear a woman's intention': Truth, Falsehood, and Fiction in Aphra Behn's *Oroonoko*," *Texas Studies in Literature and Language* 30 (Winter 1988): 513.

29. Michael McKeon, *The Origins of the English Novel 1600–1740* (Baltimore: Johns Hopkins University Press, 1987), especially 1–98, which explain the antinomy of "overarching pattern" and "individual life" and its effects on writing in Behn's period.

respectively. Spengemann relates the text's generic instability to Behn's goals and to the ideology of her audience:

> The prose romance was in every sense [Behn's] *métier*. Not only was she thoroughly practiced in its conventions, having read romances all of her life and modeled most of her plays (to say nothing of her own behavior) upon them, but, like most persons of her class and education, she regarded them as accurate pictures of reality and as dramatizations of her own most cherished values. The Brief True Relation, on the other hand, simultaneously evaded her busy middle-class readers' distrust of idle fictions and met their demands for useful information about current affairs in brief compass. What is more, because the Brief True Relation rested the authority of its statements upon the writer's experiences rather than upon his or her social station or sex, the form allowed Behn to assume an authority that had been begrudged her in the masculine, courtly domains of drama and poetry.[30]

In his last sentence Spengemann links the genres of *Oroonoko* to the question of experience already examined. Rose Zimbardo, as well, in suggesting that *Oroonoko* is "the design of heroic tragedy novelistically rendered," identifies these genres essentially through the effect their "high heroic" and "low realistic" styles, respectively, have on the reader:

> She uses the high heroic style in discourse for the purpose that it served in heroic drama and romance—to elevate our minds to an appreciation of *ideas* of heroic greatness embodied in her protagonists, who are figures of majesty and virtue. She uses the low realistic mode to serve the very purpose for which the novel was invented—to admit us into a fictional world that, while it is exotic, is, above all, probable, and to explore subtle nuances of thought and feeling in characters, and, by admitting us into their unspoken, interior lives, to force us to share their emotions and participate in their actions. In short, Behn's low realistic style opens a channel from the distant epic world of valorized action into the familiar world of the reader's experience.[31]

30. Spengemann, "The Earliest American Novel," 390. Spengemann's helpful generic positioning of Behn suffers only from his decision not to mention her other short fictions, such as "The Black Lady," which are Brief True Relations of London life.

31. Rose A. Zimbardo, "The Late Seventeenth-Century Dilemma in Discourse: Dryden's *Don Sebastian* and Behn's *Oroonoko*," in *Rhetorics of Order/Ordering Rhetorics in English Neoclassical*

Less important than the differences between the specific generic names that Spengemann and Zimbardo use to characterize *Oroonoko*'s instability is the similarity in the use-values and ideologies which they perceive as shaping the differences between them. In placing these two opposing genres side by side in the same narrative, Behn has carried out an operation similar to Lévi-Strauss's rewriting of Corneille on the back of his anthropological data. Generic instability becomes Behn's way of bridging the gap between the familiar and the alien while maintaining their incommensurability.

The writing in the first part of *Oroonoko* is lucid and transparent; having established the truth of her story through her corporeal presence then and now, the storyteller for the most part hides herself in the background. In the second part, the "true brief relation," the writing becomes confused and self-referential as Behn turns into a character in her own story. Michael McKeon argues incorrectly that "no tension exists in [Behn's] dual role as narrator and character, because both roles are dedicated to the single end of physically witnessing, and thereby authenticating, a central character [Oroonoko] whose personal history is distinct from her own."[32] McKeon, seduced by Behn's repeated invocations of presence, fails to note how often and at what crucial junctures she is absent. Behn's writing fails to authenticate her narrative (as the debate over its truth-value, discussed above, demonstrates). Lévi-Strauss intentionally produces such failure in *Tristes tropiques* but also controls it.

These failures seem intimately bound up with the confrontation between orality and literacy. Behn returns again and again to this topic. As a first step, she questions the role of writing as a tool for expanding knowledge in her odd characterization of the nonliterate Oroonoko's learning: "He knew almost as much as if he had read much" (135). Both the "almost" and the "much" create slippage in this sentence, allowing us to construct the following logical inference: "He knew as much as (or more than) if he had read little." By leaving us in a logical no-man's-land, Behn's formulation undermines the absolute difference between literate and nonliterate cultures in terms of intelligence or learning—a difference on which the ideology of slavery would come to be partly based. Nearly three centuries later, Lévi-Strauss hypothesizes that the attribution of cultural superiority and extensive knowledge to writing is ideological:

Literature, ed. J. Douglas Canfield and J. Paul Hunter (Newark: University of Delaware Press, 1989), 65, 60–61.

32. McKeon, *Origins*, 112.

Si mon hypothèse est exacte, il faut admettre que la fonction primaire de la communication écrite est de faciliter l'asservissement. L'emploi de l'écriture à des fins désintéressées, en vue de tirer des satisfactions intellectuelles et esthétiques, est un résultat secondaire, si même il ne se réduit pas le plus souvent à un moyen pour renforcer, justifier ou dissimuler l'autre. (344)

(My hypothesis, if correct, would oblige us to recognize the fact that the primary function of written communication is to facilitate slavery. The use of writing for disinterested purposes, and as a source of intellectual and aesthetic pleasure, is a secondary result, and more often than not it may even be turned into a means of strengthening, justifying or concealing the other [function]. [299])

Both books proceed to recount allegories in support of this hypothesis. Lévi-Strauss's begins as he conducts an experiment by distributing pencils and papers among the nonliterate Nambikwara Indians: "Un jour, je les vis tous occupés à tracer sur le papier des lignes horizontales ondulées. Que voulaient-ils donc faire? Je dus me rendre à l'évidence: ils écrivaient, ou plus exactement, cherchaient à faire de leur crayon le même usage que moi" (340; "One day I saw that they were all busy drawing wavy, horizontal lines. I wondered what they were trying to do, then it was suddenly borne upon me that they were writing, or, to be more accurate, were trying to use their pencils in the same way as I did mine" [296]). But the chief of the Nambikwara goes one step further, teaching the anthropologist that writing is not so much a matter of communication as of domination. He draws a number of lines on a piece of paper and "reads" from them in order to facilitate the exchange of gifts between his clan and another. The exchange is dangerous; one side may feel cheated and start a brawl. Yet the appearance of the chief "reading" off the list of gifts allows for a peaceful exchange, as the other clan accepts the chief's rulings without hesitation on the basis of the technologization of their presentation. The chief knows nothing of the technique of reading or writing. He realizes not so much that the wavy lines hold information as that they hold power. He reads his own writing in much the same way as the police in Martinique "read" Lévi-Strauss's data. The title of the chapter in which Lévi-Strauss recounts this fable—"La Leçon d'écriture" ("The Writing Lesson")—reveals the same instability of subjects with which we began this chapter. Who is the teacher here, and who the pupil? The chief seems to be giving a false "reading" of writing, to be appreciating it only as a surface phenomenon, to be perceiving the wavy lines and ignoring their meaning or content. This superficiality, however, shows the literate Lévi-Strauss an ideological dimension of writing which he had hitherto missed. The content of writing, available only to the trained, is revealed as covering up a deeper form of domination beyond or below the literal. And there is yet another lesson, a generic lesson that perhaps Lévi-Strauss himself did not catch, as the chief's charade, like the mime in *Hamlet*, raises the shadowy question of guilt. "Does the narrator's work, in the final analysis, really mean anything more than wavy lines on paper made for the purpose of dominating or impressing other groups?"[33]

The Indians whom Aphra Behn meets in Surinam show a similarly "superficial" conception of writing, associating the graphemes with power over nature. Her kinsman plays a trick with a magnifying glass, and the Indians immediately ask him for the letters of his name: "They were like to have ador'd him for a God, and begg'd he would give 'em the Characters or Figures of his Name, that they might oppose it against Winds and Storms: which he did, and they held it up in those Seasons, and fancy'd it had a Charm to conquer them, and kept it like a holy Relique" (186). Here, as in Lévi-Strauss, writing is literally superficial, a source of power rather than knowledge. And it would be difficult to find a better or more explicit working-out of Lévi-Strauss's thesis than Behn's depiction of Oroonoko's progressive enslavement by means of language, specifically of writing—an enslavement inseparable from Behn's attempts to free him. Though one genre that few modern critics assign to *Oroonoko* is the antislavery tract,[34] certainly slavery is an important and sustained theme in

---

33. McNelly, "Natives," 27. With some justification, Jacques Derrida has attacked Lévi-Strauss's scenario of an innocent speech corrupted by the invasion of writing. He points to the "violence of difference, of classification, and of the system of appellations" among the Nambikwara Indians who are simultaneously pupils and teachers in the "Writing Lesson"—and who are, after all, "des empoisonneurs experts" ("expert poisoners"). *De la grammatologie* (Paris: Minuit, 1967), 298; translated by Gayatri C. Spivak, under the title *Of Grammatology* (Baltimore: Johns Hopkins University Press, 1976), 263. In other words, the arrival of literacy cannot account for the origin of violence among people. Tobin Siebers has also pointed to the contradiction between the incommensurability of writing and speech as developed in the "Writing Lesson," and Lévi-Strauss's structuralist philosophy, which "assert[s] the similarity between Western and non-Western thought in general." "Ethics in the Age of Rousseau: From Lévi-Strauss to Derrida," *MLN* 100 (1985): 764.

34. Jürgen von Stackelberg is one of the exceptions: "Le roman de Mrs Behn peut . . . susciter chez le lecteur un état d'esprit hostile à l'esclavage" ("Mrs. Behn's novel can arouse in the reader a hostility to slavery"). "*Oroonoko* et l'abolition de l'esclavage: Le Rôle du traducteur," *Revue de littérature comparée* 63 (April–June 1989): 238. Interestingly, Stackelberg is drawn to argue for the English *Oroonoko*'s antislavery effect in order to strengthen his thesis that the French translation

the work, and one can read Behn's treatment of the theme as an assertion that Oroonoko is enslaved by writing.

The logic of the deviousness of writing presented in *Oroonoko* runs something like this: an honest man should never need to sign a contract because he is as good as his word; hence, men who run around signing contracts or foisting them off on others must be dishonest, up to no good, after more power like the chief in Lévi-Strauss.[35] For the written word, as Socrates explains by reciting an Egyptian "writing lesson" at the end of Plato's *Phaedrus,* is a "receipt [*pharmakon*] for recollection, not for memory. And as for wisdom, your pupils will have the reputation for it without the reality: they will receive a quantity of information without proper instruction, and in consequence be thought very knowledgeable when they are for the most part quite ignorant. And because they are filled with the conceit of wisdom instead of real wisdom they will be a burden to society."[36] According to Plato, then, people who read much always know less than people who don't read at all. Behn cleverly introduces this conservative attack on writing at the beginning of her text by relating the Golden Age enjoyed by the indigenous cultures of Surinam to their orality. The following attitude toward the spoken word, then, is the obverse of the Native Americans' attitude toward the written word. Where they apprehended the latter only at the surface, they perceive the former in more depth than the English:

> And these People represented to me an absolute *Idea* of the first State of Innocence, before Man knew how to sin. . . . They once made Mourning and Fasting for the Death of the *English* Governor, who had given his Hand to come on such a Day to 'em, and neither came nor sent; believing, when a Man's Word was past, nothing but Death could or should prevent his keeping it. (131–32)

---

removed all antislavery sentiment, and hence was not partly responsible, as is commonly believed, for the antislavery sentiment in France, which led to abolition in 1794.

35. This belief is widespread in essentially oral cultures. My mother-in-law, who grew up in the north of Minas Gerais in Brazil, would eulogize her father as a man that "nunca precisou assinar um papel; a palavra dele valeu mais do que qualquer contrato" ("never had to sign a piece of paper; his word was worth more than any contract"). This statement shows the dilemma of a culture that is controlled by literacy (the Bible, legal documents, a newspaper or two) but is still essentially oral.

36. Plato, *Phaedrus*, translated by Walter Hamilton (London: Penguin, 1973), 96–97. As Walter Ong points out, Plato's is above all an antitechnological stance, familiar to us today in the form of tirades against calculators and computers as sappers of our intellectual vitality. *Orality vs. Literacy* (New York: Methuen, 1982), 79–81.

This turns out to be Oroonoko's story in miniature. Behn establishes a similar sacredness of the Word for Oroonoko and contrasts it with English deviousness. Oroonoko, who has been tricked onto the slave ship and clapped in irons, is further tricked by the English captain into enduring his voyage because he is incapable of understanding what a lie is. In order to break Oroonoko's hunger strike, the captain promises him that he shall be set ashore on the first land they touch at: "And *Oroonoko*, whose Honour was such, as he never had violated a Word in his Life himself, much less a solemn Asseveration, believ'd in an Instant what this Man said" (163). The phrase "violate a Word" stands out both for its physical double entendre — Oroonoko has violated ("ravished") Imoinda, and the violation of his person forms the gruesome end to the story — and for its invocation of *logos*. Behn does not write that Oroonoko never violated "*his* Word," which would be just another way of saying he never broke a promise, an evaluation of the felicity of his performative utterances. Rather, Oroonoko never violated "*a* Word," never sinned against the realm of "absolute Idea" as embodied in oral language. This notion of the spoken word's sacrosanct quality and of its violation is confirmed by the continuation of the incident, for the lying captain, asked to remove Oroonoko's chains on his promise that he will not rebel again, "could not resolve to trust a Heathen, he said, upon his Parole, a Man that had no Sense or Notion of the God that he worshipp'd" (163–64). Oroonoko responds that "the World takes no Cognizance whether this GOD has reveng'd 'em or not, 'tis done so secretly, and deferr'd so long: while the Man of no Honour suffers every Moment the Scorn and Contempt of the honester World, and dies every day ignominiously in his Fame, which is more valuable than Life" (164). The two worlds presented here are distinguished by the function of language in each: in Oroonoko's, language and action are inevitably one; in the captain's, language and action are separate, the word is shadow to the deed. The difficulty comes in saying whether these two worlds can be located geographically (Africa versus Europe), chronologically (preliterate versus literate), socially (aristocratic versus common speech), or generically (romance versus novel). All four oppositions are important in Behn's text, but none is held consistently. For example, Oroonoko's grandfather lies to him just as the English do when he tells him that Imoinda is dead. (In fact, all the evils to be found in the West are encountered first in Africa, though they are ideologically transformed by the genre of their telling.) But the English — including Aphra Behn — bring to their game of deception the supplementary technology of writing.

Like the Nambikwara chief, Oroonoko proves adept at learning this technology—on its surface. When offered a guarantee of safe conduct after his rebellion, Oroonoko refuses several times, but finally agrees to it if a contract will be signed, "and demanding what he desired, and that it should be ratify'd by their Hands in Writing, because he had perceived that was the common Way of Contract between Man and Man amongst the Whites" (196–97). As Michael McKeon puts it, Oroonoko has "embrace[d] the decadence of literacy and documentary objectivity."[37] As if to prove this decadence, Oroonoko is immediately seized and tortured against the provisions of the contract.

We shall see that Behn, like Oroonoko, links the Word to her fame and honor. Her position subverts the distance between the lying literate and the honest oracles. However, her own writing in this story eventually becomes complicit with the discourse of slavery. Some have seen this complicity already in her first physical description of Oroonoko. If, as we have seen, Behn takes care to inscribe her own body in the text, she also inscribes Oroonoko's, but *by means of erasure*. We saw earlier how Behn's description of Oroonoko's learning effectively avoided the question of his literacy. His physical description avoids his Africanness: "His Face was not of that brown rusty Black which most of that Nation are, but a perfect Ebony, or polished Jet. . . . His Nose was rising and *Roman*, instead of *African* and flat: His Mouth the finest shaped that could be seen; far from those great turn'd Lips, which are so natural to the rest of the Negroes" (136). "Not"'s and "instead"'s abound in a description in which Oroonoko's "typical Negroid characteristics are purged almost wholly in adapting him to the traditional hero. His face, although black, is Roman in contour, his hair is straightened artificially to hang to his shoulders like a periwig."[38] Although Katherine Rogers has argued for the potential realism of Oroonoko's appearance, it is Behn's *strategy* for describing him which reveals her uneasy complicity with the discourse of the West.

An even more powerful act of simultaneous writing and erasing is Behn's and Surinam's renaming of Oroonoko as Caesar, a move that places him symbolically within the West's second-most famous story of tyranny, betrayal, murder, and retribution and obliterates his otherness by replacing his proper name (though not so proper either, since what is supposed to be an African name is readily identifiable as that of one of South America's great rivers), a name so unique that it cannot be pronounced (Behn calls such proper names "barbarous," no doubt in the etymological sense of

37. McKeon, *Origins*, 113.
38. Woodcock, *The Incomparable Aphra*, 202–3.

"babble") by an eponym. As Derrida points out in his reading of Lévi-Strauss—and his insight is based on the anthropologist's own hypotheses in *The Savage Mind*—naming (and not just writing) is an act of violence, one in which Behn participates.[39] She depicts Oroonoko's reception on shore as his inscription into slavery, and then submits to its terms: "For the future therefore I must call *Oroonoko Caesar*; since by that Name only he was known in our Western World, and by that Name he was received on Shore at *Parham-House*, where he was destin'd a Slave" (169). This statement stands literally at the center of Behn's narration (on the forty-first page of my eighty-page edition), dividing once and for all the genre of romance from that of novel. Two ambiguous terms, "future" and "Western World," highlight its importance within her narrative. On one level, the future is encompassed within the story, and the Western World is Surinam or the New World in general. On another level, the future is the future of writing or the future of slavery, the Western world is what we take to be the opposite of the non-Western world, of what the Germans call the South, of what Lévi-Strauss calls the sad tropics. "I must," says the narrator; but whence that "must"? Why must Behn's discourse repeat the historical act of Oroonoko's renaming? Behn's invocation of Parham-House as justification for her onomastics—one name is used to justify another—is particularly odd, since she will later locate the illegitimate use of political force and a great deal of the blame for Oroonoko's ill-treatment there: "All Hands were against the *Parhamites* (as they called those of *Parham-Plantation*) because they did not in the first place love the Lord-Governor; and secondly, they would have it that *Caesar* was ill-used, and baffled with" (193). Both Trefry (the good guy) and the Lord-Governor (one of the bad guys) are alternately associated with Parham. Why must the discourse system be tied so closely to that of Parhamite Surinam, as though the audience for this story were the same as that which roamed the jungles of the New World, to whom the use of the signifier "Oroonoko" in place of "Caesar" would appear at best a breach in decorum, at worst an act of rebellion? Unless it is the written record, the inscription in the plantation ledger, the reincarnation of Oroonoko in writing?

39. "To name, to give names that it will on occasion be forbidden to pronounce, such is the originary violence of language which consists in inscribing within a difference, in classifying, in suspending the vocative absolute. . . . [A]rche-violence, loss of the proper, of absolute proximity, of self-presence, in truth the loss of what has never taken place." Derrida, *Of Grammatology*, trans. Spivak, 112. Derrida is commenting not only on "La leçon d'écriture," but also on Lévi-Strauss's analysis, in *The Savage Mind*, 35–74, of the reasoning behind clan names: "One . . . never names: one classes someone else." On the violence of naming, see also Susan D. Cohen, "An Onomastic Double Bind: Colette's *Gigi* and the Politics of Naming," *PMLA* 100 (1985): 793–809.

Oroonoko is enslaved with a name that if the Word were not constantly violated in the New World, would imply his absolute power. But "Caesar" is a classic example of the hidden commonality of proper nouns. There is a hint that the narrator also participated in the reeducation of Oroonoko, as she "entertained [Oroonoko and Imoinda] with the Lives of the *Romans*, and great men, which charmed him to my Company" (175). Out of the two categories, it is inevitable that some one or other of the Caesars be mentioned, and Oroonoko's reaction hints at the narrator's success in creating his complacency with the onomastic elevation within history which contrasts so strongly with his present misery. In spite of Behn's efforts, however, Oroonoko does not remain blind to this politics of naming, for when he is contemplating revenge after his whipping he says: "You shall see, that *Oroonoko* scorns to live with the Indignity that was put on *Caesar*" (69). The distinctiveness of Oroonoko's renaming in Surinam is underlined by the totally opposite one that his wife goes through. Imoinda has been christened "Clemene" by the English in Surinam. Yet when it is revealed that she is Oroonoko's long-lost bride from Coraman-tien, the English willingly return her African name of "Imoinda." And so Behn too must write a sentence symmetrically opposed to her previous erasure of the name "Oroonoko": "Tho' . . . we took her to be of Quality before, yet when we knew *Clemene* was *Imoinda*, we could not enough admire her" (174). However, the reinscription of Imoinda does effect Imoinda's (self-willed) enslavement to Oroonoko. Clemene, after all, is described in a position of dominance: "Her Task of Work, some sighing Lover every Day makes it his Petition to perform for her; which she accepts blushing, and with Reluctancy, for Fear he will ask her a Look for a Recompence, which he dares not presume to hope; so great an Awe she strikes into the Hearts of her Admirers" (171). Imoinda, on the other hand, "despised Grandeur and Pomp, those Vanities of her Sex, when she could gaze on *Oroonoko*" (173). Oroonoko later cuts off her head in an intended *Liebestod* whose ideal of mutual death is spoiled by the inequalities of gender and race: like Imoinda who must yield her life to her husband's hand, Oroonoko does not even have the power of death over himself, and can be killed only by *his* masters, the English.

Thus, Behn's writing enslaves and erases precisely where it promises to liberate and preserve. Or perhaps it is writing itself that enslaves by rebelling against the author's control, because Behn soon begins to lose control over her own hard-earned presence within the narrative. This loss of control comes at precisely those points where action would be required of her to save Oroonoko. Behn presents herself as two parallel and interdependent personae: the (younger) Great Mistress who wishes to save Oroonoko from torture and death, but who is always absent when the deeds of violence are carried out; and the (older) Female Pen, whose inability to control the narrative matches the Mistress's inability to control events. An example is the beautifully incoherent and contradictory sentence explaining why she was away when Oroonoko was caught and whipped mercilessly. She points out that there was fear among the settlement that the revolting slaves would murder all the settlers: "This Apprehension made all the Females of us fly down the River, to be secured; and while we were away, they acted this Cruelty; for I suppose I had Authority and Interest enough there, had I suspected any such Thing, to have prevented it" (198). Behn here uses "shifters" for all they are (not) worth. The use of "us" is all-inclusive, the use of "we" refers only to the females, and "they" appears as an alienated form of what had before been the referent of the first-person plural. Finally, all these pronouns are contrasted against the "I" of the subjunctive part of the sentence. It is only in the subjunctive that Behn can maintain her role as "Great Mistress," as an authority, for the indicative part of the sentence shows instead the obligatory female behavior of flight before danger. The subjunctive clause, in which the "I" appears to be in command, compensates Behn for her inability to help Oroonoko, whereas the shifting pronouns disperse the responsibility for her failure. Whenever the references come from without, from the third-person as it were, they deny Behn her authority (in both senses of the word) and even place her in the camp of the enemy. Note, for example, the easily missed reference to Behn in Oroonoko's speech inciting his fellow-slaves to rebellion:

> "And why (*said he*) my dear Friends and Fellow-sufferers, should we be Slaves to an unknown People? Have they vanquished us nobly in Fight? Have they won us in Honourable Battle? And are we by the Chance of War become their Slaves? This would not anger a noble Heart; this would not animate a Soldier's Soul: no, but we are bought and sold like Apes or Monkeys, to be the Sport of Women, Fools and Cowards. (61)

The only women Behn mentions in the Surinam part of the story are herself and Imoinda; by her own account, she was with Oroonoko most often, was his "Great Mistress," and her reports of Oroonoko's activities have all been of the "sporting" kind, including hunting, fishing, Indian visiting, and storytelling. What other woman could he be referring to?

Behn's direct quotation of Oroonoko's speech would seem to be a remarkable self-indictment and undermining of her own position both as narrator of his story and as his supposed liberator. Oroonoko's speech also amounts to an indictment of women in general, who become the vilest of slaveholders because they cannot be soldiers. That is, the entire slave-holding process of the West is seen here as a feminine occupation because it is not a by-product of martial activity as in Coramantien. But we have also seen above that the process of enslavement in the West is linguistic. Thus, Oroonoko indirectly raises here the same nexus of issues—language, gender, domination—as Behn does when she refers to herself as a "Female Pen" (169).

All of the shifting and contradiction in the position of the writer are brought together with the politics of naming in the last sentence of the story: "Yet, I hope, the Reputation of my Pen is considerable enough to make his glorious Name to survive all ages, with that of the brave, the beautiful and the constant *Imoinda*" (208). Oddly, it is Imoinda rather than Oroonoko whose name is preserved, providing a cadence to the end of Behn's writing. "*Caesar*" last appears a few sentences above the final one, and "Oroonoko" has all but left the reader's mind. Which name does Behn mean then, "Oroonoko," or "Caesar"? This confusion of names is symptomatic of the confusion of the text, of its striving to resolve the paradox of a discourse of liberation. But the word "Name" had a paradoxical meaning when applied to women in England at this time, as Angeline Goreau explains: "The double meaning of 'name' in Aphra Behn's century—'name' for modesty and 'name' for renown—created a split in women of literary ambitions that forced some into anonymity, others into denial of responsibility for publication, and still others into constant apology and humble appeal."[40] Like Oroonoko, Behn in making a name for herself cannot keep her good name. Earlier in the story, in fact in the middle of the description of Oroonoko's own renaming, we read the lament that breaks the surface of genre and interrupts the progress of Oroonoko's inscription in the Western world: "[Oroonoko's] Misfortune was, to fall in an obscure World, that afforded only a Female Pen to celebrate his Fame" (169).

Negative associations accrue to both the noun and the adjective in this epithet. The substantive "pen" points to the decadence of all writing, a

40. Angline Goreau, *Reconstructing Aphra: A Social Biography of Aphra Behn* (New York: Dial Press, 1980), 155.

problem we have seen addressed directly in *Oroonoko*. But then there is the adjective: Only a *female* Pen; only a *female* Behn.[41] Behn died in 1689, a year after the publication of *Oroonoko*. Her final years, according to R. A. Day, were spent "in poverty, grinding out at a frantic rate short novels, translations from the French, and occasional poems for the few pounds a dedication might bring."[42] Thus, one could read Behn's sentence as sincerely gloomy. Also, Behn apparently believed that the act of writing, regardless of who undertook it, was inevitably masculine. In the preface to her play *The Lucky Chance,* whose main purpose is to defend herself against charges of indecency that stemmed mainly from her gender, she speaks of "my Masculine part the Poet in me."[43] Angeline Goreau has seen this gendered view of writing as so important to Behn that she titles one chapter of her study "Double Binds; or, the Male Poet in Me." Goreau claims that Behn's outbursts on the gender of her writing, so to speak, are both sarcastic and serious:

> From the very beginning, she had acknowledged the definitions of her time in assigning beauty to the feminine domain and wit to the masculine. Elsewhere she maintained that it was women's education and not their innate capacities that excluded them from the field of wit, but a part of Aphra persisted in seeing herself as divided between the woman admired for her beauty, and the "masculine part," the writer. In doing so, she refused the woman writer whose rights she was defending, a literary "identity": if the activity of writing belonged to man's province, then the Aphra who wrote was a masculine self in a woman's body.[44]

Plagiarism, harlotry, and bad writing were constantly linked in the male attacks on Behn's writing. Behn's invocation of the Female Pen is thus

41. I am deeply indebted to Lincoln Faller of the University of Michigan for this horrendous pun.

42. Robert Adams Day, "Muses in the Mud: The Female Wits Anthropologically Reconsidered," *Women's Studies* 7 (1980): 61.

43. Aphra Behn, *The Lucky Chance,* in *The Works of Aphra Behn,* ed. Montague Summers, vol. 3 (New York: Benjamin Blom, 1967), 187; quoted in Judith Kegan Gardiner, "Aphra Behn: Sexuality and Self-Respect," *Women's Studies* 7 (1980): 68. For an adumbration of Behn's sexual philosophy, see also Larry Carver, "Aphra Behn: The Poet's Heart in a Woman's Body," *Papers on Language and Literature* 14 (Fall 1978): 414–24.

44. Goreau, *Reconstructing Aphra,* 266.

oxymoronic, a gesture both of defiance and of tragic acceptance of the failure of a writing of liberation, whether for herself or for Oroonoko.

Robert Chibka has related the gender question raised in *Oroonoko* to the work's problematic pronouns and generic status: "[Behn's] intentionally divided sense of womanhood images ambiguous social status. Thus, the pronouns that place her half in and half out of colonial society tell an important truth about her situation, just as the oxymoron 'Royal Slave' defines Oroonoko's contradictory position. . . . [Oroonoko's] race and her gender make their words less valid, allowing an illusion of power but requiring that they continually 'prove' themselves."[45] Thus, although *Tristes tropiques* and *Oroonoko* both are characterized by a generic instability that interferes with the act of describing, *Tristes tropiques* sublates that instability into a theoretical structuralism, whereas the conflicting genres of Behn's text become the signifiers of its conflicting races and genders.

Yet Lévi-Strauss shared Behn's liminal status—an explanation, perhaps, of his predilection for the verb *franchir* (to cross a limit) in his writings. As a Jew—we learn early in *Tristes tropiques* that his grandfather was the rabbi of Versailles—Lévi-Strauss belonged, as did Aphra Behn, to a group that could claim both to be an integral part of European culture and at the same time to exist only on its margins. References in *Tristes tropiques* to persecution come sporadically and at times are transposed metaphorically, as in the famous chapter title "A Little Glass of Rum" ("Un Petit Verre de rhum"). Had the translators been more attuned to the function of the glass of rum—the last comfort administered to a prisoner facing the guillotine— rather than to its literal status as an object, they might have translated the title as "A Cigarette and a Blindfold."

Such ironic invocations of the author's own liminal status recur over the entire breadth of his writings, even in the most complex, abstract, "scientific" works. For example, the *Elementary Structures of Kinship* closes with the following dreamy invocation of the presocietal fantasies of Freud's *Totem and Taboo* and Rousseau's *Discourse on Inequality:*

> Jusqu'à nos jours, l'humanité a rêvé de saisir et de fixer cet instant fugitif où il fut permis de croire qu'on pouvait ruser avec la loi d'échange. . . . Aux deux bouts du monde, aux deux extrémités du temps, le mythe sumérien de l'âge d'or et le mythe andaman de la vie future se répondent: l'un, plaçant la fin du bonheur primitif au moment où la confusion des langues a fait des mots la chose de

45. Chibka, "Woman's intention," 529.

tous; l'autre, décrivant la béatitude de l'au-delà comme un ciel où les femmes ne seront plus échangées; c'est-à-dire rejetant, dans un futur ou dans un passé également hors d'atteinte, la douceur, éternellement déniée à l'homme social, d'un monde où l'on pourrait vivre *entre soi.*

(To this very day, mankind has always dreamed of seizing and fixing that fleeting moment when it was permissible to believe that the law of exchange could be evaded. . . . At either end of the earth and at both extremes of time, the Sumerian myth of the golden age and the Andaman myth of the future life correspond, the former placing the end of primitive happiness at a time when the confusion of languages made words into common property, the latter describing the bliss of the hereafter as a heaven where women will no longer be exchanged, i.e., removing to an equally unattainable past or future the joy, eternally denied to social man, of a world in which one might *keep to oneself.*)[46]

To keep to oneself, to flee the law of exchange, is to flee the writing lesson, to maintain the proper name (to remain "Oroonoko," for example, if that is indeed a proper name) free of repetition and inscription. But a human being outside the system of exchange is like a text outside the system of genre. Both are oxymorons, uninterpretable, unusable nonentities. They are unable to do anything, and in a certain sense, do not exist. The fantasy of a private language could not exist without a public language, the form of exchange it dreams of escaping. Yet the phrase *entre soi,* whose ambiguity must be lost in the English translation *keep to oneself,* points beyond the individual to the family, clan, or perhaps race—after all, *entre* means "between," and thus requires more than one person. In fact, the idea of being *entre soi* is the idea of having secrets that the nonmembers do not share.

Which is to say that Lévi-Strauss chooses methods that allow him to hide and reveal at the same time. First, the generic instability of *Tristes tropiques,* and then the route of a structuralist anthropology, based on linguistics, which sought not so much to describe "primitive" peoples as to unite them with Europeans at the level of the "savage mind," for example, of totemic and binary thinking. Arthur Hertzberg has posited a type of

---

46. Claude Lévi-Strauss, *Les Structures élémentaires de la parenté* (Paris and The Hague: Mouton, 1967), 569–70; translated by James Harle Bell and John Richard von Sturmer, under the title *The Elementary Structures of Kinship* (Boston: Beacon, 1969), 496–47.

"modern Jew," beginning with Spinoza and including such figures as Marx and Freud, who responded to their alien tradition by reversing it and creating universal theories of human behavior.[47] Surely we must add the name of Lévi-Strauss to this list. Born on the margin between two cultures, it is only natural that Lévi-Strauss would conduct a long examination of the concept of *franchir*, of the penetration of boundaries in the quest of visions; and only natural that this transgression would include the collapsing of so many generic boundaries in a necessary struggle against the "writing lessons" of those cultures in order to portray others.

47. Arthur Hertzberg, "Spinoza, the Fount of Jewish Modernity" (Spindel Lecture, Bowdoin College, Brunswick, Maine, 4 November 1984).

3

Writing Lessons:
Representation Versus Rhetoric
in the *Ars Dictaminis*

Voyez donc à soigner davantage votre style. Vous écrivez toujours comme une enfant. Je vois bien d'où cela vient; c'est que vous dites tout ce que vous pensez, et rien de ce que vous ne pensez pas. . . . Vous voyez bien que, quand vous écrivez à quelqu'un, c'est pour lui et non pas pour vous.

(Try to take more care with your style. You still write like a child. I see why that is: it is because you say everything you think and nothing you do not think. . . . You can see that when you write to someone it is for him and not for yourself.)

— Letter of Madame de Merteuil to Sophie Volanges,
in Choderlos de Laclos, *Les Liaisons dangereuses*

LET US ASSUME FOR THE NONCE that Richard Rorty is correct in reducing the history of philosophy to a battle between two alternate goals, one representational, the other "conversational." Let us also assume for the moment that these opposing goals give rise to two philosophical "genres." They certainly would if genre is thought of in the pragmatic sense that I propose. For the two philosophies can only differentiate themselves if readers "use" their discourses in different ways. In other words, what Rorty's differentiation implies are different use-values for philosophical discourse. Representational philosophy is rather simple to understand: it seeks to give us the most truthful *picture* of the world possible. It is the second, conversational type that is more difficult to describe. Let us watch Rorty wrestle with the problem: adherents of the second type of philosophy "do not think that when we say something we must necessarily be expressing a view about a subject. We might just be *saying something* — participating in a conversation rather than contributing to an inquiry. Perhaps saying things is not always saying how things are. . . . We must get the visual, and in particular the mirroring, metaphors out of our speech altogether. To do that we have to understand speech not only as not the externalizing of inner representations, but as not a representation at all."[1] Thus, these two genres of philosophy can be distinguished by certain surface features, such as the presence or absence of visual metaphors.

I do not intend to argue that Richard Rorty is correct in the opposition he sets up, and I am certainly not in a position to judge the validity of his more radical claim that the second kind of philosophy is somehow "better" (less futile, perhaps) than the first. Instead, let us note that his dismissal of interiority, of our "glassy essence," sounds suspiciously like the epistolary advice given to Sophie Volanges by the Marquise de Merteuil in our epigraph. The Marquise argues against the representation of the self in the letter; language is not to show any relation to the thoughts of the writer, but is to be produced according to its desired effect on the reader. Moreover, to show the writer's mind is to diminish the power of the letter over the reader. I wish to argue that these two views of language, which I call the representational and the rhetorical, can give rise to different genres, not only of philosophy, but also of literature. In what follows I talk about two genres, the letter-writing manual or *ars dictaminis* and the epistolary novel. What should distinguish the two, I argue based on the preceding, is that the generic task of the manual is, like Merteuil's ideal letter writer, to present its particular forms of written language as rhetorical strategies to be used with no mimetic claims or essential relationship to the writing subject. The novel is representational; it gives us a picture of the world.[2] And of course the first genre should be pragmatic and openly

1. Richard Rorty, *Philosophy and the Mirror of Nature* (Princeton: Princeton University Press, 1979), 371.

2. The precise definition of the novel is one of the oldest and most hotly contested generic debates. I choose the term for two reasons: one is that the term "epistolary novel" is an accepted critical concept readily understandable to everyone and hence easily placed in contrast to

didactic, giving rules and models to be followed, whereas the latter's picture of the world is, for its very realism, more difficult to consider as advice. The ideological stakes in the writing lessons of the epistolary manual have been formulated succinctly by Janet Altman: "A une époque où les médias modernes n'existaient pas, le manuel épistolaire projette *un code de représentation* et un *inconscient politique* capable d'exercer un contrôle social à travers le contrôle de la langue" ("At a time when the modern media did not exist, the letter-writing manual projected a code of representation and a political unconscious capable of exercising social control through the control of language").[3] However, in looking at the French *artes* of the eighteenth century, Shelley Yahalom finds that "at the same time that the novel chose the letter as a form of 'authentic' discourse not subject to the restrictions associated with literature, the letter-writing manual adopted certain 'literary' techniques with regard to themes that it shared with the novel."[4] The novel uses the letter in order to survive its legitimation crisis, whereas the *ars* becomes more novelistic in order to broaden its use-value to that of *Bildung* in general. In this way, the two genres profit from their mutual generic instability. Let us turn now to an *ars* in which the ideology of this generic instability is more clearly visible. As the *ars dictaminis* takes on aspects of the epistolary novel, the boundary between two genres is crossed, and each such crossing reveals the workings of ideological split.

I

Medieval rhetoric, of which the *artes dictaminis* formed one branch, is known for teaching its readers how to "just say something," how to participate in the game of writing. Let me give an extreme example, a kind of skeletal epitome of the genre. Johannes Bondi's fourteenth-century *Practica sive usus dictaminis* is divided into seven *tabulae* or templates, the

---

"epistolary manual" or *ars dictaminis*. Second, however, if there is one thing that Georg Lukács, Michael McKeon, Ian Watt, Sheldon Sacks, and Terry Peavler all agree on (see my bibliography for their studies), it would seem to be that the novel foregrounds "individuals" against a social backdrop, which is precisely what happens in the fictionalized *artes* that are the subject of this chapter.

3. Janet Altman, "Pour une histoire culturelle de la lettre: L'Épistolier et l'État sous l'Ancien Régime," in *L'Épistolarité à travers les siècles*, ed. Mireille Bossis and Charles A. Porter (Stuttgart: F. Steiner, 1990), 115.

4. Shelley Yahalom, "Du non-littéraire au littéraire," *Poétique* 11 (November 1980): 413.

principle of division being the general rank of addressee for the letter: the first for the pope; the second for cardinals; the third for emperors, kings and princes; the fourth for the minor orders of clerics and nobility; the fifth for friends and scholars; the sixth for heretics, infidels, and so on; and the seventh for the miscellaneous. Each table offers a "menu" of salutations, narratives, and petitions (see Figs. 3–1 and 3–2), which can be combined to yield a message. The user of the manual can then choose one from several choices for subject, verb, indirect object, and so on. Putting them together gives him a sentence. Bondi's is a purely rhetorical, in fact purely grammatical *ars*, one that corresponds to the "conversational" pole in Richard Rorty's schema of philosophy. In Bondi, there is as much representation of the letter writer as there is representation of the chemist in the formula for a benzene ring. To write is to combine, according to the needs of discourse itself, *formulae* that together will produce sentences capable of achieving certain effects—the emperor will be convinced to come with his army and battle the hostile knight, for example. Nor is this approach unusual for rhetorical theory. Though in *Phaedrus* Plato had made the claim, echoed by Cicero and Quintilian, that rhetoric cannot be taught without knowledge of the soul, the vast majority of rhetorical *artes* taught their subject with as much ideational content as a computer program for filling out tax forms. But what about that other pole, that of representation? What would such an *ars dictaminis* look like?

It would look like an epistolary novel. The close relationship between the letter-writing manual and epistolary fiction has not escaped the attention of critics, most notably Bernard Bray, who argues, as the subtitle of his monograph *Des manuels aux romans (1550–1700)* would indicate, that the French epistolary novel originated as the narrative organization of fictions already endemic to letter-writing manuals.[5] Katherine Hornbeak has also written, in the context of English literature, of the uneasy alliance between fiction and rhetorical didacticism in the manuals.[6] Bray is con-

5. Bernard A. Bray, *L'Art de la lettre amoureuse: Des manuels aux romans (1550–1700)* (The Hague and Paris: Mouton, 1967).

6. It is worth quoting Hornbeak on this uneasy alliance: "From the earliest English letter-writer containing original English models, the authors of such compilations have felt—and succumbed to—the temptation to abandon their original purpose of supplying models general enough to be adapted to universal use, and to try their wings in a short flight of fiction." Katherine Hornbeak, "The Complete Letter-Writer in English 1568–1800," *Smith College Studies in Modern Languages* 15, nos. 3–4 (1934): 49. See also Jean Robertson, *The Art of Letter-Writing: An Essay on the Handbooks Published in England during the Sixteenth and Seventeenth Centuries* (Liverpool: University Press, 1943). This relation between (general) models and (specific) fictions is a mutually reinforcing one.

cerned with the diachronic development *between*, Hornbeak with the synchronic heterogenity *within*, two supposedly distinct genres: what is supposed to be a guide to rhetoric and conduct becomes novelistic, whereas novels take on the characteristics of guides to conduct. An excellent example of this is provided by the English author who perhaps had the greatest impact on European fiction of the eighteenth century, Samuel Richardson. Richardson began his career with a letter-writing manual, from whose 138th and 139th letters ("A Father to a Daughter in Service on Hearing her Master's Attempting her Virtue" and "The Daughter's Answer") arose his novel *Pamela* (1741), which in turn led to other novels intended to function as conduct books.[7] Richardson makes it absolutely clear that the letter writing his manual teaches is aimed not only at effecting a response from the addressee, as Bondi's was, but also at effecting a change in the "glassy essence" of the sender. Letter writing has ceased being a skill and become *Bildung* itself. The writing lesson has become an acting lesson. Richardson states this plainly enough in his preface:

> [These letters] may not only direct the *Forms* requisite to be observed on the most important occasions; but, what is more to the Purpose, by the Rules and Instructions contained in them, contribute to *mend the heart*, and *improve the Understanding*. NATURE, PROPRIETY OF CHARACTER, PLAIN SENSE, and GENERAL USE, have been the chief Objects of the author's attention in the penning of these Letters.

In short, Richardson insists "that the Letters may serve for Rules to THINK and ACT by, as well as Forms to WRITE after." Whereas Merteuil in our epigraph from the *Liaisons dangereuses* tries to draw Sophie's language from outside of herself, to reduce her writing to its reception by others,

7. The full title of Richardson's manual shows the relationship between fiction, rhetoric and ideology that I explore here: *Letters Written To and For Particular Friends, on the most Important Occasions. Directing not only the Requisite Style and Forms To be Observed in Writing Familiar Letters; But How to Think and Act Justly and Prudently, in the Common Concerns of Human Life* (London: Rivington, Osborn, & Leake, 1741). Further citations in text. On this work, see Hornbeak, "Complete Letter-Writer," 100–125. On fiction as social didactic in this period, see J. Paul Hunter, " 'The Young, the Ignorant, and the Idle': Some Notes on Readers and the Beginnings of the English Novel," in *Anticipations of the Enlightenment in England, France, and Germany*, ed. Alan Charles Kors and Paul J. Korshin (Philadelphia: University of Pennsylvania Press, 1987), 269–70. For an examination of one of Richardson's novels as a conduct book, see Sylvia Kasey Marks, *Sir Charles Grandison: The Compleat Conduct Book* (Lewisburg, Pa.: Bucknell University Press, 1986).

Tercia tabula.

Salutaciones ad imperatores reges principes duces comites marchiones potestates milites barones castellanos et alios quoscumque magnos laycos.

Serenissimo prin-	Fridrico Romanorum imperatori et semper augusto	
Illustrissimo cipi	Pbylippo diuina magnificencia Francie regi	
Excellentissimo do-	christianissimo	
Victoriosissimo mino	Roberto potentissimo principi Tarentie	
Illustri et excelso viro		
Magnifico et potenti domino	domino P	duci
Sublimi et excellenti domino	comiti	talis loci
Fauorabili et benigno	marchioni	
Strennuo et potenti viro milicie cingulo decorato		potestati
Nobilissimo vel strennuissimo viro	domino	capitaneo	talis
Nobili et potenti vel egregio vel strennuo viro		militi	loci
Multe probitatis et inmense sapiencie viro	P	castellano	
Titulis adhornate prudencie viro		baroni	
Honoratissimo viro et inter honorabiles educato		
Nobilibus et prudentibus viris dominis A potestati consilio et conmuni		

rex
dux
magnus

talis

minor
quicunque

equalis
quicunque

salutem et de inimicis gloriam et triumphum.
salutem et parcere prostratis et debellare superbos.
salutem et robore accingi fortitudinis et virtutis.
salutem et opinere quod placet.
salutem et honorum felicium hubertatem.
honoris habitum et salutis.
salutem in eo qui regibus dat salutem.
cum reconmendacione se ipsum ad perpetuum famulatum.
se totum ad omnia beneplacita et mandata.
successus ad vota felices.
se ipsum ad queque beneplaciorum mandata.
voluntariam seruitutem.
cum reuerencia se ad pedes.
honoris et glorie famulamen.
salutem et feliciter gubernare cingulum glorie militaris.
salutem et contra spirituales nequicias viriliter debellare.

Narraciones ad eosdem.

talis comes ciuitatem nostram municiones et castra cum exercitu congregato proponit hostiliter occupare.
in votis habemus potissimum de vestre celsitudinis manibus succingi gloria militari.
intelleximus plurimorum relatibus, quod noua superueniente causa nuper cum talibus deuenistis ad rixam, et hinc inde pro viribus armatorum congeries aggregatur.
Petrum ioculatorem expertum, qui nostra militari curia suum officium exercuit eleganter, vestre nobilitatis affectui duximus conmendandum.

Imperatorie } maiestati
Regali } corone
Sacre regie
Celsitudini
Excellencie } vestre
Nobilitati
Strennuitati

tenore presencium {
clarius innotescat,
limpidius reseretur, } quod
lucidius patefiat,

Peticiones ad predictos.

imperatorie } maiestati
regali } corone
excellencie
magnificencie
nobilitati
strennuitati

Ideoque } celsitudini
vestre

cuius gesta magnifica per mundum resonant vniuersum,
que non consueuit aures auertere a querelis,
que consueuit preces supplicancium exaudire,
que benigne audit et exaudit precamina inpotentum,
in qua locauit tocius fiducie fundamentum,
cui quisque tenetur grata famulamina exhibere,
cuius brachio protegente iura defensantur viriliter subditorum,

supplico reuerenter,
preces porrigo subiectiuas,
assisto humiliter et deuote,
} quatenus

ad tantam violenciam repellendam et superbiam edomandam nobis vestrum subsidium porrigatis.
tali festo si placet nos ad tante nobilitatis gloriam admittatis.
si opportunum esse videritis, non tedeat vos nobis quam cicius intimare, paratis cum belligere gentis exforcio vestram adire presenciam quandocunque mihi declaratum extiteriti relatu nuncii vel serie litterarum.
sic liberaliter prouidere velitis eidem nostris precibus et amore quod de vestra prouisione largifhia ferat vbilibet gratum nomen.

Fig. 3-1. Johannes Bondi, Table 3 of the *Practica sive usus dictaminis* (Ludwig Rockinger, ed., *Briefsteller und Formelbücher des elften bis vierzehnten Jahrhunderts*, vol 2 [New York: Burt Franklin, 1961], 962).

To the imperial
To the regal
To the sacred kingly } majesty of your crown

To your { Highness's
Excellence's
Nobility's
Activity's

by means of the present document } that

{ let it become more clearly known
let it be more limpidly disclosed
let it be more lucidly discovered

a certain count, having gathered an army, is intending to occupy our city, walls and camp with hostile action. we would like to be invested with military honor, preferably by Your Highness's hand.

we have understood from several reports, that for a sudden new reason you recently became involved in a quarrel, with so and so, and from here and there, according to our abilities, a group of soldiers is being mustered.

We thought we ought to recommend to your nobility's affection Peter, an experienced entertainer, who has already skillfully exercised his profession for our military staff.

Figure 3.2 Narration Section, Table 3 of Johannes Bondi's of the *Practica sive usus dictaminis* (Ludwig Rockinger, ed., *Briefsteller und Formelbücher des elften bis vierzehnten Jahrhunderts*, vol. 2 [New York: Burt Franklin, 1961], 962).

Richardson emphasizes the impossibility of separating the ethical from the rhetorical. One can observe their close connection in several of this manual's fictions—and, with Bondi in mind, in the fact that this *ars* needs to create such fictions. Dorothea von Mücke has defined the genre of epistolary fiction as particularly appropriate to the creation of *Anschauli-chkeit,* which is more or less the transparency of the aesthetic object. This transparency implies a particular disciplinary method.[8] One can certainly see this disciplinary method at work in Richardson's manual.

For example, consider the complicated social situation adumbrated in Letter 28, "From a Maid-servant in Town, acquainting her Father and Mother in the Country, with a Proposal of Marriage, and asking their Consents." The story consists of three letters describing the engagement and marriage of the servant. In the following quotation I have inserted my own commentary in bracketed italics in order to bring out the "deep" rules of ACTION implied in the writing. The daughter begins by describing her fiancée, a glazier:

> He is a young Man of sober Character, and has been set up about two Years, has good Business for his Time, and is well beloved and spoken of by every one [i.e., *I am marrying upward, but not so exorbitantly that the groom's motives must be doubted*]. My Friends here think well of it, particularly my Master and Mistress [i.e., *he is a demonstrably good catch, and I will continue on good relations with my employers*]; and, he says, he doubts not, by God's Blessing on his Industry, to maintain a Family very prettily: and I have fairly told him, how little he has to expect with me [i.e., *honest and humble that I am, I have cleverly released my parents from an expensive dowry; this will not be one of those typical mercenary marriages*]. (40–41)

The whole letter, of course, speaks to the qualities of obedience and respect in the daughter, as she properly asks her parents' blessing for the wedding. Their response is equally proper, as they relinquish their right of choice: "Our distance from you must make us leave every thing to your own Discretion [i.e., *we are preserving our role as decision-makers in theory, while relinquishing it in practice*]. . . . We are only sorry we can do no more for you. But let us Know when it is done, and we will do some little matters, as far as we are able, towards House-keeping [i.e., *we are recipro-*

8. See Dorothea von Mücke, *Virtue and the Veil of Illusion: Generic Innovation and the Pedagogical Project in Eighteenth-Century Literature.* [Works of general theoretical interest in the field of genre studies are cited in full in the Bibliography—AUTHOR.]

cating our release from the dowry with a small gift]" (41). The daughter responds that she has married, and "My Master and Mistress have been very kind, and have made me a Present towards Housekeeping of Three Guineas [i.e., *I am a good worker*]. I had saved Twenty Pounds in Service, and that is all [i.e., *all I will bring to the marriage, that is. Good saver. Steady, as I must have been employed a long time to have saved so much. My economy and industry are almost seven times more important than charity of the upper-class*]. I told him the naked Truth of every thing [*honesty again*]. . . . Pray don't streighten [*sic*] yourselves out of Love to me [i.e., *I know you will, out of love to me*]" (42).

The connotations of each sentence show that only an industrious, loving, economical, serious, and honest young woman could have written these two letters. Thus, whereas Bondi's generative model of letter writing was syntactical, Richardson's is psychological and social. The meaning of each letter is not restricted to rhetoric, but rather functions as a mimesis of the letter writer. Letter writing becomes an affirmation of the self at the same moment that the letter becomes the embodiment of social rules. Thus, a prominent historian of English literature can affirm that its letter-writing heroes, "Pamela, Clarissa, Evelina, the dramatis personae of *Humphry Clinker*—all, writing their endless letters, assert their presence moment by moment. Affirming their identities in action, they help us to affirm our own by claiming the comprehensibility and continuity of experience."[9] We are already in the realm of epistolary fiction, to which Richardson will now devote himself full time, with astonishing results.

Given that this letter-writing self is socially constructed, it makes sense that one would find such epistolary fictions being used as a vehicle for the expression of a covert political ideal, for the representation of a form of power. For example, one could point to the interrelated representations of the power of money and the power of a self-conscious morality which permeate the example cited from Richardson. The servant's letter is a particularly clear example of ideological split, simultaneously affirming the power of wealth and denying its influence on "human relations." However, for a directly political fiction, I prefer to move to Germany and to Christian Fürchtegott Gellert's immensely popular and influential *Briefe, nebst einer Praktischen Abhandlung vom guten Geschmacke in Briefen*.[10] Richardson exerted

9. Patricia Meyer Spacks, *Imagining a Self: Autobiography and Novel in Eighteenth-Century England* (Cambridge: Harvard University Press, 1976), 11.

10. Christian Fürchtegott Gellert, *Briefe, nebst einer Praktischen Abhandlung vom guten Geschmacke in Briefen* (Leipzig: Bernhard Christoph Breitkopf, 1751); reprinted in Gellert, *Die epistolographischen Schriften* (Stuttgart: Metzler, 1971). Further citations in text.

an immense influence on Gellert, but Gellert's letters mediate the English preference for representation with the French preference for conversation. And by focusing on letter writing as a *social* activity, Gellert's *ars* shows a singular preoccupation with letter writing as an activity, that is, as an end in itself. Gellert uses the structure of the *ars dictaminis* to develop a veiled representation of the political subject in eighteenth-century Germany.

Gellert's title already rejects the rhetorical *ars dictaminis* in favor of the much more subjective concept of "taste" (*Geschmack*). Accordingly, his theoretical treatise, though placed first in the volume, occupies the second place in the title, behind Gellert's letters. The most important theoretical idea of all, then, is that letter writing can no longer be taught rhetorically. Rather, one must provide the reader with good examples, and above all cultivate the reader's self by providing a representation of the model letter-writing subject. Hence, all of the model letters are by one author, Gellert himself. They will provide the model for *Natürlichkeit*, a concept repeated throughout the manual:

> Wenn auch meine Leser mit diesen Briefen nicht ganz zufrieden seyn sollten: so wird ihnen doch die Absicht nicht misfallen können, die ich dadurch zu erreichen wünsche; nämlich junge Leute, und insonderheit das Frauenzimmer, zu einer natürlichen Schreibart zu ermuntern. (2)

> (Even if my readers should not be satisfied with these letters, still my purpose which I hoped to achieve through them should not displease them: which is to encourage young persons, and especially young ladies, to use a natural style.)

This idea of the natural style sounds similar to the Richardsonian ideas of style encountered above. But Gellert's letters represent a kind of dialectical sublation of Bondi and Richardson: that is, Gellert is preoccupied with presenting a "self" through his letters—indeed, a presentation of the self seems to be the only reason for writing letters. But the "self" presented is purely rhetorical, the perfect pupil of Merteuil.

Gellert's treatise has generally been read as a declaration of war against German *Kanzleistil*, the Bondian, bureaucratic form of writing which had dominated German prose and poetry, and particularly German *artes*, throughout the seventeenth and eighteenth centuries.[11] Recently, however,

---

11. On Gellert's relation to the German *ars* tradition, see Dieter Brüggemann, "Gellert, der gute Geschmack und die übeln Briefsteller," *Deutsche Vierteljahresschrift für Literaturwissenschaft und Geistesgeschichte* 45 (1971): 117–49.

Bernd Witte has distinguished another, more overtly political objective in Gellert's letter collection. He analyzes Gellert's collection under the assumption that it is really a novel in disguise—a not unwarranted assumption, given Gellert's enthusiasm for Richardson. As in Richardson, the social positioning of the letter writer far outweighs his rhetorical positioning. Some letters reject the life of an officer, others that of a nobleman, still others the self-conscious "Idylle" of a life in the countryside modeled on Virgil's *Georgics*. What is left is life as a letter writer. To be a correspondent is neither to fall into the straitjacket of military or noble etiquette nor to abandon the social world and progress for an isolated existence in the woods. Similarly, neither private meditation nor political action are seen as viable definitions of the self. As Witte puts it, "The individual is defined through this social ideal of an unhindered communication in the private sphere. The individual is not defined through his interior self. The self remains interdicted just as much as does the public sphere."[12] To write letters is to call forth a "Gelehrtenrepublik," to exercise the only form of political power with which the bourgeoisie was entrusted, the power of *Bildung*. Gellert abandons the exterior form of the writing lesson only to relocate it at a deeper, more hidden level of the writing subject.

Thus, in contrast to both Bondi and Richardson, Gellert's letters have no other ultimate theme than writing itself as a social process. Take, for example, the following letter, addressed appropriately enough to a *Sekretär:*

> Wenn Sie wüßten, wie lieb ich Sie hätte, und wie lieb ich Sie stets haben werde, und wenn Sie zugleich wüßten, daß ich künftig eben nicht fleißiger an Sie schreiben werde, als zeither: so würden Sie etwas wissen, das nicht recht zusammen hängt, und das dem ungeachtet sehr wahr ist. Ich weiß nicht, was ich für ein ungezogener Mensch werde. Ich schreibe gar nicht gern mehr Briefe. Es liegen ihrer mehr als ein halbes hundert auf dem Fenster, die ich seit Ostern hätte beantworten sollen. Ich weiß nicht, wie viel darunter von Ihnen sind; allein ich mag es auch nicht wissen. Ich müßte suchen, und wenn ich suchte; so würde ich viele andre finden, die ich gar nicht sehen mag. Also mögen sie alle liegen. (201)

12. Bernd Witte, "Die Individualität des Autors: Gellert's Briefsteller als Roman eines Schreibenden," *German Quarterly* 62 (Winter 1989): 13. My whole discussion of Gellert is heavily indebted to Witte's analysis.

(If you only knew how I love you, and how I will always love you, and if you likewise knew, that I will not write to you any more regularly in the future than I have done so far, then you would know something which is paradoxical, and which nevertheless is very true. I can't believe what an impolite person I am becoming. I don't like to write letters any more at all. Half a hundred of them that I should have answered at Eastertime are lying on my windowsill. I don't know how many of these are from you; but then again, I don't want to know. I would have to search them out, and when I searched, I would find many more that I don't want to see. Let them all lie there, then.)

When one realizes that in Germany secretaries were most often employed by aristocrats (this was Werther's employment in the epistolary novel by Goethe), this letter saves itself from becoming an act of political insubordination only through its lightheartedness. Just as Gellert's *ars* has no readily identifiable didactic value, so too we see its rejection of any sort of "business" letter in favor of idle paradoxes. Thus it redefines the letter's use-value away from business and toward *Bildung*. Though on the surface Gellert's would seem to be an anti-letter, rejecting correspondence in general as Gellert promises not to write any more letters to the secretary, we must keep in mind that we are in fact *reading* such a letter and that Gellert is indulging himself in the art of creating something out of nothing — which shows how artificial Gellert's *Natürlichkeit* can be. Gellert's letter thus gives us the perfect image of Rorty's "conversation" about nothing, carried on for the sake of conversation. But as Witte points out, such conversations, though they be about nothing and get nothing done, can for that very reason be invested with political consequences.

II

The idea of *Bildung*, which emerges in the eighteenth-century *artes* of Richardson and Gellert, is carried to its furthest point in nineteenth-century France. Henri Fresse-Montval's letter-writing manual *Nouveau Manuel complet et gradué de l'art épistolaire* will be my example. Henri-François-Marcel-Alphonse Fresse-Montval was a member of the Institut Historique and a teacher at the Athénée Royal in Paris. Born in Perpignan to a royalist father, Henri would remain a legitimist in political orientation.

He tried monastic life several times, but became instead a Parisian poly-graph; his most popular work was to be a book on the French navy, *Beautés des annales de la marine française,* with twelve editions between 1839 and 1880. He had also published one romance, *Angelino, ou le Bandit sicilien* (1829), and a political novel, *Jules-Joseph, pensée intime* (1834), of which I will speak later. In 1838 and 1839 the first edition of his *Nouveau Manuel* appeared in two volumes.[13] A second edition followed in 1842–44, a third (from which I quote) in the revolutionary year of 1848, a fourth in 1858, and a fifth in 1869. Undoubtedly, both Fresse-Montval's own position as a teacher and the dramatic increase in *internats* (boarding-schools) during this period helped make this book a relative bestseller.[14]

Thus, the *Nouveau Manuel* was one in a long line of school publications of Fresse-Montval, one obviously similar in title, audience, and purpose to his *Nouveau Manuel complet et gradué de la composition.* Both works are set up with each *matière* followed by a *corrigé,* so that the task of the student is given in great detail as an assignment (*matière*) and then followed by a perfected version (*corrigé*) drawn from the writings of famous authors such as Jean-Jacques Rousseau, Alfred de Vigny, Jules Janin, or Alain-René Lesage. This textbook format corresponded to the structure of the French classroom, which served as a relay point for the dictation (*matière*) and the handing-in (*corrigé*) of assignments. One section of Fresse-Montval's com-position book is called "amplifications," and this is basically the idea of the whole: to fill a predetermined structure with beautiful writing: "Le dis-cours est le développement d'une «matière» longue et détaillée, que dicte le maître et à laquelle il ne faut rien changer: il suffit de la mettre en phrases harmonieuses" ("The discourse is the development of a long and detailed 'subject matter' dictated by the teacher and in which nothing should be changed: one has only to render it in a harmonious style").[15]

13. Alphonse Fresse-Montval, *Angelino, ou le Bandit sicilien,* 3 vols. (Paris: Pigoreau, 1829); *Beautés des annales de la marine française, ou Combats, traits héroïques, services signalés . . . des marins français de toutes les époques* (Paris: P. Maumus, 1839); *Nouveau Manuel complet et gradué de la composition,* 2 vols. (Paris: A. Poilleux, 1835); *Nouveau Manuel complet et gradué de l'art épistolaire,* 2 vols., 3d ed. (Paris: A. Poilleux, 1848). Citations from this third edition appear in the text with volume and page number.

14. Antoine Prost gives the figure of 50 percent of secondary schools being *internats* in 1842, as opposed to 45 percent in 1830. *Histoire de l'enseignement en France, 1800–1967* (Paris: Armand Colin, 1968), 48. However, both Philippe Ariès, *Centuries of Childhood: A Social History of Family Life,* translated by Robert Baldick (New York: Alfred A. Knopf, 1962), and Michel Foucault, *Technologies of the Self,* ed. Luther H. Martin, Huck Gutman, and Patrick H. Hutton (Amherst: University of Massachusetts Press, 1988), place the real growth period for *internats* in the middle to late eighteenth century.

15. Prost, *Histoire de l'enseignement,* 53.

Thus, the *artes* of this period all taught writing as the *mise-en-scène* of certain infinitely repeatable ideas. What is unique about Fresse-Montval's work is how little amplification this *mise-en-scène* requires. Indeed, so long and detailed are his *matières* that they often differ only in the minutest details from their *corrigés* (see Fig. 3–3).

The two volumes of the *Nouveau Manuel* are clearly divided according to the age of the letter writer, the subject of the letter, and the method of instruction. The second volume is devoted to *L'Age mûr* (adulthood). It contains no prolonged fiction, but uses many more letters from well-known writers than does the first volume. There are a number of business letters, such as exchanges between a buyer in the provinces and a seller in Paris. (We will see that this process of epistolary exchange between center and margin also structures the epistolary novel contained in the first volume.) There is a section of correspondence with the king, with princes, and with ministers. Then there is general correspondence. Some *matières* are culled from Voltaire, from Jean-François Ducis, from Jean-Jacques Rousseau, and, as one might expect, the largest number from and to Madame de Sévigné and her cousin, the Comte de Bussy. Only in the eighteenth century did Sévigné's correspondence achieve the status of model, replacing the more literary efforts of writers such as Vincent de Voiture and Edme de Boursault. Janet Altman maintains that the rise of Sévigné as the premier letter writer reflects a return to the domestic, to the private, and to Erasmian principles of epistolary writing as a reflection of the formation of the whole person.[16] The difference is precisely that between rhetorical and fictional ideas of epistolarity, the first concentrating on the letter and the latter on the letter writer. Several of the letters touch on the poignant ethical situations we have seen in Richardson, for example, "Lettre d'une fille à son pére, prisonnier, pour l'engager à revenir de ses égarements" (2:283; "Letter from a daughter to her jailed father, to get him to return from his vagabondage"). Yet the climactic letter in this volume is a banal one, "Relative à une vente de blé, demandée par un ministre à un propriétaire" (2:296; "On the subject of a sale of wheat, requested of a landowner by a minister").

There is a remarkable heterogeneity—typical, however, of the *ars*—of letters and purposes in this second volume, which contrasts with the more easily identifiable purpose of the first one. In that first volume, Fresse-Montval deals with "l'enfance" and "l'adolescence," that is, with the school

16. Janet Altman, "The Letter Book as a Literary Institution 1539–1789: Toward a Cultural History of Published Correspondences in France," *Yale French Studies* 71 (1986): 49–57.

semble toutes nos journées, de n'avoir ni amusements, ni occupations qui ne nous soient communs!

C'est alors que tu n'auras besoin de me souhaiter ni bonjour, ni bonne année, car c'est à toi que je devrai l'une et l'autre.

Adieu, cher cousin, et reçois, avec ton amitié ordinaire, l'expression de mon dévouement,

ERNEST.

29. Matière.

Un Cousin à une Cousine.

Un cousin, souhaitant une bonne année à sa cousine, lui dira d'abord qu'elle ne trouvera dans ses vœux pour elle, ni l'emphase, ni l'imposture dont tant de bouches se font les interprètes, mais seulement l'expression franche d'une vive et sincère amitié. Il lui souhaitera un bonheur aussi solide que les qualités qui la distinguent, aussi durable que l'amabilité dont elle est pourvue, et cela, non pas seulement pour cette année, mais encore pour un grand nombre d'autres.

Pour la convaincre de la vérité de ses sentiments, il lui rappellera l'inaltérable affection qu'il n'a cessé de lui témoigner depuis son enfance, et qui, au lieu de s'affaiblir avec le temps, n'a fait que se fortifier.

Il terminera sa lettre en priant sa cousine d'accepter une légère marque de son attachement, laquelle tire tout son prix, non de sa valeur réelle, mais du sentiment dont elle est le gage. Il ex-

primera le désir que ce cadeau soit cher à sa cousine, et lui rappelle quelquefois les jeux de leur enfance, leur douce et fraternelle amitié, et le dévouement avec lequel il est, etc.

Corrigé.

Un Cousin à une Cousine.

Ma chère Cousine,

Dans les souhaits que cette époque m'autorise à vous adresser, vous ne rencontrerez, ni l'exagération, ni l'imposture dont tant de bouches se font les interprètes. Mes vœux, simples et naturels, ne sont que l'expression vive et franche de ma sincère amitié pour vous. Puisse cette année, puissent encore toutes celles qui lui succéderont, vous voir goûter un bonheur aussi solide que les qualités qui vous distinguent, aussi durable que l'amabilité dont vous êtes pourvue!

Si j'avais à craindre de vous trouver incrédule à la vérité de mes sentiments, je n'aurais, pour vous en convaincre, qu'à vous rappeler l'inaltérable affection que, depuis notre première enfance, je vous ai toujours témoignée, et qui, loin de s'affaiblir avec le temps, n'a fait, au contraire, que se fortifier.

Permettez-moi, chère cousine, de joindre à cette lettre une légère marque de mon attachement : c'est un de ces mille hochets inventés par la mode, et qui, sans valeur réelle, n'en empruntent une qu'au sentiment dont ils sont le gage. Puisse ce modeste cadeau être de quelque prix à vos yeux! puisse-t-il vous rappeler parfois les jeux de notre enfance, notre douce et fraternelle amitié, ainsi que le dévouement avec lequel je suis,

Très-chère cousine,

Votre bon et affectionné cousin,
....

Paris, ce 28 décembre 1841.

Fig. 3-3. *Matière* and *corrigé* from Fresse-Montval's *Nouveau Manual*, 106-7.

ages that might use his manual as textbook rather than as reference work. Indeed, Fresse-Montval's conception of separate letter-writing handbooks for adults and for young people seems to be new in the history of the genre—older texts, such as Jean Bourlier's *Style et manière de composer toutes sortes de lettres missives* (1575), show a complete heterogeneity not only in style and subject, but also in the categories of letter writers and addressees.[17] Fresse-Montval's giving children a volume of their own corresponds to their being confined to a separate space, that of the *internat*. This implied separation of adults from children makes the *Nouveau Manuel* what Mikhail Bakhtin calls a chronotope, an image linking space and time.[18] Philippe Ariès, in his study of changes in the concept of childhood in French society, speaks of other manifestations of this same chronotope, which for the first time defined "childhood" as something essential by making its chronological borders (school age) and by physically isolating it from society within the walls of the *internat*:

> The development of the boarding-school system after the end of the eighteenth century bears witness to a different concept of childhood and its place in society. Henceforth there would be an attempt to separate childhood from the other ages of society: it would be considered important—at least in the middle class—to shut childhood off in a world apart, the world of the boarding-school. The school was substituted for society in which all the ages were mingled together; it was called upon to mould children on the pattern of an ideal human type.[19]

Ariès's last sentence gives us our first clue to the reason for the existence of a novel within a letter-writing manual. The "ideal human type" the schools were called on to produce cannot be delineated through formularies or rhetorical rules: it can only be depicted as a fiction.

The relative homogeneity of the readership for his first volume allows Fresse-Montval to address epistolarity as a social theme. That this letter-writing manual was intended for young people is amply demonstrated by the list of correspondents. All letters are written by children and are

---

17. Jean Bourlier, *Style et manière de composer toutes sortes de lettres missives* (Antwerp: Jean Waesberg, 1575).

18. Mikhail Bakhtin, "Forms of Time and of the Chronotope in the Novel," in *The Dialogic Imagination*, ed. Michael Holquist, translated by Caryl Emerson and Michael Holquist (Austin: University of Texas Press, 1981), 84–258.

19. Ariès, *Centuries of Childhood*, 284–85.

addressed either to parents or to adolescents: "Un Petit-Fils à son grand-père," "Un Petit-Fils à sa grand-mère," "Un Fils à son père," "Un Fils à sa mère" ("A Grandson to His Grandfather," "A Grandson to His Grandmother," "A Son to His Father," "A Son to His Mother"). The whole series is then repeated with a girl as the writer. No older person writes to a perceptibly younger one in this volume. The list just given, combined with others, delineates an extended bourgeois family as the number of family roles multiplies—niece, nephew, stepson, and stepdaughter are progressively added. The next letters are titled "Une Jeune Personne en pension à son tuteur" and "à sa tutrice" ("A Young Lady to Her Chaperone"), followed by ones from students to their teachers. These letters, full of praise for the recipients' powers to educate and discipline, intensify this book's remarkable if understandable self-reflexivity, intended as it was to be a school text. This further extension shows us that Fresse-Montval is interested in portraying the family not as an isolated, autogenous social unit, but rather the family as one structure within a nested series of social relationships, which are of course power relationships. The family thus is split ideologically, constituted and disintegrated in this book, as it was in real life, by other institutions such as public education.

For example, it turns out that the letters between family members, which exhibit the expected tenderness of the domestic sphere, exist only because of a separation imposed by the schools. Take, for example, a letter written by a young girl to her mother.

Ma chère Maman,
Je te souhaite une bonne année. Elle serait bien meilleure pour moi, si je pouvais te le dire en te sautant au cou. J'écris à papa pour lui faire mon petit compliment. Dis-lui que je travaille bien, que je suis bien sage, et qu'il faut m'envoyer des joujoux et des bonbons.
Adieu, ma chère Maman; je t'embrasse et je t'aime de tout mon coeur,

Eugénie
(1:69)

(Dear Mommy,
I wish you a happy New Year. It would be a much better one for me, if I could only say it while giving you a big hug. I wrote daddy to give him my kind regards. Tell him that I am working hard, that

I am being very good, and that he should send me toys and candies.

Goodbye, dear mommy; I send you kisses and love you with all my heart,

Eugénie)

Besides demonstrating obedience, discipline, and the necessary indirection for petitioning an all-powerful *paterfamilias*, this young letter writer also shows the pathos and longing for a loved one so typical of both epistolary literature and of students interned in the French boarding schools of this period. The school (which has given Eugénie this writing lesson) becomes imbricated in the family romance just as the *ars* becomes imbricated in the novel.

These schools themselves are then shown to be enclosed within an even larger and more powerful social network. In letters such as "Une Enfant à la fille de sa protectrice," "Un Jeune Homme à un conseiller d'État, son protecteur," "Une Jeune Personne à sa protectrice, femme d'un fonctionnaire public," "Un Jeune Séminariste à un évêque, son protecteur" ("A Child to the Daughter of Her Patroness," "A Young Man to His Patron, a Senior Member of the Council of State," "A Young Lady to Her Patroness, the Wife of a Government Worker," "A Young Seminary Student to His Patron, a Bishop"), Fresse-Montval has carefully chosen representatives of various "états": government, church, military, and fine arts. The last letter in the series is even more explicit about the function of these patrons and patronesses, being "Une Jeune Personne à Madame B— —, célèbre cantatrice, qui l'avait fait entrer au conservatoire de musique" ("A Young Lady to Madame B., Noted Singer, Who Got Her Admitted to the Music Conservatory"). The tone of these letters can be gathered from a single example. A young lady writes to "Madame la Maréchale de * * *, sa Protectrice, qui l'avait fait entrer à la Maison royale de Saint-Denis." The most likely explanation for her gratitude is that her father had been a legionnaire and her protectress has arranged for her acceptance at Écouen or at another "Maison impériale":

> Madame la Maréchale,
> Puisse le ciel, durant cette année et toutes celles qui la suivront, répandre sur vous tout le bonheur que je dois à vos bontés!
> Sans vous, Madame la Maréchale, les services que mon père avait rendus à l'État seraient demeurés inconnus, ou sans utilité pour moi; jamais je n'eusse joui des bienfaits de l'éducation; et,

pauvre fille sans instruction comme sans fortune, j'aurais vu ma jeunesse se passer dans l'ignorance. C'est vous, Madame la Maréchale, qui m'avez dérobée à ce malheur: grâce vous en soit rendue! C'est à votre protection que je devrai un avenir prospère, une vie qui ne sera inutile ni à moi-même, ni aux autres, et l'avantage de rendre à la societé une partie de ce qu'elle a fait pour moi.

Voilà ce qui remplit mon coeur d'une connaissance qui ne finira jamais, et avec laquelle je suis,

Madame la Maréchale, etc.
(1:132)

(Madame Marshall,
May Heaven bless you during this year and all those that follow with all the happiness which I owe to your goodness.

Without you, madame, my father's services to the state would have remained unrecognized, or would not have done me any good. I would never have enjoyed the benefits of an education; and, poor girl that I was without knowledge or fortune, I would have spent my youth in ignorance. It is you, Madame Marshall, who have saved me from this misfortune, and may you be rewarded for what you have done! I owe my promising future to your patronage, as well as my life which will never be useless, neither to myself, nor to others, with the advantage of giving back to society a part of that which it has done for me.

Such is the infinite gratitude which fills my heart, and with which I am,
Madame Marshall, etc.)

This theme of patronage, as all the themes recounted in these didactic examples, is essential to understanding the novel that fills the middle pages of this manual: we shall see that Gustave, one of the novel's protagonists, is expelled from school for taking part in a rebellion, but reinstated thanks to the efforts of his *protecteur*.

Much of each letter is devoted to expounding the writer's motivations, which amounts to describing either the distance between the writer and recipient or the special motivations of that dependence which necessitate the production of the letter as a sign for it. The latter subjugation is seen in the letter from a student in a pension to her tutor (*tutrice*). As in the Maréchale letter, this writer is an orphan:

A un enfant privé des caresses et de l'amour d'une mère, que peut-
il arriver de plus heureux, si ce n'est d'obtenir cet amour et de
recevoir ces caresses de ceux qui ont bien voulu se charger de
remplacer les parents qu'il a perdus?

C'est là le bonheur qui m'est échu en partage, et c'est à vous
que je le dois. Agréez donc, pour un si grand bienfait, l'expression
de toute ma reconnaissance, et permettez qu'elle se manifeste à
vous par l'hommage des voeux que j'addresse au ciel pour votre
bonheur, chaque fois que revient votre fête. (1:169)

(What more fortuitous thing can happen to a child deprived of the
caresses and the affection of her mother than to obtain this love
and receive these caresses from those who have been willing to
take on the task of replacing the parents she has lost?

This is the happiness which has been accorded me, and I owe it
to you. Accept then, for such a great kindness, the conveying of
my future gratitude and permit me to show it to you by the
homage of the prayers which I address to Heaven for your
happiness, at each recurrence of your patron saint's day.)

Why portray an orphan in this letter? Was it so dangerous to be a parent
in nineteenth-century France? I would argue that this writer's orphanage
is a metaphor for the general orphanage that society imposed on children
of the middle and upper classes of this period. Though obviously there
were plenty of parents in this period who really did die before their
children were grown, all statistics available indicate that they did so at a
slower rate than in the eighteenth century, when orphanage had not been
such a popular *matière* for the *artes*. Historian Lynn Hunt has argued that
the French Revolution can be analyzed in Freudian terms, as a killing of
the father and the subsequent reconstitution of a new family order. In this
context, she describes the preoccupation among the novels of the late
1790s with orphans as a symptom of the problematic status of such a new,
fatherless familial order.[20] If this is accurate, then surely the phenomenon
of boarding schools, as well as this manual, which grew out of them, must
represent not so much an actual as an ideological orphanage. The children
of the bourgeoisie were to realize their full humanity not in the bosom of
the family but in the isolation of the schools.

20. Lynn Hunt, *The Family Romance of the French Revolution* (Berkeley and Los Angeles:
University of California Press, 1991).

As can be seen from the examples given so far, the occasion of all these letters is to give best wishes for the New Year or to congratulate the recipient on his or her birthday. Like Richardson and Gellert, Fresse-Montval gives neither rules for nor rhetorical analyses of his model letters. Rather than teach the proper phrases for a number of different social occasions, our author limits himself to a few such occasions and uses them as pretexts for recitations of the phrases expressing the correct social relations. The object of the writing lesson becomes not a description of the social occasion, but the creation of a social relation through letter writing. Unlike Gellert's, this manual does not try to teach letter writing as a form of communication (in the more restricted sense of the word), for no real information is given in these letters; rather, the letter is meant to cement relations of dominance and subjugation by expressing them as unambiguously as possible. What rules for writing Montval does give are concerned with the proper form of self-abasement to be carried out by the letter writer.

The most extreme and instructive example of this concerns the proper margins for a letter, whose width should be proportional to the gap in social standing between the two correspondents: "Cet espace [marginal] doit être d'autant plus large qu'on doit plus de respect à celui auquel on s'addresse" (1:9; "The margin should be wider in accordance with the respect owed to the person addressed"). This particular sign, whose signifier is physical space and whose signified is social hierarchy, appears in other letter-writing manuals as well. For example, the German epistolary theoretician Johann Christoph Stockhausen recommends folio-size sheets for letters to princes, large quarto-size when writing to "vornehme Gönner" (essentially the equivalent of Fresse-Montval's *protecteurs*), and small quarto-size when writing to friend and equals. In the same passage Stockhausen also notes that, when writing to the upper classes, the top and bottom margins should be large enough that "kaum etliche Zeilen kommen" ("a few lines will barely fit").[21] The obligatory inscription of these social relationships provides another example of Claude Lévi-Strauss's controversial dictum, examined in the previous chapter, that writing was invented for the purpose of enslavement: "La fonction primaire de la communication écrite est de faciliter l'asservissement" ("The primary function of writing, as a means of communication, is to facilitate the enslavement of other human beings").

---

21. *Johann Christoph Stockhausens Grundsätze wohleingerichteter Briefe, Nach den neuesten und bewährtesten Mustern der Deutschen und Ausländer; Nebst beygefügten Erläuterungen und Exempeln* (Helmstedt: Weigand, 1751), 391–92.

Interestingly, Lévi-Strauss's statement itself does not specify whether writer or reader is enslaved, but the allegory of the Nambikwara chief makes clear that writing puts the writer in a dominant position, a thesis we have seen illustrated in *Oroonoko*. However, in the "La leçon d'écriture," Lévi-Strauss refers to the teaching of writing as a form of enslavement, citing the period of French history during which Fresse-Montval's manual was written:

> L'action systématique des États européens en faveur de l'instruction obligatoire, qui se développe au cours du XIXe siècle, va de pair avec l'extension du service militaire et la prolétarisation. La lutte contre l'analphabétisme se confond ainsi avec le renforcement du contrôle des citoyens par le Pouvoir."
>
> (The European-wide movement towards compulsory education in the nineteenth century went hand in hand with the extension of military service and the systematization of the proletariat. The struggle against illiteracy is thus indistinguishable, at times, from the increased powers exerted over the individual citizen by the central authority).[22]

Here, power is exerted by the central authority not through writing, but through commanding its citizens to write. Similarly, in Fresse-Montval, the enslavement of writing takes a rather surprising form, with the writing subjects dominated by their obligation to write to superiors. In the *Nouveau Manuel* it is always the powerless who must write to the empowered, whose power is further demonstrated by their not needing to respond.

These letters from the *Nouveau Manuel* give a narrative of self, the purpose of which is to disclaim any responsibility for the letter writer's having made that self. The marshall's wife and the school system she has made available have allowed the education of this young woman—in letter writing among other things—who otherwise would have neither self nor destiny. And so in the end she agrees to render a part of herself to society, to submerge her personal interests in the social context from which they emerged. Actually a resubmergence, for Madame Marshall's interest in Eugénie is really due to her father's services to the state, for which the title "Maréchale" serves as a metonym. Need one mention the way "utility,"

22. Claude Lévi-Strauss, *Tristes tropiques* (Paris: Plon, 1955), 344; translated by John Weightman and Doreen Weightman, under the title *Tristes tropiques* (New York: Atheneum, 1974), 293.

the bourgeois word *par excellence*, equally at home in the world of industry and in the positivist philosophy of Auguste Comte, informs nearly every sentence of this letter?

The relation of writing to the subject as outlined in Fresse-Montval's manual makes it an excellent example of what Michel Foucault would call a technology of the self.[23] As Foucault points out, the perception of the need for a monastic school order, in which individuals could be monitored and disciplined, began in the early eighteenth century and culminated in Napoleon's desire to have complete surveillance over every detail of his subjects' lives, to become the paterfamilias of his political family.[24] In making this statement Foucault no doubt drew on Ariès, who had described the gradual development of the *internat* beginning in the sixteenth century:

> Schoolboys boarded in burghers' homes, free of all authority, whether paternal or academic: hardly anything in their way of life distinguished them from unmarried adults. Soon teachers and parents decided that this freedom was excessive. An authoritarian and hierarchical discipline was established in the school; and after that it was decided that it should extend even further and reach the schoolboy where he spent most of his time. The result was the birth of the boarding-school system outside the school, at first fairly lax in character.[25]

Demonstrably, this lax discipline grew rigorous in response to the French Revolution. During the Napoleonic regime, an early if ambiguous supporter of the French Revolution, the aristocrat A. C. L. Destutt de Tracy, formulated the necessity of schooling for French children in its clearest and most politicized terms. Tracy, along with Honoré-Gabriel de Mirabeau, Charles-Maurice de Talleyrand, and the unfortunate Antoine-Nicolas de Condorcet, favored a centralized and universal schooling that would replace the feudal aristocracy with a new, more efficient aristocracy of intellectuals. It is no accident that one legislative plank of this anti-Jacobin platform, the creation of public secondary schools, could be enacted only after the end of the Terror, on 25 October 1795. Tracy's later pamphlet on

---

23. See Foucault, *Technologies of the Self*.

24. Michel Foucault, *Surveiller et punir: Naissance de la prison* (Paris: Gallimard, 1975), 192; translated by Alan Sheridan, under the title *Discipline and Punish: The Birth of the Prison* (New York: Vintage, 1979), 132.

25. Ariés, *Centuries of Childhood*, 284.

the subject, *Observations sur le système actuel d'instruction publique* (1801), was conceived not as idealized speculation on the most practical method of schooling, but as a polemic, an antidote to the chaos of the past twelve years: "Philosophy and education were to remedy the 'barbaric anarchy' of the Terror. At stake was not a vague *philosophie* of the Enlightenment, but a rigorous discipline in need of a name."[26]

In Destutt's scheme, which became *mutatis mutandis* the reality of the French school system, only children of the intellectual class (*classe savante*) would need confinement and surveillance. Those of the laboring class were to have only the most rudimentary and necessary schooling, relieving them of the necessity of leaving their homes. The children of the intellectuals, however,

> peuvent d'ailleurs sortir de la maison paternelle et se transporter près des écoles. Il faut même qu'ils soient dans des maisons d'éducation ou qu'ils aient chez eux des instituteurs particuliers; car le genre d'étude qui leur est nécessaire exige que des répétitions surveillent et dirigent le travail qui doit suivre les leçons qu'ils reçoivent, sans quoi elles ne seraient d'aucune utilité.

> ([The children of the intellectual class] can then leave their homes and be taken to schools. It is even necessary that they be in institutions or that they have private teachers living with them. This is because the type of study that they need requires that *repetition* control and direct the work which should follow the lessons, without which the lessons would be useless.)[27]

Repeating the same idea later in his essay, Destutt is more specific about the necessity of boarding schools for the education of the "intellectual class": "Nous sommes . . . convenus que la nature de ces études exigeait, pour qu'elles fussent utiles, que les jeunes gens eussent des maîtres qui les

26. Emmet Kennedy, *A "Philosophe" in the Age of Revolution: Destutt de Tracy and the Origins of "Ideology"* (Philadelphia: American Philosophical Society, 1978), 40.

27. A. L. C. Destutt de Tracy, *Observations sur le système actuel d'instruction publique* (Paris: Panckoucke, an 9 [1801]), 4; cited in Prost, *Histoire de l'enseignement*, 13. It is interesting to note that Destutt also addresses his *Élémens de l'idéologie* "surtout aux jeunes gens, parcequ'ils n'ont point encore d'opinions fixées" ("above all to young people, because they have no fixed opinions yet"), that is, because they can still be politically influenced. *Élémens d'idéologie*, vol. 1 (Paris: Courcier, 1801), 418. If the school system was to be the main bastion against anarchy, ideology was to be the main pillar of education itself, replacing a politically and intellectually defeated theology as the queen of sciences (cf. Kennedy, *A "Philosophe,"* 44–51).

fissent travailler en conséquence des leçons qu'ils recevaient, et qui surveil-lassent leur conduite; il faut donc des pensionnats" ("We have agreed on the fact that, in order for them to be useful, the nature of these studies requires that the young have teachers who will make them work on the basis of the lessons received, and who will supervise their conduct. We must, then, have boarding schools").[28] Destutt thus gives the *internat,* which had evolved by historical accident over the centuries, a new ideological justification.

These quotations explain the motivations behind the peculiar structure of Fresse-Montval's textbook. In French boarding schools, the classroom was merely a relay station between exercises carried out in solitude. The classroom was a place where old assignments could be handed in, new ones dictated, and surveillance and discipline carried out more effectively. Compositions (including letters) were to be written not for a practical purpose or as an opportunity for the pupils to express their individual opinions or personalities, but rather as the proper formulation of their social roles. French pupils were expected to learn through their writing the essential ideas of the good, the courageous, the brave, the bourgeois. Thus, this writing was to be nothing but a rewriting, as expressed in the *matière-corrigé* structure of the *Nouveau Manuel,* a doubleness that extends even to the novel that lies at its center. That doubleness hinges on the difference between the command to write and the writer's attempt to make some improvement to an already finished text. For example, the hero of our novel is to write an amusing description of his disagreeable coach ride from Valence to Paris. At one point in the letter, a flash of difference appears between the theme and its completion. The *matière* says that Gustave "ajoutera que, pour surcroît d'agrément, il avait à côte de lui une vieille demoiselle d'environ soixante-dix ans" (1:236; "will add that, to increase his pleasure, he was seated beside an old maid of about seventy years"), whereas the *corrigé* embellishes a bit: "J'avais à côte de moi une jeune personne parvenue à sa majorité depuis un bon demi-siècle" (1:237; "I was seated beside a young lady who had arrived at adulthood a good half-century ago"). But in discussing Gustave's ride we have already arrived at the navel of the *Nouveau Manuel,* its novel.

III

Just as a novel—particularly a nineteenth-century novel—often opens with general social and historical background before it introduces its main

28. Destutt de Tracy, *Observations sur le système actuel,* 36.

characters, the disconnected letters analyzed above have served as necessary background to the adventures of Zoé and Gustave. The double plot of Fresse-Montval's novel is as symmetrically arranged as the social relations of the writers and the addressees: Zoé and Gustave are students in *internats* who write to confidants of their own age (fifteen, a traditionally dangerous age) who are wiser than themselves. Such an arrangement is of course typical of the epistolary novel.[29] Elisa must respond to Zoé's desperation at being torn from her parents by saying that she will not cry with her; instead, she will applaud her departure. Curiously, Zoé's letter causes Elisa to take the side of authority and discipline whose signs are correct orthography and proper style:

> J'ai eu de la peine à lire ta lettre, mais uniquement par la manière dont elle est orthographiée. A chaque mot, je me disais: Zoé écrit ainsi à quinze ans, et elle ne bénit pas la main qui lui procure le pouvoir de s'instruire! Ah! ma Zoé, quel est ton aveuglement! (1:213)

> (I was saddened in reading your letter, but only because of the manner in which it is written. At each word I told myself: Zoé writes like this at the age of fifteen, and yet she does not kiss the hand of the person who seeks to give her the power of learning! Oh, my Zoé, how blind you are!)

At this point, Fresse-Montval's manual begins to indict itself, by telling us that it has just presented us with an execrable letter—the preceding one of Zoé's which has called forth such severe censure from Elisa. Oddly, the manual prints the writings of this young and unpolished person in their degenerate state, though the arrangement of *matière* and *corrigé* attempts to tell us otherwise. If this dichotomy were truly one of correction rather than an empty formalism, we should see two broadly different versions of Zoé's faulty letter. But this is not the case, and the suspicion arises that we are no longer meant to take this correspondence as a model. This, then, is the point of no return, the point at which the manual must become a novel, and rhetoric give way to representation.

Elisa's remark linking Zoé's age to her lack of writing skill can even be seen as a citation of the most famous French epistolary novel, *Les Liaisons*

---

29. On the idea of the confidante, see Janet Altman, *Epistolarity* (Columbus: Ohio State University Press, 1982), 47–86.

dangereuses, in which, as seen in the epigraph to this chapter, the fifteen-year-old Cécile Volanges is charged by the Marquise de Merteuil with similar faults. The parallel between these two works is no accident. *Les Liaisons dangereuses* is a novel that continually invokes the letter-writing manual, whereas our manual has just become a novel.[30] The negative symmetry applies to other areas of these two profoundly educational works as well: Cécile at fifteen returns home from the convent and is ruined; Zoé leaves her home for the *internat* and is saved, according to Elisa's prediction; *Les Liaisons dangereuses* is critical of society and revolutionary, with a touch of feminism in the figure of Merteuil; our novel upholds the social order and its asymmetrical gender roles.

Along the other epistolary axis, Ernest also accuses his friend Gustave of ingratitude, but Gustave's error is the opposite of Zoé's: he is too impatient to leave his home for the academy. At every point, the advice of Ernest contradicts that of Elise, just as Gustave's eagerness contradicts Zoé's timidity. Elise assures her confidante that "tu peux avoir de véritables jouissances dans ton pensionnat" (1:221; "You can have some really pleasurable experiences in your boarding school"); Ernest, on the other hand, cautions Gustave that "plus tu aura espéré de jouissances, plus les chagrins qui les remplaceront te sembleront poignants" (1:224; "The more you hope for pleasurable experiences, the more heartbreaking the unpleasant ones that replace them will be").

The young people depart for Paris. Zoé is impressed by the Tuileries and the Champs-Elysées, but an incident darkens her stay by foreshadowing the solitary discipline to which she will soon be exposed. She and her mother are dining at the home of an old friend of her father's, whose daughter resides at the very school where Zoé is destined to stay:

> On espérait me faire connaître cette nouvelle compagne, mais on n'a pu obtenir la permission de la faire sortir. Je me suis récriée sur cette sévérité, et je m'en suis bien repentie. Il y avait dans le cercle une vieille dame, élève de Sait-Cyr, qui a beaucoup applaudi à cette mesure rigoureuse. (1:236)

---

30. For example, Bernard Bray argues convincingly that the epistolary novel developed out of the collections of letters, so popular during the seventeenth century, which have precisely the same purpose as do Valmont's letters to Tourvel: to obtain power over a member of the opposite sex. Valmont could just as well have lifted his rhetorical exercises from manuals such as Pierre de Deimier's *Lettres amoureuses, non moins pleines de belles conceptions que de beaux désirs* (Paris: Sevestre, 1612) or Jean Puget de la Serre's *Le Secrétaire à la mode* (Paris, 1640). The hackneyed, "schoolbook" nature of Valmont's interminable rhetorical hammering on Tourvel's defenses would have been immediately obvious to any eighteenth-century reader.

(They were hoping to introduce me to this new classmate, but were unable to obtain permission for her to leave the school. I cried out against this severity, and I came to regret having done so. At the gathering was an elderly lady, a graduate of Saint-Cyr, who loudly approved of this strict measure.)

This mention of Saint-Cyr, the first public (in the British sense) educational institution for women in France, founded on a model of monastic discipline by Madame de Maintenon during the reign of Louis XIV, establishes both a continuity and a contrast with Zoé's nineteenth-century *internat*, which has filled Saint-Cyr's purpose with a new pedagogical content. A description of the daily routine at Saint-Cyr serves to illustrate the resemblance to monastic life: "The young ladies get up at six, attend mass at eight, breakfast at nine, have lunch at eleven, take turns reading during the meal, have recess until one, work until six, when the whole community goes to dinner, and they can only go to the reception room for two weeks at the end of each quarter (every three months) because of the distractions which an excessive number of visits would cause."[31] The last point shows a confinement experienced by the matron comparable to the present situation, thus explaining her agreement with the measures taken by the school.

Similarly monastic are the complete discipline and egalitarianism that reign in Zoé's school. On finally entering into her *pension*, Zoé is immediately separated from her younger sister, as the girls are segregated by age and skills. Zoé's first writing lesson consists mainly of the command *not* to write. Her report of it is rendered in the "writing-to-the-moment" style so familiar to readers of the epistolary novel:

> Je viens d'être interrompue par une petite malicieuse qui s'est assise auprès de moi pour me dire: Mademoiselle, vous écrivez une bien longue lettre à votre maman, et elle vient de vous quitter. — J'écris à une de mes amies, lui ai-je dit. — Ah! ne prenez pas cette peine, a-t-elle répliqué; le règlement nous le défend. — Cela est vrai, m'a dit une dame qui faisait une bourse, et qui me paraît être la surveillante de la classe. Vous voudriez bien aussi me rendre le papier à vignettes que vous avez dans votre écritoire; on

---

31. Laurent Anglivel de La Beaumelle, *Mémoires pour servir à l'histoire de Madame de Maintenon et à celle du siècle passé* (Amsterdam, 1755–56); cited in Louis Chabaud, *Les Précurseurs du féminisme, Mesdames de Maintenon, De Genlis & Campan. Leur rôle dans l'éducation chrétienne de la femme* (Paris: Plon-Nourrit, 1901), 119.

vous en donnera de plus simple pour écrire à vos parents, c'est-à-dire, seulement à Monsieur votre père, à Madame votre mère, à vos grands parents, à vos tantes et à vos oncles. (1:242–43)

(I have just been interrupted by a little troublemaker who sat down next to me in order to say: "Miss, you are writing a very long letter to your mama, and she has just left you." — "I am writing to one of my friends," I said to her. — "Ah! don't waste your time doing that," she replied, "the rules forbid such writing." — "That's true," said a lady who was making a purse; she seemed to be the class monitress. "Also, please give me the fancy stationery you have in your writing desk; we'll give you a plainer sort for you to write to your family, that is, solely to your father, your mother, your grandparents, and your aunts and uncles.")

This quotation defines an interesting role for the *surveillante*, whose eye must penetrate every detail of the circumstances of writing. She must observe the practice of writing down to the minutest details of paper and of the allowable boundaries of the bourgeois family (three generations, including aunts and uncles but not cousins). Monitoring and teaching blend into a single task in Zoé's first writing lesson, as Foucault claims they did for French education in general during this period: "A relation of surveillance, defined and regulated, is inscribed at the heart of the practice of teaching, not as an additional or adjacent part, but as a mechanism that is inherent to it and which increases its efficiency."[32] After Destutt, Madame de Campan, one of the most prominent educators of adolescents in this period, had extensively theorized the role of surveillance: "La discipline doit s'accroître en raison du nombre d'élèves: rien ne doit être négligé; l'oeil de la maîtresse doit se porter partout, pour que le règlement soit observé dans les moindres détails" ("Discipline should increase in proportion to the number of pupils; nothing ought to be neglected; the eye of the mistress should penetrate everywhere, so that the regulations may be observed in the slightest affairs").[33] This novel, part of that educational

32. Foucault, *Discipline and Punish*, 176. Or, more bluntly, Antoine Prost: "Sauf une minorité de pédagogues, tous se méfient de la spontanéité des enfants: c'est un danger plus qu'une promesse, et Durkheim définit l'éducation, comme . . . 'une œuvre d'autorité' " (*Histoire de l'enseignement*, 9; "With the exception of a minority of pedagogues, everyone distrusts the spontaneity of children: it is a danger more than a promise, and Durkheim defines education as . . . 'an act of authority' "). These are less interpretations of the period than direct quotes from Destutt and others.

33. Jeanne de Campan, *De l'éducation, suivi des conseils aux jeunes filles, d'un théâtre pour les jeunes*

system, is to be read in such a way that surveillance can specify its pedagogical efficiency. Indeed, this is the most specific scene of teaching to appear in the novel. Later depictions of wonderful soirees with the school director are much less descriptive, with no direct quotations of principles.

Zoé's writing has been restricted in two ways: in her choice of paper and in her choice of correspondents. In its preoccupation with the sensual aspect of writing—here expressed in the luxury or simplicity of the paper—this restriction takes us back to the manual's introduction, in which margins and paper were regulated by the social relations obtaining between the correspondents. In the restrictions of Zoé's correspondents to people older than herself (note the absence of brothers and sisters from the list of approved readers), one is reminded of the beginning of the manual and of the endless letters of fealty from son to father and grandfather, daughter to uncle, and so on. Many of these letters were written from the school to home. Now we see why in that first section there were no letters between friends. The forming of friendships between young people was forbidden by the school. It could lead to the weakening of discipline, to conspiracy, and ultimately to revolt, as Fresse-Montval will show us in the acquaintance of Gustave with Auguste de L. More danger still if the friend happens to reside outside the walls of the boarding school. The pendant to this censorship of outside communication is the "leçon d'écriture" that Zoé highlights as a part of her daily routine at the school, and for which the *Nouveau Manuel* could have been the textbook— a sort of *mise en abîme* of the *ars dictaminis* takes place here. The command not to write is inseparable from the command to write. The proscription of Zoé's correspondence with Elisa makes it more interesting by giving it a tinge of the forbidden. It is clear that the correspondence now represents freedom to Zoé: "Tu dois juger combien il est affreux d'être soumise à un pareil despotisme. Ecris-moi donc, ma chère Elisa, sans tes lettres je perdrais la raison; ne m'abandonne pas à ma tristesse" (1:259; "You must be able to guess how awful it is to be subjected to such despotism. Write to me then, my dear Elisa, without your letters I would lose my mind; don't abandon me in my sorrow"). In a surprising twist, though, the intended source and pillar of Zoé's rebellion denies that rebellion's validity. Elisa responds that she and her mother both laughed at Zoé's letter. That

personnes et de quelques essais de morale, vol. 1, ed. M. F. Barrière (Paris: Baudouin, 1824), 250; translated anonymously under the title *The Private Journal of Madame Campan* (London: Colburn, 1825), 409.

the mother read the letter emphasizes the public nature of these private missives and further multiplies the theme of surveillance, which is now carried out by the two recipients as well as at the source of writing by the monitress.

In opposition to Zoé, and contrary to his own expectations, Gustave is so exhausted by his journey that he goes to bed immediately after writing and is completely dissatisfied with his sightseeing the next day. Gustave is also disappointed with his boarding school, although he does not give exact reasons beyond the paucity of nourishment: "Il m'a semblé bien pénible de n'avoir que du pain sec à ce premier repas" (1:364; "It seemed wretched enough to have nothing but dry bread at my first meal here"). The complaint shows our novel to be realistic, as food deprivation was a common enough complaint against the schools in this era. A historian of the period writes, "Il semble que, dans tous les internats, les élèves, filles ou garçons, n'avaient pas la nourriture qui convenait à leur âge et qu'ils devaient, entre autres regrets, avoir celui bien vif de la table familiale" ("It seems that in all the boarding schools the pupils, girls or boys, did not have the nourishment necessary for their age, and that among other things they must have missed the family dinner-table quite a bit").[34] Even Madame de Campan came to regret the nutritional status of the boarding schools she had helped make so popular: "Il y a trop peu d'écoles où les enfans soient bien nourris; il en est même où ils ne le sont pas suffisamment" ("There are very few schools in which children are well fed; there are even some in which they are not adequately fed").[35] Yet at the same time, the lack of nourishment could not be called a deficiency or breach in the educational plan; rather, it was another realization of the school's monastic discipline and of its imposition of equality on its pupils. For after denouncing the lack of food, Campan feels called upon to defend its plainness and to condemn any system that allows the wealthier students to purchase extra delicacies. She develops the boarding system into an allegory of the general political and economic realm, and the *ressentiment* that its injustices caused into a foreshadowing of the Revolution, which nearly killed her:

> On assure que des gens, qui ont marqué de la manière la plus funeste à l'époque sanglante de notre révolution, avaient puisé leurs fureurs démagogiques, étant boursiers, dans de grands col-

---

34. Maurice Allem, *La vie quotidienne sous le Second Empire* (Paris: Hachette, 1948), 127.
35. Campan, *De l'éducation*, 1:231; *The Private Journal*, 397.

léges de Paris, parce qu'on n'y accordait de dessert qu'aux pen-
sionnaires payant, et que la seule vue de fruits donnés au fils d'un
riche dont ils venaient de faire le thème ou la version pour le
sauver du plus honteux châtiment, avait allumé dans leurs coeurs
les premiers sentimens d'une haine que les injustices du monde
avaient accrue et portée jusqu'aux plus criminels excès.

(We are assured that people who have signalized themselves, in
the most melancholy manner, at the bloody epoch of our revolution, were revenging their school affronts while *boursiers*, in great
Parisian schools, because desserts were granted only to boarders
paying for them; and that the mere sight of a fruit, given to the
son of a wealthy man, whose exercise or translation they had just
written to save him from the most shameful punishment, had
kindled in their hearts the first sentiments of a hatred which the
injustice of the world increased and carried to the most criminal
excess.)[36]

In this remarkable passage, Campan manages to unite the themes of social
status, hunger, scholarship, and revolution, which are also the essence of
Fresse-Montval's novel, and which are linked here as there to the writing
lesson—the "exercise or translation" that the poorer student is *compelled* to
write. And thus it is a sign of decadent authority in Gustave's boarding
school that he can take advantage of his financial situation in order to buy
the extra food he craves, and it is a sign of his friend Auguste's subversive
nature that he encourages Gustave in the practice of buying such extra
food.

Gustave's friendship with Auguste becomes his main solace. After all,
Auguste is "doué d'une verve intarissable de malices et de bons mots,
fécond en heureux expédients, quand il s'agit de tromper les maîtres ou de
s'égayer à leurs dépens, . . . le sujet le plus distingué que renferme notre
collége" (1:363; "gifted with an inexhaustible brilliance in practical jokes
and witticisms, full of ready strategems when it comes to fooling the
teachers or making fun of them, . . . our school's most distinguished
individual"). Ernest counsels his intern as Elisa had hers, by contrasting
his own writing lessons and his own attempts to change and restrain
Gustave's behavior through writing with Auguste's base strategy to "ap-

36. Campan, *De l'éducation*, 1:233; *The Private Journal*, 399.

prouv[er] toutes ses idées et flatt[er] tous ses penchants" (1:267; "approve all his ideas and flatter his every whim").

The last two letters of the novel show the asymmetrical accommodation of the two students to their prisons. Zoé ceases to be alienated, rises in rank, and is allowed to take tea with the director. Her last letter, though still full of regrets for the maternal home, nevertheless effects an accommodation with if not a total affirmation of the system. Its last lines affirm the writing lesson as a necessary form of surveillance: "Mais peut-être que le temps où je dois arriver à la classe des grandes viendra bientôt. Je ne m'en croirais pas éloignée, si tu pouvais suivre de près ma conduite, et me communiquer chaque jour tes précieux conseils" (1:273; "But perhaps the time for me to join the upper class will come soon. I wouldn't feel far away, if you could follow my conduct closely, and give me your valuable advice every day").

Gustave achieves ideological enlightenment in a much more violent and decisive fashion. A teacher whom the students thought to be easily manipulated has suddenly been dealing out *pensums* and study halls. Auguste and Gustave plan to revenge themselves with a rebellion, which resembles nothing so much as a failed coup attempt, and which thus must have seemed to the contemporary reader a miniature reproduction of French history since 1789. Gustave's sad letter recounting the incident is therefore minutely, perhaps satirically, detailed about the chain of command in his school:

> La fréquence et la multitude des petites réunions qui eurent lieu à partir de ce moment, l'air de mystère qui planait sur toute notre division, peut-être aussi quelques faux frères, tout cela éveilla l'attention du maître d'étude, et, par suite, celle du censeur. Le proviseur fut averti, tous les moyens de répression se trouvèrent en disponibilité. Aussi, lorsqu'à un signal donné par Auguste, pendant l'étude du soir, toutes les lumières s'éteignaient à la fois, la porte de la salle était barricadée, et tous les encriers volaient à la tête de notre tyran, c'est ainsi que nous l'appelions; tout-à-coup, les fenêtres sont enfoncées, des domestiques avec des flambeux, et suivis de la force armée, se précipitent au milieu de nous; les plus mutins, et j'étais du nombre, sont saisis et jetés dans un cachot; la conspiration est en même temps déjouée et punie. (1:277)

(The number and frequency of small meetings that took place from this moment on, the air of mystery that hung over our entire group, perhaps also some stool pigeons, all this alerted the teacher's attention, and in turn that of the deputy headmaster. The headmaster was informed, all the means of repression were made ready. Thus, when at a signal given by Auguste, during evening class, all the lights were extinguished, the door to the classroom barricaded, and all the ink pots flew at the head of our tyrant [as we called him]; all of a sudden the windows were smashed open, servants with torches followed by armed troops rushed into our midst; the leaders of the rebellion, and I was among them, were seized and thrown into a cell; the conspiracy was foiled and punished at the same time.)

Fresse-Montval apparently knew student rebellions firsthand. Gustave's story corresponds at every point to Antoine Prost's historical narrative of student rebellions in this period: "Most of the school histories record some insurrections. . . . The pattern of the rebellions changes very little: teachers or headmasters are threatened, roughed up, locked up. The police chief or the principal intervenes. Sometimes police are needed to restore order. Sometimes the rebels, barricaded, refuse to surrender: holes must be made in the partitions in order to reach them."[37]

That school mutinies could have served as a model for this scene does not eliminate its ability to function as an allegory for the "real" political events of the day as well, particularly for the failed republican uprising of 1834, which forms the background to Fresse-Montval's novel *Jules-Joseph, pensée intime*. Fresse-Montval has been remembered as a legitimist, but he treats the titular republican hero of this novel with sympathy; the real villain is neither republicanism nor monarchism, but the surveillance that represses all political ideas, as incorporated in the policeman Buget who takes furtive revenge on Joseph when the latter refuses to spy for him. (The implication is that there are only two possibilities: to spy or to be spied on.) In the penultimate scene of this novel Jules, who has already been arrested once for conspiracy, finds himself on the barricades in a situation similar to that of Gustave, revolting against oppression without being aware of the true source of his misery: "Nous avons vu quelle absolue confiance Jules-Joseph avait mise dans M. Buget; il ignorait d'ailleurs que le quartier où s'était cantonées les républicains fût aussi étroitement cerné par les agens du pouvoir" ("We have seen the absolute confidence that Jules-Joseph had placed in Mr. Buget; moreover, he

37. Prost, *Histoire de l'enseignement*, 53.

didn't know that the neighborhood where the republicans had barricaded themselves was surrounded so closely by agents of the authorities").[38] Joseph is betrayed by Buget just as the students are by their fellow students and by a teacher they thought to be their friend. In the *internat* as in the outside world, "les instruments d'oppression sont partout." *Jules-Joseph* ends tragically, with the murder-suicide of Jules, his wife, and their daughter, "trois vies qui, dans la réalisation de leurs plus chers désirs, ne recontrèrent que des piéges" ("three lives which encountered only snares on the path to realizing their most cherished desires").[39] Tragedy is an inappropriate genre for textbooks, however. Gustave and Zoé are allowed to save themselves in return for learning to conform and to write to dictation as they ought.

And for learning to write to the correct protector. Gustave is pardoned for his part in the rebellion only after he seeks the aid of "quelques anciens amis [du père], aujourd'hui fort influents" (1:278; "some old friends [of his father's], today highly influential"). Similarly, Gustave is able to get back in the good graces of his teachers by achieving twelfth place in composition—that is, by finding the correct *corrigé* for his given *matière*. Thus, though the novel would seem to contradict the intentions of Fresse-Montval's textbook by showing a scene of insurrection that challenges all the demands of pedagogy, the failure of that insurrection preserves and even reinforces the importance of the writing lesson, underlining the necessity for writing letters filled with all the tokens of subjugation at the author's command. By placing letter writing within the general framework of surveillance, the novel allows the reader to understand it as merely one form of that principle of society which triumphs over any other. The message is double-edged: Fresse-Montval at once expresses the less abstract power relations (for example, the "force armée") that enter the scene when language fails, those which therefore make of linguistic control a kind of shell game, while at the same time counseling the players to adhere to that language game as a way of avoiding the other, more brutal forms of control.

Similarly, Fresse-Montval himself seeks the "protection" of his better-known predecessor in the field of education in the didactic epistolary novel. At the end of each of Zoé's and Elisa's letters the name of "Madame Campan" appears, and well it should, because the female half of this novel is simply a rewriting—a *corrigé*—of Campan's own boarding-school novel

---

38. Alphonse Fresse-Montval, *Jules Joseph, pensée intime,* vol. 2 (Paris: Dentu, 1834), 323.
39. Ibid., 2:328.

Lettres de deux amies, ou correspondance entre deux élèves d'Écouen.[40] By comparing original and adaptation, one can discern even more clearly the ideological formation of Fresse-Montval's didactic fiction as a product of Campan's writing lessons.

Jeanne Genet de Campan has already appeared in this essay as one of
the best-known figures in French education. She attempted to improve the
methods of Madame de Maintenon's Saint-Cyr.[41] She was an important
transitional figure between the ancien régime and the Empire, as her
biographers point out: "She preceded Bonaparte in reconciling the old
with the new France, in welcoming aristocrat and bourgoisie, French-
woman and foreigner, in combining moral education with intellectual
formation and practical training."[42] Campan was appointed official reader
to Marie Antoinette from an early age; her *Mémoires* of the queen would
be her bestselling and most extensively translated book.[43] Having barely
escaped the Terror with her life—her sister had committed suicide as she
was about to be arrested—by 1794, Campan had somehow managed to
open her first school, the Institution Nationale de Saint-Germain. She
reached the height of her influence during the period 1807–14, establishing
and directing the Maison impériale at Écouen for the daughters of killed
or wounded soldiers.[44] The *maisons impériales* were conceived following the
battle of Austerlitz, where Napoleon observed the decimation of his troops
and searched for methods to compensate, encourage, and replenish his
soldiers.

In rewriting Campan's novel, Fresse-Montval felt the need to erase its
Napoleonic setting, more precisely from 20 March 1808, when Zoé
receives permission to matriculate at Écouen, to 14 August 1809, when her

40. Jeanne de Campan, *Lettres de deux amies, ou correspondance entre deux élèves d'Ecouen* (Paris:
Baudoin Frères, 1825). Further citations in the text.

41. A biographer describes the relation between Saint-Cyr and Écouen in the following terms:
"Madame Campan . . . envied Madame de Maintenon's honor of having founded the royal school
of Saint-Louis, [but] did not stop thinking that that admirable establishment had ended up being
excessively out of step and far behind the innovations of the century." Chabaud, *Les Précurseurs du
féminisme*, 276.

42. Yvan David and Monique Giot, *Madame Campan 1752–1822* (Paris: Éditions des Musées
Nationaux, 1972), 11.

43. Jeanne de Campan, *Mémoires sur la vie privée de Marie Antoinette, reine de France et de Navarre,
suivis de souvenirs et anecdotes historiques sur les règnes de Louis XIV, de Louis XV et de Louis XVI* (Paris:
Baudoin, 1822). Further editions in 1823 and 1826. There are fifty-six published translations of
this work into English.

44. The most extensive history of Écouen remains Louis Bonneville de Marsangy's *Madame
Campan à Écouen, Étude historique et biographique* (Paris: H. Champion, 1879). Unfortunately,
Marsangy never mentions Campan's novel.

friend Elisa joins her there. For obvious reasons, Campan names her own school of Écouen and stresses its alliance with the French military; for equally obvious reasons, Fresse-Montval deletes these details from the *Nouveau Manuel*. Fresse-Montval has also elided all references to Zoé's father, an epitome of French military pride and sacrifice. Here is Campan's depiction of him as he receives the news that, due to his being a legionary, his daughters have been admitted to Écouen—despite Zoé's advanced age. Zoé contrasts her own dejection at being admitted to Écouen with his patriotic elation:

> J'avais les yeux fixés sur mon père; je vis sa physionomie s'épanouir successivement, et j'entendis ces mots terribles: *mes filles et mon fils sont placés!* Alors, ma chère, comme s'il n'était plus boiteux, comme s'il ne criait pas sans cesse, *Ma blessure! ma blessure!* voilà mon père qui retire sa jambe emmaillotée du tabouret qui la soutient, qui prend sa canne, se lève, ôte son chapeau et se met à crier: «Voilà un général, mes amis, sous les ordres duquel il est glorieux de vivre et de savoir mourir!» (*Lettres* 6)

> (I had fixed my eyes on my father; I saw his face light up, and I heard the terrible words: *my daughters and my son have been admitted!* Then, my dear, as though he were no longer crippled, as though he never used to cry out ceaselessly *My wound! My wound!* there was my father taking his cast-bound leg off the stool which supported it, taking his cane, getting up, removing his hat and breaking out with "There is a general, my friends, under whose orders it is glorious to live and to be able to die!)

The father is especially overjoyed about Zoé, since girls of her advanced age are rarely admitted to Écouen. And there were good reasons for such an age limit. Zoé's sister is only eight, and the difference between her acceptance and her older sister's rejection of confinement is explicitly related to their varying ages in the following scene, when they visit notables in Paris before entering school. A monsignor asks the eight-year-old,

> Êtes-vous bien aise d'aller à Écouen? lui a-t-il demandé en la prenant par la main. — Très-aise, Monseigneur, a répondu la petite sotte . . . — Voilà l'âge d'être admise à la maison impériale, a dit M. le grand-chancelier; la réponse naïve et gaie de la petite, les larmes de l'aînée . . . en sont les preuves. (33)

> ("Are you happy to be entering Écouen?" he asked her in taking her by the hand—"Very happy, Monseigneur," replied the little

fool . . . —"Here is the age at which one should be admitted to
Écouen," said the chancellor, "the proof is in the frank and happy
answer of the younger sister and the tears of the older one.")

The naive and joyful response of the eight-year-old contrasts with the tears
and anxiety of the fifteen-year-old. The years from seven to nine are
universally considered the borderline between cultural accommodation
and a certain naïveté that allows for ideological molding.[45] At Écouen this
dividing line was drawn with special rigor because the girls' training there
was to be the counterpart of the training in the male lycées, "which were
intended to insure the formation of a class of leaders, civil servants, and
officers, so thought Napoleon: to which contemporaries added the classes
of merchants and lawyers."[46] Following the Napoleonic era, particularly
after the July Revolution and the installation of a "bourgeois king," the
latter two classes took precedence over Napoleon's. In a different historical
context with different goals for and different methods of education, Fresse-
Montval no longer emphasized the role of age distinctions in ideological
formation the way Campan had.

The rhetorical carapace (the *ars*) within which Fresse-Montval has
placed his novel functions as an indispensable guide for the proper reading
of the "fiction" of the boarding school. This fiction, however, was also the
quotidian reality of the novel's eventual readers, the boarders and teachers
in such schools. Given this readership, Fresse-Montval has drastically
narrowed the range of characters originally found in Campan's novel.
Campan, who was writing a didactic novel rather than a textbook, included
descriptions of other characters, such as Elisa's father, and also allowed
other characters to write letters. For example, there is an exchange
between Elisa's mother and the directors of the school, in which the former
asks permission for her daughter to write to Zoé, and the latter grants it,
knowing that Elisa is merely a puppet voicing the words of the directress
herself. The granting of permission amounts to deceiving Zoé, who believes
that she will be allowed news from *outside* the school, since all of Elisa's

45. For example, Native Americans tended to keep white prisoners under the age of nine only,
knowing that the older children could not be assimilated. See J. Norman Heard, *White Into Red: A
Study of the Assimilation of White Persons Captured by Indians* (Metuchen, N.J.: Scarecrow Press,
1973), 1–15. In her *Private Journal*, Campan expresses the same idea, though since she is writing
for a general audience she specifies the male sex: "At seven years of age the indispensable
separation takes place; a mother places her son in the hands of men" (*Private Journal* 1:137).
46. Georges Duby and Robert Mandrou, *Histoire de la civilisation française, XVIIe–XXe siècle*
(Paris: Armand Colin, 1958), 175.

thoughts have been preapproved by the system. This conformity is shown in the directress's phrase "sous mon couvert": "Je ne suis pas moins persuadée que le commerce de lettres entre Zoé et Elisa ne peut être qu'extrêmement utile à la première. Vous pouvez donc, Madame, lui adresser ses lettres sous mon couvert" (44; "I believe, however, that the exchange of letters between Zoé and Elisa could only be extremely useful for the former. Therefore, Madame, you may send her letters under the pretext of writing to me").[47] The strategy works, as we have seen already in our examination of Fresse-Montval's version—which, however, fails to explain the lifting of the ban on correspondence with friends. Campan also knows more explicitly that Elisa is partly responsible for Zoé's turnaround at the school: Zoé sends four of her five good report cards home; she sends the fifth to Elisa, "ma plus précieuse institutrice," without whose advice "les soins des maîtresses m'eussent été inutiles" (146–47; "my most valuable teacher; without your advice the cares of the teachers here would have availed me nothing").

Fresse-Montval has also eliminated everything in Elisa's letters that does not bear on Zoé's situation at school. Campan had taken care to make Elisa undergo her own process of enlightenment, thus establishing a parallel between intramural and extramural education. Elisa wears a flashy dress at a country banquet and laughs and talks too much with a young officer. The whole of her letter describing her conduct is doubtless read by Zoé with the sighs of a prisoner looking out her window. But enclosed within Elisa's letter is one written to her by her uncle, the *curé* who gave the banquet. The letter blames her conduct and places her in a position of confinement similar to that of Zoé—notice the future-tense commands like those in the *matières:* "Nous avons décidé, votre mère et moi, de couper court aux liaisons que votre légèreté vous a fait contracter. A l'époque des vendages, vous reviendrez à Fréville et vous y passerez l'hiver" (98; "Your mother and I have decided to cut off the contacts your giddiness made you take up. At grape-harvest time, you will return to Fréville and you will spend the winter there"). Later the same uncle will write to Elisa with suggestions on how to conduct herself in the society of the *maréchale* she is visiting. And later, Elisa will show this authority figure the first of Zoé's letters and her most recent one, in order that he might note the latter's progress in writing: "Je suis allée lui chercher ta première lettre; en la comparant à la dernière, il ne pouvait comprendre comment, en si peu de

---

47. Combining two meanings of "sous le couvert": (1) to send something through an intermediary; (2) to use a pretext.

temps tu as pu acquérir une orthographe aussi correcte: il pense très-avantageusement de la méthode d'enseignement de la maison d'Écouen" (177–78; "I went and got your first letter for him; in comparing it to the last one you wrote, he was amazed at how you had been able to learn such perfect spelling in such a short time: he regards the teaching methods of Écouen very highly").

In Campan's novel, when Elisa's brother is finally accorded the legion of honor, thus assuring her entrance at Écouen, she makes sure that her uncle continues her own epistolary surveillance. Her letter makes clear once again that virtue can be obtained and maintained only through the writing lesson:

> On me fait trop d'honneur en accordant à mes jeunes années le mérite d'une raison que vous avez fait éclore, et qui s'affaiblirait bien vite par les défauts naturels à mon âge, si votre bien-veillante sollicitude se ralentissait. Continuez, mon cher oncle, à guider cette Elisa qu'une ambition pardonnable éloigne pour quelque temps de celui qu'elle révère comme son père. Je vous communiquerai mes plus secrètes pensées, comme si je jouissais encore de vos entretiens; combattez mes jugemens [*sic*] lorsqu'ils seront faux ou légèrement portés, et grondez-moi quand je le mériterai. . . . Soutenez-moi, mon cher oncle, par vos utiles conseils, et diminuez par vos lettres la tristesse que notre séparation fait déjà naître dans mon coeur. Écrivez-moi le plus souvent qu'il vous sera possible. Je devrais dire, écrivez-nous, car Zoé partage et mes sentimens [*sic*] et l'admiration que vous avez fait naître dans le cœur de votre Elisa. (205)

> (They praise me too much in attributing to my tender years the merits of a rationality which you have made bloom, and which would be quickly blighted by the weaknesses common to my age if your beneficent solicitude ever were to slacken. Continue, my dear uncle, to guide this Elisa, whom a pardonable ambition will take away from you, whom she reveres like a father. I will tell you my most secret thoughts, just as if I still had the pleasure of your conversation; oppose my opinions whenever they seem falsely or lightly assumed, and scold me when I deserve it. . . . Preserve me, my dear uncle, by your useful advice, and by means of your letters lessen the sadness which our separation already is giving rise to in my heart. Write me as often as possible. I should say, write to us,

for Zoé shares both my feelings and the admiration which you
have awakened in Elisa's heart.)

Elisa's plea to her uncle to become her "surveillant" repeats in substance
Zoé's request to Elisa of 19 May 1808: "Aide-moi de tes avis, encourage-
moi par tes conseils, ma chère Elisa" (66; "Help me with your opinions,
Elisa, encourage me with your advice"). Thus the uncle's letters will have
not one but several recipients, just as did Zoé's (Elisa *and* her mother) and
Elisa's (Zoé *and* the school director). Given the similarities in age and sex
between Zoé and Elisa and the dictum that physical presence communi-
cates more than distant writing, it is surprising that Elisa does not look to
Zoé for the oral communication of her most intimate and secret desires,
but prefers the epistolary route provided by her uncle. The triumph of
epistolarity dominates Campan's novel; Fresse-Montval has maintained
that triumph and expanded it into pedagogy.

So far we have focused on what Fresse-Montval has deleted from
Campan's text in order to have it conform to the ideology of his readership.
But of course, Fresse-Montval has also *added* something to Campan, namely
the male plotline. The parallel series of letters by our hero and heroine
show two similar, bittersweet, uneasy accommodations. The letter writers
differ precisely in what their gender roles expect of them. The male
adventurer exults in leaving home and seeks to destroy physically the
instruments of repression as he himself defines them; the shy female clings
to mama and retreats from the horrors of incarceration into the supposed
privacy of adolescent correspondence. The more severe dissatisfaction and
punishment of Gustave compared to Zoé's fate reinforces the asymmetry
between men and women, which helps organize the manual. As pointed
out earlier, the power of writing in this *ars* derives from its function as a
bridge between unequal social positions. Although it should be noted that
women often wield power and are certainly not confined to the domestic
sphere in the *Nouveau Manuel*, their most powerful roles are derived either
from their husbands (for example, the *maréchale*) or from areas of compe-
tence traditionally assigned to women (as in the case of the singer).
However, the perceived difference between the genders here is also a
product of the novel's editorial history. Fresse-Montval presumably invented the exchange between Gustave and Ernest and, as it were, merely
adapted that between Zoé and Elise from Campan and the Napoleonic
period. Thus, despite the *matière* versus *corrigé* dichotomy in which he
places Campan's letters, Fresse-Montval has not used the letters merely as
textual models. Unlike so many authors of letter-writing manuals who raid

epistolary history in order to sprinkle letters by Balzac, Voiture, and Sévigné over their texts as illustrations (as this author also does in the second volume of the *Nouveau Manuel*), Fresse-Montval lets the skeleton of Campan's epistolary novel shape his own. Perhaps in reaction to Campan's own penchant for fiction, Fresse-Montval has handled these letters as a "strong reader" of a literary text: he has produced a countertext, a parody or adaptation in which the silencings and additions resonate with ideology. Thus, Fresse-Montval's novel must be placed in a different generic category from Campan's. For Campan's is a "girls' school novel" in the manner of Sarah Fielding's *Governess, or Little Female Academy* or Hannah Foster's *Boarding School; or, Lessons of a Preceptress to her Pupils*.[48] Like Campan's novel, these are didactic fictions in which conversation between pupils forms the basis of the story—thus favoring the epistolary mode. In all of these novels it is the students who educate each other, without much help from and certainly without repressive measures on the part of the teacher.

The male epistolary axis, however, tells a story of repression and rebellion typical of works of the late-nineteenth and early-twentieth centuries, such as Robert Musil's *Verwirrungen des Zöglings Törless*, Raúl Pompeia's *O Ateneu*, and even the German film *Mädchen in Uniform*.[49] Each of these works depicts the boarding school as a system of surveillance and control, usually personified in a tyrannical headmaster; each ends with a student revolt—Pompeia even shows his boarding school being razed by its disgruntled inmates. In these latter boarding-school fictions, discipline has replaced conversation as the guiding principle of education. Indeed, even as late as 1933 the extraordinary French motion picture *Zéro de conduite* revisits most of Fresse-Montval's themes: *conduite, surveillance,* lack of nourishment, student friendships and false friendships, rebellion, the lax or friendly professor, all have their place in Jean Vigo's masterpiece.[50] The reception history of Vigo's film also demonstrates the ideological link between school and the larger political world: the film was banned on

---

48. Sarah Fielding, *The Governess or, Little Female Academy* (1749; reprint, New York: Pandora Press, 1987); Hannah Foster, *The Boarding School: or, Lessons of a Preceptress to her Pupils: Consisting of Information, Instruction, and Advice, Calculated to Improve the Manners and Form the Character of Young Ladies. To Which is Added a Collection of Letters, Written by the Pupils, to their Instructor, their Friends, and Each Other. By a Lady of Massachusetts* (Boston: I. Thomas and E. F. Andrews, 1798).

49. Robert Musil, *Die Verwirrungen des Zöglings Törless* (1906), in *Prosa und Stücke, Kleine Prosa, Aphorismen, Autobiographisches, Essays und Reden, Kritik, Gesammelte Werke,* ed. Adolf Frise, vol. 2 (Berlin: Rowohlt, 1978), 7–140. Raúl Pompeia, *O Ateneu* (1888; reprint, Rio de Janeiro: Edições de Ouro, n. d.); *Mädchen in Uniform,* directed by Leontine Sagan, screenplay by F. D. Andam and Christa Winsloe (Deutsche Film Gemeinschaft, 1931).

50. *Zéro de conduite,* directed by and screenplay by Jean Vigo (Argui Films, 1933).

release in 1933 on the grounds that its attacks on the school system might have political consequences. The confluence of these two subgenres, of girls' school novel and boarding-school novel, within Fresse-Montval's work indicates his uneasy historical position between two ideas of education and politics.

Whatever the aesthetic merits and demerits of Fresse-Montval's novel, it remains interesting for the way it exposes a different reading situation for aesthetic works than we are used to—or than we are willing to admit. If one accepts Stanley Fish's contention, made most forcefully in *Is There a Text in This Class?* that texts are "a function of interpretation,"[51] Fresse-Montval's novel can be seen as an overt example of the operations of appropriation that are present in every reading of a text. Since it deliberately invokes the classroom, one could apply Fish's title question to the *Nouveau Manuel.* That is, what was the real shape of this novel as used within the classroom? We have already seen how the story of Zoé and Gustave announces itself as a rewriting, but this process of rewriting continued through two more levels: the teacher and the students. The *Nouveau Manuel* was undoubtedly purchased not by the students of the *internats,* but by their teachers (otherwise, why include the *corrigés?*). The double plot may be an indication of the author's desire to market his book to boarding schools for both sexes. The novel was to be given to the students not as reading, but as writing, as dictation, letter by letter over a period of weeks or months. At the discretion of their teacher, the students may have gotten the whole of this novel, part of it, or none of it. However much of it they got, our interest focuses on the concrete conditions of reception for this text: students were specifically assigned to rewrite it by turning *matière* into *corrigé.* The novel was not their reading, but their writing lesson. This sort of reading, of course, is classical; it is implicit in the teaching of letter writing (a subgenre of the teaching of rhetoric). It aims at the production of discourse rather than at its absorption. The novel thus came into being differently for each pupil in each classroom lesson in each school, its never-ending variety the product of a series of readers who were themselves the products of the writing of ideologies, products the novel depicts in the process of being formed.[52]

51. Stanley Fish, *Is There A Text in This Class?* (Cambridge: Harvard University Press, 1980), 342.

52. The classic statement of the reader as himself a product of writing is by Roland Barthes: "Ce «moi» qui s'approche du texte est déjà lui-même une pluralité d'autres textes, de codes infinis, ou plus exactement perdus (dont l'origine se perd)" ("This 'I' which approaches the text is already itself a plurality of other texts, of codes which are infinite or, more precisely, lost [whose origin is

In Chapter 2, the genres of ethnography were shown to be arranged around the different use-values of fiction and nonfiction. In this case, how can we characterize the relation between the fiction of Zoé and Gustave and the rhetorical training in the rest of the *Nouveau Manuel*? It would seem that merely teaching the rhetorical principles of letter writing is not enough. One must also show the *couvert*, the outside of the letter and the media of its writing and its reception, by placing it within a context. One must construct the ideal letter writer, as "glassy essence" (Richardson, Gellert) or as an inventory of socially oriented rhetorical stratagems (Fresse-Montval). One can do this within the model letters themselves, thus giving such models a double function, rhetorical and fictional. Such is the case for many of Richardson's letters, as we have seen. Fresse-Montval has taken the additional step, however, of adding pure fiction. He allows his students to write about themselves in order to better position themselves within the economy of epistolary exchange. Even more striking is the abstract principle that remains constant throughout these different strategies of representation: the rhetorical manual must correspond to the social and political circumstances of its readers; it must represent the letter writer in order to produce good letters. In other words, in order to fulfill the rather explicit function this genre has been assigned, it must do something else beyond the limits of its genre: it must become literature, create a (fictional) excess. In doing so, the *ars* becomes something other than itself.

Several interrelated views of the political dimensions of epistolary discourse, founded in part upon the efforts of Richardson and Gellert, are contradicted by Fresse-Montval's opus. By reading epistolary fictions in which "each [epistolary] discourse . . . combines writing and revolt, defiance and desire," Linda Kauffman has put forward the thesis that letters are the discourse of desire, in which "writing is the revolution."[53] In a similar vein, Elizabeth MacArthur finds a "non-closural" dynamics in epistolary fiction: "In an epistolary novel a series of present moments of letter-writing predominates and the future is yet to be decided," thwarting society's desire for closure, which is itself an "attempt to preserve the moral and social order which would be threatened by endlessly erring narratives."[54] The *Nouveau Manuel* provides the negative example for all

lost]"). Roland Barthes, *S/Z* (Paris: Seuil, 1970), 16; translated by Richard Miller, under the title *S/Z* (New York: Hill & Wang, 1974), 10.

53. Linda S. Kauffman, *Discourses of Desire: Gender, Genre, and Epistolary Fictions* (Ithaca: Cornell University Press, 1986), 20.

54. Elizabeth J. MacArthur, "Devious Narratives: Refusal of Closure in Two Eighteenth-Century Epistolary Novels," *Eighteenth-Century Studies* 21 (Fall 1987): 2–3.

these ideas. Writing, whose power and danger lie in its being a form of freedom, as Jean-Paul Sartre's famous argument runs,[55] is here made to function instead as the auxiliary of repression. Letter writing, already foreclosed and staged, is the repression of desire in the dictation of a self, a self as *corrigé,* the writing subject reduced to the narrow gap between the command "il écrira que . . ." and the "je" with a first-person form, a self inscribed within an economy of epistolary exchange which describes and is inscribed by nineteenth-century French bourgeois ideology.

55. Jean-Paul Sartre, *Qu'est-ce que la littérature?* (Paris: Gallimard, 1948); translated by Bernard Frechtman, under the title *What is Literature?* (Gloucester, Mass.: Peter Smith, 1978).

4

The Birth of the Prose Poem from the Spirit of Japanery

The whole of Japan is a pure invention. There is no such country, there are no such people.

— Oscar Wilde, "The Decay of Lying"

BEFORE HE LEFT PARIS FOR ARLES, Vincent Van Gogh painted a picture that might be considered unusual within the corpus of his painting (see Fig. 4-1). Rather than working from life, Van Gogh copied this painting (and the other two in the "Japonaiserie" series) from Japanese prints that he admired. The main figure is reproduced from *The Actor* by Kesaï Yeisin, a print that had appeared on the cover of the journal *Paris Illustré* for May 1886. Considering the painting's origins, it is not certain whether the subject is a woman or a male actor impersonating a woman. The bamboo that frames the actor derives from another illustration in the same magazine. The cranes have been taken from another print, this time by Hokusai, and the frogs from yet another. Van Gogh did everything he could to reduce his own role in the production of this painting to that of the *bricoleur*, the dandyist collector of Oriental images. Unlike the Orientalist works of Eugène Délacroix (*Women of Algiers*, 1834) and of Jean-Léon Gérôme (*The Slave Market*, 1867), which give an impression of transparent immediacy, Van Gogh emphasizes the gaze of the viewer by letting his woman/man return the viewer's stare. The beholder's touristic presence is interrupted, made uncomfortable, and finally negated by the distancing devices of the gaze and by the framing of the painting within another painting. Again, the device of the painting within a painting is

Fig. 4-1. Vincent Van Gogh, *Japonaiserie Oiran*, 1887. Collection Vincent van Gogh Foundation/van Gogh Museum, Amsterdam.

unusual for Van Gogh. The Japanese "woman" is shown clearly to be a mere image through the incongruous placement within a forest of bamboo. She is "encadrée dans [son] analogie" ("framed in the analogy of [herself]") of exoticism, as Baudelaire put it in another (similar, as I will argue) context.[1] It is as though Van Gogh felt compelled to inform his viewer that this Oriental woman was not the "real thing"—*pace* Heidegger, who argues Van Gogh's *Peasant Shoes* are the "truth" in art.[2] The frames for the other two "Japonaiserie" paintings consist of rows of fictitious Japanese characters invented by Van Gogh, a little parody of the "writing lesson," and another message to the viewer that there is no message, that what operates in this particular brand of Orientalism is a *vide de parole* focused on itself.

Japan, and to a certain extent the Orient in general, has often functioned less as an object of mimesis than as a group of connotations and associations intended to create difference, to empty out language, to allow a formalism without content, to embark on a project known today as modernism. Japan as an absence or as the negation of everything Western had appeared in literature as early as Voltaire's *Candide*, in which a Dutch sailor is featured who has "marché sur le crucifix dans quatre voyages au Japon" ("trampled on the crucifix four times in four trips to Japan").[3] Through the middle of the nineteenth century, Japan's chief peculiarity among the countries of the Orient lay in its isolationism, which made it unavailable to the West. Rather than lying open to colonization and dismemberment, like China or the Levant, Japan removed itself from the map, becoming a cipher to be more richly filled in by the imagination. Thus, more than any other Oriental country, Japan was not "an actual place to be mystified with effects of realness, [rather] it existed as a project of the imagination, a fantasy space or screen onto which strong desires—

---

1. Charles Baudelaire, "L'Invitation au voyage," in *Petits Poèmes en prose (Le Spleen de Paris)* (Paris: Garnier, 1973), 90; translated by Michael Hamburger, under the title "Invitation to the Voyage," in *Twenty Prose Poems. Charles Baudelaire* (London: Jonathan Cape, 1968), 34, "L'Invitation au voyage" is number 18 of the prose poems. Further citations in text.

2. Martin Heidegger, "Der Ursprung des Kunstwerks," in *Holzwege*, 4th ed. (Frankfurt am Main: Klostermann, 1963), 22–26; translated by Albert Hofstadter, under the title "The Origin of the Work of Art," in *Poetry, Language, Thought* (New York: Harper & Row, 1971), 33–37.

3. Voltaire, "Candide," chap. 5, in *Romans et contes*, ed. Henri Bénac (Paris: Garnier, 1960), 147. This fiction of making Christians trample on the cross, which puts the Japanese beyond the pale, is an exaggeration of the ceremony that the Japanese apparently made any of their own who worked for the Dutch perform. Voltaire's source was a French translation of the English version of Engelbert Kaempfer's *History of Japan*, translated by J. G. Scheuchzer, 2 vols. (London: Woodward, 1727–28).

erotic, sadistic, or both—could be projected with impunity."[4] After Japan reestablished relations with the West in 1854, the English, Americans, Russians, and Dutch divided most of the trade; France, however, kept the lead in the use of Japan as a literary motif, for example, in the novels of Judith Gautier.[5]

Linda Nochlin has identified in Western depictions of the Orient "a presence that is always an absence: the Western colonial or touristic presence."[6] In paintings of the Middle East by Délacroix, Gérôme, and others, that Western presence was a reality and hence, according to Nochlin, was repressed by the artist for ideological reasons. Painting disguised the mastery of its gaze. In the case of Japan, however, absence was a reality that became the subject for painting and poetry. Thus, Van Gogh's painting of the frame reminds us that we are viewing a painting, whereas the paintings of Gérôme seek to make the viewer into an invisible tourist. In one reading, we might say that Van Gogh's subject was not Japan itself, but images of Japan that had already been placed under the gaze of the West. It is this process I call japanery.

From its earliest moments, that peculiar genre known as the *poème en prose*, exemplary for the construction of a poetics of Modernity, was drawn by some elective affinity to scenes of the Orient.[7] I examine the Orient not as a real place, but as a metaphorical engine that played a small part in the production of a "new" genre, the prose poem, in the writing of Charles Baudelaire (1821–67), Julián del Casal (1863–93), and Roland Barthes (1915–82). Many years before Van Gogh, Louis Bertrand, often considered the inventor of the prose poem in the collection *Gaspard de la Nuit* (1841), had been quite content to make his first effort in this new genre a concatenation of Orientalist clichés. Perhaps he was even aware of the solecism when he moved "Le Soir, aux portes de Schiraz" farther East by renaming it "Scène Indoustane." (He even considered "Scène turque.") Different cultures, same repertoire of effects: "Les paons roucoulent sur les toits du caravansérail; la famille de la cigogne crie dans les combles de la mosquée; les tourterelles jouent au bord des murs élevés du jardin de

---

4. Linda Nochlin, "The Imaginary Orient," *Art in America* 71 (May 1983): 123. Nochlin is speaking of the Orient in general.

5. See G. B. Sansom, "The End of Seclusion," in *The Western World and Japan* (New York: Alfred A. Knopf, 1962), 223–74. Belying his title, which implies a balanced discussion, Sansom's book treats only Western influences on Japan.

6. Nochlin, "The Imaginary Orient," 122.

7. Fritz Nies, *Poesie in prosaischer Welt*, Studia Romanica 7 (Heidelberg: Carl Winter, 1964), 47.

l'Émir" ("The peacocks coo on the roofs of the caravansary; the stork's family cries in the heights of the mosque; the turtle-doves play at the edge of the lofty walls of the Emir's garden").[8] Despite the plethora of other place-names, this prose poem too is really japanery.

I

Nearly a century after Van Gogh's painting, Roland Barthes recapitulated the metaphor of japanery by claiming that he could make the Orient speak only by converting its complex and incomprehensible formalities into an arbitrary system. In an earlier chapter we examined Lévi-Strauss's *Tristes tropiques* as the writing of a travel book that escapes from its own categories. The restless paradoxes of Lévi-Strauss's opening sentences and of his various writing lessons are also present in the beginning of *L'Empire des signes*, Barthes's own "travel book" about Japan:

> Je puis aussi, sans prétendre en rien représenter ou analyser la moindre réalité . . . prélever quelque part dans le monde *(là-bas)* un certain nombre de traits . . . et de ces traits former délibérément un système. C'est ce système que j'appellerai: le Japon.

> (I can also—though in no way claiming to represent or to analyze reality itself . . . isolate somewhere in the world *[faraway]* a certain number of features . . . and out of these features deliberately form a system. It is this system which I shall call: Japan.)[9]

Richard Howard has translated *là-bas* as "faraway," but there is evidence from Barthes's other writings that he is more interested in the word's basic meaning of "there" as opposed to "here." The term belongs to a linguistic category termed "shifters," that is, words such as pronouns whose referent changes with the situation of the speaker. We have seen Aphra Behn make remarkable use of such shifters in order to confuse ethnic and national categories and avoid responsibility. Barthes calls that aspect of language

8. To my knowledge, the authoritative modern printing of this text occurs in Cargill Sprietsma's critical biography, *Louis Bertrand dit Aloysius Bertrand* (Paris: Champion, 1926), 59.

9. Roland Barthes, *L'Empire des signes* (Geneva: Albert Skira; Paris: Flammarion, 1970), 7; translated by Richard Howard, under the title *The Empire of Signs* (New York: Hill & Wang, 1982), 3. Further citations in text.

which finds definite categories for its subjects and their discourses the "legal." Thus, the following quotation encapsulates Barthes's revulsion toward legalistic use-values of language:

> Imagine-t-on la libertè et si l'on peut dire la fluiditè amoureuse d'une collectivité qui ne parlerait que par prénoms et par shifters, chacun ne disant jamais que je, demain, là-bas, sans référer à quoi que ce soit de légal, et où le *flou de la différence* (seule manière d'en respecter la subtilité, la répercussion infinie) serait la valeur la plus précieuse de la langue?

> (Can we even imagine the freedom and, so to speak, the erotic fluidity of a collectivity which would speak only in pronouns and shifters, each person never saying anything but *I, tomorrow, over there*, without referring to anything legal whatsoever, and in which the *vagueness of difference* (the only fashion of respecting its subtlety, its infinite repercussion) would be language's most precious value?)[10]

Though it sounds like a statement abjuring all responsibility for one's utterances, Barthes's statement on Japan "lays bare" the devices of Orientalist strategy, as traced by Edward Saïd back to the eighteenth century and to scholars such as Silvestre de Sacy and Ernest Renan. For Saïd, as for Barthes, the Orient is a function of authorship:

> The Orient . . . was modernized, restored to the present; the traditional disciplines too were brought into contemporary culture. Yet both bore the traces of power—power to have resurrected, indeed created, the Orient, power that dwelt in the new scientifically advanced techniques of philology and of anthropological generalization. In short, having transported the Orient into modernity, the Orientalist could celebrate his method, and his position, as that of secular creator, a man who made new worlds as God had once made the old.[11]

At the front of *L'Empire des signes* Barthes places the power of his own "strong desire," different from and yet perhaps foundational to the eros

---

10. Roland Barthes, *Roland Barthes par Roland Barthes* (Paris: Seuil, 1975), 169; translated by Richard Howard, under the title *Roland Barthes by Roland Barthes* (New York: Hill & Wang, 1977), 166.

11. Edward Saïd, *Orientalism* (New York: Pantheon, 1978), 121.

identified by Nochlin: the desire in language, the will to text. The energy of this will seeks to transform reality at its weakest point, the point that is farthest away and hence most malleable. Barthes's *là-bas* echoes an earlier one, Baudelaire's declaration in the prose poem "L'Invitation au voyage" that the Ideal and the Beautiful are always *là-bas*: "Oui, c'est dans cette atmosphère qu'il ferait bon vivre,—là-bas, où les heures plus lentes contiennent plus de pensées, où les horloges sonnent le bonheur avec une plus profonde et plus significative solennité" (88; "Yes, in this atmosphere it would be good to live, over there, where the slower hours contain more thoughts, where the clocks toll of happiness with a deeper and more meaningful solemnity" [33]).

Thus, in creating his japanery, critic and theorist Barthes merely repeats the attempts of many nineteenth- and twentieth-century poets also disillu-sioned with their here-and-now. And, given this similarity, I argue that the short texts (none of them longer than five pages) that comprise *The Empire of Signs* belong to the genre of the prose poem created by those earlier poets. But Barthes's awareness of the ideology of genre causes him to choose a different name for what he is writing: he calls them *haiku.*

The phrase "empire of signs" refers not only to Barthes's ironic attempts at constructing a semiotics of Japanese culture and to the place of Orientalism as a sign-system serving the interests of a Western empire, but also to the author's inability to leave his native language and writing lessons behind, the inescapability of which are bound to transform Japan into a Western product in any literary or theoretical rendering. As one critic puts it, the title of Barthes's book "refers not merely to the 'empire of signs' as a site or geographic location. It emphasizes the sense of the term 'empire' as dominance or mastery. For as much as this trip abroad takes the form of a search for difference, its account is very much the account of the impossibility of shaking the dominance of cultural values and habits that appropriate difference into sameness."[12]

Each text of the *Empire*, whether it be on tempura, *Bunraku*, street addresses, or *haiku*, reiterates the book's chief lesson—that there is an absence of content, of a signified, in Japanese culture. This absence allows Barthes to uproot all these signifiers and construct his own system with them. The missing signified is the forbidden, immobile "imperial" palace

---

12. Steven Ungar, *Roland Barthes: The Professor of Desire* (Lincoln: University of Nebraska Press, 1983), 50.

in the center of Tokyo, which all are forced to detour around and to ignore. The signifiers without signifieds themselves are like the empty packages the Japanese constantly carry:

> Ce que les Japonais transportent, avec une énergie formicante, ce sont en somme des signes vides. Tout citoyen a dans la rue un baluchon quelconque, un signe vide, énergiquement protégé, prestement transporté, comme si le fini, l'encadrement, le cerne hallucinatoire qui fonde l'objet japonais, le destinait à une translation généralisée. (13)

> (What the Japanese carry, with a formicant energy, are actually empty signs. Every citizen in the street has some sort of bundle, an empty sign, energetically protected, vigorously transported, as if the finish, the framing, the hallucinatory outline which establishes the Japanese object destined it to a generalized transport. [46–47])

On an objective level, the reader must recognize once again that Barthes founds his view of Japan more on fantasy and the hallucinatory *vertige du déplacement* (disorientation of displacement) experienced by a confused, linguistically inept tourist than on what most of us would recognize as the "facts" of a culture. Barthes needs this Japan as an escape from the (for him) Western utilitarianism of language. One can see this desire to escape use-value even more clearly in Barthes's writing on China. For Barthes, China is the world's largest and most powerful "resistance to sense":

> Nous croyons que notre tâche intellectuelle est toujours de découvrir un sens. La Chine semble résister à livrer ce sens, non parce qu'elle le cache mais, plus subversivement, parce que (en cela bien peu confucéenne) elle défait la constitution des concepts, des thèmes, des noms; elle ne partage pas les cibles du savoir comme nous; le champ sémantique est désorganisée; la question posée indiscrètement au sens est retournée en question du sens, notre savoir en fantasmagorie: les objets idéologiques que notre société construit sont silencieusement déclarés **im-pertinents.** C'est la fin de l'herméneutique.

> (We believe that our intellectual project is always to discover a meaning. China seems to resist giving this meaning, not because it hides it but, more subversively, because [hardly Confucian in this]

China deconstructs the composition of concepts, themes, names; China does not divide its objects of knowledge the same way we do; the semantic field is disorganized; the question indiscreetly posed to meaning is turned into a question of meaning in general, our knowledge is turned into a fantasmagoria: the ideological objects constructed by our society are silently declared **im-pertinent.** It is the end of hermeneutics.)[13]

Barthes next equates these "Oriental" processes of constant deferral of meaning and lack of a center with his favorite notion of *écriture:* writing as self-referential object. As its title and cover indicate, virtually everything Japanese appears in *L'Empire des signes* as a form of writing: food, the geography of Tokyo, Sumo wrestling, student riots, each appears as another form of *écriture* in its Barthesian definition, that is, as a particular emptiness, a special vacuum, a *satori:*

> Le Japon l'a mis en situation d'écriture. . . . l'écriture est en somme, à sa manière, un *satori*: le satori (l'événement Zen) est un séisme plus ou moins fort . . . qui fait vaciller la connaissance, le sujet: il opère un *vide de parole.* Et c'est aussi un vide de parole qui constitue l'écriture. (17)

> (Japan has afforded him a situation of writing. . . . Writing is after all, in its way, a *satori; satori* [the Zen occurrence] is a more or less powerful . . . seism which causes knowledge, or the subject, to vacillate: it creates *an emptiness of language.* And it is also an emptiness of language that constitutes writing. [4])

The literary genre that for Barthes best represents this emptying out of meaning is the *haiku,* that shortest of rigorous poetic forms. Though many Japanese when they read *haiku* search either for an allegorical or a biographical resonance to be expressed through the text, Barthes argues that the meaning of the *haiku* lies in its recording of an unforeseen event that cannot be incorporated into the regulated patterns of quotidian life. *Haiku's* use-value has nothing to do with meaning—Barthes claims the poems have no meaning outside their ability to disrupt the mechanisms of communication and perception. (In order to arrive at this use-value, Barthes pretends that *haiku* is a more homogeneous genre than it really is.

13. Roland Barthes, *Alors la Chine* (Paris: Christian Bourgeois, 1975), 8.

In reality, various origins and different use-values of a single verse form make the *haiku* an unstable genre.) Thus, devoid of a signified, *haiku* only become meaningful in relation to each other; their meaning becomes their generic status:

> On pourrait dire que le corps collectif des haïku est un réseau de joyaux, dans lequel chaque joyau reflète tous les autres et ainsi de suite, à l'infini, sans qu'il y ait jamais à saisir un centre, un noyau premier d'irradiation (pour nous l'image la plus juste de ce rebondissement . . . serait celle du dictionnaire, dans lequel le mot ne peut se définir que par d'autres mots). . . . Ainsi le haïku nous fait souvenir de ce qui ne nous est jamais arrivé; en lui nous reconnaissons une répétition sans origine, un événement sans cause, une mémoire sans personne, une parole sans amarres. (104)

> (One might say that the collective body of all haikus is a network of jewels in which each jewel reflects all the others and so on, to infinity, without there ever being a center to grasp, a primary core of irradiation [for us, the clearest image of this ricochet effect without motor and without check, of this play of reflections without origin, would be that of the dictionary, in which a word can only be defined by other words]. . . . Hence the haiku reminds us of what has never happened to us; in it we *recognize* a repetition without origin, an event without cause, a memory without person, a language without moorings. [78–79])

Barthes's descriptions of the *haiku* continually draw attention to the dislocation between *haiku* and the Western genres that serve him as points of comparison. In the above quotation, the dictionary seems a rather shocking choice for comparison with *haiku*, due to its nonliterary and (from the point of view of the signified) aleatory nature. The comparison recalls one of the most commonly used examples for the claims of semiotics and deconstruction that there is no outside the text, that is, that language is completely self-referential: the referents for words provided by a dictionary are simply other words with their own entries, signifieds that are themselves signifiers. According to the dictionary, there is no chance or need to move outside the realm of the signifier. To Barthes, this situation is analogous to the genre of *haiku*, whose use-value is to provide not definitions, but *vides de parole*.

In his epigraph, Barthes claims that the *Empire of Signs* is itself a collection of *haiku*. A Westerner's ability to write something resembling *haiku* derives from the similarity between the phenomenological flatness of description in *haiku* and the modernist experience of the Baudelairean *flâneur*:

> Là-bas, dans la rue, dans un bar, dans un magasin, dans un train, il advient toujours quelque chose. Ce quelque chose—qui est étymologiquement une aventure—est d'ordre infinitésimal: c'est une incongruité de vêtement, un anachronisme de culture, une liberté de comportement, un illogisme d'itinéraire, etc. Recenser ces événements serait une entreprise sisyphéenne, car ils ne brillent qu'au moment où on les lit, dans l'écriture vive de la rue, et l'Occidental ne pourrait spontanément les dire qu'en chargeant du sens même de sa distance: il faudrait précisément en faire des haïku, langage qui nous est refusé. (105)

> (There, in the street, in a bar, in a shop, in a train, something always *happens*. This something—which is etymologically an adventure—is of an infinitesimal order: it is an incongruity of clothing, an anachronism of culture, a freedom of behavior, an illogicality of itinerary, etc. To count up these events would be a Sisyphean enterprise, for they glisten only at the moment when one *reads* them, in the lively writing of the street, and the Westerner will be able to utter them spontaneously only by charging them with the very meaning of his distance: he would in fact have to make haiku out of them, a language which is denied us. [79])

The writer of haiku is a *flâneur*, a poet whose difference from ordinary souls resides in his ability to take a bath in the multitude, as Baudelaire proclaimed in his prose poem "Les foules" ("Crowds"): "Il n'est pas donné a chacun de prendre un bain de multitude: jouir de la foule est un art" (57–58; "It is not given to everyone to take a bath in the multitude: to enjoy the crowd is an art" [28]).

In order to show this denial of language, Barthes tries and fails to write *haiku*. In his own texts, his own *haiku*, his own prose poems, Barthes plays out the misery and splendor of a refused language, of a genre stuck halfway between incongruent ideologies. That is, Barthes's *haiku* are so different from even the translated Japanese product that his effort only unmasks his inability as a Westerner to exit the insistence of meaning. Take the surreal sensuality (vaguely reminiscent of the opening sequence of Luis Buñuel

and Salvador Dali's film *Un Chien andalou*) in Barthes's fanciful description
of the Japanese eyelid, for example:

> On dirait que le calligraphe anatomiste pose à plein son pinceau
> sur le coin interne de l'oeil et le tournant un peu, d'un seul trait,
> comme il se doit dans la peinture *alla prima*, ouvre le visage d'une
> fente elliptique, qu'il ferme vers la tempe, d'un virage rapide de sa
> main; le tracé est parfait parce que simple, immédiat, instantané
> et cependant mûr comme ces cercles qu'il faut toute une vie pour
> apprendre à faire d'un seul geste souverain. (134)

> (As if the anatomist-calligrapher set his full brush on the inner
> corner of the eye and, turning it slightly, with a single line, as it
> must be in painting *alla prima*, opens the face with an elliptical slit
> which he closes toward the temple with a rapid turn of his hand;
> the stroke is perfect because simple, immediate, instantaneous,
> and yet ripe as those circles which it takes a lifetime to learn to
> make in a single sovereign gesture. [99])

Barthes turns his description of the eyelid into a *salon*, that peculiarly
French genre of lyrical writing about works of art cultivated by Denis
Diderot, Théophile Gautier, and Baudelaire, and which John Simon
suggests may have served Louis Bertrand as the starting point for his
landmark collection of prose poems.[14]

A *salon* cannot be a *haiku*. Barthes's is almost an anti-*haiku* in the length
and heaviness of its description and the exoticism of its subject matter—
the *haiku* always makes familiar objects fresh. These little poems, which
will inevitably remind his Western readers of *haiku*, are in fact heavily
laden with a meaning beyond description, which, according to Barthes,
the *haiku* studiously avoids. This persistence of meaning can best be seen
in the book's photographs, which are not allowed to stand by themselves,
since they must be "explained" by short texts, even though Barthes takes
as particularly Japanese the disjunction between different sign systems
(the text should not explain the picture, nor the picture the text).

Since genres can only be defined by what they are not, Barthes's failed
attempts to write *haiku* describe the Japanese genre in the clearest possible
manner. They locate the essence of the form in its extreme, in its rejection

---

14. John Simon, "The Prose Poem as a Genre in Nineteenth-Century European Literature"
(Ph.D. diss., Harvard University, 1959; reprint, New York: Garland Press, 1987), 96–98.

of a meaning that the West is unable to shed. This unusual explanation of a genre through a failed writing of it—somewhat analogous to Eco and Höllerer's examinations of semiology through fiction—avoids the trap of universalism found in the French comparatist René Étiemble's attempt at constructing a comparative genre criticism. In the following example of how such a methodology might work, Étiemble's project becomes a tautology: "A systematic study of the novels produced by civilizations far removed from our own . . . would help us demonstrate on the one hand the *invariants* of the genre 'novel,' i.e., those elements without which there is no novel, and on the other hand those characteristics of the genre which arise more or less arbitrarily from the historical circumstances."[15] It is impossible to separate the historically contingent from the accidental if one already decides a priori that *roman, novela, romance,* novel, and *monogatari* all refer to the same essence.[16] Barthes's dislocation, his inability to formulate an adequate, convincing Western equivalent for the Japanese genres, is his way of expressing the ideology of genre, its use-value, which cannot be translated from one culture to another—nor from one historical epoch to another, even if the same name is preserved. Thus, the use-value of the arbitrary genre that Barthes warns us he is constructing serves as an antidote to those genre studies which presuppose a universality of genre, and emphasize the similarities between Western novels and Japanese *monogatari.* Not that the latter method cannot also yield insights, but Barthes's approach has been upheld by Japanese scholars using the title *Empire of Signs* for their own volume of semiotic analyses of their culture.[17]

Given that they are not *haiku,* to what genre do the short texts that make up this book belong? What familiar generic categories can we turn to for help? Philip Thody has lighted on the *textes philosophiques* of the eighteenth century, feeling that in *Empire of Signs* Barthes, like Montesquieu in the *Lettres persanes* and Voltaire in the *Essai sur les moeurs,* is using the "supposedly more rational standards prevailing outside Europe as a stick with which to beat the obviously imperfect society in which the writer himself actually lived."[18] Thody's idea of grouping these texts

15. René Étiemble, "Histoire des genres et littérature comparée," 206. [Works of general theoretical interest in the field of genre studies are cited in full in the Bibliography—AUTHOR.]

16. Precisely in the area of the novel we have an excellent counterstudy that indicates the ideological modification undergone by the genre in its Arabic and Japanese forms. See Mary N. Layoun, *Travels of a Genre: The Modern Novel and Ideology.*

17. Ikegami, Yoshihiko, ed., *The Empire of Signs: Semiotic Essays on Japanese Culture* (Amsterdam and Philadelphia: John Benjamins, 1991).

18. Philip Thody, *Roland Barthes, A Conservative Estimate* (London: MacMillan, 1977), 121.

through their use-value is correct, even if the actual use-values of the *Lettres persanes* and *L'Empire des signes* differ a great deal. For as Thody himself points out, the eighteenth-century *text philosophique* implies an instrumentality of language—the idea of "political and moral education"—which Barthes scorned throughout his career. Thus, whereas Voltaire and Montesquieu create fictions—historical and novelistic—in order to achieve their purposes, Barthes's approach is discursive and able only to break fictions, principally the fiction that he is writing about something real called Japan.

We can see Barthes wrestling with this problem of the use-value of discourse in *Alors la Chine*. Barthes here struggles to define the genre of what he has written about China, settling finally on that of the "no comment" commentary:

> Sur la Chine, immense objet et, pour beaucoup, objet brûlant, j'ai essayé de produire—c'était là ma vérité—un discours qui ne fut ni assertif, ni négateur, ni neutre: un commentaire dont le ton serait: **no comment:** un assentiment (mode de langage qui relève d'une éthique et peut-être d'une esthétique), et non forcément une adhésion ou un refus (modes qui, eux, relèvent d'une raison ou d'une foi).

> (I have tried to produce a discourse about China—an immense object and for many a burning issue—which was neither assertive, nor negative, nor neutral: a commentary whose tone would be: **no comment:** an approval [a mode of speech which proceeds from an ethic and perhaps from an aesthetic] and not necessarily an acceptance or a refusal [modes of speech which proceed from a reason or from a belief].)[19]

If Barthes saw Japanese culture as a process of emptying out the sign, here he applies this procedure to his own discourse. Barthes continues with the remark that his approach is a response to those occidentals who are only able to see a political discourse in China: "N'est-ce pas finalement une piètre idée du politique, que de penser qu'il ne peut advenir au langage que sous la forme d'un discours directement politique?" ("After all, isn't it a mediocre idea of politics to think that it cannot enter into language except in the form of a directly political discourse?")[20]

19. Barthes, *Alors la Chine*, 13–14.
20. Ibid., 14.

We tend to associate the discursiveness favored by Barthes with the essay. And in what is probably the single most detailed generic approach to Barthes's texts, Réda Bensmaïa has chosen the *essai* as the essential generic "handle" for getting at Barthes's writings. More important than Bensmaïa's choice of the essay, however, is the necessity he feels of defining the essay itself as a model of generic instability, as a verbal collage. Bensmaïa's description of the essayistic process as a montage of heterotopic elements reproduces Barthes's own account of japanery as an emptying of the sign:

> The "objects" used by the essayist are not drawn from a particular genre or domain: they can be taken from any semantic or cultural register: history, literature, painting, philosophy, sports, film, cooking—whatever you like. . . . But, generally, they are constituted as specific objects by the gap they manifest in relation to a semantic or rhetorical norm. . . . In this sense the essay falls essentially into the same category as works of collage—montage of heterotopic elements.[21]

His description also fits perfectly the texts of that most famous of collections of prose poems, Baudelaire's *Spleen de Paris*. From the fantasmagoria of its crowds to the rhythm of its prose, it would seem that Barthes's book is a collection of *poèmes en prose*, a *Spleen de Japon*. In an interview with Raymond Bellour for the weekly *Les Lettres Françaises*, Barthes indicated that the purpose of *L'Empire des signes*, and also of the book *S/Z* published in the same year (1970), was to promote the destruction of language through *sémioclastie:* "It is Western speech as such, in its very basis and elementary forms that we have to destroy."[22] (This remark was hardly calculated to please Marxists, and it shows along with his voluble "no comment" on his visit to Communist China that he regarded Marxists and the bourgeoisie as two versions of the same enemy, since both insist on the instrumentality of language.) To destroy language is a peculiar "use-value" indeed. How does it correspond to that of the prose poem as practiced by Baudelaire?

21. Réda Bensmaïa, *Barthes à l'essai* (Tübingen: Gunter Narr, 1986), 38–39; translated by Réda Bensmaïa, under the title *The Barthes Effect* (Minneapolis: University of Minnesota Press, 1987), 18–19.

22. Roland Barthes, "Sur *S/Z* et *L'Empire des signes*," interview by Raymond Bellour, *Des Lettres Françaises*, 20 May 1970.

II

If the essay is a collage, the prose poem is a dehiscence between two opposing use-values of language. The prose poem is born out of the paradox of generic classification. If genres are only recognizable in their opposition to other genres, the prose poem questions this operation by belonging to neither prose nor poetry. It comes into existence by categorizing itself out of existence. The genre is often defined as a lack. *The Princeton Encyclopedia of Poetry and Poetics* (second edition, 1974), for example, in its article "Prose Poem," defines the genre as a "composition able to have any or all the features of the lyric, except that it is put on the page—but not conceived of—as prose." This makes the prose poem sound like a slip-up at the printer's. Ulrich Fülleborn also writes of the prose poem's lack: "Es fehlen [dem Prosagedicht] als stabilisierende Faktoren die rein ästhetischen Formen des Verses und der Strophe, und ihm eignet wegen des Bezuges zur vorwärts gerichteten prosaischen Rede ein grösserer sprachlicher Expansionsdrang" ("The prose poem lacks the stabilizing factors of the purely aesthetic forms of the line and the stanza, and because of its relationship to prose discourse, which is always moving forward, it accommodates greater linguistic expansion").[23] Here again the prose poem is merely poetry without aesthetics.

Then there are the dialectical approaches. Dedicating the *Spleen de Paris* to Arsène Houssaye in 1864 (the collection was not actually published until after the poet's death), Baudelaire speaks of the form this new genre would possess: "le miracle d'une prose poétique, musicale sans rythme et sans rime, assez souple et assez heurtée pour s'adopter aux mouvements lyriques de l'âme, aux ondulations de la rêverie, aux soubresauts de la conscience" (7; "the miracle of a poetic prose, musical without rhythm and without rhyme, supple and abrupt enough to adapt itself to the lyric movements of the soul, to the undulations of reverie, to the sudden leaps of consciousness"). In the prose poem, poetic form is no longer capable of being mapped onto the printed page, nor even of striking the inner ear. Rather, the prose poem occurs within the mind of the reader. The reader's consciousness, not an arbitrary number of feet, render the form. Form and content cease to be a dichotomy. Since the consciousness of the reader is shaped at the time of reading by the content of the poem, the text that can achieve this symbiotic relationship with the movements of the soul is the

---

23. Ulrich Fülleborn, *Deutsche Prosagedichte des zwanzigsten Jahrhunderts* (Munich: Wihelm Fink Verlag, 1976), 24.

self-referential one, the one that openly investigates its own form as Van
Gogh's painting does. Thus Baudelaire could just as well be addressing his
poem when he writes: "Ne serais-tu pas encadrée dans ton analogie, et ne
pourrais-tu pas te mirer, pour parler comme les mystiques, dans ta propre
correspondance?" (90; "Shall you not be framed in the analogy of yourself,
and can you not be mirrored, in your own *correspondence*, as the mystics
say?" [34]). Though Michael Hamburger translates *se mirer* as "to be
mirrored," the emphasis in the French is on gazing at oneself. The prose
poem is poetry regarding itself in the act of creation and affirming the
empire of signs, the *mise en abîme* of poetry. It carries out this function on
one level, as J. A. Hiddleston points out, by constantly referring to other
kinds of poetry: "Very many of the [Baudelairean prose] poems make fun
of more established poetic and literary attitudes and can be read as a kind
of intertextual debunking."[24] Certainly, the *Spleen de Paris* contains a large
number of texts that explicitly concern themselves with poetic creation:
"Le «confiteor» de l'artiste," "A une heure du matin," "Les foules," to
name just the more obvious ones. But the prose poem does not just reflect
on poetry as a genre, but on itself as well.

For example, each individual prose poem's self-referentiality, its newness and restlessness within the corpus, requires its independence from all
the others. Baudelaire expressed the *haiku*-like relation between prose
poems thus: "Je ne suspends pas la volonté rétive de celui-ci au fil
interminable d'une intrigue superflue" (7; "I do not make the restive will
of this depend on the interminable thread of a superfluous plot").[25] In
other words, the prose poems of *Spleen de Paris* should be related to each
other like the words of a dictionary. Each piece would ideally become its
own history and its own genre; hence, the idea of the prose poem has
become one of an antigenre. And thus begins the long history of the genre
to escape all genres, at least in theory. In practice, as Suzanne Bernard
amply demonstrates, the prose poem has wavered between recuperation
into the literary and downright impossibility:

> The prose poem wants to go beyond language, and it makes use
> of language; it wants to smash form, and it creates forms; it wants
> to escape from literature, and here it has become a catalogued
> literary genre. It is this internal contradiction, this essential antin-
> omy which gives it the character of an Icarian art, bent on an

24. J. A. Hiddleston, *Baudelaire and "Le Spleen de Paris"* (Oxford: Clarendon, 1987), 75.
25. Baudelaire, *Petits Poèmes*, 5–6.

impossible transcendence of itself, bent on the negation of its own conditions of existence—and, doubtless for just this reason, entirely representative of the efforts of all French poetry since the 19th century.[26]

The prose poem is an artificial paradise, an ideological vacuum located *là-bas*, between disillusionment and belief. Perhaps it was this "Icarian" quality of the prose poem that caused Baudelaire to look on his own efforts in the genre as not having measured up to his desires. Like Bernard, Barbara Johnson also uses the idea of an Icarian "fall" to define the prose poem. However, she denies that the genre is a fall from the realm of poetry: "The fall recounted in the *Petits Poèmes en prose* is not that of a subject who falls from poetic paradise into the prosaic world, but rather that of the paradise itself, which differentiates itself from itself."[27] The differentiation takes the form of a dialogue between genre and text. The poem becomes poetry squared, the poetry of poetry. It becomes that instability which the systematicity of genre itself has created: "Neither antithesis nor synthesis, the prose poem is the place from where the polarity—and therefore the symmetry—between presence and absence, between prose and poetry, *disfunctions*. The description of the prose poem is only possible when one departs from the principle that any attempt to describe it ends up subverting itself."[28]

Baudelaire's attempt to get outside genre paralleled the desire of French literati to escape the constraints of a social order seemingly bent on self-destruction, on self-immolation in the lust for money, a social order of which Balzac became the foremost journalist: "Discerning young artists in France of the 1840s, perhaps like their counterparts in Vienna before 1914, saw that the world of their youth was doomed. France was beginning a social revolution; industrialization and the railroads would inevitably destroy the old agrarian, rural, hierarchical society. They were moved to find new modes of expression, and their art reflected both their interests in the emerging new world and their hopes and anxieties."[29]

Baudelaire opposed to this mutable world of material progress and spiritual impoverishment that of art and *correspondences*. The incomprehen-

26. Suzanne Bernard, *Le Poème en prose de Baudelaire jusqu'à nos jours* (Paris: Librairie Nizet, 1959), 13.

27. Barbara Johnson, *Défigurations du langage poétique: La Seconde Révolution Baudelairienne*, 86.

28. Ibid., 37.

29. David H. Pinkney, *Decisive Years in France, 1840–1847* (Princeton: Princeton University Press, 1986), 105.

sion of the unfeeling bourgeois for this world of correspondences parallels their stupefaction in the face of Oriental art objects:

> Que dirait un Winckelmann moderne . . . en face d'un produit chinois, produit étrange, bizarre, contourné dans sa forme, intense par sa couleur, et quelquefois délicat jusqu'à l'évanouissement? Cependant c'est un échantillon de la beauté universelle: mais il faut pour qu'il soit compris, que le critique, le spectateur opère en lui-même une transformation qui tient du mystère, et que, par un phénomène de la volonté agissant sur l'imagination, il apprenne de lui-même à participer au milieu qui a donné naissance à cette floraison insolite. Peu d'hommes ont, — au complet, — cette grâce divine du cosmopolitanisme.

> (What would a modern Winckelmann say . . . were he confronted by a product of China — something strange, bizarre, contorted in form, intense in color, and sometimes so fragile as to be almost evanescent? Yet it is an example of universal beauty; but in order to understand it, the critic, the spectator must effect within himself a mysterious transformation, by means of a phenomenon of the will acting on the imagination, he must learn by himself to participate in the milieu which has given birth to this strange flowering. Few men possess to the fullest degree this divine grace of cosmopolitanism.)[30]

As he says more simply later in the review, *"Le beau est toujours bizarre"* (956; "The beautiful is always strange" [81]). Perhaps Baudelaire felt that he belonged to this cosmopolitan group due to the long sea voyage he had embarked on in 1841, going as far as Mauritius. Yet it is indicative of the role of the imagination in his aesthetic attitude toward life that Baudelaire always enlarged the trajectory of this voyage — to Sumatra and beyond — when writing about it later. The importance of the imagination indicates that the prose poem may be one vehicle for taking this journey. However, the privileged group of cosmopolitans who can grasp this aesthetic does not include the academics, who remain entombed within their rules and doctrines (including the law of genre):

30. Charles Baudelaire, "Exposition Universelle — 1855," in *Oeuvres complètes* (Paris: Pléiade, 1961), 954; translated by Francis E. Hyslop, Jr., under the title "Exposition Universelle, 1855," in *Baudelaire as a Literary Critic* (University Park: Pennsylvania State University Press, 1964), 79. Further citations from both works in text.

Que dirait, qu'écrirait,—je le répète, en face de phénomènes
insolites, un de ces *modernes professeurs-jurés* d'esthétique? . . . [I]l
blasphémerait la vie et la nature, et son fanatisme grec, italien ou
parisien, lui persuaderait de défendre à ce peuple insolent de jouir,
de rêver ou de penser par d'autres procédés que les siens
propres;—science barbouillée d'encre, goût bâtard, plus barbares
que les barbares, qui a oublié la couleur du ciel, la forme du
végétal, le mouvement et l'odeur de l'animalité, et dont les doigts
crispés, paralysés par la plume, ne peuvent plus courir avec agilité
sur l'immense clavier des *correspondances!* (955)

(What would be said, I repeat, what would be written by one of
those *narrow-minded modern professors* of aesthetics? . . . [H]e would
blaspheme life and nature, and his fanaticism, whether Greek,
Italian, or Parisian, would induce him to prohibit that impudent
people from enjoying, dreaming, or thinking in any way other than
his own; with his ink-smeared knowledge, his bastard taste, more
barbarous than the barbarians, he has forgotten the color of the
sky, the forms of plants, the movement and the smell of animal
life, and his stiffened fingers, paralyzed by the pen, can no longer
run with agility over the immense keyboard of *correspondences!*
[80])

Unlike Edward Saïd, who gives primary responsibility for the judgments
of a dismissive Orientalism to academics as a power elite, Baudelaire
makes all *citoyens* academics inasmuch as they judge: "Tout peuple est
académique en jugeant les autres, tout peuple est barbare quand il est
jugé" (954; "All peoples are academic when they judge others, all peoples
are barbaric when they themselves are judged" [79]).
    The antidote to academic views of art and of the Orient is the invitation
of the voyage extended to the ordinary man. After the first shock,
comparable perhaps to the physiological disorientation caused by a dose
of hashish or absinthe, this ordinary man would be able to construct his
own empire of signs: "Si, au lieu d'un pédagogue, je prends un homme du
monde, un intelligent, et si je le transporte dans une contrée lointaine, je
suis sûr que, si les étonnements du débarquement sont grands, . . . la
sympathie sera tôt ou tard si vive, si pénétrante, qu'elle créera en lui un
monde nouveau d'idées" (955; "If, instead of a pedagogue, I were to take
a man of the world, an intelligent man, and transport him to a distant land,
I am sure that, despite the shock of disembarkation, . . . his sympathy

would sooner or later be so keen, so acute, that it would create in him a new world of ideas" [79]). It is as though Baudelaire were describing the process by which Roland Barthes came to write *The Empire of Signs.*

The remainder of the paragraph is devoted to a catalog (to be repeated in the prose poem "L'Invitation au voyage") of objects that would appear in an entirely new light. Unlike Barthes, for whom the use-value of absolute difference is to disable language, Baudelaire imputes revolutionary effects to these impressions:

> Ces formes de bâtiments, qui contrariaient d'abord son œil académique . . . ces fleurs mystérieuses dont la couleur profonde entre dans l'œil despotiquement, pendant que leur forme taquine le regard . . . tout ce monde d'harmonies nouvelles entrera lentement en lui, le pénétrera patiemment, comme la vapeur d'une étuve aromatisée . . . et même il est possible que, dépassant la mesure et transformant la justice en révolte, il . . . brûle ce qu'il avait adoré, et . . . il adore ce qu'il avait brûlé. (955)

> (Those strangely shaped buildings which at first annoyed his academic eye . . . those mysterious flowers whose deep color enslaves his eye and tantalizes it with its shape . . . this whole world of new harmonies will slowly enter into him, will patiently penetrate him, like the vapors of a perfumed bath . . . and it is even possible that, overstepping the line and transforming justice into revolt, he will . . . burn what he had adored, and adore what he had burned. [79–80])

In his comparative study of the European prose poem, Jonathan Monroe suggests that the hint of revolution in the last line of this quote is sincere and that it has a relation to the prose poem as a genre. Using Bakhtin's concept of dialogism, Monroe argues that Baudelaire turned to the prose poem for its ability to "incorporate discourses other than the predominantly literary and philosophical. This broadening of the dialogical from a virtually exclusive focus on struggles *within* high culture to include a concern with struggles *between* high and low culture is crucial to the social reinscription of the lyric that the prose poem advances as it emerges with Baudelaire."[31] Monroe goes on to analyze the incorporation of the culture

---

31. Jonathan Monroe, *A Poverty of Objects: The Prose Poem and the Politics of Genre* (Ithaca: Cornell University Press, 1987), 102.

of the poor in prose poems such as "Le Joujou du pauvre" ("The Poor Child's Toy"), "Les Yeux des pauvres" ("The Eyes of the Poor"), and "Assommons les pauvres!" ("Let's Beat Down the Poor!"). One can certainly see the struggle between high (the academics) and low (the man of the world) in the passages just quoted; moreover, one can see the translation of this vertical struggle (high versus low) into a horizontal one (here versus *là-bas*, Occident versus Orient). Monroe's notion of the politics of the prose poem is supported by the fact that the ideas of the passages we have just examined are repeated so closely in "L'Invitation au voyage" that one might almost say that the prose poem (published just two years later) is a generic transformation of the review or that Baudelaire had left the bounds of the review genre and plunged into the realm of the prose poem in "Exposition Universelle—1855." Indeed, in some sense, his review has turned into an invitation, and we will now examine how the invitation turns into the voyage.

One important difference between "L'Invitation au voyage" and "Exposition Universelle—1855" is that in the prose poem, the movement is no longer toward the Orient, but rather toward "L'Orient de l'Occident, la Chine de l'Europe":

> Il est un pays superbe, un pays de Cocagne, dit-on, que je rêve de visiter avec une vieille amie. Pays singulier, noyé dans les brumes de notre Nord, et qu'on pourrait appeler l'Orient de l'Occident, la Chine de l'Europe, tant la chaude et capricieuse fantaisie s'y est donné carrière, tant elle l'a patiemment et opiniâtrement illustré de ses savantes et délicates végétations. (86–87)

> (There is a majestic country, a Land of Cockaigne, they say, which I dream of visiting with an old friend; a unique country, drowned in the mists of our North, and which one might call the Orient of the Occident, the China of Europe, so greatly has fervent and capricious phantasy indulged itself there, so patiently and so obstinately has it illustrated the land with its learned and delicate vegetations. [32])

Baudelaire later combines the two oxymorons, "l'Orient de l'Occident, la Chine de l'Europe," into one, "la Chine occidentale": "Il est une contrée qui te ressemble, où tout est beau, riche, tranquille et honnête, où la fantaisie a bâti et décoré une Chine occidentale" (88; "There is a land that resembles you, where all is beautiful, rich, restful and decorous, where phantasy has built and furnished a China of the West" [32]).

Why choose to write about the China of Europe rather than about the real thing? Ideologically speaking, one cannot sail for the Orient itself, since as we have seen it exists only as absolute difference, as japanery. Also, as Barbara Johnson points out, the subject of the Baudelairean prose poem moves not from Spleen (World, Prose, Nature, Occident) to the Ideal (Paradise, Poetry, Art, Orient), but rather toward the structure of their opposition, the Orient in the Occident or the *poème en prose*. Instead, several clues in the text (tulips, florins, the mists of the North) point to Holland as the "real" referent of this poem. If this is accurate, Baudelaire's invitation is also an homage to "Harlem," the first prose poem of Bertrand's collection *Gaspard de la Nuit.* (In the preface to the *Spleen de Paris*, Baudelaire specifically mentions this collection as a model for his own efforts). But even Bertrand's Holland, to which Baudelaire is perhaps referring, is self-consciously defined in the former's prose poem, which like Barthes's remains close to the genre of the *salon* as a series of painted images: "Harlem, cette admirable bambochade qui résume l'école flamande, Harlem peint par Jean Breughel, Pieter Neefs, David Téniers et Paul Rembrandt" ("Harlem, that admirable bacchanal painting which epitomizes the Flemish school, Harlem painted by Jean Breughel, Pieter Neefs, David Téniers, and Paul Rembrandt").[32]

After all, referring to a real Holland would remove the possibility of this being the "vrai pays de Cocagne" (87; "a true country of Cockaigne"[33]) the poem speaks of. The French phrase "pays de Cocagne" is used to describe a hedonist utopia, similar to the English "Never-Never Land" or the American "Big Rock Candy Mountain." The "true" Cockaigne can only be unreal, a construction lying always further *là-bas*. As soon as it became real, this Cockaigne would cease to exist, would no longer be, as it is now, "supérieur aux autres, comme l'art l'est à la Nature, où celle-ci est réformée par le rêve, où elle est corrigée, embellie, refondue" (89; "superior to all others, as Art is to Nature, where Nature is reformed by the dream, where it is corrected, embellished, remodelled" [34]). The Cockaigne, like the Orient and the prose poem, is defined and in fact created by its own absence.

Thus the process of endless deferral, which is a constant theme throughout the text, is already implicit in the figural existence of this Cockaign-

---

32. Louis Bertrand, "Harlem," in *Gaspard de la nuit*, ed. Roger Prévost (Paris: Delmas, 1953), 53.

esque China of Europe. This theme begins in the text's title, which implies that we will stop in the antechamber of true voyage, that everything will be described in anticipation rather than in retrospect. Baudelaire highlights this deferral by recursively invoking his own poem within the poem: "Oui, c'est là qu'il faut aller respirer, rêver et allonger les heures par l'infini des sensations. Un musicien a écrit l'*Invitation à la valse;* quel est celui qui composera l'*Invitation au voyage,* qu'on puisse offrir à la femme aimée, à la soeur d'élection?" (88; "Yes, this is the place where we must breathe, dream and lengthen the hours through an infinity of sensations. A musician has written the *Invitation to the Waltz;* where is he that [*sic*] shall compose the *Invitation to the Voyage,* which one may offer to the woman he loves, to the sister of his choice?" [33]). The question posed here is a *mise en abîme* of the prose poem's possibilities of existence, coming as it does in the middle of a piece entitled "L'Invitation au voyage" which seems to be offered to the beloved. Like the prose poem in general, we see that this invitation must constantly question its own status as a genre. It is simultaneously the question and the answer to the question.

The art of horticulture provides another figural register for the processes of deferral and difference, as the narrator describes the efforts of those who practice this profession:

> Qu'ils cherchent, qu'ils cherchent encore, qu'ils reculent sans cesse les limites de leur bonheur, ces alchimistes de l'horticulture! Qu'ils proposent des prix de soixante et de cent mille florins pour qui résoudra leurs ambitieux problèmes! Moi, j'ai trouvé ma *tulipe noire* et mon *dahlia bleu!*
>
> Fleur incomparable, tulipe retrouvée, allégorique dahlia, c'est là, n'est-ce pas, dans ce beau pays si calme et si rêveur, qu'il faudrait aller vivre et fleurir? (89–90)

> (Let them search, let them search still, let them incessantly defer the entry into their happiness, those alchemists of horticulture! Let them offer a prize of sixty and a hundred thousand florins to the man who shall solve their ambitious problems! As for me, I have found my *black tulip* and my *blue dahlia!*
>
> Incomparable flower, tulip lost and found again, allegorical dahlia, it is there, is it not, in this country so calm and dreamy, that we must live and blossom? [34])

The mention of tulips reinforces the poem's reference both to Holland and to the Orient, since tulips were unknown to Europeans until an ambassador to Suleiman the Magnificent first saw them in 1554. The tulip market subsequently became responsible for the rise and fall of numerous Dutch fortunes. Similarly, the dahlia, indigenous to Mexico, was not introduced into Europe until 1789.[33] The value of both flowers depended on the relative rarity of their various strains or variants. The object of the searches of the horticulturists cannot be specified; it seems to be purely the production of difference, an infinite regression of the limits of happiness. We do not know what is sought, what the reason for happiness is, what the subject of the contest might be. The poet then seems to directly address his own flower, which we understand as the woman addressee of his poem. But in doing so, he undermines the very allegory he has set up by calling attention to it as a figure: "allegorical dahlia" is straight prose, the literal unmasking of a previously allegorical relationship. Here, as everywhere in the poem, the "effect of the figure is to undermine figurality and the whole notion of poetry upon which it rests, and far from being projected into a reverie in which oppositions are reduced through correspondence and analogy as when reading the verse poems, the reader is confronted with a grotesque world of incompatibilities."[34] That is, in performing this unmasking the poet has produced more difference, has expanded the realm of signification by contrasting blue dahlia (a "natural" object) with allegorical dahlia (an "artificial" product of rhetoric). On another level, this is the contrast between a paradoxical allegorizing (there is no blue dahlia in the world) intended to express the uniqueness of the woman, and the demolition of figuration (the epithet "allegorical dahlia" is not in itself allegorical, but rather a straightforward naming). Barbara Johnson calls this latter process *défigurations du langage poétique*. For Johnson, the paradoxes and deflation of rhetorical figures, which abound in "L'Invitation au voyage," are paradigmatic for the prose poem as a genre. (For example, Johnson devotes several pages to analyzing how this prose poem demolishes its similarly titled lyric double in the *Fleurs du mal*.)[35]

The addressee of the poem takes up this contradictory status of reference. She is both the subject and its representation. A basic interpretation of the text must take into account how woman becomes the allegory for country and for poem. Yet these allegories are also called into question at various points within the text by the instability of the poem's addressee. Baudelaire begins in the third person ("une vieille amie" [86]; "an old

33. Alice M. Coates, *Flowers and Their Histories* (New York: Pitman, 1956), 249–56, 66–68.
34. Hiddleston, *Baudelaire*, 69.
35. Johnson, *Défigurations*, 108–14.

friend" [32]), shifts to the second-person formal ("où tout vous ressemble, mon cher ange" [87]; "where all resembles you, my dear angel" [32]), and finally adopts the informal *tu* ("Tu connais cette maladie fiévreuse?" [87]; "Do you know the febrile malady?" [32]). Where, then, is the object of the analogy to be located? In the *tu*, in the *vous*, in the third person? The person addressed is as incapable of definition as the land to which she is being compared. How to explain these shifting pronouns, familiar to us from Behn's *Oroonoko?* Borrowing from the analysis there, I would say that the writer shows by the pronoun slippage his power (or lack of power) to create the addressee through her relation to himself expressed in the pronoun. It is he who will create and define her. Moreover, the pronouns show the writer becoming more and more familiar with the addressee as the invitation takes shape. This increasing familiarity would make most sense if the addressee were the text itself.

If one addressee of the text is the text itself (and writing in general), then such an addressee would provide the final step in lifting the text out of the dichotomy of nature versus art. Through the correspondence between the country described and the addressee the text is able to become a mimesis of itself, thereby fulfilling the expectations that Baudelaire had for the prose poem in general—particularly if one refines the idea to include the movements of the soul the prose poem seeks to represent. In any case, the more obvious mimetic tendencies of the text are consistently undermined in a continual redoubling of figuration which leads *inward* into the infinite, as in the infinite *in*breeding that continually produces new types of plants.

The final paragraph contains another redoubling and another deferral, this time of the voyage itself. By a leap of the imagination we have landed at the destination, and everything is described as being the woman herself. Here, Baudelaire undermines the figural language with which he has previously invoked both country and woman by making a simple statement of equivalence: "Ces trésors, ces meubles, ce luxe, cet ordre, ces parfums, ces fleurs miraculeuses, c'est toi. C'est encore toi, ces grands fleuves et ces canaux tranquilles" (91; "Those treasures, that furniture, that luxury, that order, those perfumes, those miraculous flowers, they are yourself. So also are those wide rivers and those calm canals" [34]). At this moment, when the specular imagery has been stabilized by a simple equation, a new figure for departure springs up. The author's thoughts are the ships in the harbor of the city, which then depart for the Orient. Here we see stated explicitly for the first time that the Orient lies in the Infinite: "Tu les conduis, doucement vers la mer qui est l'Infini, tout en réfléchissant les profondeurs du ciel dans la limpidité de ta belle âme; — et quand, fatigués par la houle et gorgés des produits de l'Orient, ils rentrent au port natal, ce sont encore mes pensées enrichies qui reviennent de l'infini vers toi" (91; "You guide them softly to the ocean that is Infinity, while reflecting the depth of the sky in the limpidity of your pure soul; and when, wearied by the surge and gorged with products of the Orient, they return to their native port, these are still my thoughts, enriched, returning from the Infinite towards you" [35]). Logically speaking, this infinite can never be reached: nevertheless, thoughts return from there enriched, perhaps only with the desire to burn what they had previously caressed or with the knowledge of the arbitrariness of cultural values we have seen Baudelaire propose in the "Exposition Universelle" where he first mentioned the "produits de l'Orient." Once the Orient of the Occident has been reached, it ceases to be the (always eastward-lying) Orient. There is an interminable movement in this prose poem away from the place reached, which is the place of achieved ("poetic") allegory and of the stable linking of signifier with signified. The Orient can never be reached because it is realized only as absence, as absolute difference, but it is precisely this absence which produces a surplus of signification, which allows the *vide de parole* to operate, enriching thought.

This concept of absence as productive of meaning is present throughout the text, as for example in the phrase "Le bonheur est marié au silence" ("Happiness is wedded to silence"), or more precisely a bit later when the narrator declares: "Les meubles sont vastes, curieux, bizarres, armés de serrures et de secrets comme des âmes raffinées" (89; "The furniture is vast, curious, bizarre, equipped with locks and with secrets like a subtle mind" [33]). The subtle mind of the cosmopolitan takes care to hide its own cleverness. Baudelaire may be working here with the stereotype of the "inscrutable Oriental" as a prototype for the poet himself, whose meanings depend on their being preserved from the scrutiny of the observer. As the Orient must never be reached else it lose its own identity, so must meaning never be completely divulged, but rather kept locked up. In this text, the meaning which is to be unavailable is above all that ideological one which the genres of either prose or poetry give to texts. Those genres, too, are deferred in this prose poem and by this prose poem. And, like the Orient, they are deferred because they are nothing but difference (or "différance," as Derrida would say).

III

"L'Invitation au voyage," then, shows how paradoxical and disingenuous Baudelaire's previous invitation in the "Exposition Universelle—1855" had been. There, Baudelaire had challenged the viewer of the Oriental "floraison insolite" to follow the object back into its original surroundings in order to appreciate its beauty: "Le spectateur opère en lui-même une transformation qui tient du mystère, et que, par un phénomène de la volonté agissant sur l'imagination, il apprenne de lui-même à participer au milieu qui a donné naissance à cette floraison insolite" (954; "The critic, the spectator must effect within himself a mysterious transformation, by means of a phenomenon of the will acting on the imagination, he must learn by himself to participate in the milieu which gave birth to this strange flowering" [79]). But such an operation would destroy the object's beauty, which derives precisely from its bizarreness within the European context, with its inability to be forced into any of the known genres. It is thus not the Orient that is beautiful, but Orientalism or japanery. Baudelaire's Latin American disciple Julián del Casal, learning this lesson from his master, went even farther than Baudelaire in treating the Orient as a synecdochical, fetishized object in his life and in his prose poetry.

Julián del Casal was one of the first *modernistas* and also one of the first Orientalists of Latin America. The Spanish term *modernismo*, more restricted than its English cognate (and rather different from its Brazilian cognate), refers to a literary movement whose aesthetic values resemble those of French Symbolism and Parnassianism, so that Jean Franco has termed it the "Symbolist Revolt."[36] Its proclamation both of the eternal status of art and of the independence of the artist from the profane world can be interpreted ideologically both as a rejection of quotidian Spanish and as a fear of the rapid economic and social transformations taking place in the last decades of the nineteenth century. Casal's family had been victimized by these transformations in Cuba in being forced out of its small sugar-holding by the large companies. Casal's reaction was to turn to poetry, to plan a novel whose hero "would travel from place to place, finding each nation intolerable,"[37] and finally to locate the tolerable in an Oriental utopia.

One of the results of the increasing role of Latin America and of Casal's

36. Jean Franco, "A Symbolic Revolt: The Modernist Movement," in *The Modern Culture of Latin America* (Middlesex: Penguin, 1970), 25–51.

37. Ibid., 31.

Havana in the world economy was an increased availability of goods from the Orient. Latin America had lagged behind in the adoption of Orientalism as a fashionable pursuit; the actual artifacts of the other world, carried by ships returning "wearied by the surge and gorged with products of the Orient," took longer to arrive in the shop windows of Havana, Buenos Aires, and other large Latin American cities than in those of Paris. However, by the end of the nineteenth century, "operettas like *El Gran Mogol* were as popular in Cuba as elsewhere in the West . . . spectaculars such as the *Circo Oriental* were immediate sellouts in Havana, and . . . interest in the Orient was extensive enough for bookstores to have ordered several copies of Louis Gonse's *L'Art japonais* . . . and an even larger number of Pierre Loti's *Madame Chrysanthème*."[38] The epoch of the increasing availability of these objects corresponds closely with the first efforts of the *modernistas*. For example, Latin America's appreciation for the works of Baudelaire dates from this period, though Casal's writing itself shows that Boyd G. Carter and James K. Wallace have overstated their case somewhat in claiming that "before the height of *modernismo*, which one generally dates to around 1896, the author of the *Fleurs du mal*, although his name was known in Latin America, had no disciples and exerted no positive influence."[39] For Casal, as for Baudelaire and Van Gogh earlier and for Barthes much later, Orientalism did not take the form of extensive scholarly investigations into the history and culture of the East. Casal's Orientalism, like the movement of *modernismo* in general, was an attempt to find (or create) a world different from that of Havana, a world stripped of human vulgarity: "El joven y desafortunado escritor cree encontrar en el Oriente un sello distintivo que lo diferencia de la vulgaridad humana" ("The young and unfortunate writer believes that in the Orient he finds a distinctive stamp which differentiates it from human vulgarity").[40] Beyond the creation of poems such as "Kakemono," "Sourimono," and "Japonería," Casal made sure that his daily life also partook of the Orient. In order to insulate himself from the real world, to which he reacted with the utmost disgust and nihilism, Casal transformed his rooms into an exotic

38. Robert Jay Glickman, *The Poetry of Julián del Casal*, vol. 2 (Gainesville: University Presses of Florida, 1978), 334.

39. James K. Wallace and Boyd G. Carter, "Baudelaire au Mexique: Les revues du *Modernismo*," *Bulletin Baudelairien* 12 (Winter 1977): 22. The statement is also inexplicable in light of the poet José Juan Tablada's demonstrable enthusiasm dating from 1890. See Hans-George Ruprecht, "Aspects du baudelairisme mexicain," *Comparative Literature Studies* 11 (June 1974): 99–122.

40. Luis A. Jiménez, "Elementos decadentes en la prosa casaliana," in *Julián del Casal: Estudios críticos sobre su obra*, ed. Esperanza Figueroa (Miami: Ediciones Universal, 1974), 108.

grotto: "He used to read and write on a divan with cushions where gold, red, and vermilion would shine forth like they do in oriental screens, archways, and vessels. In one corner sandalwood incense sticks burned before a buddhist statue. He had transformed that little corner into the modest but authentic habitation of a Japanese man."[41]

The colors and objects that Ramon Méndez describes here will reappear in the prose poem "Japonería." The term "authentic" is paradoxical here, because Casal himself admitted that it was not the Orient as such which fascinated him, but rather its transformations in the hands of Baudelaire, Judith Gautier, and other Parisians: "Pero yo adoro . . . el Paris exótico, delicado, sensitivo, brillante y artificial; el Paris que tiene representado el Oriente en Judith Gautier y en Pierre Loti" ("But I adore the exotic Paris, delicate, sensitive, brilliant and artificial. The Paris which has represented the Orient in Judith Gautier and Pierre Loti").[42] Like Baudelaire, Casal preferred not the Orient itself, but the Orient of the Occident, the Japan of Europe. Thus Casal titled his prose poem not "Japón," but "Japonería." It was published in the same newspaper (*La discusión* of Havana) that later printed his translation of Baudelaire's "L'Invitation au voyage" (both works appeared in the year 1890), and it shares with that prose poem the concept of the *vide de parole* and its association with woman and with the Orient.

The poem opens by admitting both the unnaturalness of its referent and the connection between economic fetishism and sexual desire. The speaker situates himself within the text, and we find that he, like Baudelaire, is a casual stroller. The artifact from the Orient then appears to him within a shopwindow, and he attempts to construct a context within which the randomly encountered vessel may produce meaning:

> Dentro del escaparate de una tienda lleno de brazaletes de oro, esmaltados de zafiros y rubíes, que fulguraban en sus estuches de terciopelo azul; de rosarios de coral engarzados en plata, que se enroscaban en sus conchas nacaradas; y de lámparas de alabastro con pantallas de seda rosada; que aguardaban la noche para abrir sus pupilas amarillas; he visto esta mañana, al salir de paseo, un

---

41. Ramón Meza, "Julián del Casal," in *Edición del Centenario, Poesías*, by Julián del Casal (Havana: Consejo Nacional de Cultura, 1963), 225.

42. Julián del Casal, *Edición del Centenario, Prosas I* (Havana: Consejo Nacional de Cultura, 1963), 229.

búcaro japonés, digno de figurar en tu alcoba blanca ¡oh, espiritual
María!

(Within the display window of a shop full of gold bracelets
adorned with sapphires and rubies which fulgurated in their cases
of blue velvet, full of coral rosaries linked in silver, which twist
themselves in their mother-of-pearl-colored shells; and full of
alabaster lamps with shades of rose-colored silk, which wait for
the night to open their yellow pupils; I saw this morning, upon
taking a walk, a Japanese vessel, worthy of figuring in your white
bedroom, oh, spiritual Maria!)[43]

What Casal describes is a vase made of odiferous earth: hence we must
return to Barthes's description of the Japanese package, which he says
functions as an empty sign. Once again the description is of a vacuum, an
absence. "Maria" is Maria Cay, who was in fact the sister of the Japanese
consul in Havana, Raúl Cay, and who thus becomes like the vessel a
synecdoche for the Orient.

The poem reveals, as does Baudelaire's, an amorous intent, here rather
ironic and resentful, as if the poet had been rejected and were exercising
his revenge in this playful form of writing. Sexual desire substitutes for the
idle curiosity of the Orientalist:

> . . . un búcaro japonés, digno de figurar en tu alcoba blanca ¡oh,
> espiritual María! donde no se han oído nunca las pisadas de tus
> admiradores o el eco sonoro de los besos sensuales.
>
> Sobre el esmalte verde Nilo fileteado de oro, que cubría el barro
> del búcaro japonés, se destacaba una Quimera de ojazos garzos,
> iluminados por el deseo de lo prohibido; de cabellera rubia
> destrenzada, por las espaldas; de alas de pedrería, ansiosas de
> remontarse; y de dedos de uñas largas, enrojecidas de carmín,
> deseando alcanzar, con el impulso de la desesperación una flore-
> cilla azul de corazón de oro, abierta en la cumbre de un monte
> nevado sin poderlo conseguir.

> (. . . a Japanese vessel, worthy of figuring in your white bedroom,
> oh, spiritual Maria! where the footsteps of your admirers have

---

43. Julián del Casal, "Japonería," *La discusión*, 2 April 1890. Text taken from *Prosas I. Edición del Centenario*, vol. 2 (Havana: Consejo Nacional de Cultura, 1963), 97.

never been heard, nor the sonorous echo of sensuous kisses. Over the green Nile enamel, adorned with fillets of gold, which covered the earthenware of the Japanese vessel, a Chimera stood out with blue eyes, illuminated by the desire for what is prohibited; with long blond untressed hair spread over his back; with wings of precious stones, anxious to soar, and with fingers having broad fingernails, carmine-red, wishing to reach, with the impulse of desperation, a little blue flower with a heart of gold, open in the peak of a mountain covered with snow, without being able to obtain it.)

Alternatively, we can observe the spiritual dimension of the name of Maria, the interest of the speaker in her fate, and the fact that it is she who is being compared to this vessel of earth. Like the vessel, Maria Cay also appeared to Casal as a product of the Orient removed from its context and deposited in Havana. Her erotic attraction lay in her liminal status between worlds, a status which Rubén Darío expressed more directly in these lines in his sonnet "A la misma":

> Miré al sentarme a la mesa,
> bañado en la luz del día
> el retrato de María,
> la cubana japonesa.

> (As I sat at the table
> I gazed at the portrait,
> bathed in sunlight
> of Maria, the Japanese Cuban.)[44]

The ethereal nature of Maria's beauty is further reinforced by Darío's mention of the portrait (rather than of having met her personally, even though he had done so during a visit to Havana). The final tercets of Darío's sonnet explicitly name her ethereal nature as that of the art object, specifically of the Japanese vessel:

> Diera un tesoro el Mikado
> por sentirse acariciado
> por princesa tan gentil,

44. Rubén Darío, "Para la misma," in *Prosas Profanas*, 6th ed. (Madrid: Espasa-Calpe, 1967), 41.

digna de que un gran pintor
la pinte junto a una flor
en un vaso de marfil.

(The Mikado would give a fortune
to feel himself caressed
by such a gentle princess,

worthy of having a great painter
paint her together with a flower
on a vase of ivory.)

Darío's association of the admired woman with a delicate vase is also the governing analogy of Casal's text. This central analogy of woman as vessel (Casal's version of Baudelaire's blue dahlia), is then echoed in the many other objects listed, which are meant to enclose and are mostly circular in shape: bracelets, cases, shells, lamp-shades, and pupils. (The latter are especially important because what they enclose is a void, but a void which provides the power of vision.)

In his last sentence Casal adds one further hollow space, Maria's "alcoba," whose double meaning of alcove (the origin of the word is from the Arabic for vault, and it is generally used for a monk's cell) or *boudoir* invokes both the spiritual and sexual sides of Maria:

> Y al mirar el búcaro japonés, he sentido el deseo de ofrecértelo, para que lo coloques en tu alcoba blanca ¡oh, lánguida María! donde no se han oído nunca las pisadas de tus adoradores o el eco sonoro de los besos sensuales; porque tu destino, como el de esa Quimera, te ha condenado a perseguir un ideal, tan alto y tan bello, que no lo podrás alcanzar jamás.

> (And upon looking at this Japanese vessel, I felt the desire of offering it to you, so that you might place it in your white bedroom, oh, languid Maria! where the footsteps of your adorers have never been heard, nor the sonorous echo of sensuous kisses: because your destiny, like that of that Chimera, has condemned you to follow an ideal so high and beautiful that you will never be able to reach it.)

The most erotic aspect of Maria is that as a vessel she is unfilled ("unfulfilled"), and this fact is represented in a series of absences: "En tu alcoba blanca donde no se han oído nunca las pisadas de tus admiradores o el eco sonoro de los besos sensuales" ("In your white bedroom where the footsteps of your admirers have never been heard, nor the sonorous echo of sensuous kisses"). As in Baudelaire, there is a continuous displacement of the referent here. Sexuality is first metonymized to admirers and kisses, then this metonymy is again metonymized into the sounds with which these acts are associated. Finally the whole is negated: these sounds have never been heard. Virginity is represented as an absence, a vacuum which is meaningful and turns into an ideal when combined with the concept of the Virgin Mary.

On the empty sign, the vessel, is inscribed a scene that will serve to allegorize the paradox of Maria's sexuality: a chimera grasps at a flower it cannot reach. In an interesting reversal of expectations, it is not the male poet who is the monster striving to pluck the flower of maidenhood, but rather the woman who is striving for what she can never reach since she is always already there. There is another, paradoxical reason for the identification of the chimera with Maria: it is blue-eyed and blond-haired, that is, distinctly non-Oriental. In fact, the very use of a chimera removes us from the already idealized setting of Japanese art to the realm of mythology. Once again it is a question of the continuous production of difference: the vessel is different because it is Oriental, but what is depicted is not the Orient, but the Orient's mythologization of some Occidental features. Thus, the line describing the vessel as "digno de figurar en tu alcoba blanca" ("worthy of figuring in your white bedroom"), where "figurar" means not only "to be there," "to play a role," but also "to figure forth," tells us of the capacity of the vessel to produce meaning when, an empty sign, it is placed within another empty sign such as the bedroom. (The earthen vessel suggests graphite, whereas the whiteness of the bedroom suggests the blank page.) The line is self-referential: it has itself already produced a figure of ambiguity based on the double meaning of *figurar*. As pointed out above, the speaker spends a great many words trying to empty the room of significance, in this case explicitly of sexual knowledge: his every effort works to ensure his failure (the rhetorical figure of paralipsis).

In comparing Maria to the chimera, the poet has made her a part of his imaginative system (taking chimera in its alternate meanings of "notion," "fancy," "Utopia"); she becomes for him, as Baudelaire's addressee became, the equivalent of the Orient, never attainable because attainment would halt signification. The distance between the chimera and the flower then becomes a series of unbridgeable differences: between poet and woman; between woman and virginity, and between Occident and Orient, where the final difference indicates the Orient's importance as an absence. The latter is never described, but still functions as the "origin" of difference itself. Thus the title "Japonería" can refer to the vessel, to the woman it is compared to, or to the prose poem itself, which does *not describe* Japan and is not *Japanese*, but is merely "japanery," the "Oriental" process of constant deferral and *écriture*. Both Baudelaire and Casal present us with a scene of sensual luxus and with an ostensible referent, the woman being addressed by the speaker. Yet on closer examination, we realize that any attempts at defining these referents produce only more difference, that the Orient which is a supposed allegory for the woman is defined as absence, as a vacuum or unfilled vessel that is then free to produce figures, figures that refer not to a referent but to the process of figuration itself and which become a continual redefinition of that process. Thus, in its very unfolding, the prose poem is in the process of transforming its own rules, eluding definition endlessly as does the absent, empty, unattainable Orient.

The poem is signed "Hernani." In alluding to the title figure of Victor Hugo's 1830 verse drama, Casal defines himself as the indefinable antihero of a play whose main purpose and achievement was to protest all the laws (the unities, the alexandrine) of the genre of Parisian drama. Inevitably, then, whether by a Roland Barthes writing a literature of exhaustion in the twentieth century, by a Charles Baudelaire founding modernism by turning poetic form against itself in the nineteenth century, or by a Julián del Casal observing Japan through the optic of Parisian literature and helping found Latin American modernism on this doubly distanced image in his prose poem "Japonería," japanery embraces the artificiality of writing, and eschews by means of the prose poem both the reality-driven empiricism of prose and the academicism of poetry.

5

What Is Legal Discourse
Made Of?

LAW is a Rule of Action, prescribed by a superior Power.
— William Blackstone, *An Analysis of the Laws of England*

IT IS HARD TO THINK OF TWO GENRES more opposed in their
use-values than the prose poem and the law (or what I will be calling legal
discourse). The prose poem, as I have argued, was designed to escape the
writing lesson, to neutralize the pragmatics of prose for which legal
discourse is the most visible example. After all, William Blackstone, that
most influential of legal theorists, defines law as a form of discourse whose
particular use-value is that of regulating human actions.[1] We move then to
the question of how we are to recognize such illocutionary language when
we hear it. Which kinds of language will be admitted as legal discourse?
This question can be looked at in many ways, or subdivided into many
smaller questions, for example, into the root metaphors that every legal
theory must make use of or the debate over the admissibility of children's
testimony (essentially a disguised debate on the peculiar semiotic status of
children's *discourse*). One could write a history of legal discourse in, say,

1. William Blackstone, *An Analysis of the Laws of England*, 5th ed. (Oxford: Clarendon Press,
1762), 1. The definition of law by Blackstone's successor, Sir Robert Chambers, differs only
slightly: "Any kind of rule or canon whereby actions are directed." *A Course of Lectures on the
English Law, 1767–73*, ed. Thomas H. Curley, vol. 1 (Madison: University of Wisconsin Press,
1986), 84. In both cases, law is defined very narrowly as the set of rules, with no reference to
their interpretation or to who is to carry them out.

Anglo-American jurisprudence as the history of successive kinds of heterogeneity, of admissions of and defenses against varieties of discourse; one
chapter of such a history would discuss the shifting boundaries between
the genres of aesthetic and legal discourses. Yet what truly makes the
creation of a legal genre ideological is that it intentionally forgets its own
history, and that this forgetting gives it the power to act.

Aesthetic discourse, however, suffers from a similar amnesia. For example, editor George Sherburn cut the entirety of the title figure's last will
and testament out of his modern abridgment of Samuel Richardson's
Clarissa (1748), one of the greatest novels of the eighteenth century.
Sherburn explained his twentieth-century decision thus: "Gentlefolk of the
eighteenth century found wills especially fascinating. Thus Richardson
naturally printed Clarissa's entire will, which ran to fourteen pages of print
and which is here omitted."[2] Substituting the phrase "aesthetically pleas-
ing" for "especially fascinating," reveals Sherburn's real perspective, that
of the post-Kantian reader shocked at finding language in this novel which
is other than pure form, which refuses to be categorized as a literary style.
One can demonstrate this assertion by noticing the other elements of
Richardson's art that Sherburn also refuses to accept: he excises from his
abridgment the various death scenes that Richardson took almost un-
changed from Protestant didactic literature, which also represented rules
of action for many people of the period. Sherburn also reduces the letters
of this epistolary novel to the bare bones of plot, thereby eliminating all
traces of the letter-writing manual or conduct book, which, as we saw in
Chapter 3, "taint" the novel's aesthetic purity. Sherburn's characterization
of the eighteenth-century reader gives us the photographic negative of the
twentieth-century reader, who finds wills, and legal language in general,
alien to literary aesthetics. Sherburn's statement implies a general impatience with Richardson's extensive use of legal language throughout the
novel, an impatience that in turn functions as synecdoche for our general
incomprehension in the face of eighteenth-century society, which had not
yet learned, in its prose at least, to seal off the boundary and squelch the
intercourse between legal and fictional styles.

For while he was writing *Clarissa,* Richardson could have and probably
did read the last work of Alexander Pope, his will and testament, which
was published in full between the parliamentary debates and the poetry
selections of the *Gentleman's Magazine* in 1744. Legal language was generally available to those who could read (about half the adult population)

2. George Sherburn, ed., *Clarissa or the History of a Young Lady,* by Samuel Richardson
(Boston: Houghton Mifflin, 1962), 494.

and devoured by a public that was indeed fascinated by both the power of legal art and the art of legal power. In what follows, I wish to restore the wills and the rest of its legal language to Richardson's *Clarissa* to show that the relation between legal and fictional discourses constitutes a dialectic: the legal dialect, which invades and appropriates the language of this novel, is itself presented as heterogeneous, as composed of the different semiotic systems of theater and art.

If Richardson decomposes legal discourse by including it within the genre of the novel, Roland Barthes in his *Mythologies* does the opposite by repeatedly finding literature at the heart of law: "Justice et littérature sont entrées en alliance, ont échangé leurs vieilles techniques, dévoilant ainsi leur identité profonde, et compromettant impudemment l'une par l'autre" ("Justice and literature have made an alliance, they have exchanged their old techniques, thus revealing their basic identity, and compromising each other barefacedly").[3] A comparison of these two writers reveals a similar concern with the generic purity of legal discourse, as well as a difference in their approaches caused by the very different kinds of law they critique.

I

Legal language functioned as a socially privileged form of discourse in England in the middle of the eighteenth century. The religious wars of the previous century, in which, as T. F. T. Plucknett points out, lawyers had thrown their weight behind Parliament and the supremacy of law rather than behind the king and royal prerogative, had ensured that the law would become the ultimate and most significant instrument for governance.[4] According to E. P. Thompson, the law was "elevated during [the eighteenth] century to a role more prominent than at any other period of [English] history . . . serving as the 'impartial,' arbitrary authority in place of a weak and unenlightened monarchy, a corrupt and ineffective bureau-

3. Roland Barthes, *Mythologies* (Paris: Seuil, 1957), 55; translated by Annette Lavers, under the title *Mythologies* (New York: Hill & Wang, 1972), 44.
4. Plucknett claims that the civil war of the seventeenth century "made clear issue between tradition, common law and the medieval view [that the king was under God and the law] on one hand and, on the other, the newer idea of statecraft, absolutism and a supreme royal equity," with the former set of values triumphing. See T. F. T. Plucknett, *Concise History of the Common Law*, 5th ed. (London: Butterworth, 1956), 283; cited in Peter Stein, "Common Law," *Dictionary of the History of Ideas*, vol. 2 (New York: Scribner, 1973), 695.

cracy and a democracy which offered to the real intrusions of power little
more than rhetoric about its ancestry."⁵ The power of the law was by no
means limited to or even located primarily in the legislative branch. In his
social history of the period A. S. Turberville sees fit to mention the
eighteenth century's "sense of the majesty of the law; the fact of the
extraordinary ascendancy exercised, not only over the judicature, but over
the politics and general life of the time, by . . . great lawyers [and] the
immense influence and authority of Sir William Blackstone's *Commentar-
ies*."⁶

The elevation of legalism over regalism and over religion gave rise to
conceptions of the English law as a structure or organism that had reached
its entelechy. Let us examine a metaphor for the law used by Blackstone
in his *Analysis*, one of the period's most influential works of legal theory.
Significantly, Blackstone uses architecture for his metaphor, an art form
in which the aesthetic and the practical are of equal importance: "The
common law of England has fared like other venerable edifices of antiquity,
which rash and unexperienced workmen have ventured to new dress and
refine, with all the rage of modern improvement. Hence frequently it's [*sic*]
symmetry has been destroyed, it's proportions distorted, and it's majestic
simplicity exchanged for specious embellishments and fantastic novelties."⁷
The metaphor of architecture is used here without its concomitant notion
of construction. Any interference by workmen is condemned. We are to
presume that this edifice has come into being entirely on its own; its actual
constructedness is obscured and made ineffable by locating it in the remote
past. Although Blackstone's comment seems negative, its defense of common versus statutory law and its conservatism depend on a positive view
of the law as an independent organism with its own entelechy, rather than
as the product either of a legal science or of the conflicts between opposing
social and political interests. This independence is by necessity also
linguistic. Legal discourse constructs its own edifice and converses only
with itself. There is in this building of the law no room for its interpreters.

Blackstone's successor at Oxford, Sir Robert Chambers, made use of an
equally complex and even more organic metaphor in the introduction to
his Vinerian lectures: "The laws of a civilized and flourishing people, like
mature and vigorous fruit-trees, though they afford shade, ornament,

5. E. P. Thompson, "Eighteenth-Century English Society: Class Struggle Without Class?"
Social History 3 (1978), 144.
6. A. S. Turberville, *English Men and Manners in the Eighteenth Century*, 2d ed. (Oxford:
Clarendon Press, 1929), 8.
7. Blackstone, *An Analysis*, xxvii.

shelter and sustenance, to their proprietors, are yet rooted in obscurity, and derive their juices, life, and beauty from sources which it is toilsome to search after, and not always possible to discover."[8] In making his analogy between flourishing people, mature and vigorous flora, and healthy laws, Chambers evokes an edenic, pastoral world, a land with a past (only dimly perceived) but no future. Any departure from the present moment would turn the vegetative cycle into decay and death. This is a vision of the common law, of the discourse of a collective memory, rather than of articulated priorities of values in conflict. These two quotations describe and condone what Roberta Kevelson, wielding similes rather than metaphors, has referred to as the legal system of a "closed society": "In a closed society, the dominant, prevailing legal code has become *as though* canonized. It is represented by the guardians of the legal order as embodying fixed and eternal values, somewhat like the holy texts which religious leaders of communities safeguard. In an open society it is assumed that codes of law are man-made, and that new laws must be enacted to fit changes in the times."[9] Kevelson's language ("canonized," "holy text") reduces the legal order to its texts and its language; the legal genre is identifiable not by its intrinsic features, but by its difference from other genres. Again, however, those features are not found "within" the law itself, but in the way it is handled, preserved, and above all guarded from contamination by other forms of discourse. Both Blackstone and Chambers, whom I take to be representative of eighteenth-century English legal theory, specifically construct models that deny the possibility of other genres conversing with the law.

An opposing view of the law would deconstruct it into the various genres that would have to compete and interact with each other in order to ajudicate human desire. This latter view comes closer to the pragmatics (as opposed to the theory) of the English legal system in the eighteenth century, at least according to social historians John Brewer and John Styles:

> On the one hand the courts were powerful regulatory mechanisms, dealing not only with crime but numerous aspects of social and economic life. It is no exaggeration to argue that the long arm of the law was the strongest limb of the body politic. But, on the

---

8. Chambers, *A Course of Lectures*, 83–84.

9. Roberta Kevelson, "Prolegomena to a Comparative Legal Semiotic," in *Frontiers in Semiotics*, ed. John Deely, Brooke Williams, and Felicia E. Kruse (Bloomington: Indiana University Press, 1986), 194.

other hand, law enforcement varied in its intensity and efficiency.
. . . The absence of a class of legal administrators, the tensions
between centre and locality and the remarkable variations in law
enforcement make it extremely difficult to generalize about either
state power or the exercise of authority. Because they both
manifested themselves primarily through the law, they were mediated by a complex, varied, almost idiosyncratic process.[10]

Clarissa examines this side of the law, in which Eden and architecture give
way to the unregulated and unmemorable entanglements of conflicting
desires.

    Clarissa undermines the organic concepts of a closed legal system with
alternative views of the law as but one genre competing against others in a
world ruled by heteroglossia. In other words, in *Clarissa* legal discourse
becomes "dialogized," to use Mikhail Bakhtin's critical term. Although the
term "dialogic" has by now been shown to apply to virtually every literary
genre — including the prose poem — Bakhtin originally argued for the novel
as the most convincing modern example of dialogism: "The novel orches-
trates all its themes, the totality of the world of objects and ideas depicted
and expressed in it, by means of the social diversity of speech types
[*raznorechie*] and by the differing individual voices that flourish under such
conditions. Authorial speech, the speech of narrators, inserted genres, the
speech of characters are merely those fundamental compositional unities
with whose help heteroglossia [*raznorechie*] can enter the novel."[11] On the
level of genre, this means that the novel can only be defined recursively, as
a "collection" of genres. Whereas poetry can be characterized as an
attempt at creating a genre independent of any other, the novel as a genre
can only be characterized by its recursivity, by its definition as a diversity
of speech types or dialects, including the language of such nonliterary
genres as the law. In terms of my theory of genre as use-value, the purpose
of the novel would be to provide a discursive space for different genres to
critique one another. Thus, legal language enters *Clarissa* not as a rule of
action, but only as *raznorechie*, as one dialect arguing with other dialects.
    Yet the novel is not the only genre to be defined recursively. In his essay
"The Problem of Speech Genres," Bakhtin establishes a fundamental
difference between "primary" and "secondary" speech genres:

    10. John Brewer and John Styles, *An Ungovernable People: The English and Their Law in the
Seventeenth and Eighteenth Centuries* (New Brunswick: Rutgers University Press), 12–13.
    11. Mikhail Bakhtin, "Discourse in the Novel" [Works of general theoretical interest in the
field of genre studies are cited in full in the Bibliography — AUTHOR.], 262–63.

Secondary (complex) speech genres—novels, dramas, all kinds of scientific research, major genres of commentary, and so forth—arise in more complex and comparatively highly developed and organized cultural communication (primarily written) that is artistic, scientific, sociopolitical, and so on. During the process of their formation, they absorb and digest various primary (simple) genres that have taken form in unmediated speech communion. These primary genres are altered and assume a special character when they enter into complex ones. They lose their immediate relation to actual reality and to the real utterances of others.[12]

Bakhtin's designation of secondary genres as "ideological" a few lines later probably refers to this process of absorption and digestion, which is not without social implications and cannot be carried out neutrally. In the genre of legal discourse, for example, theological language and "statements of fact" are allowed to coexist but can never have equal weight—the former was more important in the medieval period, the latter is predominant today.

Whereas the ideological solidity of the English common law is derived from its projection as the communal memory of a people, the ideological solidity of French law is derived from its projection as the rationality of legal reasoning. Roland Barthes has devoted several of his *Mythologies* to showing how heteroglossia undermines this abstract rationality. In "Le Procès Dupriez" ("The Dupriez Trial"), Barthes concerns himself with the trial as a kind of text, a specimen of dialogue, which he analyzes into its striations of unequally weighted genres. To view a trial in this way is immediately to remove oneself from any Blackstonian notion of the law as a "rule of action" or an architectural structure. The case is one of familial murder: Dupriez is supposed to have murdered his parents because they opposed his wedding. That is its shock value. What makes it a "hard case" in Barthes's opinion is that the defendant maintains strict silence about the crime; the defendant Dupriez's language ultimately disturbs because it cannot interface with the discourse of the court. The whole trial, according to Barthes, revolves around the issue of the apparent lack of a motive, without which, it would appear, the crime would itself become a nullity. And, as Barthes notes, the concept of a *mobile* (motive) is merely the reconstruction of an interior discourse for the defendant according to

12. Mikhail Bakhtin, "The Problem of Speech Genres," 62.

Aristotelian rules of logic and *mythos*. In this way, crime itself becomes merely a function of discourse:

> Il se trouve donc que le crime est toujours *construit* par la Justice selon les normes de la psychologie classique: le fait n'existe que comme élément d'une rationalité linéaire, le crime a besoin, pour être, d'une cause ou d'une fin; il doit être *utile*, faute de quoi il perd son essence, on ne peut le reconnaître. Pour pouvoir nommer le geste de Gérard Dupriez, il fallait lui trouver une origine.

> It happens that crime is always *constructed* by Justice according to the norms of classical psychology: the phenomenon exists only as an element of a linear notionality, must be *useful*, or else it loses its essence, cannot be recognized. To be able to name Gérard Dupriez's action, we had to find an origin for it.[13]

The analysis of Dupriez begins to resemble the Barthes of *L'Empire des signes*, and *Alors la Chine,* for whom the most radical political act imaginable is to create a language without use-value. Dupriez's silence about his motives cannot be used by the court. Without the criminal's discourse, neither crime nor criminal can be made to fit any of the necessary legal categories. Again and again in the three brief pages Barthes dedicates to this judicial anomaly, we read of different processes of categorization usually carried out by naming, renaming, and unnaming: "Il ne restait plus à la défense . . . [que] d'en faire un *crime sans nom*" (117; "There was nothing left for the defense . . . except . . . to make it, precisely, a *crime without a name*" [67]); "Il suffit donc que le geste soit abstraitement utile, pour que le crime reçoive un nom" (117; "Hence it suffices that the action be abstractly useful for the crime to receive a name" [68]); "Il suffit que la démence ait une origine *raisonnable* pour que l'on puisse la nommer crime" (117; "It suffices that madness have a *reasonable* origin for us to be able to call it a crime" [68]);[14] "Pour [les psychiatres] l'absence de causalité

<hr>

13. Roland Barthes, "Le Procès Dupriez," in *Mythologies,* 116; translated by Richard Howard, under the title "The Dupriez Trial," in *The Eiffel Tower* (New York: Hill & Wang, 1979), 67. Howard's translation pulls Barthes's text into the genre of philosophy rather than that of legal discourse. *Construit* is rendered as "constructed" rather than "construed," *fait* as "phenomenon" rather than "deed," *rationalité* as "notionality" rather than "rationality," and so on. The rendering of *il fallait* as "we had to" further weakens the impression of the French text that Barthes is critiquing an action by the court. Further citations in text.

14. The translation of *raisonnable* by "reasonable" is tricky. Clearly, Barthes is here using *raisonnable* in its etymological sense, "that which can or must be reasoned about," which here means "that which the discourse of reason (e.g., of logic) can recuperate." The word "reasonable"

n'empeche nullement de nommer l'assassinat crime" (117; "for [the psy-chiatrists] the absence of causality in no way prevents us from calling the murder a crime" [68]); "La psychiatrie, elle, du moins la psychiatrie officielle, semble vouloir reculer aussi loin que possible la définition de la folie . . . elle joue le rôle de l'Église livrant aux laïcs (la Justice) les accusés qu'elle ne peut récupérer faute de pouvoir les inclure dans aucune de ses «catégories»" (118; "Psychiatry, at least our official psychiatry, seems to want to postpone the definition of madness as long as possible . . . it plays the role of the Church handing over to the secular arm (Justice) the accused it cannot [save or] include in any of its 'categories' " [69]).[15] But is it not the case that "to name an action" is to classify it generically?

It would seem, according to Barthes, that before the law can become a rule of action it must name and categorize using methods and nomenclature derived from other genres (philosophy, psychiatry, theology), of which it has been recursively constructed. The even more unstable genre in this analysis is that of psychiatry. As can be seen from the examples above, Barthes depicts it as floundering about for a discourse with which it can name Dupriez's crime. One can demonstrate this instability by simply listing the different kinds of discourse (often coupled with the verbs of naming listed above) to be found in Barthes's three-page analysis: "des sciences nouvelles d'exploration psychologiques" ("new sciences of psy-chological exploration"); "code pénal" ("penal code"); "psychologie clas-sique" ("classical psychology"); "catégorie théologique" ("theological cat-egory"). The final genre is that of exorcism, a speech act with a readily recognizable use-value.

A more thorough demonstration of the meanderings of genre in this essay must examine how these different generic names constantly but subtly supplant each other from first sentence to last. As though, like Lewis Carroll, he had come directly to literature from mathematics and symbolic logic, Barthes structures his essay around a series of equations that together can be analyzed as syllogisms. Thus, a phrase like the following, "une Justice née dans les temps bourgeois, dressée par consé-quent à rationaliser le monde par réaction contre l'arbitraire divin ou monarchique" (118; "a Justice born in the bourgeois era, trained conse-quently to rationalize the world by reaction against divine or monarchic

---

in English seems to me to have the sense just mentioned only in diminished force, in favor of others such as "moderate in price" and "not extravagant," which hardly apply to crime. However, the English translation does have the virtue of "making strange" our word "reasonable."

15. Howard omits *récupérer*.

arbitrary action" [69]), together with other statements in the essay, engenders the following substitutions:

1. Legal discourse ≈ bourgeois discourse
2. Bourgeois discourse ≈ discourse of rationality
3. Psychiatric discourse ≠ discourse of rationality (it is by definition the discourse of irrationality), *ergo*
4. Legal discourse will not listen to, cannot converse with, the language of psychiatry.

Thus the first paradox is achieved through logic: psychological examination, embedded in the legal proceedings, negates itself and takes on the discourse of the Church, handing over to the secular arm (Justice) the accused it cannot recuperate via any of its genres of dementia. By this point, then, another form of discourse, that of theology, has entered the legal arena. It will lead to another syllogism, which will complete the vicious circle:

1. Legal discourse ≈ psychological discourse (the responsibility of the subject)
2. Psychological discourse ≈ theological discourse (the shared category of free will or "ego")
3. Theological discourse ≈ discourse of sorcery (Satan as explanation of *lack* of free will), *ergo*
4. Legal discourse ≈ the discourse of sorcery (and hence of the irrationality it hopes to avoid)

Through this series of substitutions, legal discourse becomes as arbitrary and irrational—as fictional—as the divine and monarchical power it came to oppose: "La défense elle-même hésite entre la revendication d'une psychiatrie *avancée* . . . et l'hypothèse d'une «force» magique qui aurait investi Dupriez, comme aux plus beaux temps de la sorcellerie" (118; "The defense itself hesitates between the claim of an advanced psychiatry . . . and the hypothesis of a magical 'force' which apparently seized upon Dupriez, as in witchcraft's finest hour" [69]).[16]

16. The discourse of exorcism conflicts continually with other genres. Such conflicts have also been examined by Stephen Greenblatt in "Shakespeare and the Exorcists," in *After Strange Texts*, ed. Gregory S. Jay and David L. Miller (Tuscaloosa: University of Alabama Press, 1985), 122–45.

Given the generic instability of legal discourse, how does it affect the action of *Clarissa?*

II

A complex, varied, and idiosyncratic series of legal and illegal acts—wills, marriage contracts, abduction and sequestration, imprisonment for debt, a duel—comprise the backbone of *Clarissa*'s plot. Testaments frame the beginning and end of the novel; in the middle is the villain Lovelace's rape of Clarissa. Readers of *Clarissa* have often noted the importance of legal discourse for the novel, but have disagreed over its implications. David Demarest believes that Richardson presents a rigorist conception of law and that legal language, in particular that of Clarissa's will, ultimately triumphs over other forms of discourse in providing the rules of action for its characters.[17] Charles Knight argues, on the contrary, that the law's failure is most noticeable, and that this failure reflects the fact that "the institutions of society cannot deal with the moral needs of individuals."[18] As with nearly every other aspect of *Clarissa*, the extremities of these two positions are anticipated within the novel itself. As Jocelyn Harris writes, they are embodied in the opposing ideologies of Clarissa and Lovelace: "Like Portia in *The Merchant of Venice* Clarissa turns to law, her ultimate guarantee of fixed meanings and protective contract. She implicitly subscribes to Locke's belief that the law preserves and enlarges that 'Liberty [which] is to be free from restraint and violence from others,' just as Lovelace maintains a definition that Locke calls its opposite, a 'Liberty for every Man to do what he lists.' "[19] Clarissa shares Blackstone's conception of law as a set of rules governing or prohibiting action; for Lovelace, however, law is but one variety of rhetoric used to obtain power. Thus the law is presented within the novel not as an unchanging institution or fixed canon, but as an object open to interpretation and as a social dialect in eternal competition and dialogue with other language systems that form and deform it.

17. David P. Demarest, "Legal Language in the Eighteenth-Century Novel" (Ph.D. diss., University of Wisconsin, 1963).

18. Charles A. Knight, "The Function of Wills in Richardson's *Clarissa*," *Texas Studies in Literature and Language* 11 (1969): 1190.

19. Jocelyn Harris, *Samuel Richardson* (Cambridge: Cambridge University Press, 1987), 92–93. The quotation that characterizes Clarissa's view of the law is taken from John Locke's *Of Civil Government* (1690), chap. 6, par. 57.

We may hear echoes of the philosopher John Locke and foreshadowings of Blackstone and Chambers when Clarissa's mother, responding to the fears of her daughter that the family may be injured by the wrath of Mr. Lovelace, assures her that "the law will protect us, child! offended magistracy will assert itself."[20] Like Chambers, Mrs. Harlowe metaphorizes the law as an organism; like Blackstone, she declares that it is better left to its own devices. Mrs. Harlowe's statement consists of two clauses expressing the same idea, which therefore equate the two subjects: "law" is equivalent to "the magistracy." By equating an abstract concept with a term designating a professional and social group, Mrs. Harlowe endows the law as abstract concept with will and purpose.

Yet even before Mrs. Harlowe has spoken, her statement has already been undermined by the events of the novel, which are predicated on its first specimen of legal language, the will of Clarissa's grandfather. Realizing that the bequest of his whole estate to his youngest granddaughter Clarissa conflicts with the legal tradition of primogeniture, the grandfather fills the preamble of the will with extralegal appeals to his other survivors:

> Wherefore it is my express will and commandment, and I enjoin my said three sons, John, James, and Antony, and my grandson James, and my granddaughter Arabella, as they value my blessing, and will regard my memory, and would wish their own last will and desires to be fulfilled by *their* survivors, that they will not impugn or contest the following bequests and devises in favour of my said granddaughter Clarissa, although they should not be strictly conformable to law or to the forms thereof; nor suffer them to be controverted or disputed on any pretence whatsoever. (1:30)

A religious form of illocutionary act (the blessing) is made contingent on the acceptance of the will's terms ("as they value my blessing"). Added to this are an emotional appeal (the regarding of the will-writer's memory) and one of self-interest (the Harlowes should respect the terms of this will so that their own testaments will be respected). Most striking, however, is the paradox invoked by placing within a legal document the writer's desire that the law be disregarded. Legal language is used in order to wrench the

---

20. Samuel Richardson, *Clarissa, Or, the History of a Young Lady*, vol. 1 (Oxford: Clarendon Press, 1930), 122. This is the so-called Shakespeare Head edition in eight volumes, based upon Richardson's third edition of 1751, in which Lovelace's important rape/trial fantasy first appeared. Future references will be given in the text by volume and page number.

document out of the legal sphere and into those of religion and family sentiment, which are apparently to be considered as sacred and above the law. Thus Margaret Doody's view that "the will of Clarissa's grandfather bequeathing her all that property . . . is an example of a legal and social contract, easily definable in Locke's language about the nature of property, but absurdly frail in the world of active wills engaged in the struggle for power," although correct in terms of the novel's thematics, perhaps under-estimates the paradoxical nature of the document itself.[21] The will is generically unstable because it confronts legal discourse with that of religious and familial ideology.

Clarissa's sister Arabella's view of the law opposes those of her mother and sister. For her, the law is not architecture or organism. Its power derives from its subjective interpretation by living beings enmeshed in a particular set of social relations. Arabella taunts Clarissa: "Your Father's *living* Will shall controul your Grandfather's *dead* one" (1:337). The pun between "will" as a legal document and "will" as human desire both establishes and complicates the connection between those spheres. Though a will is always a "Rule of Action," the source of the "superior power" is obscure. Clarissa's grandfather, deceased, can have a hand neither in the interpretation of his own will nor in the maintenance of its interpretation. Clarissa remembers this when she comes to write her own testament. The Harlowes, however, not content with their legal challenges to the bequest, use other means to wrest the property from Clarissa. Their plan is to marry her to the odious Mr. Solmes, whose property lies adjacent to hers. Once she is married, Clarissa's property will devolve to her husband, who has agreed to cooperate with the rest of her family in forming a single great estate to be used as a basis for the political ambitions of her brother. Clarissa's only possible counter to this power play is to run off with the villain of the novel, the rake Robert Lovelace.

"The law was not made for such a man as me," boasts Lovelace to his fellow rake Belford (4:45), meaning of course that a lively man like him can remake the law at will. Lovelace, though he is hardly interested in Clarissa for her property, and though he is a mortal enemy of her family, shares with the Harlowes a view of the law as the enabling faculty of possession. Thus John P. Zomchick, in a thorough study of Lovelace's legal language and ideas, can group him in the same category with his enemies: "The law that is meant to constitute society and protect it informs

---

21. Margaret Doody, *A Natural Passion* (Oxford: Clarendon Press, 1974), 123.

the behavior of the Harlowes and the Lovelaces of the world, suggesting
tactics and establishing a protective armor of self-interest as they ready
themselves to enter the arena where the battles for possession rage."[22]
Lovelace is the character who has most fully realized that the law is not
the self-perpetuating organism described by Blackstone and Chambers,
but rather a machine that must be driven. He knows furthermore that this
driving of the law requires—besides wealth and lineage—the careful
control of appearance and language. And so Lovelace must himself remake
the law by manipulating legal dialect and writing courtroom drama for his
own benefit.

One of the many paradoxes of *Clarissa* is that Lovelace, who is never
brought to trial for his rape (he is punished outside the law, falling to
Clarissa's cousin Morden in a duel), is nevertheless continually engaged in
preparing his own defense. Thinking ahead to possible legal action that
will stem from his abduction and violation of Clarissa, Lovelace wishes to
plant some evidence that could help him in court. Having brought his
victim to London, Lovelace convinces Clarissa that she should let everyone
call her "Mrs. Lovelace," thinking that this will serve as *prima facie*
evidence that she had consented to cohabit with him. After the collation at
which this form of address is used, Lovelace writes an imaginary piece of
testimony for his trial. But the testimony comes to the reader in the form
of heteroglossia, that is, embedded within Lovelace's "normal" discourse,
the rakish dialect—full of "thou"s and "thee"s—in which he couches all
his letters to his friend Belford:

> No less than four worthy gentlemen, of fortune and family, who
> were all in company such a night particularly, at a collation to
> which they were invited by Robert Lovelace, of Sandown-Hall in
> the County of Lancaster, Esquire, in company with Magdalen
> Sinclair widow, and Priscilla Partington spinster, and the lady
> complainant; when the said Robert L addressed himself to the
> said Lady, on a multitude of occasions, as his wife; as they and
> others did, as Mrs. Lovelace; every one complimenting and con-
> gratulating her upon her nuptials; and that she received such their
> compliments and congratulations with no other visible displeasure
> or repugnance, than such as a young Bride, full of blushes and
> pretty confusion, might be supposed to express upon such contem-

22. John P. Zomchick, "Tame Spirits, Brave Fellows, and the Web of Law: Robert Lovelace's
Legalistic Conscience," *ELH* 53 (Spring 1986): 116.

plative revolvings as those compliments would naturally inspire. (3:335)

Lovelace, Sinclair, and Clarissa herself are transfigured by this language into carefully defined objects. For example, the naming of Lovelace's residence supposedly identifies him more precisely than does his name. In fact, an opposite process of obfuscation is occurring: the procuress Sinclair, in whose brothel Lovelace has lodged the unwitting Clarissa, becomes "Magdalen Sinclair widow"; the prostitute Partington is transformed into a "spinster"; Belford and the other rakes have somehow become "worthy gentlemen." In his legal parody Lovelace has achieved more than irony; he has created drama or masquerade. Familiar people and familiar events now appear strange and unrecognizable—indeed they must, if their testimony is to carry any weight. Legal discourse for Lovelace is drama. The stock legal phrases add no new information to the descriptions. Rather, they mark off a particular genre that elevates the subjective into the objective, hardens style into content, and transforms mere language into the legal "facts" Lovelace will need to win his case. Yet the embedding of this testimony within Lovelace's other dialects causes its legal language to fall apart. The final sentence of his quote falls back into the genre of rakish dialect. The preciosity and gallantry of "pretty confusion," the cozy salaciousness of the "contemplative revolvings," alienate it from the "real" legal language it attempts to appropriate. Lovelace cannot sustain his performance or, perhaps, does not try to at this preliminary stage (before the rape has occurred).

In this example, Lovelace creates a legal drama that has no real existence. In our next example, on the other hand, Lovelace himself enters into dialogue with an existing legal text. The document is a marriage license that Lovelace obtains so that he may convince Clarissa of the sincerity of his plans to marry her. Through his influence Lovelace has obtained a dispensation of the banns, which, if published, would undoubtedly bring Clarissa's family into the arena.[23] Again, the effect of the legal dialect is heightened by its being quoted within a rake's letter. Belford reads not the original license, but an annotated copy, which Lovelace sends to his friend permeated with his cynical comments (in brackets):

23. A parallel to Lovelace's dispensation, which seems more explicable from the perspective of Brewer and Styles than from that of Blackstone and Chambers, is found in the fifth of William Hogarth's series of eight engravings, *The Rake's Progress* (1739). In the background of Rakewell's wedding to a rich spinster, we can make out his former lover Sarah Young holding his illegitimate daughter, while Mrs. Young objects vociferously to the marriage. They are being silenced by the sacristan.

Whereas ye are, as is alleged, determined to enter into the holy
State of Matrimony [*This is only alleged, thou observest*] by and with
the consent of, &c. &c. &c. and are very desirous of obtaining
your marriage to be solemnized in the face of the Church: We are
willing that such your honest desires [*Honest desires, Jack!*] may
more speedily have their due effect: And therefore, that ye may be
able to procure such Marriage to be freely and lawfully solemnized
in the parish-church of St. Martin in the Fields, or St. Giles's in
the Fields in the County of Middlesex, by the Rector, Vicar, or
Curate thereof, at any time of the year [*At any time of the year,
Jack!*] without publication of banes: Provided, that by reason of
any precontract [*I verily think that I have had three or four precontracts
in my time; but the good girls have not claimed upon them of a long while*]
consanguinity, affinity, or any lawful course whatsoever, there be
no lawful impediment in this behalf. (5:289–90)

Here we have most literally an example of heteroglossia, of a dialogue
between rakish dialect and the language of law. It is a true conflict, in
which Lovelace's cynical language punches holes in the contract's ecclesi-
astical solemnity. The document's relation to action is no longer that of a
rule, since nearly every legal statement is followed by a comment that
negates its validity. Lovelace first notes that the word "alleged" is convenient for him, since he does not really plan to marry Clarissa — the marriage
license is but a hook. He then notes that the word "honest" is hardly
consonant with his desires. He finds that the dispensation of the banns and
of any time limits for the marriage is convenient, since now Clarissa's
family will have no chance to intervene should he go on with the wedding.
Finally, he confesses that he actually is in violation of one of the provisions
of the license: he has already promised marriage to a number of women,
apparently by signing precontracts with them. (The precontract was a
time-honored device for solidifying marriages before the actual ceremonies
took place.) Those contracts are insignificant for the purposes of the
present document, because the women who signed them have no legal
voice. They are merely "girls," and he their "guardian."
    Lovelace's most elaborate composition of courtroom drama follows a
similar strategy of silencing women. He plans an elaborate defense not for
his real rape of Clarissa, but rather for his imagined rape of her friend
Anna Howe, her mother, and their servant. Here, a completely unstable
legal genre is engulfed by the semiotics of spectacle. As John Zomchick
describes it, "In [his] rape/trial fantasy, Lovelace directs the spectators

and the *dramatis personae* of the juridical theater to his own advantage."[24] The use-value of theater, however, lies in the effect the spectacle has on its audience, not as a Rule of Action but as catharsis, not as reason but as emotion. Lovelace revels in the apprehension that "Women will be five-sixths of the spectators" (4:274), and his defense is based entirely on his physical beauty causing those women in the audience to intercede for his acquittal. The theatrical parallel is completed by his inserted stage direction indicating the "scene" and the reactions of the audience (as always, Lovelace is writing to Belford):

> How bravely shall we enter a court, I at the head of you. . . . What brave fellows! —What fine gentlemen! —There goes a charming handsome man! —meaning me, to be sure! —Who could find in their hearts to hang such a gentleman as that? whispers one lady, sitting perhaps on the right hand of the recorder. [I suppose the scene to be in London.] (4:273)

Lovelace's drama resembles the fatal mime show in *Hamlet*, with the stage silent and the spectators all a-flutter. Indeed, the comments from the women translate the gestures of the actors into "legal" language—thus the proximity of one speaker to the recorder, suggesting that the transcription of this trial will contain far more "extraneous" material than most. Then again, Lovelace's fantasy, coupled with the actual events of the novel, denies that such material is alien to legal discourse to begin with.

So far in this imagined scene Lovelace has not spoken a word, and it is with a gesture that he will win his case, a gesture that will prohibit the plaintiff Anna Howe from speaking and turn her into an object of spectacle. Indeed, throughout the passage, we only hear the voices of the spectators:

> But every eye dwells upon Miss [Anna Howe]! —See, see, the handsome gentleman bows to her!
> To the very ground, to be sure, I shall bow; and kiss my hand. See her confusion! See! She turns from him! —Ay! that's because it is in open court, cries an arch one! —While others admire her—Ay! that's a girl worth venturing one's neck for!
> Then we shall be praised—even the judges, and the whole crowded bench, will acquit us in their hearts! (4:274)

24. Zomchick, "Tame Spirits," 109.

On the one hand, we should not take Lovelace's courtroom drama for legal reality, not even for the novel's legal reality. On the other hand, *Clarissa* never allows us a real trial with which we might compare Lovelace's fantasy, so that in a curious way this *is* the novel's legal reality. The trial we have seen here is really the suppression of a trial. The fantasy fulfills Lovelace's theory of rape prosecution, that "what a modest woman will suffer rather than become a *viva voce* accuser, lessens much an honest fellow's apprehensions" (5:340). The negated phrase "viva voce" returns us once again to the idea of Lovelace's legal power as dependent on his ability to silence women in court. This concept is totally appropriate not only to his fantasy, but also to another, more "realistic" representation of an eighteenth-century English rape trial from a very different source.

Transcripts of eighteenth-century rape prosecutions published in popular books such as the *Select Trials* (1742) demonstrate both the theatrical nature of the proceedings and the confrontation of the woman with a discourse system to which she should, as woman, remain alien. In order to prove rape, a woman was forced to describe the act in terms that, as a woman, she should not have had in her vocabulary. The graphic description needed to prove the rape, according to contemporary rules of feminine decorum, tended to prove her unvirtuous and hence a dubious plaintiff. In trial after trial the question of what exactly happened was posed to the woman, and she in turn attempted to evade, to circumlocute, to use a woman's language to (not) describe what had been done to her. The moment of truth for a Mrs. Batten is typical. She is forced to graphically describe her rape:

> BATTEN. And must I speak plain English then? — and before all these Gentlemen. — I vow I am ashamed. — I don't know how to say such a word. — But if I must, I must. They two held me while the Prisoner_____.[25]

If *Select Trials*, which was not a genteel publication, felt the need to censor the language here, we may imagine how self-demeaning and self-implicating it was for plaintiff Batten to speak those words. We see the plaintiff in this short passage examining the role assigned her, questioning its language, becoming aware of her male audience, in short, struggling against

25. *Select Trials for Murder, Robbery, Burglary, Rapes, Sodomy, Coining, Forgery, Pyracy, and Other Offences and Misdemanours, at the Sessions-house in the Old Bailey, to Which are Added Genuine Accounts of the Lives, Exploits, Behaviour, Confessions, and Dying-Speeches, of the Most Notorious Convicts, from the Year 1720 to this time,* vol. 2 (London: G. Strahan, 1742), 319.

the generic requirements of her legal writing lesson. The rhetorical device of hesitation (hers or the editor's?) heightens the effect of her final sentence, whose expurgated verb in turn heightens the reader's perception that this woman has crossed the boundary of decency, has been forced to speak another, untranslatable dialect. The trial has repeated the rape.

Let us observe this in one more example from another case in order to show the court's insistence on graphic description:

> COURT. In what manner did he use ye?
> M.H. He forced my body with what he had.
> COURT. You must explain yourself.
> M.H. _____. _____.[26]

The *Select Trials*, which always presented its legal proceedings in dialogue form, might be considered a forerunner of American television's *People's Court* or *Divorce Court*. The popularity of the series is indicated by the number of editions it went through. Besides the two 1742 editions, references can be found to a 1764 edition, a 1734–35 edition, and an undated, probably earlier one. The inclusion in these books of the "Genuine Accounts of the Lives, Exploits, Behaviour, Confessions, and Dying-Speeches, of the Most Notorious Convicts" indicates that they also belonged marginally to the extremely popular genre of criminal biography, which, as Lincoln Faller has demonstrated, had the use-value of confronting the deepest social and political anxieties of the English middle classes.[27]

A comparison between the courtroom scenes in *Clarissa* and those in *Select Trials* reveals a clear symmetry. If Mrs. Batten is but a poor player, forced to speak her lines before an all-male audience, Robert Lovelace is by birth and by gender entitled to the role of playwright or stage manager of his drama. Whereas Batten is forced to enter a signifying system alien to her self-definition as a lady, Lovelace silences his accuser and provokes language on the part of the now predominantly female spectators through the semiotics of gesture. In one scene, a woman is forced to speak against her will, while in the other Anna Howe is forced into silence; both women are overpowered by a discourse alien to their own.

After Clarissa's rape, her friends and family urge her to appear in court against Lovelace. Clarissa voices similar intentions in the famous "penknife" scene: locked in her room and overhearing Lovelace plotting

26. Ibid., 2:345.

27. Lincoln Faller, *Turned to Account: The Forms and Functions of Criminal Biography in Late Seventeenth- and Early Eighteenth-Century England* (New York: Cambridge University Press, 1987).

another rape attempt, Clarissa appears and makes a magnificent speech, near the climax of which she holds a knife to her breast, threatening to use it if anyone comes near her. Lovelace later describes to his friend Belford the paradoxical way in which Clarissa invokes the law: "You, sir, and ye women, are safe from every violence of mine. The LAW shall be all my resource: the LAW, and she spoke the word with emphasis, that to such people carries natural terror with it. . . . The LAW only shall be my refuge!" (4:68). With the phrase "such people," Lovelace once again notes his own position above the law. Clarissa, on the other hand, while invoking the law, uses the emotional effect of suicidal gesture to achieve her effects. Paradoxically, the legal power which Clarissa creates for herself in this scene is based, like Lovelace's, on theater and gesture. Rather than prevent crude violence, it invokes it in the threat of suicide.

Her invocation of LAW never leaves her script. Later in the novel, Clarissa comes to realize that a rape prosecution resembles a theatrical performance in which the woman is forced to assume a dialect of direct description which annihilates her status as a "lady." When Clarissa decides not to prosecute Lovelace for rape, the reader is meant to remember all these scenes and understand the motives for Clarissa's decision. From the Batten case we recognize that legal punishment of Lovelace for the rape he has committed depends entirely upon Clarissa's willingness and ability to testify, that is, to manipulate or be manipulated by legal discourse. These two scenes help explain why Clarissa in the end prefers to construct her own work of literature — including her coffin, Biblical quotation, the book *Clarissa*, and her will — rather than submit to the law's.

Moreover, Clarissa's use of familiar genres makes her will a Rule of Action. Indicative of the importance that Richardson attributed to this last testament of Clarissa is the fact that he originally thought of naming his novel *The Lady's Legacy*.[28] The will, then, represents *Clarissa* in miniature, both because the collection of letters that constitutes the novel is Clarissa's real legacy, and because the problems of legal interpretation addressed in the will are equivalent to those faced by readers of the novel. Charles Knight points out that Clarissa's will serves the purpose of redefining relationships between characters — reflected particularly in Clarissa's appointment of the previously unthinkable triumvirate of Lovelace's friend Belford, Clarissa's chauvinist cousin Morden, and her feminist confidante Anna Howe to interpret jointly dubious points in her will.[29] Indeed, the

---

28. This was one of several suggestions by Richardson's friend Aaron Hill. See Ben D. Kimpel and Duncan Eaves, "The Composition of *Clarissa* and Its Revision Before Publication," *PMLA* 83 (1968): 422.

29. Knight, "The Function of Wills in Richardson's *Clarissa*," 1188.

will does even more, functioning as a closural device for the novel as a whole. Virtually every character in the novel is remembered in Clarissa's will. The fact that the will does *not* mention Clarissa's brother and sister, who were largely responsible for Clarissa's ostracism and death, speaks more about them and their transgression than any direct rhetorical intervention could. The reader of *Clarissa*, then, is led to balance the possible failure of the will as a legal document against its success as an aesthetic device with moral effects.

Because of the will's generic instability, the question of whether it (and hence law in general) "works" or not cannot be answered for the document as a whole. Both sides of the debate over whether the will achieves its purpose or not share the implicit premise that it belongs to a single genre, that it is a single (if complex) speech act. But Clarissa feels free to use various forms of discourse (legal, religious, familiar) within her document. She makes no attempt to limit her will to the bounds of what the law can carry out, writing for example a provision for giving a divine warning to Lovelace, should he wish to view her body. In this and in other provisions, such as the elaborate carrying home of her body, Clarissa's will constructs the same legal theater as we have seen in Lovelace's letters and in her own pen-knife scene. Her description of the disposition of her body is not a legal arrangement, but stage directions for a spectacle. As though in response to Lovelace's own legal fantasies, she makes provisions to exclude him and his impromptu performances from her passion play:

> And I could wish, if it might be avoided without making ill will between Mr. Lovelace and my executor, that the former might not be permitted to see my corpse. But if, as he is a man very uncontroulable, and as I am nobody's, he insist upon viewing her dead, whom he once before saw in a manner dead, let his gay curiosity be gratified. Let him behold, and triumph over the wretched remains of one who had been made a victim to his barbarous perfidy: but let some good person, as by my desire, give him a paper, whilst he is viewing the ghastly spectacle, containing these few words only; — "Gay, cruel heart! behold here the remains of the once ruined, yet now happy, Clarissa Harlowe! — See what thou thyself must quickly be; — and REPENT!" — Yet, to show that I die in perfect charity with all the world, I do most sincerely forgive Mr. Lovelace the wrongs he has done me. (8:107)

The first verb, a modal "could," signals that we are now in the realm of the subjunctive, and Clarissa piles hypothesis on hypothesis, thereby passing from the instructions of a will to a theater of the mind. The legal text of the will thus contains within it a drama (Clarissa's corpse as prop, Lovelace and a "good person" as actors) that in turn contains a religious text (the *memento mori*). Only the emphatic present indicative of the last sentence brings the reader back to the legal "reality" of *Clarissa*.

The contrast between the rhetorical violence of Clarissa's legal theater and the sudden cheerfulness of her forgiving Lovelace in that last sentence is almost comic and makes the legal status of the forgiveness ambiguous. Clarissa may be making a statement rather than performing an act of forgiveness, especially since she also forgives Lovelace "privately" in a letter addressed to him. In other words, this last sentence can also be read as a continuation of Clarissa's theater. The emphasis is still on performing as acting, and just as in her passion play or Lovelace's rape trial the objective is to move the audience in order to achieve a desired action, which in this case is the end of action, the silencing of retribution. In fact, Clarissa's forgiveness does not succeed in preventing her cousin Morden from avenging her by killing Lovelace in a duel.

In its generality the sentence contrasts with the disposition of Clarissa's body, for which every detail is prepared, including a prompter to hold up a cue card for Lovelace. If Lovelace insists upon performing in Clarissa's spectacle, he must play the role she assigns him. He must be subjected to language (religious discourse) rather than triumph over it through the visual. Such a scene is supralegal, the translation of an ideology of divine punishment (which operates in the world of the novel) into the human legal world. It is an attempt to go beyond the law and control the very mind and will of Lovelace as part of a struggle that has been carried on over the course of the novel. Here the language of theater, of religion, and of piety replace the supposed neutrality of legal discourse, which has already been fragmented in the course of the novel into the various idioms that compose it. Legal discourse is used here in order to compose the scene, to hire the actor, and to ensure the performance of another perlocutionary act outside the bounds of legality. If Lovelace imagines himself able to silence legal discourse with the semiotics of gesture, Clarissa, anticipating Lovelace's penchant for spectacle, insists on returning it to the realm of language proper. Interestingly, this passage is the only one in the will which is never realized. Lovelace never visits the body, never repents, and is never forgiven by the living, who hound and kill him.

III

Clarissa's theater, in revealing a symmetrical legalization of the aesthetic and dramatization of the legal, would seem to support Susan Sage Hein-

zelman's contention that "fictionally . . . a woman is legitimate; jurispru-
dentially, however, she is illegitimate."[30] The examples of legal theater we
have been analyzing here could also be used to bolster Susan Brownmiller's
(and others') claim that in rape prosecutions it is always the victim who is
on trial, and that "from the humblest beginnings of the social order based
on a primitive system of retaliatory force . . . woman was unequal before
the law."[31] Brownmiller would undoubtedly see in these eighteenth-century
presentations a pattern endemic to all Anglo-American jurisprudence
dealing with rape, a pattern related in the end to the arrangement of power
between men and women in society. Law cannot defend itself against
literature. If law turns into a theater in which *logos* is subordinate to
spectacle, then women must become playwrights. But one could also read
Richardson as pointing out the general inequality between discourse
systems in any legal proceeding—indeed, the domination of one genre by
another is portrayed as the very *modus operandi* of the court. If theoretically
the law's power derives from its unambiguous identification as a particular
variety of speech-act, that is, the Rule of Action, Richardson's fiction
portrays its power as deriving from generic instability as a function of its
ideological split, the necessary conflict between different modes of expression.

Roland Barthes gives a similar view of legal heteroglossia in his analysis
of the real case of "Dominici ou le triomphe de la littérature," which
becomes another of the *Mythologies* of French culture. In the trial of
Dominici, an alpine peasant condemned for the murder of an English
aristocrat, a judicial French replete with the syntax and vocabulary of
rationalité competes against a regional (Provençal) peasant dialect. Barthes
first quotes from the transcript of the trial in order to give an idea of the
disparity between these dialects. For example, there is the misunderstand-
ing faintly reminiscent of a Marx Brothers movie, where Domenici takes a
question about the substantive *allée* ("path") to be about the past participle
from *aller* ("to go"). The trial thus appears to be more a lesson in proper
grammar than an investigation of facts. Barthes summarizes the tortuous
application of the judicial writing lesson:

> La disparité des langages, leur clôture impénétrable, ont pourtant
> été soulignées par quelques journalistes. . . . On y constate qu'il
> n'est pas besoin d'imaginer des barrières mysterieuses, des malen-

30. Susan Sage Heinzelmann, "Women's Petty Treason: Feminism, Narrative, and the Law," *Journal of Narrative Technique* 20 (Spring 1990): 89.
31. Susan Brownmiller, *Against Our Will: Men, Women, and Rape* (New York: Simon & Schuster, 1975), 16.

tendus à la Kafka. Non, la syntaxe, le vocabulaire, la plupart des matériaux élémentaires, analytiques, du langage se cherchent aveuglement sans se joindre, mais nul n'en a scrupule. . . . Ce sont tout simplement deux particularités qui s'affrontent. Mais l'une a les honneurs, la loi, la force pour soi.

The disparity of both languages, their impenetrability to each other, have been stressed by a few journalists. . . . Their remarks show that there is no need to imagine mysterious barriers, Kafka-like misunderstandings. No: syntax, vocabulary, most of the elementary, analytical materials of language grope blindly without ever touching, but no one has any qualms about it. . . . These are in actual fact two particular uses of language which confront each other. But one of them has honours, law and force on its side.[32]

For our purposes, Barthes's most interesting point, consonant with Richardson's depiction of legal heterglossia, is that this language of law which triumphs, which must triumph over all other social dialects, is itself a literary construction: "Tout le procés Dominici s'est joué sur une certaine idée de la psychologie, qui se trouve être comme par hasard celle de la Littérature bien-pensante" ("The whole Dominici trial was enacted according to a certain idea of psychology, which happens to be, as luck would have it, that of the Literature of the bourgeois Establishment").[33] Thus Barthes is concerned not only with exposing legal procedure as heteroglossia, but also with exposing the "winning" language as being composed of something that should be alien to it. For Barthes, not only are legal and aesthetic language two different genres, but the former is actually created out of the latter, exactly as in Lovelace's fantasy.

IV

If Barthes and Richardson note a similar generic instability in the law, they themselves resort to different genres for their critiques. Yet the genres they choose show a similar instability. Though today we have few reserva-

32. Barthes, *Mythologies*, 54–55; Lavers, trans., *Mythologies*, 44–45.
33. Barthes, *Mythologies*, 53; Lavers, trans., *Mythologies*, 43. The English translation unfolds or interprets Barthes's sentence, particularly *bien-pensante*, rather boldly, but the translation is certainly in consonance with the ideas expressed throughout *Mythologies*.

tions about calling *Clarissa* a novel, Richardson himself rejected such a generic term because it excluded the kinds of social critiques he wished to make in this massive work of prose fiction. As we might expect from the publisher of an edition of Aesop's fables, Richardson believed in the possibility of moral instruction through fiction, a use-value few could find in the novelistic genre in his era. In turn, the generic instability inherent in the act of writing a non-novel probably helped Richardson make unconventional moves like including an entire will in his text.

If Richardson was able to conduct an ideological critique of the law through fiction (as long as he could fit his work "between" the recognized genres of his day), there are various reasons why Roland Barthes did not see that option as open to him. "J'aime le romanesque," Barthes has said in an interview, "mais je sais que le roman est mort" ("I love the novelistic, but I know that the novel is dead").[34] By which Barthes means that the use-value of the novelistic genre has changed such that it can no longer critique language and culture the way Richardson did.[35] The use-value of the novel had been reshaped by Alain Robbe-Grillet and other *nouveau romanciers*. Or, to put it differently, the postwar novel in France had turned into a different genre while continuing to carry the same name. Philip Thody has characterized Barthes's essays in *Mythologies* as filling a gap left open by the retreat of the novel into phenomenological description:

> What is . . . fascinating about *Mythologies* is the portrait which it gives of French society in the 1950s, and in this respect it is almost as though Barthes were compensating for the deliberate refusal of the "nouveaux romanciers" to offer any account of what their own or indeed any other society was like. For central to the theory which Alain Robbe-Grillet put forward in his essays and fiction was the view that the novel ought to concern itself solely with physical objects and not at all with sociology or psychology. These, it was argued, were best left to the professionally qualified specialists, and the support which Barthes himself gave to Robbe-Grillet, like his attacks on supposedly realistic literature, tended to support this view. But in *Mythologies*, albeit unintentionally, he goes against his theory of what the *scripteur* should offer, and does for the

34. Roland Barthes, *Le Grain de la voix* (Paris: Seuil, 1981), 210; translated by Linda Coverdale, under the title *The Grain of the Voice* (New York: Hill & Wang, 1985), 222.

35. As if to respond to Barthes's deflation of the novel, Philippe Roger has turned the tables by giving his critique of Barthes's work and life the intriguing and incongruous title *Roland Barthes, roman* (Paris: Grasset, 1986).

France of the Fourth Republic almost what the despised Maupassant did for the first twenty years of the Third.[36]

In this sense, Barthes's text also invokes its own instability through the
mention of fiction writers such as Kafka. Barthes's defictionalization of
Kafka and Maupassant points to the failure of genre in much the same
way Lévi-Strauss's dedramatization of Corneille's *Cinna* did. And like
Tristes tropiques, *Mythologies* gives the image of a critical mind in a restless
search for the proper genre—novel? essay? *haiku?*—that would lend the
desired critical force to his writing.[37] For example, even Barthes's autobiography turned into a disconnected series of critical aperçus rather than
take on the narrative form that had developed hand in hand with the
modern novel.[38]

Another factor in the different genres of these authors is that each
"uses" legal discourse in a way that his legal tradition itself legitimates. On
the one hand, Richardson, writing on an English jurisprudence based
mainly upon custom and precedent, as Blackstone's architectural metaphor
has shown, simply invents a precedent, a rape case, which should be
adjudicated and cannot be. There is very little abstract, dry legal reasoning
in *Clarissa*. It merely goes about presenting the mimesis of law. French
law, on the other hand, has always been largely Roman, that is, codified,
written—above all in the Napoleonic promulgations. Its power thus derives
a priori from its internal consistency and logic, from its representation of
la Raison. The confrontation with such a system is less through facts
(including Richardson's fictional facts), than through discourse itself. For
example, in French jurisprudence, the opinions of law professors and other
judicial experts are placed on a par with those of judges. Thus Barthes's
claim (if we generalize from his two analyses) that French legal discourse
is recursively constituted out of literary, theological, logical, and psychol-
ogistic discourses, is not merely an invention on his part, but would seem
a necessary observation that every university-trained legal mind need
assent to. But not only that: this communication between academic and
pragmatic legal thought also means that at least these texts of *Mythologies*
sidle up, as it were, to the edges of "legitimate" legal discourse in France.

36. Philip Thody, *Roland Barthes, A Conservative Estimate* (London: Methuen, 1977), 46–47.

37. The secondary literature on Barthes repeatedly invokes the problem of genre in his
writings. Even the titles of the following works reveal the problem. Besides Roger's *Roland Barthes,
roman*, see also Réda Bensmaïa, *Barthes à l'Essai* (Tübingen: Gunter Narr, 1986); and Marjorie
Perloff, "Barthes and the Degree Zero of Genre," 510–16.

38. Roland Barthes, *Roland Barthes par Roland Barthes* (Paris: Seuil, 1975).

(Indeed, Barthes's legal essays in this volume had more legal-political than literary force. For years after the publication of this immensely popular and influential volume, Barthes still had no permanent academic home due to his failure to write a work that would satisfy the generic expectations of French academia, much as the rejection of Walter Benjamin's *Ursprung des deutschen Trauerspiels* as a *Habilitationsschrift* had much to do with the generic expectations of German academia.)

If, as Barthes argues, the law is really literature in disguise, then we might argue that literature—at least the literature of Richardson and Barthes—is really law in disguise. If Blackstone and Chambers defined law as a set of rules of action, legal literature explores the law's generic instability. Once one posits the law as generically unstable, it would be difficult to separate rule from interpretation or to stop the process of rule-formation at the doors of the courtroom or legislative hall. We have seen that if legal discourse invades the literary body of *Clarissa*, literary language in turn impinges on, interprets, and translates legal dialect. Richardson and Barthes critique the law not only as a language endlessly open to conflicting interpretations, but also as a dialect conversing with and being informed by other speech genres. As it is continually being turned into literature, legal dialect loses any pretensions to infallible memory or absolute reason. Only ideology allows us to pronounce the latter genre a Rule of Action and the former a nonbinding "revelation of reality."

Postscript

One reader of this book has already chastised my ignorance of "matters legal" in this chapter. He felt it necessary to add: "My views carry some weight; I am a lawyer." In writing this he confirms *exactly* my thesis of the legal ideology of homogenous discourse laid out above. Although all of us are continually being formed and influenced by legal discourse in its many manifestations, this containment within the law can somehow never amount to a being "inside" it; the many are made weightless in being spoken (to) by the law, but the law itself gives weight only to the few who are empowered to speak it. Like Clarissa, like Anna Howe, like Mrs. Batten, like Dominici, I was (meant to be) silenced by a legal "sentence" (formulated in an act of literary criticism). Like the man from the country in Kafka's "Before the Law," I was (meant to be) put in my place, which is neither inside nor outside a law whose generic borders cannot be fixed— as my lawyer/critic's comment shows. Case dismissed.

6

Dylan, Degenhardt, and Dissonance

So I'll make my stand

And remain as I am

And bid farewell and not give a damn. . . .

—Bob Dylan, "Restless Farewell"

THESE LINES FROM THE SONG "RESTLESS FAREWELL" illus-
trate the paradoxical consistency of the lyric of singer-songwriter Bob
Dylan (1941–   ).[1] Whereas popular art tends to force its performers to
assume a single, stable persona, which provides for infinite repetition with
small variations, Bob Dylan's presence on the popular music scene since
1961 as performer and songwriter can only be described as protean. Each
phase of his career has frustrated, angered, and alienated a large part of
his former listening public, but gained him a larger audience in the end.
This eternal leave-taking and departure into new affection and new noise
can also be seen as generic evolution, from folk to rock 'n' roll to rock to
country to gospel to pop. Yet Dylan never remakes himself out of whole
cloth, and the generic instability revealed most clearly in a comparison of
the various stages of his career can also be felt synchronically within a
particular album or even a single song.

1. From Bob Dylan, "Restless Farewell," in *Lyrics 1962–1985* (New York: Alfred A. Knopf,
1985), 105. All quotations from Dylan's works are taken from this source and will be cited in the
text. Where appropriate, references to phonograph records, which are indispensable for a full
understanding of Dylan's art, will also be given.

One way of representing the German *Liedermacher* (lit. "songmaker") Franz Josef Degenhardt's career is to describe him as the "German Bob Dylan." Thomas Rothschild certainly describes him in terms that remind one of Bob Dylan: "Degenhardt has changed through the years. That caused him to lose some fans and gain new ones. His development in the sixties and seventies is almost paradigmatic for [that of] a large group of sensitive intellectuals."[2] But although Degenhardt has used generic shifts almost as extensively as Dylan in order to create musical and political dissonance, and although Degenhardt admires Dylan and acknowledges his debt to Dylan in his songs and novels, their careers can almost be described as inversions of each other if charted according to the ideology of genre.

In his book *Bruits (Noise)*, Jacques Attali argues that new forms of music function as early warnings of social change by interfering with the established channels of communication.[3] Attali thus develops in detail the connection between dissonance and dissidence that Nietzsche had suggested in his *Geburt der Tragödie*, where he claimed that dissonance is the Dionysian principle that rejects culture:

> The joy aroused by the tragic myth has the same origin as the joyous sensation of dissonance in music. The Dionysian, with its primordial joy experienced even in pain, is the common source of music and tragic myth.
>
> . . . [R]eferring to the artistically employed dissonances . . . we desire to hear and at the same time long to get beyond all hearing. That striving for the infinite, the wing-beat of longing that accompanies the highest delight in clearly perceived reality, reminds us that in both states we must recognize a Dionysian phenomenon: again and again it reveals to us the playful construction and destruction of the individual world as the overflow of a primordial delight.[4]

Though Nietzsche and Attali are working from different paradigms of "reality," both single out dissonance or "noise" as the "wing-beat of

2. Thomas Rothschild, *Liedermacher* (Frankfurt: Fischer, 1980), 54.

3. Jacques Attali, *Bruits, L'Economie politique de la musique* (Paris: PUF, 1981); translated by Brian Massumi, under the title *Noise: The Political Economy of Music* (Minneapolis: University of Minnesota Press, 1985).

4. Friedrich Nietzsche, *Die Geburt der Tragödie* (Stuttgart: Reclam, 1953), 148; translated by Walter Kaufmann, under the title *The Birth of Tragedy* (New York: Vintage, 1967), 141–42.

longing" of music, as that aspect of music which points beyond the veil of ideology toward apocalypse. It is in this sense that Adorno speaks of the products of "Kulturindustrie," from which dissonance has been carefully and ruthlessly eliminated, as merely reinforcing the categories of the real (which Nietzsche reads as the illusion of the "self"). Only dissonance, musical "noise," can point beyond in a message that cannot be recuperated by reified language. That Dylan and Degenhardt almost always work with words *and* music allows us to examine their apocalyptic messages more closely.

I

One important aspect of noise is its self-referentiality: Noise calls attention to itself by working against the systemic in music, by deriving its meaning from its opposition to what already exists. Noise probes the unknown and unarticulated, and alludes to the apocalypse by foregrounding itself against the background of familiar form, by defining itself over against the already known, the "tradition" recognizable in the imperatives of genre. Charles Hamm, the noted historian of American popular music, describes Dylan's early music in just this way: "His singing style was nasal, rasping, declamatory . . . in no way calculated to fall easily on ears conditioned on Bing Crosby, Frank Sinatra, Burl Ives, or Joan Baez. He accompanied himself on the guitar, with ringing, percussive, harsh chords of little harmonic sophistication; sometimes he treated his guitar as a drone instrument, at other times his chord changes seemed simply wrong—to ears trained by Western harmonic music."[5] The lack of harmonic sophistication in Dylan's music derived from the same sources as did most of his apocalyptic imagery, that is, from his experience of liturgical music and from his interest in blues and other African-American music, a great deal of which does not use functional harmony. Also, a good number of the Anglo-American folk songs made popular by the figures Hamm mentions were originally modal or pentatonic, but were accommodated to the Western harmonic system in order to fall easily on the ears of urban white audiences raised on a popular music erected from the ruins of classical style. (With its modal melodies, "true" folk, like rock 'n' roll, has no classical components.)

5. Charles Hamm, *Yesterdays: Popular Song in America* (New York: Dutton, 1979), 433.

In this sense, Dylan's disregard of functional harmony contradicts his insistence that the determining influence on his style had been that of Woody Guthrie (1912–67), whose music derived entirely from the white country style made popular by the Carter Family, a style that is based upon the three major chords of functional harmony. Dylan's early songs often lacked two of these. Guthrie was idolized by the young Dylan, who appropriated Guthrie's persona more than his musical style, becoming, like Guthrie, a singer-songwriter using popular music to deliver political and social messages.[6] However, Dylan was unable to completely absorb Guthrie's writing lessons, no matter how often he visited the dying man in East Orange, New Jersey. Dylan's comfortable, upper-middle-class background did not allow him to ingenuously assume Guthrie's position as the great communicator of proletarian concerns. Instead, Dylan chose to narrate his own failure to become Woody Guthrie, thus producing a new genre whose meaning lay in its *noise*, that is, in the discord (musical, textual, political) between these new songs and Guthrie's. One can see this new genre taking shape by comparing Dylan's first two albums. Dylan's first two commercially recorded original compositions, "Talking New York" and "Song to Woody," show their ideological split in using Guthrie tunes to sing about a theme with which Guthrie (at least the canonical Guthrie) never concerned himself: the relation between the singer, his audience, and his sources. Note, for example, how the singer portrays himself as epigonal throughout "Song To Woody":

> I'm out here a thousand miles from my home,
> Walkin' a road other men have gone down. . . .
>
> Hey, Woody Guthrie, but I know that you know
> All the things that I'm a-sayin' an' a-many times more.
> I'm a-singin' you the song, but I can't sing enough. . . .
>
> The very last thing that I'd want to do
> Is to say I've been hittin' some hard travelin' too.
>
> *(Lyrics* 6)

6. In fact, the term "singer-songwriter" was coined to describe performers like Dylan. In the early 1960s a high degree of specialization had still reigned in the music business, with very few singers writing their own songs. "Tin Pan Alley developed such a high degree of specialization that one takes it for granted that there are no songs *by* Bing Crosby, Margaret Whiting, Frank Sinatra, or Fred Astaire. But Bob Dylan changed this." Hamm, *Yesterdays*, 434. We tend to forget that it was Dylan's innovation, derived from Woody Guthrie, who had done the same thing within a less commercial and more traditional context, to write songs and present them himself to the public.

All this to the tune of Guthrie's highly political "1913 Massacre." Dylan's song shows all the marks of the anxiety of influence: neither his road nor his knowledge is new. Communication fails, and tradition is broken as the singer "can't sing enough." Dylan is shy about proclaiming his hard traveling; his dues have been paid with borrowed money—after all, his peregrinations were all charades, done not out of economic necessity, like those of Guthrie's midwesterners, but solely from the motive of seeking fame and fortune as a singer. The self-mockery implied in these lyrics is further ironized by the origin of the song's tune. Guthrie's "1913 Massacre"—a masterpiece of folk narrative—laments the murder of striking miners in Calumet, Michigan, by company thugs. Its last line is "See what your greed for money has done." Dylan, on the other hand, can think only of his own struggle to become a famous singer. This combination of tribute and parody thus becomes something new by invoking the incommensurability between Guthrie's traditionalism and Dylan's eclecticism. The song hints that Dylan's concerns will instead be with a more distanced, epigonal, secondary reading of the American musical tradition and of American culture. In other words, Dylan tells us in this parody of Woody that his goal will be to create noise and a new musical genre.

The ideological split in this early song is paradigmatic of the differences between the political folksong movement of the 1930s, of which Guthrie was a part, and the genre's more commercialized development in the early 1960s. Bill Malone has described the conscious appropriation of the traditional ballad to leftist politics in the thirties:

> Through the 1920s and the depression years there was a conscious effort on the part of leftists to make traditional southern ballad singing into a kind of official working class music: Southern rural songs and melodies were not only introduced to the North, they also acquired radical and intellectual connotations which they have never really lost. The folk, and their music, were glorified during the depression as they had not been since the days of Andrew Jackson. . . . The thirties saw the emergence, therefore, of that [genre] which has flourished so strongly in the sixties: "urban folk music."[7]

The second folk movement, in which Dylan took part, was not primarily a political movement, but the reaction to a stagnancy in music and culture.

7. Bill C. Malone, *Country Music U.S.A.* (Austin: University of Texas Press, 1968), 106.

As Jerome Rodnitsky puts it: "Folksingers quietly invaded the musical vacuum on college campuses in the late 1950s. While Jazz had become increasingly complex and abstract, rock 'n' roll had steadily become nonsensical and meaningless. The folk ballad, however, was extremely communicative and intelligible."[8] Thus, by the early 1960s, the folk ballad tradition had become popular not for its supposed origins among the rural proletariat, but as a response to young people's need for meaningful narrative. The ballad tradition is above all one of storytelling, with an emphasis on plot, suspense, and concrete actions, whereas rock 'n' roll had, like the blues idiom from which it was born, concentrated more on the emotional, discursive side of song. Rock 'n' roll has thereby produced few great storytellers, compared to folk and country music.

The sixties marked the end of the geographic and political isolation of folk music and its entrance into mainstream commercial markets. The journal *Sing Out!* in which many of Dylan's early songs were published, is a case in point: founded in 1946 with 500 subscribers, by 1966 *Sing Out!* had attained a circulation of 24,000.[9] Its readership, however, as the audience for folk music in general, was largely white, middle-class, and under thirty, a far cry from the working class that Guthrie and other political songwriters had attempted to reach. It is an interesting paradox that the one political movement of the period associated with folk music, that for civil rights, used spirituals and work songs to great effect, but ballads only rarely. The search for meaning and the search for justice touched each other tangentially—as when Dylan's "Blowing in the Wind" became popular—yet required different musical genres.

Today the folk genre, which exhibits an incredible heterogeneity of musical styles, is identified above all by its source in noncommercial radio. This noncommercial, alternative aspect, the refusal to become part of the culture industry, is part and parcel of the music's rejection of all the American imperatives: materialism (let's sing about the Diggers); modernization (let's sing ancient songs and use nonelectric instruments); standardization (let's sing about different geographic regions of the United States as if there weren't a McDonald's in each and every town of all of them); and urbanization (let's sing about the country). Once someone becomes a "big star," he or she no longer belongs to the "minor genre" of folk—which, in one sense, is what happened to Dylan. In the early sixties,

8. Jerome L. Rodnitsky, *Minstrels of the Dawn* (Chicago: Nelson-Hall, 1976), 12.
9. R. Serge Denisoff, *Great Day Coming: Folk Music and the American Left* (Urbana: University of Illinois Press, 1971), 119, 180.

however, the interaction between folk and its surrounding genres was more dynamic and fluid.

This complex of social forces that created the folk music scene in the early 1960s is reflected in the heterogeneity of Dylan's first album, *Bob Dylan*, which shows a generic instability foreign to the music of Woody Guthrie.[10] As discussed above, Dylan's two original texts for the album were based on Guthrie tunes. However, no complete Guthrie song appears on the album. (In fact, it is worth noting that Dylan has *never* performed a Woody Guthrie song on an album released commercially under his name; he performs three on the collective album *Tribute to Woody*.)[11] Of the eleven remaining songs on *Bob Dylan*, eight came from the African-American tradition (blues or gospel), and only three ("Freight Train Blues," "Man of Constant Sorrow," and "Pretty Peggy-O") from the Anglo-American tradition. Dylan's unreleased material from this period shows an even greater emphasis on blues sources, though he also performed some Guthrie tunes. What becomes evident is not so much that Dylan's musical identity derived in large part from rock 'n' roll and the black tradition—though this has in fact been well documented—as that any single, "pure" musical genre was from the beginning inadequate to his creativity.[12] Dylan's apocalyptic visions, for example, represent a strain rarely found in Guthrie or in the Anglo-American tradition. Dylan wanted both the communicative, message-oriented ballad form and the emotional lyricism of blues and rock 'n' roll. Dylan's use of both traditions reflects a position outside of either, a position from which to examine each tradition in terms of the other. This split characterizes the originality of songs such as "A Hard Rain's A-Gonna Fall" and "All Along the Watchtower."

"Hard Rain" brought together for the first time all the discrete elements in Dylan's artistic background: the ballad tradition, Scripture, the political lyrics of Bertolt Brecht, the moral and spiritual visions of T. S. Eliot, and the hallucinatory poetry of Arthur Rimbaud. Let us begin to unpack these elements at the most obvious level: "Hard Rain" as a transformation of the English ballad "Lord Randall." The connection between "Lord Randall"

10. Bob Dylan, *Bob Dylan* (Columbia CS 8579, 1962).

11. "I Ain't got No Home," "Dear Mrs. Roosevelt," and "Grand Coulee Dam," *Tribute to Woody Guthrie* (Warner Brothers 4–26036, 1972).

12. "By the time he was sixteen, Bobby had already opened up his ears to rhythm & blues, gospel, rockabilly, country & western, show tunes, and jazz." Mark Spitz, *Bob Dylan* (New York: McGraw-Hill, 1989), 48. See also Toby Thompson, *Positively Main Street* (New York: Coward-McCann, 1971), 74–75 and especially Wilfrid H. Mellers's *Darker Shade of Pale: A Backdrop to Bob Dylan* (New York: Oxford University Press, 1985), passim.

and "A Hard Rain's A-Gonna Fall" becomes apparent in any side-by-side reading or listening. Take the similarities in the first stanzas, for example:

> "Oh, where have you been, Lord Randall, my son?
> Oh, where have you been, my handsome young man?"
> "I have been to the greenwood; mother, make my bed soon,
> For I'm weary with hunting and I want to lie down."[13]

> Oh, where have you been, my blue-eyed son?
> Oh, where have you been, my darling young one?
> *I've stumbled on the side of twelve misty mountains,*
> *I've walked and I've crawled on six crooked highways,*
> *I've stepped in the middle of seven sad forests,*
> *I've been out in front of a dozen dead oceans,*
> *I've been ten thousand miles in the mouth of a graveyard,*
> And it's a hard, and it's a hard, it's a hard, and it's a hard,
> And it's a hard rain's a-gonna fall.
>
> (*Lyrics* 59; emphasis added)

If we take out the italicized lines, we are left with the structure and many of the words of "Lord Randall." Yet previous studies have failed to delve adequately into the particular artistic and cultural vision implied in the musical and structural transformations that Dylan makes in the ballad form. Even musicologist Wilfrid Mellers is reduced to vaguely calling "Hard Rain" a "refashioning of the ballad of Lord Randall. The sinister story is remade in universal terms."[14] At this point, then, I wish to define Dylan's "refashioning" more precisely as the inmixing of a different musical tradition, which brings with it the theme of apocalypse, and as the creation of a different role for the narrator of the ballad, which links that apocalypse to the theme of self-reference. This linkage begins, however, with the polysemy of the title "Hard Rain."

Whereas the title "Lord Randall" serves merely to identify the song's protagonist and hence points to its worldly context, the phrase "hard rain" is thematic, encompassing three important and interrelated areas elaborated in the song's text: politics, religion, and art. "Hard Rain" was first

---

13. Bertrand H. Bronson, *The Traditional Tunes of the Child Ballads,* vol. 1 (Princeton: Princeton University Press, 1959), 217. I use number 76 of the Bronson collection. Number 77 is even closer to "Hard Rain" in its second line: "Where you been, Willie Ransome, *my own darling one?*" (Bronson 1:217; emphasis added). Of course, Dylan's source may have been yet another version not contained in Bronson.

14. Mellers, *A Darker Shade of Pale,* 132.

released on Dylan's second album, *The Freewheelin' Bob Dylan*.[15] The song's first critical interpretation, expounded in Nat Hentoff's liner notes to that album, was a purely political one. Hentoff, one of the period's most influential music critics, claimed that the song was Dylan's response to the Cuban missile crisis of October 1962. For many listeners, then, "Hard Rain" instantly became the *memento mori* for a narrowly avoided war, which had revealed to Americans their vulnerable position on the edge of nuclear catastrophe. The song's meaning was easily recuperable by assigning it to the "protest" subgenre of folk. In fact, however, the song was written *before* the missile crisis, and it makes no graphic or realistic references to nuclear war. Furthermore, such a "protest" motive for the song's writing does little to explain its meaning or its continuing power as a work of art even for those who know nothing of its supposed origin.

The song's imagery continually shifts between the sacred and the profane. The title "A Hard Rain's a-Gonna Fall" begins this process of shifting by superimposing the political on the archetypal: "hard rain" refers both to radioactive fallout *and* to the Flood of Genesis, representing God's will to eradicate a sinful world. For example, the singer reports that he has seen "a white ladder all covered with water." This image is Jacob's ladder, which angels used in order to ascend into heaven and come down to earth (Genesis 28:12). It is now deserted and useless, inundated by the Flood.[16] By linking these two incidents, the Flood and Jacob's ladder, Dylan invokes apocalypse as yet another version of the familiar biblical cycle: man's covenant with God, man's breaking of the covenant, and God's subsequent punishment of man. But there is little one can say about a white ladder on the political level. For a listener starting from Hentoff's liner notes, nuclear war, stripped of its political context, becomes during the song's unfolding a mere signifier of apocalypse, that is, a perceptible component allowing the listener to picture the unthinkable. Dylan's imagery thus follows a pattern described by R. W. B. Lewis as typical of modern American apocalypses: "The bomb, when it has been mentioned at all in our imaginative literature, has usually been taken as a symptom and an instrument: the inevitable product of the diseased energies of mankind, and the physical force that can bring about that grand conflagration which mankind has long been striving to deserve."[17] The question of whether "Hard Rain" is about nuclear war is related to that other, larger

15. Bob Dylan, *The Freewheelin' Bob Dylan* (Columbia CS 8786, 1963), side 1, band 6.
16. I am indebted to Louis Renza of Dartmouth College for the identification of this allusion.
17. R. W. B. Lewis, "Days of Wrath and Laughter," in *Trials of the Word* (New Haven: Yale University Press, 1965), 184.

question concerning the overall functioning of *mimesis* within the song. I argue that due to its lack of narrative, the *mimesis* in "Hard Rain" is directed toward the depiction of the singer as creator of images and as cultural hero.

Only later, as one of Dylan's live albums received the title *Hard Rain*, would a third reference for the term "hard rain" clarify itself. The title *describes* the album's contents. That is, "hard rain," in referring to the way the words of the singer fall on the ears of his listeners, can also stand for music or poetry. Like "Song to Woody," "Hard Rain" is self-referential. Like "Song to Woody," "Hard Rain" is also a song about singing, about the ability or inability to narrate. In the liner notes to *Freewheelin'*, Dylan describes the composition of the song as follows: "Every line in it . . . is actually the start of a whole song." This quotation offers an important clue to understanding that the song's structure is really alien to that of the traditional ballad, despite the song's allusions to "Lord Randall" and, in particular, to that ballad's treatment of the theme of death.

Several critics have begun the job of defining the complex relationship between the narrative structures of the two songs. Betsy Bowden writes of "Hard Rain" as "a Child ballad being run through a projector too fast," claiming that such intensification is appropriate for a description of nuclear attack.[18] But I have suggested that the issue may not be that of how to describe nuclear war, but rather of how to *use* nuclear attack as a signifier of apocalypse. Michael Gray also notes that the effectiveness of the supposedly "cohesive moral *theme*" of "Hard Rain" depends upon the "pictures rolling past . . . without opportunity of recall."[19] Although these two visual metaphors give a certain insight into the effect that "Hard Rain" has on someone familiar with ballad tradition, they fail to recognize the presence of two different musical and narrative structures within the song. "Hard Rain" is not a ballad but an apocalyptic ballad; that is, Dylan has transformed the ballad genre in adapting it to a generation whose political aspirations were largely couched in the language of idealism. Beneath the surface of political protest in the Guthrie style there ran a deeper current of religious vision, just as beneath this song's apparent preservation of the ballad form in its appropriation of "Lord Randall" there took place an extraordinary transformation of that genre. These differences begin in how these two songs tell their stories.

18. Betsy Bowden, *Performed Literature: Words and Music by Bob Dylan* (Bloomington: Indiana University Press, 1982), 18.
19. Michael Gray, *Song and Dance Man* (New York: Dutton, 1972), 160.

There is nothing idealistic or even moralistic about most ballads. "Lord Randall" is a murder ballad told from the perspective of the victim, a young man who has been poisoned by his lover. And "Lord Randall's" question-and-answer form allows an incremental unfolding of its simple plot: "Who cooked you your dinner?" . . . "My true love she cooked it"; "What had you for dinner?" . . . "Eels fried in fresh butter"; "She's fed you snake poison" . . . "Oh, yes, I am dyin'." Specific verbs—"cook," "feed," and "die"—quickly outline a murder plot and evoke a world of sordid actions. Then Randall usually makes a series of bequests, ending with a rope for hanging his lover. The rhetoric of question and answer, the triple meter of the music, and the theme of imminent catastrophe are all adapted by Dylan. The basic structure of "Hard Rain," like that of its source, is determined by dialogue in the form of question and answer. Were we to stop at these elements, "Hard Rain" would certainly conform to the definition of a ballad as combining elements of narrative, dialogue, and lyric, in which "the confrontation is usually between a man and a woman . . . leading to decisive action" (*New Grove Dictionary of Music*, 1981 ed.).

Yet Dylan has converted the narrative structure of "Lord Randall" into the vehicle for a far different kind of vision. To begin with, the questions posed in each stanza of "Hard Rain" do not lead, as they do in "Lord Randall," to the reconstruction of an *histoire*, that is, of a probably impossible series of events that can be imagined to have taken place previous to their narration (virtually a definition of the "epic" genres). The verbs "see," "hear," and "meet," which form the questions in the middle stanzas of "Hard Rain," are verbs of sense rather than of action as in "Lord Randall." They are verbs that contribute to the action of *apo* + *kaluptein*, that is, of the uncovering or revealing that is the basis of apocalypse. Each question calls not for the narration of events, but instead for the expression of perceptions mediated by a particular sense: "What did you see, my blue-eyed son? What did you hear . . . ? Who did you meet . . . ?" They serve only to organize the enumeration of the singer's visions, which apparently cannot be assembled into a narrative. Indeed, the different senses are not even clearly separated from each other. Synaesthesia is often used to contradict our normal sensory ordering of the world: "I *saw* ten thousand talkers whose tongues were all broken"; "*Heard* one person starve, I heard many people laughin'" (emphasis added).

This difference in the quality of the questions and answers in the two songs leads in turn to their different stanzaic structures, a difference immediately discernible to any listener, and which I have emphasized by italicizing Dylan's "additions." Listening carefully to the first stanza of each song reveals more than the simple fact that Dylan's stanza is longer than that of "Lord Randall." Actually, Dylan's stanza is of a variable and potentially infinite compass. The extra length is given to Dylan's stanza by lines inserted *between* those four lines modeled on "Lord Randall." The number of these inserted, anaphoric lines (the italicized ones in the stanza above) is not constant: the first stanza has five; the second and third, seven; the fourth, six; and the fifth, twelve. The variable number of lines imparts to the song a feeling of indeterminacy and incompleteness, as though any one of the stanzas could be prolonged indefinitely, in strict contradiction to ballad tradition, in which stanza and line length never vary. The structure of Dylan's stanza points toward the infinite, whereas the ballad stanza doubles back on itself, holding both character and listener to a concrete here and now. In addition, since the individual images never show any chronological relation to each other, the ordering of the lines appears chaotic. This randomness and lack of chronology make this part of the stanza antinarrational and hence alien to ballad tradition. The reason for the absence of narrative—for narrative is not speeded up, as Gray and Bowden maintain, but actually incoherent and hence absent in the balladic sense—is that the central lines of the song belong to a different musical tradition, that of litany, in which, as Gray himself points out, moral rather than narrative coherence is at stake.

Thus, in contrast to the impulse of most ballads to tell a coherent story with objective or "epic" distance, narrative in "Hard Rain" is sacrificed to indeterminate and highly personal imagery. The structural tension between ballad and lyric is mirrored by a conflict between the public or archetypal symbolism of the ballad and the complex, hermetic imagery shared by Revelation and modern poetry (especially, in Dylan's case, that of Arthur Rimbaud, Dylan Thomas, and T. S. Eliot). Lines like "I saw a room full of men with their hammers a bleedin' " and "I saw a black branch with blood that kept drippin'," although they sound as if they were drawn from a ballad—or from Stith Thompson—do not yield up the secret of their meaning beyond a vague feeling of impending disaster. Even images borrowed directly from the Bible are revised into a more personal idiom: the archetypal flood becomes an oxymoronic "hard rain"; the symbol of Jacob's ladder is distorted by being superimposed onto the image of the Flood, as mentioned earlier.

Hence anaphora, not plot, relates the central lines of the stanzas to each other. Ballads rarely use anaphora, and it is clear that here Dylan has been influenced by the Old Testament or by the genre of litany, perhaps that of

the synagogue, where "the litany or the congregational prayers of suppli-
cation and intercession, especially on fast days, from time immemorial,
have been used as important media of musical and religious expression."[20]
Dylan may have also drawn on a knowledge of African-American religious
music. Indeed, the call-response structure of most litany has been preserved in the binary rhetorical structure of many of these interior lines —
except in the last stanza, which presents a marked variation in many other
areas as well. The relation between hemistichs is often one of opposition:
"I met a white man / who walked a black dog"; "I heard one person starve
/ I heard many people laughin'." Often the second half of the line shocks
through violent contrast with the first: "I saw a newborn baby / with wild
wolves all around it"; "I met a young woman / whose body was burning."
Occasionally, there is simple parallelism: "Where black is the color, where
none is the number." In each case, however, rather than ballad lines,
which give a single, complete thought (those of "Lord Randall" are
typical), these lines are really two half-lines. These two half-lines are in
dialogue; they depend upon each other, just as the liturgist's call and the
congregation's response together constitute a line of litany.

The genre of litany contrasts with the ballad's characteristics of stanzaic
construction and narrative impersonality. As Michael Gray has noted,
referring however only to the content of the song, "the actual tale which is
told in answer to the traditional question takes place on an altogether
different plane of reality from that of its source."[21] Accordingly, the musical
structure of "Hard Rain" is also split, working as "noise" against the
closed form of the ballad. Though each line receives four three-beat
measures and (in the first version) three instrumental measures, the song's
harmonic structure echoes its textual organization in clearly differentiating
the outer, ballad-like lines of each stanza from its central ones of litany.
The song is one of the few early Dylan pieces to show a clearly identifiable
functional harmony. Beginning on the tonic, it touches the subdominant
briefly on "blue-eyed," begins again with the tonic, and moves to the
dominant on "young one." At this point the listener can feel the distance
from the tonic and the urge to return there. But it is precisely at this point
that litany begins, with each line now receiving its own separate cadence
(IV–V–I). The repeated cadences emphasize the isolation of each line from
the others. Rather than work together to form, through the building and
release of harmonic tension, a single musical structure, each line becomes

20. Eric Werner, *The Sacred Bridge* (New York: Columbia University Press, 1959), 26.
21. Gray, *Song and Dance Man*, 158.

a kind of separate song, not interacting with the others, but enclosed within the frame of the opening fourteen measures, which leaves us harmonically suspended. Indeed, the seemingly endless repetition of the same three-chord sequence works to negate its harmonic function, making it instead into a kind of ostinato. Only the final two lines resolve the harmonic tension created in the first two. There each repetition of "hard" receives a new chord, in the sequence I–V–I–IV. Then the final "rain" is broken into two syllables, the first on the tonic and the second on the dominant, before the line falls to the tonic. Altogether, then, each stanza has the following harmonic structure:

> I   IV
> Oh, what did you see, my blue-eyed son?
>
> I   V [suspension]
> Oh, what did you see, my darling young one?
>
> IV   V   I [cadences]
> *I saw a newborn baby with wild wolves all around it,* [etc.]
>
>   I   V   I   IV
> And it's a hard, and it's a hard, it's a hard, and it's a hard,
>
>   I   V   I [resolution]
> And its a hard ra-ain's a-gonna fall.

As in the music so in the text: the first and last two lines collectively provide the overarching structure and the sense of a beginning and end, whereas each middle line is autonomous, seeming to burst the confines of the stanza as a whole. In listening to these middle lines, time itself seems to stop, or at least to lose its linear progression, to bend back upon itself like a snake biting its tail.

Music, its rhythms founded on those of the human heartbeat, expresses time. Although the words in "Hard Rain" convey the immensity of the singer's journey ("ten thousand miles," "twelve misty mountains"), they do not mention its duration. Time's "image" is given instead through the conflict between the song's two opposing musical structures: one linear (functional harmony), the other cyclical (ostinato), as discussed above. As Wilfrid Mellers has written, these two vastly different structures, which characterize modern Western and "primitive" folk music respectively, carry within them what we may describe as two radically different ideologies. (Neither of these cosmologies is in itself ideological; rather, ideology lies in one view's repression of another through the creation of musical genres):

> [Folk] tunes . . . have little sense of temporality; far from trying to "get somewhere," they live in an existential present, affirming our identity with Nature, even with the Cosmos, cradling us on the bosom of the unconscious deep, winging us into the air. They either induce acceptance—of "fate," of what life does *to* us—or offer some kind of religious sublimation. . . .
>
> The distinction between this music and more modern "Western" hymn, march and ballad is crucial. They exist in Time: both rhythmically, since metrically unitary pulse is as regularly time-dominated as a pendulum, and also harmonically. . . . Unlike earlier monodic incantations, they do not transcend the World, the Flesh and the Devil but rather attempt to control—in physiological time to repress—them by an imposition of the human will, through which alone we hope to evade chaos.[22]

Dylan's modern "refashioning" of "Lord Randall" is a return to a more primitive musical form that actually predates the ballad and its forms of temporality, both musical and narrative. The ballad "Lord Randall" is profoundly about human time, as we hear a man about to die. The words and music of its inserted litanies make "Hard Rain" transcend such temporality and its mimetic propensities. In "Hard Rain" Dylan tropes the folk movement's need for narrative and concrete political action by moving his folk composition back into the realm of disconnected images, litany, and ostinato more appropriate to religious and emotional expression. However, the absence of temporal references in the first four stanzas makes their sudden introduction in the last stanza immediately noticeable. It is no accident that in the final stanza the singer, by finally creating narrative, simultaneously creates himself as a temporal being. It is to that crucial final stanza that we now turn.

In "Lord Randall," as in most ballads, the singer is a "third person," remaining in the background to sing both parts (here mother and son) with equal dispassion. Indeed, an important performance characteristic of the ballad is precisely the invariance and dispassion of the singing style, which becomes in Dylan's 1963 performance a seemingly pessimistic

---

22. Wilfrid Mellers, "God, Modality and Meaning," *Popular Music* 1 (1981): 144. So too Wole Soyinka: "Traditional thought operates, not a linear conception of time but a cyclic reality." *Myth, Literature and the African World* (London: Cambridge University Press, 1976), 10.

monotony.[23] However, in "Hard Rain" the singer becomes the central character. If "Hard Rain" is a portrait of the singer, what are his characteristics and his actions? Does he perish as Lord Randall does? Most critics, ignoring the temporal and allusive complexities of the final stanza, ignoring the fact that the singer himself hesitates, have answered this question with an unhesitating "yes." Aidan Day, for example, feels that "Knowledge that the rain will fall does not . . . exempt the singer from submergence"; the song "identifies no ground to survive the deluge."[24] For Bowden, "Dylan's narrator is a Christlike figure, martyred in the end. . . . If this narrator had started singing sooner, without worrying quite so much about exact facts and a perfect performance . . . perhaps he would still be speaking out from atop the ocean . . . just like Jesus."[25] In fact, as the song sublimates politics within apocalypse, narrative within litany, and time within the eternal, it also sublimates pessimism within creativity and death within art.

If the first stanza has identified the singer as a *poeta vates* who has made a supernatural or catabatic journey and lived to tell about it, and the next three stanzas relate his visions, the final stanza changes the function of the singer to that of prophet, even of savior, as the "decisive action" of ballad tradition is transformed into the act of singing itself—that third, self-referential meaning of "hard rain." The fourth stanza returns us to the temporal realm as the realm of performance. Hence, it is only in this final stanza, where it becomes obvious that singer and visionary are one, that for the first time a narrative begins to form, a narrative given in the future tense, responding to the question "What'll you do now?" Even this narrative (and the answer to the interlocutor's last question) is suspended in favor of a short series of descriptive metaphors beginning with "where":

23. My use of "dispassion" here derives from Bertrand Bronson's observation that in the ballad "the relatively impassive outlines of a folk-tune suggest no latent shades of verbal meaning. Psychological implication, innuendo, irony cannot be heard in the straight rendition of a genuine folk-singer. . . . [The] almost marmoreal inviolability of the ballad as traditionally sung subdues insinuations and forbids intimacy. Suggestive inflections of stated meaning, even broadly ironic, find no foothold on this smooth surface" (1:x–xi). This puts balladry at the opposite end of the scale from genres such as blues, flamenco, or gospel, in which inflection, nuance, and the passionate involvement of the singer-narrator with what is sung (expressed through melismata, differential phrasing, etc.) can be more meaningful than whatever narrative there happens to be. And it is no accident that the latter genres have a much less rigid differentiation between individual songs. The individual song in flamenco is often ephemeral, constructed for the moment out of the conventions and the imagination and passion (not the memory) of the singer. Though blues and flamenco can be roughly classed by musical structure or theme, ballads are so individualized and fixed as to be capable of numeric classification.

24. Aiden Day, *Jokerman* (Basil Blackwell: Oxford, 1989), 90–91.

25. Bowden, *Performed Literature*, 14, 19.

I'm a-goin' back out 'fore the rain starts a-fallin',
I'll walk to the depths of the deepest black forest,
Where the people are many and their hands are all empty,
Where the pellets of poison are flooding their waters,
Where the home in the valley meets the damp dirty prison,
Where the executioner's face is always well hidden,
Where hunger is ugly, where souls are forgotten,
Where black is the color, where none is the number,
And I'll tell it and think it and speak it and breathe it,
And reflect it from the mountain so all souls can see it,
Then I'll stand on the ocean until I start sinkin',
But I'll know my song well before I start singin'
And it's a hard, and it's a hard, it's a hard, and it's a hard,
And it's a hard rain's a-gonna fall.

> (*Lyrics* 60)

One notes here again the absence of any specific reference to nuclear holocaust or to geopolitical concerns. Instead, lines such as "the people are many and their hands are all empty, / Where the pellets of poison are flooding their waters, / Where the home in the valley meets the damp dirty prison" are metonyms for problems of hunger, poverty, environmental disaster, and social injustice. Once the actual narrative begins, it presents the song's most complex problems in interpretation. The *poeta vates* will "tell *it* and think *it* and speak *it* and breathe *it*." To what can the pronoun "it" refer here, since it has no antecedent? "It" refers to the rain, to the revelation, to the Gospel, and, most centrally, to the song itself, as we apprehend in the paradoxical deferral conveyed by "its" final line. The critics who have read "until I start sinkin'" as indicating the death of the singer have neglected the grammar of the sentence: the sinking occurs in a subordinate clause opening with "until," which suspends the act of sinking. The sentence is as tautological as faith.

The idea of standing on the ocean is a reference not to Christ, as Bowden assumes, but to Peter, who walked on the water as long as his faith held him up: "But when he saw the wind boisterous, he was afraid; and beginning to sink, he cried, saying, Lord, save me. And immediately Jesus stretched forth his hand, and caught him, saying unto him, O thou of little faith, why didst thou doubt?" (Matthew 14:30–31).[26] Peter,

26. I am indebted to Ernst Schürer of Pennsylvania State University for pointing out this allusion.

Christ's favorite and his denier, is a more ambiguous and appropriate role for the singer than that of Jesus. In a move parallel to his invocation of political song as an impossible ideal in "Song to Woody," Dylan here invokes faith through an example of its failure. We might say that Dylan plays Peter to Guthrie's Christ. Only "hard travelin' " can allow him to know his song well enough to sing it. A message of faith is being preached, but it is a thoroughly modernist faith in art rather than in either God or politics. At the same time, however, the invocation of Christ through the biblical allusion foils our pessimistic readings of the song's ending. The story of Peter also encapsulates "Hard Rain's" split textual and musical structure into a single brief parable. And like those opposing structures, Peter's story reveals two kinds of time, sacred and profane. Peter's faith places him within sacred time, in which the physical laws dependent on the passage of profane time are suspended. The end of his faith, like the end of the song, means release back into a world where history can have an end, where souls can indeed sink and be forgotten.

Dylan also plays with time in the line "I'll know my song well before I start singin'." The listener is confronted in that final line with the fact that the real song has not yet begun. He must ask himself what further knowledge is needed, and what differences there would be between "Hard Rain" and the imagined song of songs. On one level, Dylan is again recalling the theme of "Song to Woody," the notion that he "can't sing enough." He is referring to his own "Hard Rain" as noise, as the tuning up before the real playing. Yet this paradox, that the song we are hearing is not the real song, also makes sense both within Jewish mystical tradition, in which God's real name is forever hidden behind a screen of false names and the one pure language is palpable only in the interstices of human tongues, and within the apocalyptic tradition, which can remain vital only because the "last things" it predicts never arrive. Most people are forced to choose between believing in the apocalypse either as a real catastrophe occurring in fixable historical time (the "Lutheran" position), or as an infinitely repeatable occurrence within each person's soul (the "Augustinian" interpretation). The artist, however, may synthesize rather than choose, just as he may synthesize tradition and noise, ballad and litany. But did Dylan ever get to "know his song well?"

II

The theme of redemption through art broached in "Hard Rain" should have been fair warning to Dylan's fans (many of whom came out of the overtly political period of folk music) that Dylan was in the business of vision rather than of politics. The "Lutheran" apocalyptics of the political left became ever more hopelessly at odds with Dylan's increasingly Augustinian concept of salvation. As George Monteiro puts it, Dylan increasingly "discovered that apocalyptic imagery said more about an individual's soul than about what happens to the physical world." Monteiro has seen these conflicting visions of apocalypse as motivating the generic instability of entire albums by Dylan. He writes: "The protest songs and the songs which can be called apocalyptic songs . . . which prophesied and described violent destruction and some sort of eschatological revelation . . . were to take turns at dominating individual albums. *Freewheelin'* can be seen as an announcement of balanced possibilities and as a presentation of thematic concerns. But the album which followed it, *The Times They Are A-Changin'*, was his most striking protest album."[27]

It is true that several of the songs on the latter album are journalistic, focusing on current events rather than on future ones. From the point of view of our analysis, however, it is more accurate to say that *The Times They Are A-Changin'* held the poles of dialogue and narrative, of ballad and Bible apart.[28] "Boots of Spanish Leather" is a typical, nonpolitical ballad, consisting almost entirely of dialogue between lovers. "The Hour When the Ship Comes In," however, is a true millennial narrative of the triumph of good over evil. "The Times They Are A-Changin' " similarly locates itself within the prophetic genre, though here the dialogue is with the listener, as Dylan constantly uses the pronoun "you" and verbs in the command form. Like "Hard Rain," this song constantly shifts between representations of real current events and more archetypal images and biblical language. Thus, the vaguely political "Come senators, congressmen / Please heed the call / Don't stand in the doorway / Don't block up the hall" gives way in the final stanza to the explicitly apocalyptic "The line it is drawn / The curse it is cast / The slow one now / Will later be fast" (*Lyrics* 91). Thus, whereas the levels of secular history and apocalypse were merged in "Hard Rain" through polysemy and the blending of musical structures from different traditions, here the song moves from one level to the other as it unfolds.

Degenhardt alludes to this 1964 song in "Nostalgia" (note the English spelling, the German word is *Nostalgie*), written in 1972, which looks back on 1968 with that sense of the loss of radical zeal familiar to ex-revolutionaries everywhere:

27. George Monteiro, "Dylan in the Sixties," *South Atlantic Quarterly* 73 (1974): 165.
28. Bob Dylan, *The Times They Are A-Changin'* (Columbia CS 8905, 1963); *Lyrics* 91–105.

Die Trauer meiner Klasse,
die mir manchmal noch so süß schmeckt,
dabei denke ich
an euch und mich
und an die, die diesen Krampf nicht
ausgehalten haben und die
losgeschossen haben,
und nicht nur auf sich.
The times they are a-changin,
und die Trauer
schläft in der Gitarre.
Weck sie nicht mit deinem Schrei.

(The sorrow of my class,
which still often tastes so sweet to me,
makes me think
of you and me
and of those who couldn't stand
this noise and who
started shooting,
and not just at themselves.
The times they are a-changin',
and sorrow
sleeps in the guitar.
Don't wake it with your shouting.)[29]

I have translated "Krampf" here as noise. The primary meaning is equivalent to the English cognate ("cramp") of a kind of convulsion that makes movement impossible. This approximates earlier, now obsolete meanings of the English "noise" (which derives from Latin "noxia," poison) and of the adjective "noisome." Like "noise," then, "Krampf" refers to a disturbance in an otherwise harmonious system. Nostalgia offers itself as an escape. The song places the feeling of nostalgia, which many might express in a personal, psychological tone, at an intersubjective and intertextual level. Consequently, whereas most nostalgia "trips" rely on the phantasmagoria created by selectively wrenching cultural artifacts out of the

29. Franz Josef Degenhardt, "Nostalgia," in *Kommt an den Tisch unter Pflaumenbäumen* (Munich: DTV, 1981), f. 90. Further citations from this unpaginated collection of Degenhardt's songs given in text by song number.

concrete social and political contexts that helped produce them, Degenhardt thinks not of such artifacts, but only of their original contexts: "Und meine heiseren Lieder, / eure scharf geschriebenen Blätter / warfen wir am Abend / auf die Strasse vom Balkon" ("And my hoarse songs, / your sharply written leaflets / in the evenings we used to throw them / from the balcony onto the street"). Degenhardt remembers not himself, but his political and artistic actions in a year when the times were indeed changing, when student revolts initiated a climate of political confrontation in Germany that would last well into the next decade.

The Adenauer era of economic recovery and political conservatism had ended in 1966 with a "Grand Coalition" between the Christian Democratic Union and the Social Democrats, which left only 10 percent of the Bundestag (parliament) in the opposition. The Social Democratic Party, to which Degenhardt belonged, no longer seemed to represent true socialism, given its cooperation with Adenauer's party. Given the absence of meaningful debate, energies for change were forced into the extraparliamentary opposition, "das Argument der Straße" ("the argument of the street") as Degenhardt put it. The word "Schrei" in "Nostalgia" alludes to the many demonstrations during this period. In 1968, the death of student Bruno Ohnesorg during one such "street argument" and the passing of repressive *Notstandsgesetze* (emergency laws) by the government provoked the final breach between West Germany's radical youth and their mentors of the economic miracle. This is the "Krampf" that caused some to start shooting (a foreshadowing of the Baader-Meinhof gang and the terror of 1977).

It was in 1968 that Degenhardt, already a famous singer, changed genres. From now on he would write songs whose use-value lay in their pamphleteering, in their throwability. In "Nostalgia," Degenhardt uses the figure of zeugma, making both "songs" and "leaflets" the objects of the verb "throw," to make clear the use-value of his songs. The line expresses the familiar Marxist idea that ideas and art are produced out of material conditions and are subject to many of the same sorts of manipulation — including "throwing" — as any other material. The conjunction of song and leaflet is metonymic for the cooperation between political radical and artist, between worker and intellectual. Degenhardt played both roles in 1968. Besides being a popular leftist singer, he also worked as a lawyer, representing radicals accused of crimes against the West German state.

Degenhardt's music in this period of political upheaval explicitly rejected the kind of song that had made him famous. Dylan had found in Woody Guthrie an unattainable model of musical and political tradition, against which his own creative talents would appear to create only noise. Degenhardt, on the other hand, growing up in postwar Germany, could only find noise in his own tradition. In one of his shortest songs (eighteen lines), "Die alten Lieder," Degenhardt made absolutely clear why *Volksmusik* could never be his musical genre. Note the images of discord in the following lines:

> Tot sind unsre Lieder,
> unsre alten Lieder.
> Lehrer haben sie zerbissen,
> Kurzbehoste sie verklampft,
> braune Horden totgeschrien,
> Stiefel in den Dreck gestampft
> (f. 51)

> (Our songs are dead,
> our old songs.
> Teachers have chewed them to bits,
> guys in short pants have mangled them on their guitars,
> brown hordes have screamed them dead,
> boots have stomped them into the mud.)

These words speak directly to the ideology of genre. The *Volkslied*—like all compounds beginning with *Volk* except the Volkswagen—has been destroyed by the use-values to which it has been put. In the classroom, in the *Wandervogel* movement,[30] and in National Socialist exercises, the *Volkslied* had functioned as a nationalistic sign, a mark of disastrous German unity. In 1960, the genres of American folk and German *Volksmusik* were incommensurable. The latter became unavailable to the uses of social criticism. The American genres of rock 'n' roll and jazz which flooded postwar Germany, however, carried their own messages of consumer capitalism and sexual freedom.

And so Degenhardt (along with Dieter Süverkrüp, Wolf Biermann, and others) created a genre that explored the detritus of both nationalism and capitalism. The models most frequently invoked by Degenhardt are non-German. He mentions his earliest musical influences as being "first of all

---

30. *Wandervogel* (lit. "wandering bird") is the name of a student movement that arose in Germany around the turn of the century. Members of this movement opposed their romantic views to the more cosmopolitan and modernist ones of their parents and mentors. In this context, the "official" songbook of the movement, Hans Breuer's collection of "authentic" German folksongs, *Der Zupfgeigenhansl* (Leipzig: Friedrich Hofmeister, 1913, with thirty-two printings by 1929), played an important role in transmitting and validating nationalist ideas.

the swing musicians. Coleman Hawkins, Fats Waller and later Bebop."[31] This jazz was almost purely instrumental. As songwriters, François Villon and Bob Dylan are most frequently alluded to in Degenhardt's music, while his early musical style derived from the French *chansonneur* George Brassens. Degenhardt's music, characterized as one of "passing tones" (*Zwischentöne*), is something of a cross between folk and jazz idiom, where text and music share the status of liminality.

Hearing Degenhardt describe his early childhood, one can see the source of this liminality. He describes himself as a "Mauergucker," (an outsider, literally a person who looks on at life while sitting on a wall). Degenhardt sat on the same wall to watch the antics of the Hitler Youth as he did to watch the Allied bombardment of Wuppertal in which thousands of people lost their lives. His parents, although totally opposed to the Nazis, did very little to fight them. Notice how the word *zwischen* also crops up in Degenhardt's description of his postwar situation: "Am sogenannten Wiederaufbau haben wir, die angehörigen meiner Zwischengeneration, auch nicht teilgenommen. Diese Zwischengeneration ist mit dem Schrecken davongekommen. Aber dieser Schrecken sitzt einigen noch heute so tief in den Gliedern, daß sie ihn nicht wegtherapieren können—wie laut sie auch schreien, brüllen, oder singen" ("We, the in-between generation, also did not help with the so-called reconstruction of Germany. This in-between generation got off with just a scare. But this scare is so deeply embedded in some of them, that they can't get rid of it through therapy—however loud they might cry, yell, or sing").[32] Here then is the origin of the *schreien* the song "Nostalgia" tries to silence. It was this in-between generation, who experienced both unrestrained fascism and unrestrained capitalism without being responsible for either, that would vent its frustration in the student revolts of the late 1960s. Similarly, the most frequent subjects of Degenhardt's early songs were powerless outcasts unable to fit themselves into the economic miracle.

A good example is one of Degenhardt's most famous songs, "Spiel nicht mit den Schmuddelkindern" ("Don't Play with the Slum Kids"), which predicted 1968 from the perspective of 1965. The refrain is made up of the anonymous imperatives of middle-class society, which tell the child protagonist: "Spiel nicht mit den Schmuddelkindern, / sing nicht ihre Lieder. /

---

31. Franz Josef Degenhardt and Matthias Altenburg, "«Ich habe mit dem Literaturbetrieb nichts zu tun und leiste mir solche Unbekümmertheiten». Franz Josef Degenhardt im Gespräch," in *Fremde Mütter, fremde Väter, fremdes Land*, ed. Matthias Altenburg (Hamburg: Konkret, 1985), 82.

32. Ibid., 78.

Geh doch in die Oberstadt, / mach's wie deine Brüder" (f. 15; "Don't play
with the slum kids, / don't sing their songs. / Go to the rich part of town, /
be successful like your brothers"). The child, who is attracted to the
bohemian life of the slums, becomes rich "aus Rache" ("out of revenge").
After an auto accident, the man begins exhibiting attributes of the *Schmud-
delkinder* such as wearing rat fur. The ending of the song is ambiguous:

> Eines Tages in aller Helle
> hat er dann ein Kind betört
> und in einen Stall gezerrt.
> Seine Leiche fand man, die im Rattenteich rumschwamm.
> Drum herum die Schmuddelkinder bliesen auf dem Kamm:
> Spiel nicht mit den Schmuddelkindern . . .
>
> (f. 15)

> (One day in broad daylight
> he seduced a child
> and dragged it into a stall.
> The body was found floating in the rat pond.
> All around it the slum kids blew on their kazoos:
> Don't play with the slum kids . . .)

Whether it was the poor child or the upper-class man who ended up dying
of his love-hate relationship with his roots, the message here is of the
violent return of the repressed. The song is almost Freudian in showing
the unstable sublimation of filth, sex, and pleasure by the "higher things"
in society: money, fast cars, socialites, and philanthropy, before the final
catastrophe. Freud's "wo Es war soll Ich werden" finds its echo in the
doings of the rich man: "Und Kaninchenställe riß er / ab. An ihre Stelle
ließ er / Gärten für die Kinder bauen" ("And he demolished rabbit hutches.
/ In their place he had playgrounds built for the children"). The social
costs of the economic miracle, hidden from everyone's view, can only
surface in this kind of "accident" or in Degenhardt's liminal genres.

As in Dylan's "Hard Rain," music itself becomes an important theme in
this song. The music of the slum kids is of the direst simplicity. Their basic
instrument is the homemade kazoo, that is, paper held up against a comb.
Their musical genre is that of "rat-catcher songs" (*Rattenfängerlieder*). There
is a prohibition against participating in these musical forms; thus, their
enforced substitution by the higher genres: "Und statt Rattenfängerweisen
/ mußte er das Largo geigen" ("And instead of rat-catcher tunes / he was

forced to play the largo on the violin"). In becoming rich he learns to love "Musik, / blond und laut und honigdick" ("music, / blond and loud and thick as honey"). But the "noise" of the rat-catcher genre has a social immediacy the largo lacks: as we have seen in the last stanza, their singing is direct, spontaneous commentary on whatever situations they are confronted with, and they sing "voller Hohn" ("full of scorn"). The social awareness and social criticism represented in their lyric is missing from the largos and the honeyed music. Indeed, it is not clear that the sophisticated genres of the rich man lend themselves to words at all.

Degenhardt accompanied himself on solo guitar for "Spiel nicht mit den Schmuddelkindern," as he did for almost all his early songs, and the rollicking, simple tune is based on the interval of the minor third (C to E-flat). It was necessary that the musical accompaniment for these songs also be detritus, neither folk nor classical, a nongenre like the prose poem, a music of passing tones. The "Rattenfängerlied" is an image of Degenhardt's own early musical style: acute in its power of observation and full of scorn, and constructed from the most basic musical elements. This genre, interestingly, has yet to receive a name, though the creators of it are referred to as "Liedermacher." It is not, as mentioned above, "folk." The term "politisches Lied," by contrast, refers more to the party-line creations of Hans Eisler and Bertolt Brecht. Degenhardt's own term, "zeitbezogenes Lied" ("timely song"), is to my knowledge not in general use. Degenhardt stresses once again this genre's "in-between" status: "Das zeitbezogene Lied wird damit heute so etwas, wie das missing-link, das fehlende Glied zwischen Nieder und Hoch, U- und E-Kultur" ("The timely song today is becoming something like a missing link, the missing part between high and low, the underground and educated cultures").[33]

"Ein schönes Lied" of 1965 is one of the best examples of Degenhardt's "Zwischentöne." Like "Spiel nicht mit den Schmuddelkindern," "Ein schönes Lied" is self-referential. In this song, the music (again, solo guitar accompaniment) wanders from complex chord to complex chord in arpeggios, just as the story wanders into an endless expansion of meaning. The story begins with obvious references to Vietnam and napalm: "Nah bei Quang Nai, fand / ein gebranntes Kind die Hand / eines Generals" (f. 17; "Near Quang Nai / a burned child found the hand / of a general"). The boy trades the stones of the general's ring for a boat and sails "zu jenem Land, / da riecht die Erde nie verbrannt, / und jeden Tag, da gibt es viele Hände Reis" ("to that land, / where the earth never smells burnt, / and

33. Ibid., 86–87.

each day there are many handfuls of rice"). The narrative ends by simply reporting the dream of earthly happiness of the boy tossed in a boat that may never arrive at its destination.

Despite the obvious references to Vietnam, the only political position taken up by the singer concerns aesthetics itself, what "ein schönes Lied" might be:

> Komm, sing uns mal ein schönes Lied
> komm, sing uns mal ein schönes Lied,
> eines, wo man sich so richtig gut nachfühlt,
> eins das nicht in Schmutzgefühlen wühlt,
> wohl makaber, aber unterkühlt,
> vertraut, verspielt,
> verspielt, vertraut
> und nicht zu laut.
>
> (f. 17)

> (Come, sing us a beautiful song,
> come, sing us a beautiful song,
> one where we feel so good after hearing it,
> one that doesn't wallow in prurience,
> macabre maybe, but laid-back,
> intimate, playful
> playful, intimate,
> and not too loud.)

Though the song begins in A minor, when it reaches the line about feeling good, a cadence on F–G–C moves it to the relative major key of C, and it stays with a major "feeling" until the last word of the stanza. The ambiguity between major and minor reproduces the conflicting demands for the song, which in turn produce a narrative that scatters its political images in the kaleidoscope of a *Märchen*-like narrative. The musical "noise" that causes the song's tonality to waver is equivalent to the "noise" in the narrative, which disturbingly confuses dream and horrid reality. An example of "noise" in this song is Degenhardt's use of enjambment, which breaks up sentences between musical phrases, thus "helping" the listener lose the narrative thread. The singer plays a frustrating game with his audience, alluding to other genres of music ("*un*schöne Lieder," we might call them) which do not disguise political reality in a beautiful dream. According to the opening stanzas, Degenhardt is merely responding to the wishes of his middle-class listeners (he tells them to prepare a gin and tonic, for example) for beautiful music. After all, "Schein und Scherz, / massiert das Herz" ("Illusions and jokes / massage the heart").

In the late 1960s, the outcasts and the powerless began to take on a clearer shape. For the first time since 1933, class struggle became a subject for discussion and dispute in Germany. Since the nonsystemic had suddenly become part of the system, Degenhardt gave up the idea of passing tones. And so in that year, Degenhardt wrote a song called "Manchmal sagen die Kumpanen" ("Sometimes My Comrades Tell Me"), which reviews his previous work against the standards of the present in musical aesthetic terms. *Zwischentöne* (passing tones) are now the target:

> Manchmal sagen die Kumpanen
> jetzt, was soll denn dieser Scheiß?
> wo sind dein Zwischentöne?
> Du malst bloß noch schwarz und weiß.
> Na schön, sag ich, das ist ja richtig,
> aber das ist jetzt nicht wichtig.
> Zwischentöne sind bloß Krampf
> im Klassenkampf.
>
> (f. 60)

> (Sometimes my comrades tell me
> now, what is this shit?
> where are your passing tones?
> now you just paint everything in black and white.
> OK, I answer, you are quite right
> but that is not important now.
> Passing tones are just noise
> in the class struggle.)

The last two lines then provide a continuing refrain for the song. Here we see that *Krampf* really can mean "noise," since Degenhardt applies the word to most of his previous songs. In doing so he reverses the normal process of music, which is to incorporate noise and dissonance into the system. Here what had been harmonious becomes unacceptable. And the actual noises in this song could not be more different from those in "Nostalgia." Degenhardt's meaning is clear enough: musical and textual ambiguities hinder the direct communication necessary in political situations. In referring to "Zwischentöne" as the generic marker of his earlier cabaret-styled music, Degenhardt denies the constructive role of musical ambiguity.

After 1968 the mild, jazz-flavored discords virtually disappear from Degenhardt's songs, which become either simplistically diatonic ("Moritat Nr. 218" [f. 101]), or harshly discordant ("Das Ereignis am Mondfalter-fluß" [f. 62]), or at times dissolve simply into a chant or monologue spoken over an obbligato ("Vatis Argumente" [f. 87]). The music of "Manchmal sagen die Kumpanen" is a good example. The song is unambiguously in the key of B minor with tonic, subdominant, and dominant guitar chords laying down the harmonic structure. The tune is close to a chant, first of all because of its almost unbroken string of eighth notes—dotted rhythms occur at only three places—and, second, because the melody consists of unbroken strings of a repeated tone: first B, then D, then B again. The second and third lines are constructed over a simple chromatic scale: F#–G–F#–E. The impression of the song as a whole is that of a hammer, of a hard rain constantly being "thrown" at the audience. (*Hammerlied*, "hammer-song") is a kenning that appears frequently in Degenhardt's novel about his artistic profession, *Der Liedermacher*.)[34] The lights are now full up, the imbibing of a gin and tonic to heighten listening pleasure is unthinkable. Yet, though the crooked has now been made straight, what remains is the self-reflexivity of Degenhardt's text. He is still singing about singing, and specifically about the political use-value of different genres of song:

> Und der Dichter, der poetisch
> protestiert in seinem Lied,
> bringt den Herrschenden ein
>   Ständchen
> und erhöht ihren (und seinen) Profit.
> Protestieren ist bloß Krampf
> im Klassenkampf.
>
> (And the artist, who poetically
> protests in his song,
> is singing a serenade to the ruling class
> and raising their [and his] profits. . . .
> Protest songs are just noise
> in the class struggle.)

34. Franz Josef Degenhardt, *Der Liedermacher* (Munich: Bertelsmann, 1982). See in particular the last chapter, which describes in detail all the necessary components of a *Hammerlied*, including its political relevance.

The lines that complain of Degenhardt's new tendency to paint things black and white echo almost word for word those of Bob Dylan in "My Back Pages." "My Back Pages," which appeared on Dylan's fourth album, *Another Side of Bob Dylan,* is the functional equivalent of Degenhardt's song, opening a direct dialogue with his critics and fans, but it moved Dylan in the opposite direction. Here, the notion that life can be painted in black and white is given the lie: "Lies that life was black and white / Spoke from my skull" (*Lyrics* 139).

III

Both "My Back Pages" and "Manchmal sagen die Kumpanen" are programmatic for their composers' later careers, which move farther and farther away from each other on the generic spectrum. As Dylan's vision became more personal, he found the musical structures we have been discussing to be inadequate for its expression. Gradually he returned to the music of his youth, to rock 'n' roll, and then became one of the creators of rock. In the dissonance of rock music Dylan found again the element of "noise" that made his art distinctive. In July 1966 a motorcycle accident caused Dylan to disappear from public view. In conversations with Dylan's brother, journalist Toby Thompson discovered that Dylan had not been seriously injured in the accident and that the reasons for his seclusion were psychological and professional rather than medical.[35] The album *John Wesley Harding,* which represented Dylan's return to the public eye in 1968, is a self-portrait and reflection on the two earlier phases of his career.[36] Neither folk nor rock, *John Wesley Harding* is something different again, combining elements of several genres. In the song "All Along The Watchtower" on this album, Dylan returned to the genre of the apocalyptic ballad.

This song, which like the album as a whole seeks the "middle ground" between folk and rock, also presents the two opposing images of the singer—the joker and the thief—which characterize the first two stages of Dylan's career. It also represents a return to the blending of ballad and Bible we examined in "Hard Rain":

35. Thompson, *Positively Main Street,* 84–85.
36. Bob Dylan, *John Wesley Harding* (Columbia KCS 9604, 1968).

"There must be some way out of here," said the joker to the thief,
"There's too much confusion, I can't get no relief.
Businessmen, they drink my wine, plowmen dig my earth,
None of them along the line know what any of it is worth."

"No reason to get excited," the thief, he kindly spoke,
"There are many here among us who feel that life is but a joke.
But you and I, we've been through that, and this is not our fate,
So let us not talk falsely now, the hour is getting late."

(*Lyrics* 252)

The archetypal possibilities for interpreting these figures of the joker and the thief recall the polysemy of such phrases as "hard rain." They are the two men who died with Christ, one of whom mocked, the other of whom believed. They are also, however, the two sides of Dylan's art—the political and the poetical, the striving for a historical millennium and the acceptance of primordial chaos—engaged in a moral dialogue. The title of the album is the name of a thief of the American West, and Dylan makes of him a benevolent folk hero, a "friend to the poor," who was "never known / to hurt an honest man" (*Lyrics* 249). But inasmuch as Harding is also a self-referential figure, aspects of the joker, of indeterminacy, of noise, creep into the portrayal in lines that recall "Restless Farewell." Notice the noise of Harding's name in the telegraph wires, which however leads to no concrete information:

All across the telegraph
His name it did resound,
But no charge held against him
Could they prove.
And there was no man around
Who could track or chain him down,
He was never known
To make a foolish move.

(*Lyrics* 249)

In "Watchtower," too, this aspect of indeterminacy and "confusion" appears as the domain of the thief, not the joker. But if Harding made no foolish move, so too the most striking aspect of the joker is his inability to laugh. Indeed, the first words he speaks, "There must be some way out of here," are stolen from the discourse of desperados rather than clowns. In a similar surprise, the concern of the joker is entirely with profit and loss as he speaks of his economic exploitation. Conversely, it is the thief who refers to life as a joke, who is kind and relaxed, who demands honesty. The reversal of roles indicates a world turned upside down, a biblical trope found both in Psalm 146 and in the same Book of Isaiah (24:1–2) which forms the basis of the third stanza of this song. The idea of reversal is a recurrent one in Dylan; we have seen it in "The Times They Are A-Changin'," in which "the slow one now / will later be fast."

As in a ballad, our interest is focused upon the linguistic exchange between these two opposing figures. Unlike the realism of the ballad, however, the dialogue between joker and thief has interest only inasmuch as it can be read allegorically, as an exchange between unbelief and faith, between politics and religion, in short between the two poles of Dylan's career. Also, whereas most ballads begin with a stanza of narrative or otherwise localize the speakers of dialogue, Dylan has left such an "establishing shot" for the last stanza. Our vista suddenly widens, and the claustrophobia of the first line is reversed as we see the two speakers on horseback approaching a city:

> All along the watchtower, princes kept the view
> While all the women came and went, barefoot servants, too.
>
> Outside in the distance a wildcat did growl,
> Two riders were approaching, the wind began to howl.
>
> (*Lyrics* 252)

Nearly every image of this final stanza derives from Isaiah's prophecy of the fall of Babylon. As befits a ballad, Dylan's narrative is dry and unemotional, his singing uninflected. The anguish the prophet Isaiah feels in viewing catastrophe has been transferred to the joker. The vision is also given as dialogue in Dylan's Old Testament source, though the participants in the dialogue are not specified:

> Prepare the table, watch in the watchtower, eat, drink: arise, ye princes, and anoint the shield . . . And he cried, A lion: My lord, I stand continually upon the watchtower in the daytime, and I am set in my ward whole nights:
> And behold, here cometh a chariot of men, with a couple of horsemen. And he answered and said, Babylon is fallen, is fallen.
> (Isaiah 21:5, 8–9)

In reshaping this text, Dylan has expanded the image of the lion—which incidentally is a misreading of the Hebrew and has been eliminated from the Revised Standard Version—into a harbinger of doom that parallels the thief's pronouncement that the hour is late. Isaiah's vision of Babylon destroyed by a great army, for which the chariot and horsemen are synecdoches, has been replaced by the more subtle invasion of chaos and anomie implied in the pair of riders. The dialogue between these two figures contrasts sharply with the silence of the city and with its rigid hierarchization, which, this song suggests, will help speed its fall. Social injustice, mentioned in the abstract by the joker, is demonstrated by the presence of servants and by the distinctly secondary position of the women. (Indeed, according to the punctuation, "barefoot servants" could be merely an appositive for women.) Of course the name of "Babylon" is left out; the parallel to Christ's entering Jerusalem merely provides another paradigm for a liberating event. The listener is left to imagine what civilization this is; to many of those in 1968 who had eagerly bought the first Dylan release in several years, Establishment America readily came to mind. Though the coming cataclysm is frightening, it is also a sign of relief. The anxiety this song provokes is due not to the prediction of cataclysm, but rather to the seemingly insurmountable distance between the riders and the city they are approaching.

For like "Hard Rain," this song invokes a curious deferral. Time here is cyclical. Both Paul Williams and Michael Gray have noticed the extraordinary difference wrought by the unexpected placement of the final stanza. Williams even describes the song as a Möbius strip:

> [The song's] ends have been twisted, and taped together. In another universe, Dylan would begin: "All along the watchtower, princes kept the view. . . . Two riders were approaching, the wind began to howl." The second and third verses would then be conversation between the two riders, the Joker and the Thief; and "let us not talk falsely now" would close the song with comfort.
>
> Because indeed, "There must be some way out of here"—what more natural reaction, caught on a möbius strip?[37]

Dylan has changed the linear narrative of the ballad into a cycle and hence posits the apocalyptic end "as lying in the very *endlessness* of the nightmare vision offered."[38] Jerusalem is never entered, and Babylon never falls. The

---

37. Paul Williams, "Tom Paine Himself: Understanding Dylan," in *Outlaw Blues* (New York: Dutton, 1969), 76.

38. Gray, *Song and Dance Man*, 211.

joker and thief (and all they stand for) are doomed to an infinite repetition of their dialogue, trapped continually before the gates of the city just as we are trapped in a perpetual nostalgia, in a history never able to turn the corner on millennium. This endlessness is the negative image of "I'll stand on the ocean / until I start sinkin'." If "Hard Rain" presented us with a song not yet sung, "Watchtower" represents a song from which there is no exit. Such a reversal is indicative of the change in the political climate within which Dylan was operating. The hope of the early 1960s had given way to bitterness and protest, largely over the Vietnam War. The dialectic between "inside" and "outside" that we see in this song had a special resonance for listeners in 1968, as the chaotic Democratic Convention took place in Chicago, and the nation's attention was split between the political princes trying to preserve their hierarchy on the inside and the jokers and thieves being plowed under by the police on the outside.

As in "Hard Rain," the endlessness of "Watchtower" is not only histori-cal, but also refers to the peculiar way in which music depends on iterability to convey meaning. The very concept of owning a record album implies that music requires repeated listenings. Self-reflexivity comes here in the subtle form of analogy between cyclical history and the repeated turnings of a record album.[39] The most convincing evidence of Dylan's intentions here is the music itself. Whereas harmonic music (like most narrative) moves through increasing tension to final resolution, this song merely repeats the same chords (A minor–G–F–G) over and over as an ostinato. The lack of a tonal center for the song causes the final harmonica solo to end on an arbitrary note, terminating the music but not bringing it to rest. Dylan was able to find release from this vision ten years later by bracketing it under the rubric of Old Testament, which would be subli-mated by the New. Dylan, trapped in history, found a temporary exit by converting from Judaism to Christianity and by moving from apocalyptic ballad to apocalyptic gospel song.

IV

"Born-Again Bob" is the name often given to Dylan in the period from 1979 to 1983 when he began attending fundamentalist Christian Bible

39. That Dylan makes such references to his medium is shown most clearly in the title of a later album, *Blood on the Tracks* (Columbia PC 33235). On the literal level the title invokes the quintessential American disaster, the train wreck; on the metaphoric level it describes the pain involved in recording the "tracks" for the album itself.

classes and producing what can only be described as gospel music, that is, music whose use-value is the production of religious exaltation. In the first of these "Christian" albums, *Slow Train Coming,* the engaged singer of "Hard Rain" has returned, but the persona has changed from prophet to preacher.[40] The dialogue between believer and nonbeliever found in "Watchtower" has also returned, but it is now a dialogue between singer and audience. The use of Scripture has returned, but the allusions are now mainly to the New Testament. Apocalypse has returned, but for the first time since "The Hour When the Ship Comes In" it is accompanied by millennium. "When He Returns," the final song on *Slow Train,* exhibits a musical structure strikingly different from those of "Hard Rain" and "All Along the Watchtower": the piano (the only accompanying instrument) opens the song with a repeated sequence of four simple chords: subdominant, tonic, first inversion of the tonic, and dominant. This sequence is paradigmatic; it sets down the harmonic structure of the song like the foundations of a building. Similarly, the first stanza of the text presents contrasting images of endurance and evanescence:

> The iron hand it ain't no match for the iron rod,
> The strongest wall will crumble and fall to a mighty God.
> For all those who have eyes and all those who have ears
> It is only He who can reduce me to tears.
> Don't you cry and don't you die and don't you burn
> For like a thief in the night, He'll replace wrong with right
> When He returns.
>
> (*Lyrics* 437)

In their study of Dylan's gospel music, Alberto Gonzalez and John J. Makay have rightly singled out the music of "When He Returns" for detailed analysis. Their term for "cadence" is "resolved structure," and they note its effect in this song: "The resolved structure of the C–G chords provides a fitting context for the 'wall,' a source of apparent strength. . . . These major chords, especially majestic on the piano, come to a solid resolution which works to confirm the conclusion of the lyric. The lyric gains credibility from the beautiful assent of this 'second opinion.' "[41] The phrase "When He returns" is also framed by such a plagal cadence (that is, V–IV–I rather than the "true" cadence V–I). Significantly, this harmonic sequence is also called church cadence because it is used so often in hymns. It is, for example, a familiar setting for "Amen" during service. Most of the other lines end with this same cadence, reinforcing the durability of this vision, which anchors the song as firmly in traditional hymnody as its words anchor it in the tradition of the sermon.

If the generic status of this song seems more stable than that of the previous ones, so too the interpretation of apocalypse has become more straightforward:

Truth is an arrow and the gate is narrow that it passes through,
He unleashed His power at an unknown hour that no one knew. . . .

Will I ever learn that there'll be no peace, that the war won't cease
Until He returns?

Of every earthly plan that be known to man, He is unconcerned,
He's got plans of His own to set up His throne
When He returns.

(Lyrics 437)

A simple listing of the nouns in this text could serve as a matrix of biblical typology: the "iron rod," the "wall," the "thief in the night," Christ's "power," the "narrow gate," the "wilderness," a "crown," a "throne"—all these are important to the story of Christ Redeemer. Yet though the sheer number of allusions tends to confirm the singer's orthodoxy, Dylan has not abandoned his tendency to personalize biblical typology. In the first line, for example, the iron rod recalls Revelation 19:13, 15: "He was clothed with a vesture dipped in blood: and his name is called The Word of God. . . . And out of his mouth goeth a sharp sword, that with it he should smite the nations; and he shall rule them with a rod of iron." This iron rod, the symbol of spiritual and, more significant, of scriptural power, is contrasted with the iron hand of secular political rule, that rigidity which characterized the city in "Watchtower." The phrase "iron hand" does not occur in the Bible, so that the very phrasing of the contrast also presents a conflict between sacred and secular genres. It occurs in the first line of the second and third stanzas as well. Christ's metaphor of the narrow gate is combined with that of truth as an arrow, a favorite image of Dylan's since "Restless Farewell."[42] In the third stanza, an archetypal invocation of

42. The image first appears in "Restless Farewell," in lines that immediately precede the epigraph for this essay: "And the dirt of gossip blows into my face, / And the dust of rumors covers me. / But if the arrow is straight / And the point is slick, / It can pierce through dust no

Golgotha is followed by the startling command to "take off your mask": "Surrender your crown on this blood-stained ground, take off your mask." The word "mask" does not occur in the Bible, but is frequently found both in Dylan's work and, as I indicated at the beginning of this chapter, in critical assessments of his career as the assumption of various personae.[43] Yet in mixing the secular with the sacred, the personal with the scriptural, Dylan keeps with the tradition of the gospel genre, whose own generic instability (the exact borders with hymn and spiritual are hard to define) has resided in its secularized religiosity, which has drawn the genre away from the strictness of psalmody and toward the vernacular and the personal mode of expression.[44]

The rhetorical structure of this song shows a remarkable balance between dialogue (this time between singer and audience) and narrative. As in "Hard Rain" this narration is fragmented, but the numerous allusions make it possible for a listener to fill in the gaps, particularly due to the relatively unproblematic links to the longer, more complete text of the Bible. The first couplet of each of the first two stanzas centers on biblical quotation. The first stanza describes the triumph of Christ over the forces of evil, which initiates the millennium. In the second stanza, in which truth and the possibility of knowledge are at stake, the central lines are rhetorical questions that point to the spiritual struggle within the singer. In the final stanza, the same kinds of question are asked, but this time they are

---

matter how thick" (*Lyrics* 105). More recently the image occurs in "Dark Eyes," where "passion rules the arrow that flies" (*Lyrics* 500). One is reminded of Blake's "arrows of desire."

43. Carolyn Sumner and Steven Scobie have provided the most useful studies of Dylan's various personae. The title of her essay, "The Ballad of Dylan and Bob" (*Southwest Review* 66 [1981]: 41–54), indicates Dylan's tendency to figure himself as two opposite personalities, which we have analyzed in "Watchtower," as paradigmatic over his career as a whole. So too Scobie's title, *Alias Bob Dylan* (Red Deer, Alberta: Red Deer College Press, 1991).

44. For characteristics of the gospel song, see, on the white tradition, William Jensen Reynolds, *A Joyful Sound*, 2d ed., ed. Milburn Price (New York: Holt. Rinehart & Winston, 1978), 94–98; and on the black tradition, Tony Heilbut, *The Gospel Sound* (New York: Simon & Schuster, 1971), and Joan R. Hillsman, *Gospel Music: An African American Art Form* (Washington, D.C.: Middle Atlantic Regional Press, 1990). There is no strict separation between the two genres ("Amazing Grace" for example is a standard in both traditions), and it is interesting to note that Dylan originally intended "When He Returns" to be sung not by himself, but by his black female backup vocalists. Dylan has said of another of his gospel compositions that "you just don't hear things like that . . . white gospel, black gospel, forget it. . . . I wanted to expose people to that sort of thing because I loved it and it's the real roots of all modern music." Liner notes to "Solid Rock," *Biograph* (Columbia PXT 38830–38835, 1985). The album *Saved* is a virtual tour de force of various gospel traditions. We see that Dylan's conversion can be seen as a *musical* conversion, a movement from the structure of ballad to that of gospel.

directed at the listener. So too in the final stanza the first couplet no longer narrates, but exhorts. This is balanced by the return to objectivity in the final couplet: "Of every earthly plan that be known to man He is unconcerned / He's got plans of his own to set up His throne when He returns" (*Lyrics* reproduces this text as three lines, but Dylan sings it as two). In the previous stanzas the first line of this final couplet had either commanded ("Don't you cry . . .") or questioned ("Can I cast it aside . . . ?"). The last line of each stanza points to the millennium:

> For like a thief in the night, He'll replace wrong with right, when
> He returns. . . .
> There'll be no peace . . . the war won't cease, until He
> returns. . . .[45]
> He's got plans of His own to set up His throne when He
> returns. . . .

A simple listing of the other titles on *Slow Train Coming* shows how central the "I-Thou" relationship has become to Dylan. Nearly all the titles constitute forms of direct address: "[You] Gotta Serve Somebody," "I Believe in You," "[You] Precious Angel," "Do Right to Me Baby," and "When You Gonna Wake Up?" (*Lyrics* 422). The dialogue at the heart of "Hard Rain" and "Watchtower" continues within a new rhetorical framework.

Indeed, the different use-value of his new genre changed Dylan's audience from the white middle- to upper-class who had bought his records before—and who now rejected his Christian orientation—to the mass of underprivileged and working-class people who have always been most receptive to the call of millenarianism. For example, the very geography and architecture of Dylan's concerts had to change:

> We'd play theaters in the mission and Times Square districts in
> some of the larger cities, in the inner cities where industry has

---

45. The topoi of Christ winning the war against Satan and ruling an earthly kingdom and of wrong replacing right in a world turned upside down (which we have seen in earlier Dylan lyrics) come directly from the popular, "Lutheran" tradition of millenarianism as described by Ernest Tuveson: "The great and lasting appeal of the millenarian idea . . . may be attributed . . . to two elements: its promise of a utopian age, when the positions of oppressed and oppressors are reversed, as the culmination of history; and its suggestive outline of a revolution and a redeemer who will be able to break down the seemingly impregnable fortress of power and injustice." Ernest Tuveson, "Millenarianism," *Dictionary of the History of Ideas* (New York: Scribner's, 1973), 3:224.

moved out and people don't have work, some of the most beautiful theaters are there—the people that would come to the shows, you know, they'd be more or less from the neighborhood, prostitutes, pimps, whatever, shady looking characters, I guess they didn't have anything better to do and most of these theaters were right in the heart where they operated but anyway in these areas, this particular show went down well, audiences would be very receptive and even if I say so myself, wildly enthusiastic, strange too because a lot of these people I don't think they'd ever heard of me before.[46]

Like Degenhardt, Dylan has finally formed an image of his true audience as outsiders, the slow ones who will later be fast. Like Degenhardt, his songs have to be thrown at the listeners in order to have their effect. But such similarities only serve to make the differences between these two singers more apparent. Their two genres of radical commitment stand at opposing ideological poles, symbolized in the distance between Marxist and Christian millenarianism.

Degenhardt punctures his own "Nostalgia" with an ironic "punchline": "Und die sangen meine Lieder, lasen eure Blätter nicht" ("And they sang my songs, and did not read your leaflets"). The self-reference, which in Dylan leads to the apotheosis of the artist in "Hard Rain," here is deflected into another attempt at politics. The songs are sung, but without the necessary knowledge of the political principles behind them. Partly as a consequence of this failure to unite art and politics, the pursuit of millennium failed, and Degenhardt has made clear that this was his hope for his art. The "revelation of the world" that his songs provide is useful only if it explains better than the genre of political discourse can:

> Wenn sie mich fragen, was Beschreibung leisten kann, bitte immer auf Lieder bezogen . . . die ja mal laut und mal leise sein können, agitatorisch und lyrisch oder beides, je nach Lage und Lautstärke der Bewegungen, die sie begleiten, so meine ich, sie leisten überhaupt nichts, wenn das Beschreiben längst bekannt ist oder besser in politischer Rede dargestellt wird.[47]

> (When they ask me what description can achieve, in songs at least . . . which can sometimes be loud and sometimes soft, sometimes

46. Dylan, liner notes to "Solid Rock."
47. Degenhardt and Altenburg, "«Ich habe mit dem Literaturbetrieb nichts zu tun»," 92.

agitating and sometimes lyrical or both at the same time, according to the situation and the volume level of the groups they accompany, then my opinion is that they don't achieve anything at all when the description is already well known or done better in political speech.)

But the song "Nostalgia," like "Ein schönes Lied," implies that the discourse of art always represses the discourse of politics. "Nostalgia" thereby also re-marks the generic differences between literary and political discourse that it expresses the wish to destroy.

At this point, at least one meaning of both nostalgia and the citation of "The Times They Are A-Changin' " becomes clear: the nostalgia is for a time when the political singer could believe himself to be a *poeta vates*, a prophet, a changer of society. It is the same nostalgia Dylan expressed in "Song For Woody," this time turned back on the singer himself. "The Times They Are A-Changin' " is not merely the reporting of political upheaval, it participates in it through exhortation. The singer not only reports his vision of the changing of the order of things, but helps bring it about through his exhortations. Song here must be thought of as powerful and capable of effecting change. If Degenhardt had used Dylan's song in 1968, either through performance, citation, or adaptation—as German popular music continually adapts Dylan—it would already have been an act of nostalgia, as Dylan had by then moved on to the apocalypse of "Watchtower." And so Degenhardt, writing this song "Nostalgia" in the seventies, silences Dylan's text by making his citation of it into a bit of noise:

> The times they are a-changin,
> und die Trauer
> schläft in der Gitarre.
> Weck sie nicht mit deinem Schrei.
>
> (The times they are a-changin',
> and sorrow
> sleeps in the guitar.
> Don't wake it with your shouting.)

Grammatically speaking, Degenhardt alludes to rather than cites the title of Dylan's song. He is merely stating—in English—that nothing is permanent. He thus implies that his music had to change as well—and ironizes

Dylan's song, which predicts both apocalypse and the prophetic role of the singer, rather than the passing of revolutionary energies. In either case, the end of revolution is also the end of noise, as an almost sacred stillness is imposed before the sleeping song and the sleeping grief. The grief of his class, which has led to his revolutionary attitude, tastes sweet to Degenhardt, even if it is now dormant. With its cause inactive, the "Schrei" becomes meaningless, and Degenhardt's wish that it be stilled is a reaction precisely against nostalgia: a nostalgic action would be to scream and yell in the streets in a historical period that is not ready for such action. The lesson here becomes one of revolutionary patience and a vision of the dialectic of history, which can cause a singer to change his music according to the needs of his age. This is again a well-known Marxist *topos*, and Degenhardt has treated it compellingly in the song "Joß Fritz" (1973, f. 104).

Thus, "Nostalgia" portrays the tension between a genuine feeling for the sixties, when revolution was believed possible, and a repudiation of that hope, which works as a kind of antinostalgia similar to that of "My Back Pages." The differences lie in the fact that for Degenhardt the rejection of the past is not absolute. Both political song and political anguish "sleep in the guitar," awaiting their reawakening just as older musical forms had been reawakened with renewed political content at the beginning of these two artists' careers. The comparison of these two artists has shown that the social energies based on a "principle of hope" (a principle I have tried to indicate with terms such as "apocalypse" and "millenarianism") always appear as noise within the existing generic system.

7

Höllerer's Echo: *Ecco* Höllerer!

Pseudo-Translator's Preface

THE FOLLOWING UNDATABLE ARISTOTELIAN DIALOGUE
has been reconstructed from a clean-catch palimpsest deposited (that is,
illegally dumped) centuries ago, in a salt mine near Gorleben, Germany.
Carbon-14 testing was obviously out of the question. Furthermore, the
dialogue had been written in a cipher that I was for the most part unable
to crack. My disappointment was relieved somewhat by the realization that
had I been able to break the first level of code, I still would have had no
idea what the original language of the dialogue was. I have therefore been
forced to reconstruct everything from my own imagination and pawn it off
as genuine.

I was, however, able to decipher the names of two venerated scholars,
Master Umberto of Bononia and Master Walter of Mussrivus. These
philosophers, building on foundations laid by Saint Augustine and Hugh
of Saint Victor, contributed much to the theory of signs, and their ideas
are certainly present in the text-to-be-deciphered, even if I cannot read
them. The *summae-centi* of these two immortals are entitled *Il nome della
rosa* (Milan: Bompiani, 1980) and *Die Elephantenuhr* (Frankfurt am Main:
Suhrkamp, 1973). Master Umberto's work has been translated into English by William Weaver as *The Name of the Rose* (San Diego: Harcourt
Brace Jovanovich, 1984). Alas, Walter's *Elephantenuhr* has not yet had the
same "honor." *Anni mirabili,* which gave to the world such a double advance
in semiotic knowledge through these two! In addition, I have also feigned
that the two discuss briefly the *summa* of another renowned scholar,
Raimundus of Camboricum. His *People of the Black Mountains* (London:
Chatto & Windus, 1989) resembles the work of the two interlocutors in its

attempt to go beyond the boundaries of the treatise in his era by combining autobiography, fiction, history, and theory. It is thus difficult to identify the genre of these works, which, like so many medieval omnibuses, seem to wish to be everything at once. All three venerables wrote something similar to Jean de Meung's *Romance of the Rose* or Dante's *Divine Comedy*, that is, a general guide to humanistic endeavor in the form of a fiction.

Perhaps because of the similar historical situations within which each scholar wrote his work, they show some remarkable parallels. Like Dante, but with a bit more dissimulation, both have written themselves into their works as faint-hearted but cerebral heroes who must go through hell. In order to accommodate the dialectical form of teaching, each has in turn split that hero into several selves. Umberto has kept things simple by having a young, semiotically naive self (Adso) be trained by a learned-semiotician older self (William of Baskerville). Walter, on the other hand, has allowed his main hero Gustaf Lorch, who works in the Jean-Paul Museum in Murrbach and is responsible for planning a semiology exhibit, both narrate his adventures and play back a tape that he had made while experiencing them. A third narrative strand has Gustaf imagining his alter ego, G, to spend his time sitting on the Testaccio in Rome talking with his girlfriend K. Adso and William make the trip to an abbey in Italy in order to mediate a religious dispute whose technicalities seem opaque to us moderns, but luckily for us they end up trying to solve a "series" of murders. Although Adso's trip is important, he remains stationary through most of the novel. Gustaf, on the other hand, travels all over Germany: to Berlin, Salzgitter, Frankfurt, and back to Murrbach.

Both of these allegories end with apocalypses. In the act of apprehending the culprit, the fanatical monk Jorge, and the treasure (the lost second book of Aristotle's *Poetics*), Adso and William accidently set the abbey library on fire. Gustaf, on the other hand, intentionally dynamites the museum and the Schiller monument next to it. Again, the exact purpose of all these excesses is a matter for interpretation, but must have something to do with the difficult and violent times in which these authors wrote.

Also not clear is the purpose of this writing which I am now giving to the world. I have the body, but not the motive or the malefactor. Is this piece satirical? Is it elegiac? There remains even the bizarre possibility that a young researcher desperate for publishable material planted a hearing device on one of these two figures and transcribed their ravings. It is even more probable to assume that the author was simply fudging (that is, feigning) her data, desperately hoping that her inferior creative effort would appear before the eyes of her tenure committee in the raiments of the loftier genre of research. (Now there's use-value for you! Expectations of the period stood at fourteen books and 165 articles at peer Japanese institutions.)

The excruciating demands of tenurable genres of writing would have also required a cumbersome textual apparatus threatening to capsize the fragile dialogue (more and more fragile, as the author's imagination disappeared exponentially during the reconstruction process, worn away by the Scylla and Charybdis of Smartie® abuse and excessive committee work). Instead, I prefer to credit here a number of writers who have filled my mind with the ideas this text echoes.

ON WALTER

D'Elden, Karl H. van. "Walter Höllerer." In *West German Poets on Society and Politics,* ed. van D'Elden, 141–61. Detroit: Wayne State University Press, 1979.

Durzak, Manfred. "Der Roman als offenes system. Walter Höllerers 'Elephantenuhr.' " In *Gespräche über den Roman: Formbestimmungen und Analysen,* 512–28. Frankfurt am Main: Suhrkamp, 1976.

Höllerer, Walter. "Aktualität von Jean Paul. Bayreuther Rede." In *Oberpfälzische Welteierkundungen,* ed. Werner Gotzmann, 57–65. Weiden: Vereinigte Oberpfälzische Druckereien, 1987.

———. *Die Elephantenuhr.* Frankfurt am Main: Suhrkamp, 1973.

———. "Das historische Bewußtsein und das Gedächtnis des Elephanten." In *Oberpfälzische Welteierkundungen,* ed. Werner Gotzmann, 46–49. Weiden: Vereinigte Oberpfälzische Druckereien, 1987.

———. Catalogue to the exhibit "Welt aus Sprache." Berlin: Akademie der Künste, 1972.

Höllerer, Walter, and Manfred Durzak. "Wir leben in einer unüberblickbaren Welt. Gespräch mit Walter Höllerer." In *Gespräche über den Roman. Formbestimmungen und Analysen,* ed. Manfred Durzak, 482–511. Frankfurt am Main: Suhrkamp, 1976.

Höllerer, Walter, and Ruth Lorbe. "Documentation Walter Höllerer." *German Quarterly* 59 (Winter 1986): 85–102.

Hunt, Irmgard, "Utopia ist Oval, oder: Weltei gegen Denkmal—der utopische Gedanke im Werk Walter Höllerers." *Germanic Review* 63 (Summer 1989): 140–46.

Krumme, Detlef. "Die Lesemodelle für 'Die Elephantenuhr.' " In *Lesemodelle. Canetti, Grass, Höllerer,* 145–87. Munich: Hanser, 1983.

ON UMBERTO

Carpino, Joseph J. "On Eco's *The Name of the Rose.*" *Interpretation: A Journal of Political Philosophy* 14 (May–September 1986): 89–413.

Coletti, Theresa. *Naming the Rose: Eco, Medieval Signs, and Modern Theory.* Ithaca: Cornell University Press, 1988.

Golden, Leon. "Eco's Reconstruction of Aristotle's Theory of Comedy in *The Name of the Rose.*" *Classical and Modern Literature: A Quarterly* 6 (Summer 1986): 239–49.

Eco, Umberto. "The Frames of Comic Freedom." In *Carnival!* ed. Thomas A. Sebeok, 1–9. New York: Mouton, 1984.

———. *Lector in Fabula: la cooperazione interpretativa nei testi.* Milan: Bompiani, 1979. Translated under the title *Role of the Reader: Explorations in the Semiotics of Texts.* Bloomington: Indiana University Press, 1979.

———. "Postille a 'Il nome della rosa' 1983." In *Il nome della rosa*, 505–33. Milan: Bompiani, 1989. Translated by William Weaver, under the title *Postscript to "The Name of the Rose."* San Diego: Harcourt Brace Jovanovich, 1983.

Eco, Umberto, ed. *On the Medieval Theory of Signs.* Amsterdam and Philadelphia: J. Benjamins, 1989.

Horn, Pierre L. "The Detective Novel and the Defense of Humanism." In *Naming the Rose: Essays on Eco's "The Name of the Rose,"* ed. Thomas M. Inge, 90–100. Jackson: University Press of Mississippi, 1988.

Richter, David H. "Eco's Echoes: Semiotic Theory and Detective Practice in the Name of the Rose." *Studies in Twentieth-Century Literature* 10 (Spring 1986): 213–36.

Stephens, Walter E. "Ec[h]o in Fabula." *Diacritics* 13 (1983): 51–64.

Yeager, Robert F. "Fear of Writing, or Adso and the Poisoned Text." *SubStance* 14 (1985): 243–48.

OTHER

Aristophanes. *The Frogs* (405 B.C.).

Aristotle. *Poetics; Politics* (ca. 330 B.C.).

Gadamer, Hans-Georg. "Lob der Theorie." In *Lob der Theorie*, 26–50. Frankfurt am Main: Suhrkamp, 1983.

Gellrich, Jesse. *The Idea of the Book in the Middle Ages.* Ithaca: Cornell University Press, 1985.

Gleick, James. *Chaos: Making a New Science.* New York: Penguin, 1987.

Goethe, Johann Wolfgang von. "Materialien zur Geschichte der Farbenlehre." In *Zur Farbenlehre*, ed. Peter Schmidt, 473–919. *Saemtliche Werke*, vol. 10. Munich: Carl Hanser, 1985.

Golden, Leon. "Aristotle and Comedy." *Journal of Aesthetics and Art Criticism* 42 (1984): 283–90.

Grass, Günter. *Die Blechtrommel.* Darmstadt, Berlin, and Neuwied: Luchterhand, 1959.

Janko, Richard. *Aristotle on Comedy: Towards a Reconstruction of Poetics II.* London: Duckworth, 1984.

Mann, Thomas. *Der Tod in Venedig.* Berlin: Fischer, 1913.

Mörike, Eduard. *Mozart auf der Reise nach Prag.* Augsburg: Cotta, 1856.

Nelson, Cary. "On Whether Criticism is Literature." In *What is Criticism?* ed. Paul Hernadi, 253–68. Bloomington: Indiana University Press, 1981.

Neumann, Robert. *Die Parodien.* Vienna, Munich, and Basel: Kurt Desch, 1962.

Plato. *The Phaedrus* (ca. 404 B.C.).

Robbe-Grillet, Alain. *Les gommes.* Paris: Minuit, 1953.

Sebeok, Thomas A. *Perspectives in Zoosemiotics.* The Hague: Mouton, 1972.

Stevens, Wallace. "The Idea of Order at Key West." In *Ideas of Order.* New York: Knopf, 1936.

Thompson, Michael. *Rubbish Theory: The Creation and Destruction of Value.* New York: Oxford University Press, 1979.

Voltaire. *Zadig ou la Destinée: Histoire Orientale.* Nancy: Leseure, 1748.

Wilde, Oscar. *The Decay of Lying: A Dialogue.* In *The Eclectic Magazine* 49 (February 1889): 184–98.

On a warm summer day two old friends, Umberto of Bononia and Walter of Mussrivus, climb Rome's Testaccio hill, near the Cestius pyramid and the Protestant cemetery, in an attempt to escape the smog and the infinite boredom of yet another international conference on the death of genre. Master Umberto was looking especially wan. He had been persuaded to take over the organization and planning of the conference, which had been delayed by strikes on the part of transportation workers, computer programmers, students and professors, postal employees, and janitors. This incident might have led Master Umberto to see life as a futile paradox, since like a good Franciscan and a bad bureaucrat he had always supported the oppressed in their attempts to win a better material life. (He himself was certainly no addict to poverty or asceticism, and his comfortably stout figure made a meaningful contrast with the lean, wiry, intense frame of his German companion.) But Master Umberto shrugged his difficulties off with a laugh and with the comment that "we are lucky to have had so few strikes this year." Inspired by a rare dose of the controlled substance oxygen, these two literati entered into their following memorable (even though apparently forgotten) discussion.

WALTER: [*Panting*] Well, Master Umberto . . . this is turning out to be quite a climb. . . . I'm quite out of breath. Or maybe I'm short of breath because I'm nervous about being discovered here, where we're not supposed to be.

UMBERTO: Master Walter, don't be so *tedesco* as to tell me you pay attention to things like gates and fences?

WALTER: No, but I do pay attention to *signs*. And there was one back there, just off the Via Zabaglia, forbidding us entrance. By the way, are we taking one of your inferential walks?

UMBERTO: No one really cares that we are here on the Testaccio. It's just that Romans have too much pride and art to bear giving people free access to their two-thousand-year-old garbage dump. The profound thing about this culture is how it constantly valorizes its own surface features. This hill is one of the first historical examples of a landfill reclamation project. It was built up out of the pottery shards of the Roman empire and the leftovers from the trading and traffic along the Tiber. The splinters and ashes of an entire civilization lie beneath our feet. Ruins that point to the redemptive end of history, as that other Master Walter would have said. And of course in telling you all this I am merely quoting from your own *Elephantenuhr,* wherein G spends most of his time on this very *testo* . . . errr . . . Testaccio, looking down on the restaurants below in the city, the wide piazzi, general meetings of corporations, universities, which at this moment are black letters, they make the places dark, uneven—pairs of letters, even combinations of letters, names, articles for names, G sees them in sets inside of parentheses, and thus he provides logistically for the incalculable conglomerations of institutions, persons.[1] But look how G has suddenly popped up in our conversation.

WALTER: Yes, he certainly appears at the most inconvenient moments. He appears suddenly in our bathrooms like a hallucination, and he seems to be ubiquitous, because time never enters the descriptions of his activities "and while I am *thinking* there in the bathtub in the Murrbach museum, G is standing arrogant, naked, in my bathtub and is *screaming:* 'a new semiology . . .' he screams, 'for a new communication . . .' he screams, 'in a new society . . .' he screams, holding out a thick stomach and a thick dick he stands, I see that under the apple tree, with my face to the wall in my tub."[2] Now there's comedy for you. I would say that Gustaf's G is something like Adso's William, a mentor, the image of a world traveler, the model for a more sophisticated semiology. Except that he may not be fictionally real at all.

UMBERTO: Well, that's a relief. I thought I was just overfatigued when I read his sections. I understand that Gustaf Lorch is a *real* fictional character who works in a museum. But I must confess that this character G has always puzzled me. I always find myself trying to guess his real name—Godibert? Gottfried? Gaspard?—

1. From time to time, the doctors lace their discourse with quotations from one another's *summae-centi,* which seem to have been the topic that our unknown *academica* placed in the centerpiece of her discussion. I will indicate those passages where appropriate: "Die Restaurants unten in der Stadt, die weiten Plätze, Vollversammlungen von Betrieben, Universitäten, sind in dieser Minute schwarz von Buchstaben, sie machen die Orte dunkel, schütter—einzelne Buchstaben, Buchstabenpaare, auch längere Buchstabenzusammensetzungen, Namen, Artikel von Namen, G sieht sie mit Kenngruppen in Klammern, so bewirtschaftet er die unüberblickbaren Anhäufungen von Institutionen, Personen." Walter Höllerer, *Die Elephantenuhr,* 18.

2. ". . . und während ich, in der Badewanne im Museum von Murrbach, *denke,* steht G, breitspurig, nackt, in meiner Badewanne und *schreit:* 'eine neue Semiologie,' schreit er, 'für eine neue Kommunikation,' schreit er, 'in einer neuen Gesellschaft,' schreit er, 'in einer neuartigen Stadt,' schreit er, nackt, einen kräftigen Bauch und einen kräftigen Schwanz vorgestreckt, steht er, das sehe ich unter dem Apfelbaum, mit dem Gesicht zur Tür in meiner Wanne" (30).

like the queen in "Rumpelstiltskin." But just who is this G? At any
rate, I found his *italienische Reise* rather funny.

WALTER: Like your hero Adso's. G is Gustaf's doppelgänger, you
know. It is essentially a romantic notion, as one finds in Jean-Paul
or E. T. A. Hoffmann, two of my favorite authors. Every German
story has to have at least one doppelgänger in it. He spends his
time doing all the things that Gustaf does not do. Gustaf is always
indoors, in the museum, in a car, in apartments. G spends most of
his time outdoors, on this very hill. Or on the beach in Sausalito.
So I split my character into two as you do, but I drop the pretense
that G is anything other than a figment of Gustaf's imagination in
order to show how real he is. I don't wish to commit mimesis,
after all.

UMBERTO: I know that there are three narrative strands in your
novel, because of the different indentations, but I don't usually
have enough energy to hold them apart from one another. I know
that on the simplest level Gustaf tells of his trip through Germany,
of his plans for a semiology exhibit in the museum in Murrbach,
and of his great crime, blowing up the Schiller monument and the
new wing of the museum. He does seem excessively contemplative,
like Adso. And he likes making lists, too, a trait that seems to
irritate most readers. I remember how instead of going out to
enjoy the night life — a temptation Adso also faces — Gustaf inven-
tories someone's Berlin apartment:

> And if I had gone out with them tonight, then I would not be
> finding in the drawers all around me buttons, and letters,
> stamps around this groaning bed; great quantities of *brain-sand*;
> old newspapers, yellowed; and in the closet: sayings in prover-
> bial fire-brick, and old cups wrapped in old headlines
>   had I gone out with them tonight into the Night-Berlin,
> then I would not be finding this collection of car accidents,
> plane crashes, kidnappings, runnings amok in the bathroom;
> then I would not be seeing the aunt-brain before me, as it clips
> the newspapers daily with a sharp scissors, searching for hand-
> cuffs, crash, for last-words, for faces in the news photographer's
> flash.[3]

3. ". . . und wäre ich mitgefahren mit ihnen in dieser Nacht, dann . . . fände [ich] hier nicht
um mich herum in den Schubladen Knöpfe, und Briefe, Briefmarken um dieses dröhnende Bett
herum; Mengen von *Hirnsand;* alte Zeitungen, gelb; und im Schrank: Motten in Motten-Schamott,

WALTER: I'm simply amazed! You memorized that whole passage, and in *tedesco*.

UMBERTO: It's not hard when you have a book in front of you, not having to instantly grasp the gist of a speech or decipher a manuscript in some bizarre handwriting. And besides, this is one of my favorite passages in the book. I find it particularly theoretical, one of the best explanations I can give my students of what semiotics is. And entirely similar to Adso's meditations and list-making, except for the different ideologies behind them, of course.

WALTER: Except for everything, in other words.

UMBERTO: All right, Gustaf and G, and what is the third strand?

WALTER: Also Gustaf, but on tape. He tape-records himself constantly, creating yet another fictional version of himself, we might say. I understand your confusion, because unlike you I wanted my book to cause unlimited semiosis. In writing this way I was challenging my readers, those who like theory and those who like fiction, to take new positions, to develop a new semiology. I allow my character to shout absurdly utopian phrases which I would never risk myself:

> Keep in mind, that you have two eyes! Use them for a semiology that takes us further!
>
> Obtain through enthusiastic, coordinated movements at least the lower boundary of future possibility! . . .
>
> Don't let yourselves be *cemented in, mummified, poisoned!* Don't trust pre-packaged paper-pushers! Don't trust a canned bureaucracy! Don't trust an eloquent offer!
>
> Listen to semiology! What gets mummified *now* can never be made good again!
>
> Haul yourself out of the old ceremonial junk, out of comfortableness! Get desire, get fresh air! Don't let thinking be driven out of you by scholastic formulations!

UMBERTO: [*To himself*] Poor scholastics! Always the bum rap!

---

und alte Tassen, in alte Schlagzeilen eingewickelt . . . wäre ich mitgefahren ins Nacht-Berlin in dieser Nacht, dann fände ich hier nicht diese Kollektion von Unfällen, Abstürzen, Entführungen, Amokläufen, in der Kommode; dann sähe ich nicht vor mir das Tanten-Gehirn, wie es täglich, mit spitzer Schere, die Zeitung zerschnippst, auf der Suche nach Handschellen, Crash, nach-letzten-Worten, nach Gesichtern-im-Blitz" (409).

WALTER: [*dithyrambically*] Let the censors censor themselves! *Look! Taste! Smell! Think!*
Come forward with semiology against hypnosis and against all the rest that is choking us! Against the binding up of land and mind![4]

As you can see, the words on the tape are exhortatory, inflammatory. They represent not doctrine, but the endless dissolution of doctrine in conversation with itself. Think of how children learn by talking to themselves. You, on the other hand, portray a whole master and apprentice relationship between your characters William and Adso.
UMBERTO: Yes, William teaches Adso quite a bit of theory.
WALTER: It really must have pained your colleagues in this country to see you bring English common sense with William and German morality with Adso in order to solve this Italian mystery. As if the Italians didn't run the abbey. Of course, the internationalism of your text (true to its medieval spirit) could never have been thought of a few decades ago. It sometimes seems like an advertisement for the European Community. . . .
UMBERTO: Most definitely, and it delighted my colleagues, precisely because William and Adso couldn't solve the mystery; it remained *cosa nostra*. They couldn't understand chaos, you see, but only order. They failed to accept the mystical experience of a *vide de parole* like Juan de la Cruz or Roland Barthes have written about. They set to work, gave order, moralized; above all, they *theorized*. [*Stops, points*] Look over there, you can see three distinctly different epochs of garbage piled on top of each other!
WALTER: Yes, how beautiful! What a find! Just by standing here one could be inspired to write a novel. But even more inspiring — do you know that there is a similar mountain in Berlin? That hill is made out of the rubble of all the destroyed buildings of World

4. " 'Beachten Sie, daß Sie zwei Augen haben! Benützen Sie sie, für die weiterführende Semiologie!' Schaffen Sie sich durch eifrige, kombinierte Bewegung wenigstens die untere Grenze der künftigen Möglichkeit! . . . Lassen Sie sich nicht *einzementieren, ausdörren, vergiften!* Vertrauen Sie nicht auf eingewickelte Routiniers! auf eine verdöste Bürokratie! auf ein schönrednerisches Angebot! Hören Sie auf die Semiologie! Was *jetzt* ausgedörrt wird, ist nicht wiedergutzumachen! Ziehen Sie sich heraus aus dem alten Zeremonien-Kram, aus der Bequemlichkeit! Holen Sie Lust für sich, holen Sie Luft! Lassen sie sich nicht das *Denken* austreiben, durch scholastischen Formulierungs-Dreh! Lassen Sie die Zensoren sich selbst zensieren! *Sehen* Sie! *Schmecken* Sie! *Riechen* Sie! *Denken* Sie! Rücken Sie mit der Semiologie gegen Hypnosen vor, und was sonst uns ersticken will!" (380–81).

War Two, and was appropriately named the Teufelsberg. On a walk there you will step on all the little plaster busts of Hitler (and now Honecker) and Nazi (and now Communist) Party pins which people rapidly threw away on May 8, if they were lucky enough not to be forced into swallowing them. You will also step on all the bones of people killed in the bombing raids. And so the two most inevitable facts of life, mortality and the production of rubbish (not all cultures have developed a tax system) have blessed us with two points of semiology, of observation of the cities, of the *tempora* and *mores* of this world.

UMBERTO: *Ecco,* two perfect examples of the semiotic labyrinth too complex for complete deciphering, like a medieval library after it has burned down and fragments of the parchments must be sewn together.

WALTER: Or like the intertextual mind of a reader, Norn-like, continually sewing together and taking apart texts.

UMBERTO: Or like a writer on the verge of re-creation. Remember the image Lévi-Strauss gives us of himself on the island of Martinique, confronted with piles of photographs, maps, note-cards, and god-knows-what that the forces of genre eventually pulled and pushed into some kind of order?

WALTER: Order, yes, but a nonlinear or dialectical order, a violent order. The beautiful shape of this hill is the result of the chaos of millions of people randomly throwing their chicken bones here. This Testaccio is the eye of the cyclone, the center of the elephant clock.[5] This silence is the apparent stillness of interfering sound waves, whose peaks and troughs cancel each other out, just as the apparent order of genre is really just a dead heat in the tug-of-war between conflicting ideologies. [*Pauses, listens. An undefinable noise is heard, like Bob Dylan with laryngitis after smoking a pack of Camels.*] And you see, it didn't last long. I now seem to hear cicadas chirping, Umberto . . .

UMBERTO: Frogs, actually: "koax! koax! koax!" The croaking is distorted by the echo, which transforms it into a different message, which you hear as the chirping of cicadas and interpret optimistically as a sign of rebirth, of the shedding of one more layer of skin, whereas the frogs, well . . .

5. ". . . der innere Kern des Zyklons, das Zentrum der Elephantenuhr" (32).

WALTER: But tell me, is it true that our colleague Raimundus of Cambridge is buried somewhere on this hill?

UMBERTO: There are many who claim it is true, but still more who call this story a fiction invented by his enemies in order to discredit him. An ideological fiction, if you will.

WALTER: A *mythologie*, perhaps.

UMBERTO: Perhaps a lie. But what's in a name?

WALTER: Different genres have different uses. But why would his enemies invent such a story, after all?

UMBERTO: I too am puzzled, and in fact I am not really sure it was his enemies who started this rumor. On the positive side, such a legend seems to correspond with how Glyn, the fictional character he created of himself, interacted with the Black Hills in Wales. On the negative side, however, to be buried on Europe's oldest historical garbage dump in continuous use is not exactly an honor in the eyes of most people. Even more to the point, for a cultural materialist to be buried in this semiotician's paradise seems ironic, like a Franciscan being buried in a Dominican cemetery. You remember how the Black Hills, through their very integrity and the preservation of their cairns and housing, call up visions of the past in Glyn. He then combines them into little narratives, which enter into the great narrative of his Welsh ancestry. Glyn's historicizing of his environment is not presented as *bricolage*. But our hill, the Testaccio, has no such narrative integrity. It is just a garbage dump; here we can find only fragments, so our narrative would also have to be fragmentary. So the rumors of his being buried here seem to have originated in a kind of anti-fiction, a search-and-destroy mission against his novel.

WALTER: Well, Master Umberto, are you happy with how your conference has gone so far? I sympathize with you immensely. After all, I nearly went crazy organizing my semiology exhibit "Welt aus Sprache" in the Berlin Academy of Arts. The only way to hang on was to make poor Gustaf go crazy.

UMBERTO: Yes, I'm burned out too. And of course, I would much rather have held it in Bologna than in Rome. Why give all that prestige to an *arriviste* upstart in the academic world, after all? Bologna has forgotten more than Rome ever knew about theory. But in the end I had to give in, for political reasons.

WALTER: For some reason, Rome sells better than Bologna. But really it should have been held in Bari.

UMBERTO: Ah, yes, Bari, home of the *maestro*, the greatest of the genre-killers . . .

WALTER: Actually, I was thinking more of the beach . . .

UMBERTO: Polluted. But yes, I understand perfectly, what would an *italienische Reise* be without a view of the smoothly undulating water, whether you're Thomas Mann's Aschenbach being rocked in a gondola or Eduard Mörike's Mozart looking out on cavorting nymphs. Every fictional German who comes to Italy must see the Mediterranean, that primordial symbol of a comforting and vital chaos . . .

WALTER: Except Nietzsche. He preferred the heights, like us. And Adso's *Bildungsreise*, I noticed, also stays in the mountains.

UMBERTO: For precisely Nietzsche's reasons. Where the air is clear, one can think better. And look what happened to Aschenbach and to Mozart, whereas Adso lived on to a ripe old age . . .

WALTER: In absolute despair, in a world that seemed to be dying all around him.

UMBERTO: Your Adso, I mean Gustaf, travels northward instead, to Berlin. And where the ocean inspires Mozart and kills Aschenbach, Berlin makes a semiotician out of Gustaf. But to get back to your question, the conference has been an exhausting success. I'm sure you realize that there's no failure like success. I chose the topic "The Death of Genre" for the conference in order to arouse controversy and provoke a response. I wanted to save genre dialectically, by proclaiming its death: "Genre is dead, long live genre!" And now I am astounded and depressed to find that everyone is on my side, repeating over and over again that genre is dead. So the conference is dead, too.

WALTER: At least you can be proud of my countryman, Markus, who has spoken up enthusiastically for the ubiquity of genre. He hates all this postmodern *Überhauptpoesie*, you know.

UMBERTO: Yes. But generally, what he has to say goes "over my head." I only notice that he makes sure always to oppose his friend Amalia, who shudders at the drop of a rubric.

WALTER: Yes, she crosses as many rubricons as possible. But on either side of the question, I notice that the Americans and the English and the Germans and the Russians take this whole thing quite seriously. They think it very important and of immense practical and political value to kill genre, and the harder they try, the more life they pump into it. Another aspect of our serious attitude is this strange expectation that theories ought to work, ought to have some sort of practical value. We have even done you, *maestro*, the disservice of turning your books into methodologies, so that you had to flee with your theory into the realm of fiction where no one would hold you accountable.

UMBERTO: A confusion of genres, as though I were writing *Surgery of the Skull Base* or some such *ars* where the wit of *fingere* played no part. How much more sophisticated the Middle Ages, who put all such *artes* below the realm of fiction, of the *Roman de la rose*, for example.

WALTER: It certainly seems hard enough just to write something that will continue our conversation or read beautifully. These converters of theory into praxis remind me of one of those detective films where the murderer tries to fit a corpse into a coffin that is too small for it. He presses down on one end and the other end sits up, ready for a meal. The only solution is to cut . . .

UMBERTO: By the way, have you noticed that our whole conversation has involved death so far? First these hills made of dead culture, that is, rubbish; then the death of genre; then the dead conference about death; then the killing of theory by converting it into "facts" . . .

WALTER: Lugubrious, aren't we? It reminds me of your book, which is all about death, with many ingenious murders. One great, deep death, like Aschenbach's, or one simple cataclysm, like the *Götterdämmerung*, seems more meaningful.

UMBERTO: Ah, but mine are generic deaths in another sense, they are what identify *The Name of the Rose* as a medieval detective novel. And those deaths are stripped of all their agonies as they are turned into the signs of an intellectual puzzle. No one has ever called Agatha Christie a great meditator on death, or even a very lugubrious person. Just a very clever one.

WALTER: [*Slyly*] So you agree with the critics and blurb-writers who keep on calling *Il nome della rosa* a detective novel?

UMBERTO: No, I only agree that, like any clever murderer of genre, I plant the corpses as false clues that there is a detective novel to be discovered inside the *Rose*, just like the many false clues that lead William closer and closer to the nontruth that he needs to finish his mission. And do I need to remind you that you also attach the palpably false label of "novel" to your *Elephantenuhr*? To me it seemed more like a five-hundred-page-long poem.

WALTER: Not just a poem, but a "poem of inconvenience." By using a very special prose, which is rhythmically arranged and at the same time includes conversational elements, I hoped to "touch" a greater number of readers. That would be one reason for the misleading designation of "novel," a genre whose use-value extends from the didactic to the pornographic. That generic label is perhaps the most important piece of sabotage in the whole work — and of course, it is not quite "in" the work at all. It is the genre-theoretical equivalent of Gustaf's blowing up the museum. But I don't want to put myself in the same camp with the many critics who have said that *Die Elephantenuhr* is not a *Roman*. They are all thinking of Heinrich Böll and Thomas Mann and the nineteenth-century novel. It is true that, like Roland Barthes, I found that form impossible to use now. But perhaps *Die Elephantenuhr* is a novel in Schlegel's sense of the word, the ultimate romantic genre, the literary absolute. It is a novel as Jean Paul wrote them, as Rabelais wrote one, as Joyce wrote them, a work of the most absolute heterogeneity. All three authors aim at including a certain playful noise created by the genre system that gave us novels but which is normally excluded from those texts. These novels are systems that try never to close themselves off; they are theories that create their facts; they are edifices that accept the odium of their ruin-like structure, are addicted to change in their very element, and thus best resemble the human brain and the processes of human society. All four authors — now I am including myself — seize on the generic instability of the novel as its essential feature. I call *Die Elephantenuhr* a novel precisely because it is so unlike a novel, so impossible to conceive of as a novel.

UMBERTO: The novel is dead, long live the novel! But now you have discovered precisely the problem people see with genres, precisely the necrotic elements of genre theory. It is this Procrustean cutting and stuffing that critics are driven to. And then they are forced to make all kinds of strange patchings to account for extraneous elements in the text. For example, one critic titles his article on *The Rose*, "The Detective Novel and the Defence of Humanism." I fail to see what the detective novel has to do with humanism. It has everything to do, however, with metaphysics, because a detective novel represents a series of conjectures in their purest state. A detective novel is *fingere* from start to finish. As such it connects with that aspect of contemplation in the thought of the Middle Ages, not with that of the Renaissance, as our critic wishes it to. That is perhaps why only a German has found the perfect generic designation for *Il nome della rosa*, which, as I said, is not a detective novel, but has been mistaken for one like *Trauerspiel* has been mistaken for Tragedy. It seems my work is a *Mönchsroman* (monk's novel). This designation, it seems to me, has the right ideological flavor to it. This monk, William of Baskerville, who comes to the monastery to solve Adelmo's murder, is not really anything like Sherlock Holmes. He is even less like Poe's Dupin, the first detective hero in fiction. For example, one might think that when William goes on and on about the rhinoceros, that he is translating Holmes's famous explanations of deductive reasoning into medieval terms. But he says the opposite, that "solving a mystery is not the same as deducing from first principles" (304).

WALTER: But this caution seems to also apply to works of theory, as we were just discussing.

UMBERTO: William is really translating Aristotle, you know, and he is really talking about reasoning as a kind of sorting procedure:

"Take the case of animals with horns. Why do they have horns? Suddenly you realize that all animals with horns are without teeth in the upper jaw. This would be a fine discovery, if you did not also realize that, alas, there are animals without teeth in the upper jaw who, however, do not have horns: the camel, to name one. And finally you realize that all animals without teeth in the upper jaw have two stomachs. . . . You then try to imagine a material cause for horns—say, the lack of teeth provides the animal with an excess of osseous matter that must emerge somewhere else. But is that sufficient explanation? No, because the camel has no upper teeth, has two stomachs, but does not have horns. . . ." (304)[6]

6. "Ma immagina il caso degli animali con le corna. Perché hanno le corna? Improvvisamente ti accorgi che tutti gli animali con le corna non hanno denti nella mandibola superiore. Sarebbe una bella scoperta, se non ti rendessi conto che, ahimè, ci sono animali senza denti nella mandibola superiore e che tuttavia non hanno le corna, come il cammello. Infine ti accorgi che tutti gli animali senza denti nella mandibola superiore hanno due stomaci. . . . Allora provi a immaginare una cause materiale delle corna, per cui la mancanza di denti provvede l'animale con una eccedenza di materia ossea che deve spuntare da qualche altra parte. Ma è una spiegazione

WALTER: Pardon me, but am I to read this as a pronouncement on theory, or on genre? And I do wish you had chosen elephants instead of rhinos and camels.

UMBERTO: Never mind. Let me continue with my demonstration of the nondetective status of my novel. Surely, you also remember how William goes on to analyze this bizarre example. It is a disappointment to all Sherlock Holmes fans: "I was trying to tell you that the search for explicative laws in natural facts proceeds in a tortuous fashion. In the face of some inexplicable facts you must try to imagine many general laws, whose connection with your facts escapes you. . . . I line up so many disjointed elements and I venture some hypotheses. I have to venture many, and many of them are so absurd that I would be ashamed to tell them to you" (305).[7]

WALTER: Pardon me again, *maestro*, but is this passage intended to show that the *Rose* is not a camel . . . errr . . . not a detective novel, or is it intended to show us the proper heuristic for determining what the *Rose* is? Unlike in London, here the law has only the most tangential relation to the facts. And this is certainly the case also for the Abbey murders, which present a false order, an order of propositions about things rather than an order of things themselves. The story of these murders is in the reader. *Fabula in lectore.* But I noticed William's Teutonic rage for order. He formulates general laws linking discrete acts: a single murderer with a clearly definable purpose and, on top of that, the seriality provided by the paradigm of the Book of Revelation. Patterns imposed on chaos, and hence ultimately ineffectual. This revelation of chaos as the ordering principle, so to speak, more than the defeat of William in the end, is what makes *Il nome della rosa* an anti-detective story.

UMBERTO: And a warning against all who would see theory as method?

---

sufficiente? No, perché il cammello non ha denti superiore, ha due stomaci, ma non le corna." Umberto Eco, *Il nome della rosa*, 307.

7. "Ma era per dirti che la ricerca delle leggi esplicative, nei fatti naturali, procede in modo tortuoso. Di fronte ad alcuni fatti inspiegabili tu devi provare a immaginare molte leggi generali, di cui non vedi ancora la connessione coi fatti di cui ti occupi. . . . Allineo tanti elementi sconnessi e fingo delle ipotesi. Ma ne devo fingere molte, e numerose sono quelle così assurde che mi vergognerei di dirtele" (307–8).

WALTER: And the unkindest cut of all is when you allow William a very minor triumph at the beginning, a truly Holmes-like discovery of the horse Brunellus.

UMBERTO: Again, a false clue, this time for the reader, since William finds Brunellus because he has read Voltaire's "Zadig," in which a similar incident occurs. Thus, the incident that most seems like a detective story is derived from another genre entirely. In a metafictional world in which books speak of other books, the best detective is the best reader. One can say that inasmuch as I am also writing semiotic theory, the detective part of my story must fail, because the detective story by itself could never be metafictional, could never question its own assumptions.

WALTER: Yes, you cannot just let the detective novel rest on its laurels. The whole genre is bound to be murdered by semiotics, by a science that finds an unbridgeable gap between sign and referent. Which is why I had the curious feeling, as I was reading your book, that I was reading two novels at once: a classic detective story and a detective story in quotation marks—the latter a postmodern fiction that calls attention to its very fictionality.

UMBERTO: Or shall we say, to follow your lead, a detective story and a postmodern detective story as practiced by Robbe-Grillet in *Les Gommes*—or by Borges in "The Garden of Forking Paths."

WALTER: Now, Master Umberto, help me with another problem, which may constitute—God help me!—a sin against genre theory, authorial intention, and political order. I myself cannot help but read the *Rose* as an *Universitätsgeländeroman* (campus novel) in disguise. The library and the protection of knowledge, the closedness of the abbey as an "ivory tower," the internecine strife between the monks, all these features seemed to correspond to academics' tendency to line up in orders of battle designated by various "isms"—Marxism, feminism, Freudianism, deconstructionism—each claiming to be a different genre of discourse capable of liberating truth from the prison in which the other genres had held it silent. And where else today can we find the search for the truth as a daily ideological struggle? Only in the university, it would seem. And the meeting of the monks that ends in fisticuffs is only a way of portraying, through a visible sign, the very real aggressions between all of us "colleagues." And how typical William is of the tenured intellectual: he loathes power as it is portrayed in the figure of the abbot, who, like most university deans and presidents, has left the world of learning behind for a life of politics, pomp, and cynical patting-oneself-on-the-back. William sympathizes instead with the Dolcinians, that is to say, the Marxists, the poor, and the Other. He supports affirmative action and diversity, but he spends all his time in the library and in theorizing, which as he himself realizes will never fit the facts. When poor Remigio and the girl are carted off to be executed, he does not lift a finger.

UMBERTO: *Ecco!* You have found it, my friend, the perfect generic designation for my book. But just remember that you have chosen this genre because it gives the book a certain use-value for you. To move from "monk's novel" to "campus novel" is something like moving from a ten-year-old girl's use of the word "brick" to a bricklayer's use of the same word. The value must inevitably change. The "monk's novel" can have no value to you. Believe me, monks still carry on their scholastic debates today, but why write about them? It does not seem to have the social power that accrues to university scholastic debates. And so, like Walter Benjamin who reads the excessively profane world of *Trauerspiel* as pointing to redemption, you take all the surface features of the *Rose* at their negative values. If the book seems to explore the past, it is in order for it to be able to work in the present; if the discussion seems to concern only monks, it is so that we university professors will be able to read it. After all, the world at large knows that the only things worth fighting over are money and sex and child custody. In the post-Gorbachev era, the only people in the world willing to kill each other over ideas are academics.

WALTER: So the Franciscans' struggle with the Dominicans over the poverty of Christ is meant to allegorize our own absurd allegiance to one theory over another?

UMBERTO: Not only the struggle, really, which is historical fact, but the impossibility of defining the real battle lines in such a struggle. For the Franciscans, you will remember, argue among themselves. Yes, I intentionally put in as many movements as I possibly could—Minorites, Umiliati, Beghards, Joachimites, Williamites, Waldensians, Dolcinians, Fratricelli, Catharists, Arnoldists, Patarines, and so on. And of course the papists fight the antipapists, the Franciscans loathe the Dominicans, and the Italians feel oppressed by all the foreigners who have consistently occupied the high offices in the abbey. But this kind of strife between denominations was inevitable, given that categorization was the method of inquiry in all things. After all, ancient science did not inquire of being or put it to the torture (as in scientific experiments); it accused, imputed "categories," and then followed their histories, awaiting results that were "largely and for the most part" true. And so all the wars in the *Rose* are sorting wars.

WALTER: Then the reader of your book is left with the impression of a process of a continual mitosis of discourse, a never-ending replication of religious genres like the production of ever-more-varied flowers: "Let them seek and seek again, let them endlessly push back the limits of their happiness, those ideological Alchemists! Let them offer prizes of sixty, a hundred thousand florins for the solution of their ambitious problems! As for me, I have found my *black rose!*"

UMBERTO: *Ecco!*—those lines sound familiar. Where have I read them before?

WALTER: Rilke perhaps, "Das Roseninnere"? At any rate, categorization dominates the center of your book the way the Aedificium dominates the monastery and the missing book of Aristotle dominates the mystery. And the kind of sorting that happens in the library is meant to confuse, to deny rather than provide access to knowledge. The library, like certain legal strategies, becomes an instrument not for distributing the truth, but for delaying its appearance.

UMBERTO: Yes, I think I had to look hardest at lawyers in order to understand the abbey. The monks, with their Latin and their incomprehensible system of classification, become like lawyers whose livelihood depends on making sure no one can speak their language. They must make sure as well that no one gets to the bottom of their system of classifying books, which is the Dewey decimal system having a nightmare. And William's big success in the book is finally getting to the bottom of that system.

WALTER: And so your book is not really a *Krimi* or a *Mönchsroman* or even an *Universitätsgeländeroman;* no, you have really written a *Gattungsroman* (genre novel). It is really a book about books, a novel about genres. How else can we put order into the novel's various discourses and dialects or explain the central role of the library and the deciphering of its classificatory system, and how else can we explain that the book that everyone is willing to kill for is Aristotle's lost treatise on comedy?

UMBERTO: This is one surprise I pulled from the detective genre. Everyone was expecting something about a false pope or some other "hard information." A new apocryphal book of the Bible, or a new and exquisitely illustrated apocalypse, maybe. No one was expecting that people would kill for theory.

WALTER: No one *ever* suspects theory. Yet Aristotle's book, had it survived, would have taken genre theory in a different direction, since it would make clear that genres can only be defined as they are opposed to other genres and as use-values.

UMBERTO: Use-values? I don't understand.

WALTER: Aristotle really defines tragedy as a use-value; it is just that without the special emphasis on catharsis that the comparison with comedy would have given, people tend to concentrate exclusively on the list of structural features, and hence they end up calling Aristotle the first formalist. In the treatise on tragedy, Aristotle mentions catharsis as the bottom line for deciding what a tragedy is. Now, if we look at his discussion of music in the *Politics*, we see that catharsis has a specific social use-value, and that use-value is only understandable in relation to the ideology of the *polis*:

> We say, however, that music is to be studied for the sake of many benefits and not of one only. It is to be studied with a view to education, with a view to a purge [catharsis] . . . and thirdly with a view to the right use of leisure and for relaxation and rest after exertion. It is clear, then, that we must use all the [musical] scales, but not all in the same way. For educational purposes we must use those that best express character, but we may use melodies of action and enthusiastic melodies for concerts where other people perform. For every feeling that affects some souls violently affects all souls more or less; the difference is only one of degree. Take pity and fear, for example, or again enthusiasm. Some people are liable to become possessed by the latter emotion, but we shall see that, when they have made use of the melodies that fill the soul with orgiastic feeling, they are brought back by these sacred melodies to a normal condition as if they had been medically treated and undergone a purge [catharsis]. . . . In the same manner cathartic melodies give innocent joy to men. (*Politics* 8.7.1341b 35–1342a 8)

Different scales or modes have different effects on their listeners, hence different use-values. The musical system as a whole reproduces all the various functions of a member of the *polis*. One of those use-values, catharsis, is then ascribed to tragedy. We see that Aristotle defined tragedy first by its use-value, catharsis, and then described the generic features that produced that use-value. This would have been more apparent if his work on comedy had survived. In that work Aristotle, *your* Aristotle at any rate, counters the fear and pity of catharsis with the use-value of laughter: "In the first book we dealt with tragedy and saw how, by arousing pity and fear, it produces catharsis, the purification of those feelings. As we promised, we will now deal with comedy . . . and see how, in inspiring the pleasure of the ridiculous, it arrives at the purification of that passion. That such passion is most worthy of consideration we have already said in the book on the soul, inasmuch as — alone among the animals — man is capable of laughter" (468).[8] No wonder Jorge feels threatened by this book. Neither faith nor reason, but only laughter differentiates man from the animals.

UMBERTO: The theme of laughter is meant to put the lie to Jorge's outmoded categorizations. Signs and language are no longer attributed exclusively to man. Ethnology demonstrates that other animals also use reason and language. Science has broken down the distinctions between man and animal to the extent that the last remaining difference between them is laughter.

WALTER: Absolutely. It is only by granting animals the full capacity to communicate and by observing that capacity fully that we can recognize the importance of our own nonintellectual channels. Only then, after first specifying the use-value that gives the genre of comedy its essence, does your Aristotle go on to assemble a list of generic markers: "We will then define the type of actions by which comedy is the mimesis, then we will examine the means by which comedy excites laughter, and these means are actions and speech. We will show how the ridiculousness of actions

8. I am not sure whether our anonymous author translated the following from Eco, or just went to Aristotle: "Nel primo libro abbiamo trattato della tragedia e di come essa suscitando pietà e paura produca la purificazione di tali sentimenti. Come avevamo promesso, trattiamo ora della commedia . . . e di come suscitando il piacere del ridicolo essa pervenga alla purificazione di tale passione. Di quanto tale passione sia degna di considerazione abbiamo già detto nel libro sull'anima, in quanto — solo tra tutti gli animali — l'uomo è capace di ridere" (471).

is born from the likening of the best to the worst and vice versa, from arousing surprise through deceit, from the impossible, from violation of the laws of nature, from the irrelevant and the inconsequent, from the debasing of the characters" (468).[9] I happen to agree with your colleague Leo Aureus, who has noticed that you left something out of this definition, namely, the probable twin of Aristotelian *katharsis*. The corresponding emotion in comedy would have to be indignation, *nemesan*.

UMBERTO: All right, all right, but didn't you notice how closely my dear colleague Leo resembles Jorge, and how he even made Aristotle resemble Jorge too, with his awful passion for truth? It is another example of how facts, discontented with merely finding a foothold in history, are now also usurping the domain of fancy, and have invaded the kingdom of the novel. Leo writes his own little fiction, where the bad rap that Truth, God, and Certainty get in my book dismay Aristotle, and evoke from him, the philosopher who gave order and clarity to the universe of knowledge at his disposal, the mocking laughter of deep discontent. So there is a laughter of truth! First of all, Aristotle is much less intimidating than Plato on this account, but second, Leo mistook the genre of my work! He only allows one kind of *fingere*, like all those critics who insist that *Oroonoko* be Aphra Behn's biography, her whole biography, and nothing but her biography.

WALTER: What a paradox! On the one hand, Leo is condemning fiction; on the other hand, he has recognized the *Rose* only as theory. One reason I wrote my *Elephantenuhr* the way I did was so that no one could slap terms like *erbaulich* (edifying) on it. The urge to get rid of literature is simultaneously the urge to repress semiotics as a self-reflexive enterprise. A number of persons, like Leo and Jorge, have wondered whether we shouldn't just *eradicate* literature (viz., semiology). What an enchanting disagreement with one's own viscera! Others, liberals and humanists, have always wanted and continue wanting to train it. One of them repeatedly dreams of a guideline within which thoroughly learned gentlemen speaking with constant sniffs can train this literature

9. Again, Eco or Aristotle? "Defineremo dunque di quale tipo di azioni sia mimesi la commedia, quindi esamineremo i modi in cui la commedia suscita il riso, e questi modi sono i fatti e l'eloquio. Mostreremo come il ridicolo dei fatti nasca dalla assimilazione del migliore al peggiore e viceversa, dal sorprendere ingannando dall'impossibile e dalla violazione delle leggi di natura, dall'irrilevante e dall'inconseguente, dall'abbassamento dei personaggi" (471–72).

(viz., semiology) to carry out noble missions. Or someone else discovers with forensic eagerness and casuistic ingenuity that literature (viz., semiology) has always worked together with mankind's very best capital, that it is enlightening and benevolent. They scratch literature's (viz., semiology's) skin made of metaphors until the zeitgeist and a disgusting white liquid, weltanschauung, spurt out.[10] And so, in your campus novel, the central conflict between this fanatic, truth-loving, aristocratic tight-ass Jorge and the semioticians is expressed as a generic conflict between poetry and Scripture, which are also separated by their use-values. Benno reports to William on Jorge's condemnation of Aristotle's *Poetics* on the grounds that it speaks of literature. Jorge has proposed metaphor as a generic marker to separate poetry from Scripture, and has received the disturbing reply that this same marker can be found in both genres. He therefore moves to the two use-values of the opposing genres that can be expressed by the same marker:

"Jorge added that the second cause for uneasiness is that in the book the Stagirite was speaking of poetry, which is *infima doctrina* and which exists of figments. And Venantius said that the psalms, too, are works of poetry and use metaphors; and Jorge became enraged because he said the psalms are works of divine inspiration and use metaphors to convey the truth, while the works of the pagan poets use metaphors to convey falsehood and for purposes of mere pleasure, a remark that greatly offended me." (111)[11]

10. "Manch einer," höre ich ihn sagen, "hat sich Gedanken gemacht, ob man die Literatur, die Semiologie nicht ganz *abschaffen* sollte. Welch entzückendes Zerwürfnis mit den eigenen Eingeweiden! Andere, Liberale und Humanisten, wollten und wollen sie *erziehen*. Immer wieder träumt einer von einem unantastbaren Leitfaden, in dem grundgelehrte Gentlemen mit näselnder Stimme die Literatur, die Semiologie zu edlen Missionen erziehen. Oder ein anderer entdeckt mit forensischem Eifer und kasuistischer Spitzfindigkeit, daß die Literatur, die Semiologie doch im Grunde schon immer mit den besten Kapitalien der Menschen zusammengarbeitet habe, daß sie *aufklärend* und *willfährig* sei. Man kratzt an ihrer Metaphernhaut, bis der 'Zeitgeist' und eine ekle, weißliche Flüssigkeit, die 'Weltanschauung' hervorquillt." (Höllerer, *Die Elephantenuhr*, 468–69)

11. " 'Ma Jorge aggiunse che il secondo motivo di inquietudine è che ivi lo stagirita parlasse della poesia che è infima doctrina e che vive di figmenta. E Venanzio disse che anche i salmi sono opera di poesia e usano metafore e Jorge si adirò perché disse che i salmi sono opera di ispirazione divina e usano metafore per trasmettere la verità mentre le opere dei poeti pagani usano metafore per trasmettere la menzogna e a fini di mero diletto.' " Eco, *Il nome della rosa*, 119.

This sounds like "Jorge" Habermas, always reminding us of the distinction between literature and "serious" discourse that solves problems. And how similar to the distinction drawn between medicine and poison just a few pages earlier: "The line between poison and medicine is very fine; the Greeks used the word 'pharmakon' for both" (108).[12]

Jorge is not dumb. When he read the text by Aristotle he immediately and instinctively recognized comedy's use-value: the removal of fear through laughter. And since Jorge, like Hobbes, thinks that only fear keeps man in line within the *polis*, he also thinks that comedy can only lead to apocalypse: "This is why Christ did not laugh. Laughter foments doubt" (132).[13] And Jorge's greatest fear is also generic. Comedy's mere existence is bad enough, but if allowed into the Aristotelian corpus it will become philosophy; comedy would have to be taken seriously.

UMBERTO: Now I see your point. And Jorge's only defense against the ideological power of Aristotle's genre system is to neutralize it with that other system of generic classification, the library.

WALTER: People tend to read the burning of the library at the end of your novel as a kind of tragic outcome, but it would have pleased my hero, Gustaf, for it is the beginning of a new placement, a new circulation (the evil of money for the monks is that it circulates), a blow against dead knowledge. For the library is made out of stone; it too is a monument which Gustaf wishes to destroy and replace with the brain, the brain as a monument or the monument as a brain, as in the thought of Karl Hartung. In such a model we could climb all over the monument, and one could conceive of it as a brain constantly altering its thoughts. The brain-monument also stores up signs and signs of signs, like a library, but it cannot be guarded by fanatics like Jorge:

> And I ask myself why at the same time this wind is blowing so many documents and books stand as if dead in the museum in assigned places. — As though it were not the fate of books to always be *further*-written, by you and by others; by whoever reads them semiotically: a book, a leap, an escape from pinned-

---

12. " 'Il limite tra il veleno e la medicina è assai lieve, i greci chiamavano entrambi *pharmacon*' " (116).

13. "Ecco perché Cristo non rideva. Il riso è fomite di dubbio" (139).

down writing; their holding on is only good enough for one thing, for the possible escape act, and when the books are no good for that, then they are worth little, almost nothing. Here he sits, the writer, in the collective brain; there you sit, the reader, in the collective brain; the brain is changing; the book, though fixed at first glance, is being transformed through its being looked at from an ever-changing brain. And the book for its part gives the detonating sentence for such processes, the trigger to a chain-transformation-flash, *if* such a thing takes place; small explosions that keep on affecting us; a blink of the eyes in the tunnel of humanity.[14]

You can see why the books in the Abbey library are extremely flammable and explode on being read. Think of the heat that possessed Adelmo and Berengar. And so, I finally recognized why you had come to write theory in the form of fiction. It was to get that element of the risible, of dialogic, carnivalesque, Bergson-esque laughter into theory. The law of genre, the Don't-Bee of history, has denied laughter the ability to create theory. Only a few wise-acres, like Schlegel and Nietzsche, have been able to overcome that prohibition.

UMBERTO: [*The two have reached the top of the hill. Umberto takes his friend by the arm and shows him Rome stretched out below them, an anthill of activity.*] Here we are at the summit. I find everything you've said up to this point utterly convincing, even if I hadn't thought of any of it that way before.

WALTER: That is, even if it is not true. [*Picks up a rusted Social Democrat election button.*] We've reached the top of the mountain and the bottom of history's slide. It's like the poet says: You'll find out when you've reached the top, you're on the bottom.

---

14. "Und ich frage mich, warum so viele Dokumente und Bücher zur selben Zeit, in der dieser Wind bläst, im Museum dastehen an festen Plätzen, wie tot.—Als ob es nicht die Chance von Büchern wäre, immer-*weiter*-geschrieben zu werden, von dir und von anderen; wer immer sie semiologisch liest: ein Buch, ein Sprung, Absprung von festgepinnter Schrift; ihr Halt ist für *eins* nur gut genug, für den möglichen Absprungs-Akt, und wenn die Bücher nicht dazu taugen, taugen sie wenig, fast nichts. Hier sitzt er, der Schreiber, im kollektiven Gehirn; dort sitzt du, der Leser, im kollektiven Gehirn; das Gehirn ändert sich; das Buch, festgelegt, auf den ersten Blick, wird verändert durch den Blick aus einem immer anders sich ändernden Gehirn. Und das Buch gibt den Zündsatz zu solchen Verfahren, andererseits; den Anreiz zu einem Änderungs-Ketten-Blitz, *wenn* es ihn gibt; kleine fortwirkende Explosionen; ein Blinken im Tunnel der Menschheit." Höllerer, *Die Elephantenuhr*, 212–13.

The Ideology of Genre

UMBERTO: And this is the most beautiful view one can get of Rome. The whole city lies beneath us, just as your G sees it, a form of writing, like everything in Japan.

WALTER: But now you, my friend, don't you see that William and Adso's long search for *the* book is a search for *any* book, a search for a defined object between two covers rather than for a generalized form of writing? The religious conceptions that you present are also the principles of modernism, the idea of the book in the Middle Ages is also Mallarmé's idea of the spirituality of the tome, the project of the book, a reverence shared by all the characters in your story.

UMBERTO: But my friend, it seems that our two books agree here, in the ideology of their genres, more than anywhere else. You are correct; all of my characters, who disagree about everything else, revere the book. Only the events themselves disagree. The library disagrees. Isn't the ecpyrosis at the end of the novel the negation of that kind of thinking? Here too, I find the parallels between our works almost exact. Gustaf blows up the museum at the end of *Elephantenuhr*. Isn't that an equivalent of the burning of the books?

WALTER: How so?

UMBERTO: After all, what use had the books been, hidden as they were from the eyes of everyone, both because they were written in code (the dead or foreign languages) and because they were stored in an impenetrably intricate order, and because no one was allowed into the fortress? And isn't the complex tapestry collected by Adso decades afterward from the library's ashes the model for a new kind of intertextual semiosis, beyond the museum, beyond the collection?

WALTER: But listen to Adso's elegiac tone as he weaves his text! He laments that he can only construct "a kind of lesser library, a symbol of the greater, vanished one: a library made up of fragments, quotations, unfinished sentences, amputated stumps of books" (500).[15] Adso still sees his compilation—which is *The Name of the Rose*, of course—as merely a "segno," a sign of something larger that is missing. His tragic (instead of comic) voice leaves readers wallowing in the emotions aroused by the old-fashioned

15. ". . . biblioteca minore, segno di quello magiore scomparsa, una biblioteca fatta di brani, citazioni, periodi incompiuti, moncherini di libri." Eco, *Il nome della rosa*, 502.

idea of reconstructing the transcendental signified, rather than moving them forward toward the *gaya scienza* of an endless, metonymic traversal of the labyrinth of signifiers. He contradicts everything in your theory as well as in Aristotle's theory of comedy.

UMBERTO: Whereas your Gustaf, though he seems to be as confused, unhappy, imaginatively unstable, and horny as my Adso, nevertheless formulates a semiotic ideal. And he *acts*.

WALTER: But you had to leave Adso—and hence your readers— unhappy, and why? Because you were writing a *Mönchsroman*, and to portray Adso with a modern semiotic perspective would have violated the limits of that genre.

UMBERTO: Whereas you have written *The Name of the Novel*, a book that deliberately violates the limits of genre, a text through which we search and search for a novel and find something different. And so the final showdown between us is finally over genre, isn't it? I had no idea, I'm really shocked, Master Walter, that two old friends like us must have our own sorting war.

WALTER: What is academia for? In Gustaf, I tried to show theory from the inside, because if theory tells us what literature is, a generalized semiology exposes the fragility of the boundaries between criticism and literature, theory and practice, leaving Gustaf with the single possibility of action. Instead of having to blow things up, I was able to write this novel, a much longer, quieter, gradual explosion of the genre of criticism.

UMBERTO: But aren't both our messages equally ideological, that the politics of information, archaic and reactionary as it is, con- flicts with the way people otherwise experience their world? Doesn't the mimetic figure of Adso in novelistic conflict with the world around him show the inadequacies of this politics too?

WALTER: Perhaps you are right.

UMBERTO: And look at all the other similarities, like the role of memory. Are our two central symbols, the library and the ele- phant, really all that different from each other? Like the memory that a library represents, the elephant's memory is a collective one and a dialectical one, as much a dismembering as a remembering. Without the elephant's memory, which goes beyond a single memory that remains within its own time frame, without this elephantine memory, which literature attempts again and again, there would be no active, passionate—*ecco! italienische Reise, kennst du das Land, wo die Zitronen blühn?*—changes in contemporary consciousness, because there would be no continuity and no comparison. The elephant's head stands there like a huge library, it stretches from London to Vienna to Siebenburgen to Tokyo to Bari.[16] The elephant's trunk, similar in shape and function to the nose and the penis, is the new monument, constantly sending and receiving nonlogical signs. The trunk, swinging back and forth, is the image of a totally sensual sign communication, uncontaminated by the intellect.

WALTER: But I still find that your desire to write something "readable" that can be sold in a supermarket has led you to some very limited semiosis.

UMBERTO: I too, in my early years, in the years you were writing your semiotic novel, objected to anything popular, to anything that appealed to nonprofessional readers. Only the avant-garde, the artistically innovative text, which would read like a nonnarrative because of its new techniques, was valid. But history puts the lie to such an attitude. Popularity, the destruction of narrative, and the death of genre are all separate questions. They do not share an ideology, and the generalized semiotics you have in mind should encompass them all.

WALTER: Still, you will forgive me for my stubbornness, but it seemed to me as if you constructed another library in which books are constantly whispering to each other, whereas I tried to construct a text with a structure like this hill, an archaeology, a *bricolage* constructed from the shards and splinters of narrative. While you have your characters—like your readers—negotiate a labyrinth in their search for a book, my Gustaf has gone long beyond the focus on script, even on words.

UMBERTO: I see, sort of. Whereas my book ends with a piecing together of texts after the catastrophe of the fire, your entire book is such an explosion of the channels of communication. Neverthe-

---

16. "Ohne das Gedächtnis der Elephanten, sagen diese Autoren, das über ein Gedächtnis hinausgreift, welches in seinen jeweiligen Zeitbezügen sich abstrampelt,—ohne den Versuch dieses elephantischen Gedächtnisses, den die Literatur immer wieder unternimmt, gäbe es keine aktive, sehnsuchtsbezogene Veränderung im zeitgenössischen Bewußtsein, weil es keine Kontinuität gäbe und keinen Vergleich gäbe. Der Kopf des Elephanten steht da wie eine große Bibliothek, sie reicht von London über Wien bis Siebenbürgen, bis Tokyo, bis Bari in Italien." Walter Höllerer, "Das historische Bewußtsein und das Gedächtnis des Elephanten," 46.

less, as a reader, I really experience Gustaf's search as a putting together of the pieces of a jigsaw puzzle. In that he is not much different from Adso. The genre of fiction allowed both of us to make a riddle rather than the riddle's answer. And in both works the riddles come in the form of labyrinths.

WALTER: But you allow your reader to experience this labyrinth from the outside, as a model, whereas I put the reader in the middle of the real thing, the torturous, labored reading of an autobiography of the collective, which must be a poem of inconvenience.

UMBERTO: Ah, but I too wanted the first hundred pages of my text to be inconvenient for the reader, so that he would really feel that he had accomplished something afterward. Yes, for me, the difference between writing theory and writing a novel was precisely that of choosing between a model of the labyrinth of reading, which was expected to correspond to the object it represented, and the labyrinth itself, which readers were free to remake at their leisure and which didn't have to be perfect, but only complex. You know, when I wrote theoretical works, my attitude toward reviewers was judicial: Have they or have they not understood what I meant? With a novel, the situation is completely different. I am not saying that the author may not find a discovered reading perverse; but even if he does, he must remain silent, allow others to challenge it, text in hand.[17] I see two very different use-values, just like you can sue someone because he wrote your biography but not because he wrote a novel based on your life, you see?

WALTER: Yes, the labyrinth. The labyrinth means the continuity of theory. The novel is a laughing answer to those who always ask what my semiology is after all, in twenty-five words or less. In a statement of principles! As if I were not continually showing, how it is in-movement! As if I were not continually-giving-fresh-starts! As if I weren't sending-out-impulses: help-me-with-it! help-me-with-it! As if something finished and dead should be delivered![18]

---

17. "Quando scrivevo opere theoriche il mio atteggiamento verso i recensori era di tipo giudiziario: hanno capito o no quello che volevo dire? Con un romanzo e tutto diverso. Non dico che l'autore non possa scoprire una lettura che gli pare aberrante, ma dovrebbe tacere, in ogni caso, ci pensino gli altri a contestarla, testo alla mano." Umberto Eco, "Postille," 508.

18. " 'Immer höre ich die Klienten darauf dringen, was denn nun meine Semiologie, in wenigen Worten gesagt, sei. In einer Grandsatz-Erklärung! Als ob ich nicht dauernd vorzeigte, wie-sie-in-Bewegung-ist! Als ob ich nicht dauernd-Anstösse-gäbe! Als ob ich nicht Impulse ausschickte: macht-mit! macht-mit! Als ob hier etwas zu liefern wäre, das fertig und tot ist!' " Höllerer, *Die Elephantenuhr*, 60.

UMBERTO: *Ecco,* my attitude exactly. Or if people say that I used to write theory and now I write fiction, I ask them where exactly they would locate the differences. I have always wondered about this thing called theory. Where is it possible, for example, to separate it from criticism? When do we call an essay a piece of criticism and when a piece of theory?

WALTER: Exactly. In my other life, in the United States, when I teach theory, I teach it out of anthologies that have some title like *The History of Criticism.* Somewhere along the way, there was an alchemical change of this critical discourse into theoretical discourse. That is, our ideological appropriation of those texts by Horace and Boileau and Schlegel is now different. They are being used for different purposes now than before. In effect, critics collectively create an institution that validates particular notions of critical practice. Both within academia and in the world of publishing, that institution exercises definite (though not identical or even always consistent) administrative and economic control over critical writers. Yet the less visible elements of the institution of criticism are equally important. It is in this almost intangible area—of criticism as an intellectual and ideological institution— that criticism calls itself into existence and valorizes itself as a certain kind of discourse. This discursive institution establishes simultaneously a zone of permission and a sense of what is taboo, as well as the unstable realm in which one can experiment; thus, while it creates opportunities for discourse that would not otherwise exist, it also excludes opportunities it rejects. My namesake, that other Master Walter from Berlin, has seen the *kunstphiloso-phisches Feld,* I mean field, in which he hoped to make a contribution with his book on *Trauerspiel,* slip between his fingers as his work was appropriated by theory. Similarly, the good old, pedantic scholarly article, compressing within the concrete walls of its objectivity a genre of discourse that has an ill-defined relationship to the works it takes as its object: is it a metaphor of those works, a continuation, a by-product, a son, a daughter? And the incredible boredom of always writing within a single genre (as if that were possible), whereas the only way of being creative and politically effective is to constantly create new genres, albeit through *bricolage,* as theory was created.

UMBERTO: You have spoken eloquently of the misery and splendor involved in generic distinctions. The undecidable difference between criticism and literature is criticism's special burden, though it is also criticism's mode of performative rigor and, for those, like Roland Barthes, who are willing to employ the resources of this problematic, criticism's form of play. I too tried turning my essays into *haiku.* Then I decided just to start writing lists and catalogs, and finally I ended up with the *Rose.* But, since you tend to be from across the great divide between literature and criticism, you choose instead to write a work of antitheory, where theory collapses back into the fiction it started from. You feign your hypotheses. You literally incorporate your theory into G. I can see in your writing the impossibility of separating a semiotic position from a political one and the necessity of the imagination in both. The critical-theoretical essay is part of the Wall that encloses and blocks off memory and imagination. The only way to become a wall-jumper is to project oneself beyond, into a homunculus such as G. Theory becomes praxis. But you are not satisfied even with that, this solidity of character is also too contrived. You will be content only when you can show us the heavens in a handful of dust.

WALTER: And now I must sing my palinode, and take back all the nasty things I have said about the genre of your work, to pray that the genre god will not be too angry with me. I will admit that I was plotting to kill both of us. I planted hundreds of sticks of dynamite under our feet, I was going to blow us both to smithereens, to allow the *sparagmos* of our bodies to become part of the semiotic labyrinth of the Testaccio, to free both of our minds from the prison of life, since both of us have written against monuments and have created them.

UMBERTO: And if you had done so, the Roman police chief would have said: "Round up the usual suspects—and the usual *corpora delicti* while you're at it." Of course, I will never know whether you are telling the truth about your murderous intentions. The relation of semiotics to truth, science, scholarship, history, and sophism is at least worth many inferential walks and arguments such as this one has been. And make sure you speak your palinode broadly enough to include Raimundus as well, whose spirit lies here on this black mountain, even if his body does not.

WALTER: And so let me sing this palinode, not my own composition, of course, but that of the greatest *italienischer Reiser* of all:

Since neither knowledge nor reflection can create a whole—for the former lacks interiority, the latter exteriority—then we must necessarily conceive of science as art if we wish it to have any kind of wholeness.

UMBERTO: And perhaps the use-value of our new genre is to give theory an interiority, the way your countryman Gellert helped give an interiority to those awful *artes dictaminis* that my countrymen, old Bondi for example, at Montecassino, had produced so many of. And, as this seems to be the best statement we can come up with on after-genre for the present, let us quit our newly achieved summit for the depths of our conference.

8

Theoretical Postlude:
The Ideology of Genre

I'm too rock for country, too country for rock 'n roll.

—Lonnie Mack

SO I EXIT THE SUPERMARKET with two bags of Smarties® (my only vice) and a paperback thriller (my only other vice). At least the book's cover, title, and blurbs have lulled me into concluding that it is a thriller. (You can't be too careful. I've heard horror stories about slasher-movie aficionados flocking to see *Henry, Portrait of a Serial Killer* and then almost vomiting at a movie that tries to take its title seriously rather than fulfill their anodyne generic expectations. And then there's all those suckers who bought *The Name of the Rose* thinking that it was Dungeons and Dragons stuff.) I hop into my car and turn on the radio, pressing one by one the buttons I have set to their various generic wavelengths: inspirational, classical, hard rock, adult-contemporary, country. . . . Wait a minute, what am I hearing? "I'm too rock for country, too country for rock 'n roll."[1] Some singer with the audacity to make a hit by lamenting the fact that he falls through the cracks of the generic system. It's them old generic-instability-blues *again!*

In the previous chapters I selectively documented the extent to which the meaning of a literary text can depend on the play between its generic categories. By now, my reader should be convinced that the truly vital meanings of a text are often contained not in any specific generic category

---

1. Lonnie Mack, "Too Rock for Country, Too Country for Rock 'n Roll," *Roadhouses & Dancehalls* (Epic 44075, 1988), side 1, band 1.

into which the text may be placed, but rather in the play of differences
between its genres. In these final pages, then, it will be useful to summarize
some of the theoretical premises behind my readings, to show that such
play is a result of the fact that genre is a system constituted by differences,
to better define the concept of use-value as the foundation of genre, and to
elaborate the link between genre and ideology. I elaborate upon these
points in reference to previous work in genre theory, making particular
use of Walter Benjamin's theory in *Der Ursprung des deutschen Trauerspiels*
(The Origin of German Tragic Drama), one of the most provocative and
difficult genre "studies" to date. The inevitable reduction of Benjaminian
mysticism may strike some readers as willful or perverse, like Benjamin's
own reading of baroque drama; indeed, it is my final example of anaclastic
comparison, "[Eine] Verbrennung des Werkes, in welcher seine Form zum
Höhepunkt ihrer Leuchtkraft kommt" (211; "[An] incineration of the
work in which its external form achieves its most brilliant degree of
illumination" [31]).[2] Perhaps my placement of Benjamin's work, which he
assigned to the genre of the philosophy of art, in the very different context
of this theoretical treatise on genre can be considered part and parcel of
this process of "rettende Kritik" ("redemptive criticism").

I

"I'm too rock for country, too country for rock 'n roll." As always, popular
speech here shows an extraordinary fondness for theoretical pronounce-
ments. The singer sings the genre(s) of his music. No need to wait for
some academic to come along and theorize it (them) for him. My first
point, then, is that genre is only secondarily an academic enterprise and a
matter for literary scholarship. Primarily, genre is the precondition for the
creation and the reading of texts.

Recent genre theory has tended to regard its objects neither as collections of texts nor as lists of essential features of texts, but rather as
processes of interpretation. A good example is E. D. Hirsch, who makes
genre a key element of the hermeneutic theory presented in his *Validity in*

---

2. Walter Benjamin, *Der Ursprung des deutschen Trauerspiels;* translated by John Osborne, under
the title *The Origin of German Tragic Drama.* [Works of general theoretical interest in the field of
genre studies are cited in full in the Bibliography—AUTHOR.] Further citations in text.

Interpretation. The successes and failures of his approach to genre are instructive. Hirsch begins by redefining the hermeneutic circle as the relationship between genre and trait. Identification of the genre of an utterance becomes the first, necessary step in the delimitation of its meaning: "All understanding of verbal meaning is necessarily genre-bound."[3] In addition to placing genre where it belongs—in the reading process—Hirsch also takes the necessary step of applying genre to all verbal utterances (which we might amplify to include all communication). Numerous theorists make the unwarranted assumption that genres only fit *within* the supergenre called literature.[4] In analyzing texts that "use" such genres as ethnography and legal discourse, I have shown that the interpretation of literary genres depends on a recognition of their nonliterary neighbors as well.

Having established the ubiquity and necessity of genre, Hirsch then negates that necessity by allowing texts to assign themselves unique genres. Hirsch calls these "intrinsic genres." A good idea of the difficulties that such a position leads Hirsch into can be gathered from his attempt to define the intrinsic genre of Milton's *Paradise Lost*. The "trait" here, the other side of the hermeneutic circle, is the poem's first lines:

> To understand those lines an immense amount of relevant knowledge is required, but the one overarching conception which determines not only the meaning and function of that long sentence, but also just what knowledge *is* relevant to its understanding is the conception [e.g., the intrinsic genre], *Paradise Lost*. No one, no matter how learned and sensitive to poetry, could possibly understand those lines if he did not rightly understand the kind of poem this is, by which I certainly do not mean "a Christian-humanist epic in blank verse" nor any other manageable compound name. To understand those lines it is necessary to grasp, in a way more specific than any label [e.g., genre as it is commonly understood] could be, the particular type of "Christian-humanist epic" this is. (84–85)

---

3. E. D. Hirsch, *Validity in Interpretation*, 76. Further citations in text.

4. The following formulation of this usually unargued axiom is unusual for its explicitness: "The division into 'poetic' and 'nonpoetic,' 'fictional' and 'nonfictional' must also be dropped as all genres acquire a right to aesthetic existence precisely through their 'poetic,' 'fictional' character. . . . Classification in accordance with the practical use of the genres—poetic, scientific, utilitarian—should be discarded because of the very extra-aesthetical, predominantly heteronomous criteria adopted." Adrian Marino, "Toward a Definition of Literary Genres," in *Theories of Literary Genre*, ed. Joseph Strelka (University Park: Pennsylvania State University Press, 1978), 41.

A problem here is that "the conception, *Paradise Lost*" is determined not by the text itself, but by its reception. Otherwise, "intrinsic genre" would be just another term for "text" and would offer neither new insight into the hermeneutic circle nor a way of penetrating it. The intrinsic genre of *Paradise Lost* that the reader must be acquainted with in order to understand its first lines can only be the unique place of the text within literary history, a place carved out in opposition to other works within the same extrinsic genre of "Christian-humanist epic." By invoking the extrinsic genre "Christian-humanist epic" as a species of writing that will at least get the reader closer to the intrinsic genre of *Paradise Lost*, Hirsch implicitly and paradoxically accepts the very shaping role of tradition in the act of interpretation he disputes when formulated by theorists such as Hans-Georg Gadamer.

But Hirsch, who began his discussion of genre by emphasizing both its universality and its interpretive power in a way few critics have done, ends up joining Benedetto Croce in arguing for the uniqueness of every literary text. For Croce, that uniqueness derived from the origin of literary expression in *intuizione* (intuition) rather than in *concetto* (concept). These generic markers, or rather the ideas that divide artistic from rational forms of discourse, are the only valid ones for Croce.[5] Hirsch arrives at essentially the same position, with authorial intention substituted for *intuizione*. Hirsch's contradictions arise from the fact that he wishes to put genre to a use antithetical to it: as a heuristic for recovering a unique authorial intention. "Christian-humanist epic" recovers not authorial intention as the object contained within a black box, but rather the uses to which society has put that text and the values society has seen it as having.

The arguments of Hirsch and Croce seem fundamentally flawed in their assumption that textual sorting operates on the basis of identity rather than similarity. One can, however, recognize both the uniqueness of each text and the possibility of grouping them together on the basis of shared features, particularly if one proceeds along Alistair Fowler's line of "family resemblance": "Representatives of a genre may . . . be regarded as making up a family whose sets and individual members are related in various ways, without necessarily having any single feature shared in common by all."[6] (The problem with this approach, as Earl Miner points out, is the question,

5. See Benedetto Croce, *Estetica come scienza dell'espressione e linguistica generale*, 8th ed. (Bari: Laterza & Figli, 1945), esp. 75–82. Also interesting are Croce's caustic remarks on genre in "I «genere letterari» a congresso." See Bibliography.

6. Alistair Fowler, *Kinds of Literature: An Introduction to the Theory of Genres and Modes*, 41. The concept of "family resemblance" is derived from Ludwig Wittgenstein.

"How is one to decide that family resemblance does *not* exist?")[7] In other words, one can allow for and even welcome the lack of "fit" between the label "Christian-humanist epic" and *Paradise Lost,* as long as one recognizes the family resemblance, and as long as one agrees with Hirsch that such discrepancies are essential to the text's meaning. But then a great deal of textual meaning would reside not in authorial intention but in the realm of generic instability created by the genre system surrounding the text. If genre is a means of understanding, as Hirsch rightly argues, then part of authorial intention dissolves into the maze of rules for generic understanding which readers always impose on texts.

Like Hirsch, Adena Rosmarin recognizes the interpretive aspect of generic classification, and she explores in greater detail the results of such impositions. To classify a text is to describe how it can mean, and thus is not idle speculation but the unavoidable first step of criticism itself: "Classification enables criticism to begin."[8] Rosmarin focuses on the critic in order to avoid what she considers to be genre theory's blind spot: "Criticism has treated genre not as the critic's explanatory tool but as a hypothesis, a probable stab at the truth, something whose inherence in a particular literary text or whose independent existence as a schema is potentially verifiable or, at least refutable" (26). Instead, argues Rosmarin, genre should be looked at as the critic's tool of interpretation, and thus as ad hoc and pragmatic. No genre classification should be expected to stand the test of time; it has done its job if it enables the critic to make interesting statements about the text under consideration: "A genre is chosen or defined to fit neither a historical nor a theoretical reality but to serve a pragmatic end. It is meant to solve a critical problem, a problem that typically involves justifying the literary text's acknowledged but seemingly inexplicable value" (50). Although the word "value" seems indispensable to her pragmatic approach, Rosmarin does not specify further which kind of value she is talking about: linguistic, aesthetic, or economic? Thus, what Rosmarin calls "the power of genre" is a very limited enabling power. A student of the genre-killer Benedetto Croce, Mario Fubini, made a very similar argument after the *maestro* had supposedly destroyed his topic. The concept of genre, writes Fubini, is "legitimate, if the genre is considered only a means or an instrument whose function is limited only to recalling to mind those notions which are necessary for determining and fixing our

---

7. Earl Miner, "Some Issues of Literary Species, or Distinct Kind," in *Renaissance Genres,* ed. Barbara Kiefer Lewalski (Cambridge: Harvard University Press, 1986), 24.
8. Adena Rosmarin, *The Power of Genre,* 22. Further citations in text.

judgment, and if it is demanded by the development of critical discourse and responds to the needs of the critic."[9] Fubini and Rosmarin's exclusive concern with critics presupposes a completely atomistic world devoid of social forces and conventions, a world in which writers write their texts oblivious to readers and their generic expectations, and readers read these texts, apparently oblivious to genre distinctions, even though such distinctions stare them in the face every time they go to the bookstore, the supermarket, or the library. Only critics are left to worry about genre. In analyzing this last group, Rosmarin envisions a critic who is able to make a single, solitary, nonideological decision about which genres apply to a text. She is able to take this approach by reducing such isolated, arbitrary generic judgments to mere critical exercises. Such critical exercises, however, as this book has shown, are only made possible by the suppression of generic instability. Reading generic instability often means simply reading the text, as in *Tristes tropiques*, for example, or in the powerful message about reading that Eco puts into his *Rose* by making it appear to be a detective story.

Rosmarin's complete isolation of the critic results in a scholastic approach to the question of genre. She uses genre to construct the following exemplary syllogism, supposedly superior to more usual classificatory schemes:

> Let us define dramatic monologues as poems that invite their readers to distinguish the characterized speaker's meaning from the poem's.
>
> Let us discuss "Andrea del Sarto" as a dramatic monologue.
>
> Let us discuss "Andrea del Sarto" as inviting its readers to distinguish the speaker's meaning from the poem's. (Rosmarin, *Power*, 46)

This syllogism is problematic for several reasons—beyond the fact that philosophy and science since the late Middle Ages have not considered syllogisms to yield new knowledge. One, as pointed out above, is the failure to account for genric instability, which would require an "and not . . ." clause after each premise. The anaphoric "let us" also becomes a deceptive phrase. It implies that the decision to mark the dramatic monologue with the particular features announced is a purely ad hoc critical

9. Mario Fubini, "Genesi e storia dei generi letterari," 131.

exercise, the construction of a *problema*. The deception lies in the fact that no one invents a term like "dramatic monologue" on the spot. It and all genre terminology are intersubjective. Individuals can produce new generic conceptions only through *bricolage*—for example, my "apocalyptic ballad" in Chapter 6. Such an invention, which has some of the goals that Rosmarin envisions for her syllogism, goes beyond being an ad hoc theoretical exercise. Even *bricolage* did not arise simply from my individual critical will, but from a dialectic among a corpus of texts, the obvious models that served for the creation of those texts, and the cultural contexts and audience expectations that influenced the variations between models and new genre. Similarly, the dramatic monologue has a long history, and so its use here is hardly arbitrary, nor is its virtual definition as having a main speaker whose words are ironized by the poem as a whole. And of course the choice of "Andrea del Sarto" by Robert Browning, the poet universally identified with the genre of the dramatic monologue, is hardly arbitrary either. Neither the genre itself, nor the example for it, has been invented by the critic; the two premises of the syllogism are spoken by someone else, and it is interesting to ask who this someone else could be.

Rosmarin finds the following benefits in her syllogism:

> The [traditional] asserted relation between [genre and example] has become explicitly definitional rather than implicitly intrinsic or "natural." No longer claiming that "Andrea del Sarto" *is* a dramatic monologue, that there is some intrinsic or natural connection between the two, we now propose a pragmatic thought-experiment: let us explore what "Andrea del Sarto" is like when we read it in terms of the genre here defined as "dramatic monologue." The syllogistic process of deducing the poem from the genre is now refined—and redefined—as the unpacking of metaphoric equivalences. (46)

I have already pointed out that this "explicitly definitional" approach simply hides rather than penetrates the hermeneutic circle of genre criticism. For example, one might ask how and why Rosmarin got from step 1 to step 2 of the syllogism? That is, why choose "Andrea del Sarto" and not "Dover Beach" as a dramatic monologue, unless one is already convinced that it fits the major premise? And how does one decide such a thing, if not by considering certain features of the poem? The "let us" Rosmarin substitutes for "is" has almost no logical force. But if it did have logical force, then it would make the syllogism—and hence genre—useless. For if

the critic is merely being arbitrary, then what could the first two parts of
the syllogism add to the statement "Let us discuss 'Andrea del Sarto' as
inviting its readers to distinguish the speaker's meaning from the poem's"?
If one is to take generic classification as merely an arbitrary decision by an
individual critic, then this new syllogism hardly seems necessary in order
for us to arrive at new critical insights. It becomes a tautology.

   In contrast, the study examples in this book proceed not tautologically,
but anaclastically, always using more than one syllogism at a time and
comparing their results, as it were, and choosing less obvious matches for
major and minor premises: "Let us look at this *ars dictaminis* as if it were
an epistolary novel." Behind this alternative method lies an alternative
conception of the uses of genre, based on the argument that critics should
be less interested in generic classification than in discovering, first of all,
the kinds of systems and intertextual relationships (rather than individual
genres) that have given them the classifications they take for granted, and
second, the tensions *within* texts between contradictory generic features.
Above all, critics should note that such tensions are of the utmost importance for authors and readers. In the case of Lonnie Mack, belonging to a
particular genre is the prerequisite for getting played on the radio. Genre
is seen here as a balancing act between alternate possibilities, rather than
as the construction of a logical syllogism. This song's unclassifiability is
indicative of the lack of positive terms in the generic system of differences.

   And therefore, "Thou shalt not define genres singly"; the linguistic
principle formulated by Ferdinand de Saussure must be applied to genre.
Saussure had written: "Dans le langage il n'y a que des différences *sans
des termes positifs*" ("In language there are only differences *without positive
terms*").[10] I write: "Genre is a system of differences without positive terms."
This is the spirit, though not the letter, of Paul Hernadi's claim that the
most useful genre investigations will always "focus on the *order of literature*,
not on the *borders between literary genres*."[11] Hernadi is only one of several
critics who have recognized the need for a systemic approach to genre.
Heather Dubrow has found a useful analogy for this systemic approach to
genre in the color spectrum:

> Much as colors appear in actual objects in different degrees of
> saturation, for example, so a work may display the characteristics

   10. Ferdinand de Saussure, *Cours de linguistique générale*, 4th ed., ed. Charles Bally and Albert
Sechehaye (Paris: Payot, 1965), 166; translated by Wade Baskin, under the title *Course in General
Linguistics* (London: Fontana-Collins, 1974), 121. Emphasis Saussure's.
   11. Paul Hernadi, *Beyond Genre: New Directions in Literary Classification*, 184. Emphasis Hernadi's.

of its genre vividly and precisely or, alternatively, offer an altered and less vivid version of generic patterns. And in a sense the opposing and paired genres that Claudio Guillén has termed "genre and counter-genre," such as pastoral and satire, resemble complementary colors—when combined they complete a spectrum of human emotions and values.[12]

Unfortunately, critics such as Hernadi, Dubrow, and Guillén have not sufficiently emphasized the lack of positive terms in these systems, even if the Saussurean principle goes a long way toward explaining the paradox of genres, namely that they seem real and at the same time indefinable. But to think of genre as a system of differences, we must obviously focus our attention on the borders between genres, because it is precisely there, in their differences, that genres exist. As Dubrow mentions, Claudio Guillén has begun this process by identifying generic pairs, but some chapters of this book have looked at more complex systems—*Oroonoko* and *Tristes tropiques* are located between ethnography, biography, and novel— and at pairs that take us outside the literary per se: *ars dictaminis* and epistolary novel, for example, or fiction and theory. Thus, grouping genres into pairs is only a start toward representing the complex relationships of generic ideas to one another, which of course also change through time. Walter Benjamin, for example, found that he needed to construct a complex system with many different terms in order to highlight the *Trauerspiel* against the web of its differences from other genres.

One of the most intriguing—and frustrating—aspects of Benjamin's *Ursprung des deutschen Trauerspiels* (henceforth simply *Ursprung*) is that it eschews Rosmarinian sentences of the type "*X* genre has *Y* features." Rather than attempt to define a single genre, the baroque *Trauerspiel*, Benjamin seeks to "pry it loose" from other, "neighboring" genres such as tragedy and comedy. Before arriving at the topic of *Trauerspiel*, Benjamin tried out this approach in an essay on the generic instability of Goethe's *Wahlverwandschaften*. In that essay, Benjamin linked the central ideas of appearance and expressionlessness to the forms of novel and novella, respectively (the feature of expressionlessness or silence being the novella's link with tragedy). In Benjamin's view, Goethe's text examines both genres, or rather the ideational conflict between them, and by doing so escapes any specific generic categorization.[13] For Benjamin, conflict and

12. Heather Dubrow, *Genre*, 29.
13. Walter Benjamin, "Goethes Wahlverwandschaften," in *Gesammelte Schriften I.1*, ed. Rolf Tiedemann (Frankfurt am Main: Suhrkamp, 1972), 125–201.

instability rather than conventional generic features alert us to the transcendental forms of literature.

Ursprung's gnomic "Erkenntniskritische Vorrede" ("Epistemological-
Critical Foreword") tries to demonstrate that genre theory cannot account
for genre on a purely phenomenal basis. A genre can never be a collection
of texts or a list of traits, since neither of these could include the idea that
genre represents: "Das Extrem einer Form oder Gattung ist die Idee, die
als solche in die Literaturgeschichte nicht eingeht" (218; "the idea is the
extreme example of a form or genre, and as such does not enter into the
history of literature" [38]). Benjamin then applies this dictum specifically
to the case of the *Trauerspiel:* "Das *Trauerspiel* im Sinn der kunstphiloso-
phischen Abhandlung ist eine Idee. Von der literarhistorischen unterschei-
det eine solche sich am auffallendsten darin, daß sie Einheit da voraussetzt,
wo jener Mannigfaltigkeit zu erweisen obliegt" (218; "In the sense in
which it is treated in the philosophy of art the *Trauerspiel* is an idea. Such
a treatment differs most significantly from a literary-historical treatment in
its assumption of unity, whereas the latter is concerned to demonstrate
variety" [38]). According to Bernd Witte, Benjamin's main point in this
passage, as in the whole of the foreword, is to distinguish between two
different uses of the term *Trauerspiel*, as word and as name: "How can one
mediate between the word, which comprehends in its abstraction the
panoply of empirically verifiable *Trauerspiel*, and the name, which symbol-
izes the totality of its idea? This task falls to the concepts."[14] Though
Benjamin apparently regarded his treatment of ideas in this foreword as
Platonist, the study itself treats *Trauerspiel* not as an unchanging idea, but
as a "durable object," to use Michael Thompson's phrase, that is, as a
man-made "eternal" object with a variable life span: "Eternal objects may
be ranged along a scale from those with immensely long life-spans involv-
ing the possibility for an astronomical number of actualities to those with
quite short life-spans encompassing the possibility for only a very few
actualities."[15] Benjamin's "ideas" do not arise from cosmological necessity.
Rather, they come about as the only possible indexes capable of expressing
the objectively necessary formation (the *Ursprung*) of the work of art.[16] In
his later work Benjamin renames such ideas "dialectical images." Thus,
Benjamin's discussion of genres as Platonic ideas seems intended not to lift

14. Bernd Witte, *Walter Benjamin—Der Intellektuelle als Kritiker* (Stuttgart: Metzler, 1976), 109.
15. Michael Thompson, *Rubbish Theory: The Creation and Destruction of Value* (New York: Oxford University Press, 1979), 75.
16. Klaus Garber, *Rezeption und Rettung* (Tübingen: Niemeyer, 1987), 84.

genre out of the realm of transience into that of transcendence, but rather to explain how ideology works in literature:

> Benjamin's decisive contribution to genre theory lies in his thought that genres are condensed world-images. If we understand genres as unified and distinct projections of the world, then the reasons behind Benjamin's use of the controversial concept of "idea" becomes apparent: "idea" identifies the unifying and distinguishing principle by means of which the wholeness and distinctiveness of the world of art is created. Organized by means of ideas, genres are pregnant outlines which contrast with the endlessness and indefiniteness of the real world.[17]

Benjamin seeks such concepts not in the multifarious features of *Trauerspiel*, but in the oppositions between *Trauerspiel* and other genres: "Die philosophische Geschichte als die Wissenschaft vom Ursprung ist die Form, die da aus den entlegenen Extremen, den scheinbaren Exzessen der Entwicklung die Konfiguration der Idee als der durch die Möglichkeit eines sinnvollen Nebeneinanders solcher Gegensätze gekennzeichneten Totalität heraustreten läßt" (227; "Philosophical history, the science of the origin, is the form which, in the remotest extremes and the apparent excesses of the process of development, reveals the configuration of the idea—the sum total of all possibly meaningful juxtapositions of such opposites [45–47]). In the *Ursprung*, Benjamin sets up a schema in which he can always relate two such concepts, and the forms they take, to each other. I have wagered a visual representation of Benjamin's system of genres (see Fig. 8–1), which may help anchor my discussion of it in the pages to follow.

For Benjamin, as for Georg Lukács in the *Theorie des Romans*, the dividing line between two forms—epic and novel for the latter, tragedy and *Trauerspiel* for the former—is the relation of the hero to the community and the cosmos. Benjamin compresses the mythical element in tragedy into the silence of the hero. Drawing on Nietzsche's blaming of Socrates for the death of tragedy, Benjamin makes Socratic dialogue the agent that divides tragedy from *Trauerspiel*: Socrates is thus the first martyr, that is, the first tragic hero with a voice. Socrates and his later reincarnations replace the wordless suffering of the tragic hero with the endless ponder-

17. Heinz Schlaffer, "Walter Benjamins Idee der Gattung," in *Walter Benjamin: Profane Erleuchtung und rettende Kritik*, ed. Norbert W. Bolz and Richard Faber (Würzburg: Königshausen & Neumann, 1985), 44.

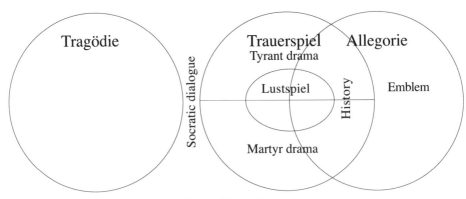

Fig. 8-1. The genres of *Trauerspiel* according to Benjamin.

ings of destiny found in the *Trauerspiel*—for example, in Corneille's *Cinna*. Though the martyr becomes the typical hero of *Trauerspiel*, he or she remains alien to the concept of tragedy. The voluble response of the martyr to his or her fate depends upon the very different notions of the world order that inhabit martyr and hero. According to Benjamin, the "Trauer" (literally "mourning") of a *Trauerspiel* is not *for* the fallen hero, but *by* the hero for a fallen world:

> Im Sinn der Märtyrerdramatik ist nicht sittliche Vergehung, son-
> dern der Stand des kreatürlichen Menschen selber der Grund des
> Unterganges. Diesen typischen Untergang, der so verschieden von
> dem außerordentlichen des tragischen Helden ist, haben die Dich-
> ter im Auge gehabt, wenn sie—mit einem Wort, das die Dramatik
> planvoller als die Kritik gehandhabt hat—ein Werk als «Trauer-
> spiel» bezeichnet haben. (268)

> (In the terms of the martyr-drama it is not moral transgression but
> the very estate of man as creature which provides the reason for
> the catastrophe. This typical catastrophe, which is so different
> from the extraordinary catastrophe of the tragic hero, is what the
> dramatists had in mind when—with a word which is employed
> more consciously in dramaturgy than in criticism—they described
> a work as a *Trauerspiel*. [89])

A fallen, "creaturely" world, a ruined landscape whose redemption is only hinted at through the process of allegory—such are the "features" that make of *Trauerspiel* a "mourning-play" rather than a tragedy. The loquaciousness of the *Trauerspiel*'s protagonists points dialectically toward language's inability to imbue their fates with a meaning. This essential difference leads Benjamin to locate the varying concepts of tragedy and *Trauerspiel* not in their surface features, but in their "rewrite rules":

> Tragik ist eine Vorstufe der Prophetie. Sie ist ein Sachverhalt, der nur im Sprachlichen sich findet: tragisch ist das Wort und ist das Schweigen der Vorzeit, in denen die prophetische Stimme sich versucht, Leiden und Tod, wo sie diese Stimme erlösen, niemals ein Schicksal im pragmatischen Gehalt seiner Verwicklung. Das *Trauerspiel* ist pantomimisch denkbar, die Tragödie nicht. (297)

> (Tragedy is a preliminary stage of prophecy. It is a content, which exists only in language: what is tragic is the word and the silence of the past, in which the prophetic voice is being put to the test, or suffering and death, when they redeem this voice; but a fate in the pragmatic substance of its entanglements is never tragic. *Trauerspiel* is conceivable as pantomime; tragedy is not. [118])[18]

In one sense, Benjamin in this passage affirms Aristotle's observation that performance is not essential to tragedy. Redemption is possible only through the *logos*, the prophetic voice, which cannot be represented visually. Since the world depicted in *Trauerspiel* is abandoned by the gods to the vagaries of history, its events can be reconstructed as mere phenomena, and hence represented in pantomime.

Thus, Milton's Samson is a tragic hero, whereas Dryden's Antony is a martyr of *Trauerspiel*. In the article "Milton, Dryden, and the Ideology of Genre," D. S. Rosenberg adapts Benjamin's system to investigate the ideology of seventeenth-century English dramatic form. Rosenberg develops a lengthy series of binary oppositions in order to specify the ideological differences between Milton's drama, which is closer to what Benjamin calls tragedy, and Dryden's, which is an incarnation of *Trauerspiel*. For example, unlike Dryden's plays, Milton's *Samson Agonistes* (1671) was written to be read rather than performed, thus emphasizing the *logos* of the story rather than its spectacular or pantomimic aspects. The act of reading presupposes a reader free of the social pressures that attend a theater performance. (Somewhat along the same lines, Rosenberg also notes that

---

18. I have emended Osborne's translation in four places: I substituted "put to the test" for "tried out" and "when they redeem this voice" for "when they *are redeemed by* this voice," and deleted the definite articles before *Trauerspiel* and Tragedy in the last sentence.

Dryden's audience consisted largely of the court, whereas Milton's was Oxford and Blackfriars.)

Finally, the idea of "closet drama" can also be interpreted as an absorption of the audience into the play itself, the way a religious ceremony is most effective precisely when it transforms all its spectators into actors. Benjamin makes tragedy an autonomous performance versus the politically inscribed pantomime of *Trauerspiel:*

> Es ist [in Tragödie], wie schon das offene Theater und die auf gleiche Weise niemals repetierte Darstellung es nahelegt, ein entscheidender Vollzug im Kosmos, was in ihr sich abspielt. Um dieses Vollzuges willen und als sein Richter ist die Gemeinde geladen. Während der Zuschauer der Tragödie eben durch diese erfodet und gerechtfertigt wird, ist das Trauerspiel vom Beschauer aus zu verstehen. Er erfährt, wie auf der Bühne, einem zum Kosmos ganz beziehungslosen Innenraume des Gefühls, Situationen ihm eindringlich vorgestellt werden. (298–99)

> (As is suggested by the open theatre and the fact that the performance is never repeated identically, what takes place [in tragedy] is a decisive cosmic achievement. The community is assembled to witness and to judge this achievement. The spectator of tragedy is summoned, and is justified, by the tragedy itself; the *Trauerspiel*, in contrast, has to be understood from the point of view of the onlooker. He learns how, on the stage, a space which belongs to an inner world of feeling and bears no relationship to the cosmos, situations are compellingly presented to him. [119])

Moving from reception to theme, Rosenberg finds that the erotic and martial themes of Restoration drama emphasize the collective, whereas Milton glorifies the religious values of individuals. Putting all these elements together, one finds that Milton has come much closer to an Aristotelian tragedy, whereas Dryden has kept to the Restoration concept of *Trauerspiel*, which could include even operatic works. As in Benjamin, the Restoration theater worked with an untragic drama of modernity: "An incomplete secularization . . . had left the world with a vacuum from which tragic freedom and tragic grandeur could no longer emerge."[19]

---

19. D. S. Rosenberg, "Milton, Dryden, and the Ideology of Genre," *Comparative Drama* 21 (Spring 1987): 18.

Rosenberg clearly states that the ideological component in generic choice lies not so much in the content of the genre, as in its opposing itself to other genres. For Rosenberg, much of the political import of Milton's *Samson Agonistes* lies in its closeness to and yet rejection of Restoration drama. These contrasts are sharpened by both playwrights' distance from yet a third genre, the native English drama: "Both [authors] closely adhere . . . to neoclassical and humanistic norms of rhetoric and decorum and thereby exclude the popular and native traditions of English drama. Nevertheless, these dramas are markedly different with respect to the interrelation of theater, society, and dramatic art. So markedly different are they that one may view Milton's dramatic poem as a deliberate rejection of the heroic play."[20] Hence, the ideology of genre is always split, for the use-value of any single genre depends on our recognition of other genres that oppose it.

Rock and not country, folk and not rock: to say a work's genre is to say what it is not. Rather than seeing fiction as something in and of itself, we judge it by its nonrelatedness to the world, by the nonillocutionary force of its speech acts.[21] The novel is a kind of biography which does not allow us to sue. Oddly, though, when we go to name fiction's opposite, the only general term we have for it (in English), "nonfiction," also denotes a lack. It is this lack, rather than a presence, which "establishes" the genre, like the double lack that established the genre of the prose poem. The systemic nature of genre foils formalist studies, because formalism is limited to describing what is "there" in the texts, whereas any generic reading of a text is based equally on what is not there, on what the text does not say, and ultimately on what cannot be done with it. Comparison has been my way of getting at this "not-said."

II

Then again, the distinction between rock 'n' roll and country that has inhibited the career of poor Mr. Mack is in one sense rather odd, since country music was so essential to the creation of rock 'n' roll in the first

---

20. Ibid., 2.

21. The idea is Richard Ohmann's. See his "Speech-Acts and the Definition of Literature," *Philosophy and Rhetoric* 4 (1971): 1–19. Mary L. Pratt, however, has turned this lack into a presence, finding the essence of literature in its assertion of tellability as a use-value. See Mary Louise Pratt, *Toward a Speech-Act Theory of Literary Discourse.*

place. Rock 'n' roll is being opposed to an idiom that brought it into being. Thus, at the same time as opposition holds genres apart, there is another epistemological claim on genre which moves in the opposite direction, away from separation and toward miscegenation.

To give an example, Gary Saul Morson has made an interesting case for the existence of a genre called metaparody, which arises out of the dialectic between an original and its parody: "As there are genres and parodic genres, there are also metaparodic genres—that is, genres of works that are designed to be interpreted as a dialogue of parody and counterparody. . . . One such genre is the rhetorical paradox, the praise of something regarded as essentially unpraisable."[22] One might say that the rhetorical paradox involves a dialectic between the twin genres of encomium and invective, with both genres displaying equally long and honored traditions. It is not merely that both genres are present in works such as Erasmus's *Praise of Folly*, but that each assumes the guise and seizes the use-value of the other until we can no longer distinguish between them. Thus, with no stable genre available to bring the reader's thoughts to a resting place, meaning plunges into an abyss. Though both encomium and invective are particularly easy genres to grasp according to their use-values (since those use-values are given in their names), when they interpenetrate in metaparody those original use-values are removed. The same instability is implicitly at work in any literary text.

Genre must be defined recursively: genres are made out of other genres. Tzvetan Todorov has formulated this plainly enough: "From where do genres come? Why, quite simply, from other genres. A new genre is always the transformation of one or several old genres: by inversion, by displacement, by combination."[23] Such transformations can be analyzed diachronically, as in the invention of the prose poem in the nineteenth century or the emergence of the epistolary novel from the *ars dictaminis*, or synchronically, as in the process which Mikhail Bakhtin has called dialogism and for which—besides Erasmus—the works of Eco and Lévi-Strauss provide clear examples.

Though the idea of recursivity, that is, of defining something in terms of itself, sounds like a paradoxical cul-de-sac, many definitions are made

22. Gary Saul Morson, *The Boundaries of Genre: Dostoevsky's "Diary of a Writer" and the Traditions of Literary Utopia*, 143.
23. Tzvetan Todorov, "The Origin of Genres," 161. Todorov makes the mistake, however, of speaking of literature "as a whole, the ultimate genre" (159). From the principle of opposition, one can see that the discussion of literary genres will never be complete without a consideration of neighboring, nonliterary genres. Cf. note 4.

recursively: a Fibonacci number can only be defined as the sum of two previous numbers in the series; the data structure called a "tree" can be defined as "a set of smaller trees, related in a particular way."[24] However, to function in the real world, every recursive definition also needs a base. The first two Fibonacci numbers must be defined outright; every tree must have a singleton root. In the case of genre, Todorov understands the base of genre as a single speech act; what we usually call genres are then different combinations of such speech acts. To tell a story about oneself, for example, given the proper transformations, becomes the genre of autobiography. Though such a view hints at the use-value of the various genres, it presupposes that verbal works can in fact be meaningfully reduced to a single speech act. However, the endless ironies of metaparody are related to the recursive entanglements of the two genres, with no indication of a more fundamental meaning for either of them. My point, as demonstrated in the chapters of this book, is that most works not only can but *must* be analyzed in more than one generic way in order for their messages to have any effective meaning or value. Put another way, Todorov momentarily ignores the Saussurean principle discussed above.

Yet Todorov's speech acts are not the logical, universalist ones found in the language philosophy of J. L. Austin or John Searle. Instead, with examples borrowed from Marxist criticism, Todorov has identified ideology as the producer of generic distinctions. Ideology forms appropriate speech acts into the network of differentiated use-values that constitute genre:

> A society chooses and codifies the [speech] acts that most closely correspond to its ideology; this is why the existence of certain genres in a society and their absence in another reveal a central ideology, and enable us to establish it with considerable certainty. It is not chance that the epic is possible during one era, the novel during another (the individual hero of the latter being opposed to the collective hero of the former); each of these choices depends upon the ideological framework in which it operates.[25]

In this passage, Todorov combines Marxist-historicist thoughts on genre with the insights of speech-act theory.[26] His invocation of ideology, absent

24. Norman Gibbs and Robert Korfhage, *Principles of Data Structures and Algorithms with Pascal* (Dubuque, Iowa: W. C. Brown, 1987), 324.
25. Todorov, "Origin of Genres," 164.
26. Todorov's contrast between epic and novel is taken from Georg Lukács's *Theorie des Romans*. See also Marx on the historicity of genre: "It is even recognized that certain forms of art, e.g. the epic, can no longer be produced in their world epoch–making, classical stature as soon as the

from speech-act theory proper, complements the analyses of Rosenberg and Benjamin, and brings us away from speech acts per se and closer to what Bakhtin calls speech genres (*rechevy zhanry*).

Speech genres are utterances that "reflect the specific conditions and goals of each such area not only through their content (thematic) and linguistic style . . . but above all through their compositional structure."[27] These utterances are to be differentiated from one another and identified according to the pragmatic criteria of goals and "felicity conditions" familiar from speech-act theory. Bakhtin argues that one can distinguish between the "primary" speech genres and the secondary genres, which are recursively constructed from them, thus making the former (presumably rather limited in number) speech genres bases for the recursive building of other genres.

The use of speech genres as a base for literary genres is not new. Aristotle discussed the recursive construction of genre out of ways of speaking in his *Poetics:*

> What is relevant is that [tragedy] arose, at first, as an improvisa-
> tion (both tragedy and comedy are similar in this respect) on the
> part of those who led the dithyrambs, just as comedy arose from
> those who led the phallic songs. . . . Then the iambic meter took
> the place of the tetrameter. For the poets first used the trochaic
> tetrameter because their poetry was satyric and very closely
> associated with dance; but when dialogue was introduced, nature
> itself discovered the appropriate meter. For the iambic is the most
> conversational of the meters—as we see from the fact that we
> speak many iambs when talking to each other, but few [dactylic]
> hexameters, and only when departing from conversational tone.[28]

production of art, as such, begins; that is, that certain significant forms within the realm of the arts are possible only at an undeveloped state of artistic development. If this is the case with the relation between different kinds of art within the realm of the arts, it is already less puzzling that it is the case in the relation of the entire realm to the general development of society. . . . From another *side*, is Achilles possible with powder and lead? Or the *Iliad* with the printing press, not to mention the printing machine? Do not the song and the saga and the muse necessarily come to an end with the printer's bar; hence do not the necessary conditions of epic poetry vanish?" Karl Marx, "Grundrisse," in *Marx-Engels Reader*, 2d ed., ed. Robert C. Tucker (New York: W. W. Norton, 1978), 245–46.

27. Mikhail Bakhtin, "The Problem of Speech Genres," translated by Vern W. McGee, 60.

28. Aristotle, *Poetiké* IV, 1449a8–28; translated by Leon Golden, under the title *Aristotle's Poetics*, 8–9.

It is possible to see three levels in this passage: primary speech genres, secondary genres, and what Thomas Kent would call the "hybrid genre" of tragedy.[29] Essentially, Aristotle states here that certain forms of speech have associated use-values: you cannot dialogue in tetrameter or hexameter; you cannot praise in iambics or tetrameter; you cannot dance in hexameter or iambics. Aristotle not only relates each genre to a basic mode of speech, but also identifies certain intermediary genres (phallic song, dithyramb, invective, epic) that the critic can analytically unfold from the genres of tragedy and comedy constituted by them.

Again and again in the *Ursprung*, Benjamin invokes not only genre's oppositional aspects, but also its recursive imbrications. If *Trauerspiel* can be opposed to tragedy, it can also be analyzed as a combination of or oscillation between two subgenres, the martyr drama and the tyrant drama. These two heroic types would seem to be interpretable from a purely oppositional scheme, as the "pity and fear" of tragedy are divided between them: "Den «gar bösen» gilt das Tyrannendrama und die Furcht, den «gar guten» das Märtyrerdrama und das Mitleid" (249; "For the 'very bad' there was the drama of the tyrant, and there was fear; for the 'very good' there was the martyr-drama and pity" [69]). But Benjamin invokes the ideology of the period (in this case, the problematical relation between temporal and eternal rule) in positing the sublation of this opposition: "Diese Formen wahren ihr kurioses Nebeneinander nur so lange, als die Betrachtung den juristischen Aspekt barocken Fürstentums übergeht. Folgt sie den Hinweisen der Ideologie, erscheinen sie als strenges Komplement. Tyrann und Märtyrer sind im Barock die Janushäupter des Gekrönten" (249; "This juxtaposition of forms appears strange only as long as one neglects to consider the legal aspect of baroque princedom. Seen in ideological terms they are strictly complementary. In the baroque the tyrant and the martyr are but two faces of the monarch" [69]). The "legal aspect" here is the idea of affective, "decisionist" government, which, according to Benjamin's source Carl Schmitt, was a subject of much

29. Kent claims that "a hybrid genre is higher in uncertainty and information content than a pure genre." Thomas Kent, "The Classification of Genres," 9. A novel, because it is less predictable than a fairy tale, contains more information. The idea is an interesting one and has potential critical uses, but the notion of a "pure genre," which requires that we believe in the eternal status of genres, their identifiability apart from neighboring genres, is problematic. Is the fairy tale identifiable apart from the myth, fables, legends, and folk tales that border it? In setting out his classification, Vladimir Propp never dealt with the interesting question of which stories to include and which to exclude from his definition of "fairy tale." The purity of the genre can only be maintained over against another corpus that has not been included.

discussion in the baroque period.[30] Tyrant and martyr are united in their ability to force a "state of emergency" on history through the affective force of their personalities.

In another surprising move, however, Benjamin also uses the principle of recursivity to insist that the most perfect examples of *Trauerspiel* contain their opposite, *Lustspiel*, within them like an embryo: "Das Lustspiel wandert ins Trauerspiel: niemals könnte das Trauerspiel im Lustspiel sich entfalten. Dies Bild hat seinen guten Sinn: das Lustspiel macht sich klein und geht gleichsam ins Trauerspiel hinüber" (306; "The *Lustspiel* enters into the *Trauerspiel:* the *Trauerspiel* could never develop in the form of the *Lustspiel*. There is a certain good sense to the following image: the *Lustspiel* shrinks and is, so to speak, absorbed into the *Trauerspiel*" [127]). The opposition between horror and delight is developed out of their deeper affinity, revealed in shared nonsystemic phenomena such as sadism. The figure of Iago is only the most famous of the clowns who, once they strut onto the scene of *Trauerspiel*, grow into dastardly plotters. (The Devil himself, Benjamin reminds us, wears the aspect of a clown.) Thus, in an example of how extremes symbolize genres, the purest examples of *Trauerspiel* become the generically unstable ones: "Das Trauerspiel erreicht ja seine Höhe night in den regelrechten Exemplaren sondern dort, wo mit spielhaften Übergängen es das Lustspiel in sich anklingen macht. Daher denn Calderon und Shakespeare bedeutendere Trauerspiele geschaffen haben, als die Deutschen des XVII. Jahrhunderts" (306; "The finest exemplifications of the *Trauerspiel* are not those which adhere strictly to the rules, but those in which there are playful modulations of the *Lustspiel*. For this reason Calderón and Shakespeare created more important *Trauerspiele* than the German writers of the seventeenth century" [127]). Whether through opposition or through recursivity, genre is shown to be what it is not. Not genre so much as generic instability now offers itself as the key to understanding the text. The question now becomes, What is it that we are reading when we read generic instability?

III

So country has always been a part of rock, and rock has also invaded country. Lonnie Mack's lament cannot be an evaluation of his music's

---

30. Carl Schmitt, *Politische Theologie* (Munich and Leipzig, 1922).

"essential" generic instability, which exists everywhere around him. Rather, he is using free indirect style to describe how his music gets "used" by others. Specifically, the ideological and commercial configurations of American culture have defined musical "format" in a way that suppresses instability and will not allow his music to be appreciated. So how did I hear this hit song on the radio? Luckily for Mr. Mack, popular culture is self-reflexive; it loves to *theorize* itself. Our struggling musician is simultaneously practitioner and victim of what Kristeva calls the "juridical function" of intertextuality.[31]

But what exactly does this juridical function judge? What Mack's text presupposes is not so much genre as the law of genre. It does not invoke a corpus of texts, but predicts the uses to which the song itself will be put, the kind of sorting that will be carried out on it. Which law of genre is being invoked? Because of the recursivity of genre, there is always an excess of generic markers to be sorted. Lévi-Strauss refers to Rousseau, writes like Montaigne, and reads like Proust. Eco alludes in his ostensible detective novel to everything nondetective from Voltaire to Wittgenstein. Once they agree that genres do indeed "exist," theorists of genre differ most radically precisely on this one point, on the "things" in the text which will be compared in order to classify works.

A popular sorting technique a few decades ago was that of the authenticity or fictionality of the "voice" one hears in the text. According to Käthe Hamburger, if that voice is authentic rather than representational, then we have a lyric. If the voice is fictional, then we have fiction. In his highly influential "Theory of Genres," Northrop Frye modifies this binary theory to that of the revelation or hiding of the implied author in terms of the audience: in lyric, the listeners are hidden from the author; in drama, the author is hidden from the spectators; in epic, both are present to each other.[32] Such views, as René Wellek points out, owe much to German idealist philosophy's emphasis on the subject-object dialectic.[33] The subjec-

---

31. The following quotation is indicative of the notion of struggle that goes into the making of any text: "In obeying the juridical function of its context, the new text aims at arrogating to or possessing for itself the juridical role; this means that it enters into a polemic with that which it presupposes in order to totalize that which it presupposes and its own polemic, and in order to make out of this polemic a new juridical act, a new law, which will be the new presupposition of the texts to come." Julia Kristeva, *La Révolution du langage poétique*, 339.

32. Northrop Frye, "Rhetorical Criticism: Theory of Genres," 243–51. Frye goes on to discuss other ways of distinguishing genre. Furthermore, the chapter that Frye feels represents his thoughts on genre is really just one of six different approaches to genre in his *Anatomy of Criticism*. Thus, perhaps contrary to his own intentions, Frye ends up celebrating generic instability.

33. René Wellek, "Genre Theory, the Lyric and *Erlebnis*," 225–52. The works by the other authors mentioned can be found in the Bibliography.

The Ideology of Genre

tive, the objective, and its dialectical synthesis have given us the tripartite division between lyric, epic, and drama, which, as Irene Behrens has shown, was virtually unknown before the eighteenth century. A similar bulwark of the tripartite division has been our ability to speak of three temporal situations: past, present, and future, which are then assigned to the three genres—differently by different theorists. Emil Staiger, for example, in his influential *Grundbegriffe der Poetik*, counterintuitively associates the lyric with the past, the epic with the present, and the drama with the future. All of these genre theories have more to say about our conceptions of authenticity, subjectivity, and futurity than about literature itself. In addition, all of these approaches suffer from their refusal to take genre as operative beyond the limits of literature. The reduction of what most readers acknowledge as a multitude of genres to just three is unnecessarily limiting; in particular, it eliminates the historical and ideological elements of genre. By locating the juridical function in the universal rather than the specific, these theorists are able to avoid the messy problems of looking at genres as they live in literary history. There, disruption and ideological drift are the rule, as the Prague structuralists recognized:

> When described formally rather than thematically, a genre emerges as a set of *fixed structural* elements, such as the metrical form (in the *chansons de geste*, for instance), the lexical selection (as in the heroic epic), or the technique of composition (as in the short story in contrast to the novel). In time, the particular combinations of such generic devices undergo considerable change. While some elements remain unaltered, maintaining the genre's continuity, the influx of new elements assures its freshness and elasticity. But in extreme cases even those elements with which the genre is primarily identified may disappear, whereas the secondary elements endure. Thanks to such permutations in the function of individual elements, a given genre may, over a long period, produce two almost unrecognizable evolutionary offshoots, such as the picaresque novel and the modern novel. Even for epic and lyric it appears impossible to design simple and unambiguous definitions adequate for literatures of every period. Thus genre is a historically conditioned concept, not a universally valid one.[34]

34. F. W. Galan, "The Prague School Theory of Literary History, 1928–48," *PMLA* 94 (March 1979): 279.

F. W. Galan's assessment reveals the necessity of a dialectic between formal and thematic approaches to genre, as the initial list of formal features slowly gives way to a situation in which generic affinity is preserved only in the name itself as the expression of an essence—a return to Benjamin's pseudo-Platonism. In moving from universal forms to historically conditioned disjunctions between name and features as determiners of genre, Galan implies that genre is a dialectic between surface and "interior."

Where to turn for this "interiority"? One could begin with José Ortega y Gassett's brief discussion of genre as he meditates on the meaning of Cervantes. He begins by noting (thinking no doubt of Horace), that the Greeks and Romans understood genres as sets of rules that had to be adhered to in poetic creation, "estructuras formales dentro de quienes la musa, como una abeja dócil, deponía su miel" ("formal structures within which the muse, like a tame bee, deposited her honey").[35] Ortega y Gassett goes on to point out, however, that such a distinction is only the surface manifestation of a more fundamental one:

> Así es la tragedia la expansión de un cierto tema poético fundamental y sólo de él, es la expansión de lo trágico. Hay, pues, en la forma lo mismo que había en el fondo. . . . Entiendo, pues, por géneros literarios, a la inversa que la poética antigua, ciertos temas radicales, irreductibles entre sí, verdaderas categorías estéticas.

> (In this way, tragedy is the expansion of a certain fundamental poetic theme and only of that theme; it is the expansion of the tragic. Form and essence are thus the same. . . . Thus, I understand by literary genres the opposite of what ancient poetics does, certain basic themes, irreducible in themselves, actual aesthetic categories.)[36]

As with Benjamin, then, Ortega y Gassett's initial equation of basic themes with aesthetic categories has led him to a notion of value. Tragedy as an aesthetic category is the historically conditioned use to which the spectator puts tragic form. Ortega y Gassett links generic development to the evolution of different concepts of man through history:

> Los géneros entendidos como temas estéticos irreductibles entre sí, igualmente necesarios y últimos, son amplias vistas que se

---

35. José Ortega y Gassett, "Meditación primera," 128.
36. Ibid., 129.

toman sobre la vertientes cardinales de lo humano. Cada época trae consigo una interpretación radical del hombre. Mejor dicho, no la trae consigo sino que cada época es eso. Por esto, cada época prefiere un determinado género. (130)

(Genres, understood as aesthetic themes which are irreducible as such, as necessary as they are final, are broad views of the cardinal directions of the human. Each epoch brings with it a basic interpretation of man. Or better, it does not bring such an interpretation with it as much as it *is* that interpretation. For that reason, each epoch favors a certain genre.)

Ortega y Gassett then goes on to analyze the seventeenth-century *novela* as a narrative focused on the present and the uninteresting, responding to a secularization of the world. It is this fundamental positioning in the world which then determines generic features. Ortega y Gassett has taken us away from the timeless and into the flux of history. As Benjamin puts it, genre leaps up from the whirlpool of history, which determines its features. That is genre's *Ursprung*—literally, its "originary leap."

Benjamin's dialectical approach to genre rejects the formal and thematic characteristics generally used for distinguishing genres from each other only in order to arrive at a deeper idea of form: the accidental character of historically conditioned literary structures is overcome in a genre poetics that emphasizes the redemption of form rather than its purposeless linear development. The task of criticism becomes that of illuminating this "symbolic form so that its pure, original essence shines through the inessential, contingent moments with which it is encumbered."[37] Benjamin's treatment of allegory is a clear example of a description of genre so intent on giving its *fondo* that it must resort exclusively to metaphors. We have seen Benjamin describe tragedy's *fondo* as a relationship between hero, audience, and *logos*. In contrast, Benjamin discusses *Trauerspiel* as the hieroglyphic of a nature that reveals only decay and death. This hieroglyphic writing lesson is allegory:

Wenn mit dem Trauerspiel die Geschichte in den Schauplatz hineinwandert, so tut sie es als Schrift. Auf dem Antlitz der Natur steht "Geschichte" in der Zeichenschrift der Vergängnis. Die

---

37. John Pizer, "History, Genre and 'Ursprung' in Benjamin's Early Aesthetics," *German Quarterly* 60 (Winter 1987): 72.

allegorische Physiognomie der Natur-Geschichte, die auf der Bühne durch das Trauerspiel gestellt wird, ist wirklich gegenwärtig als Ruine. Mit ihr hat sinnlich die Geschichte in den Schauplatz sich verzogen. Und zwar prägt, so gestaltet, die Geschichte nicht als Prozeß eines ewigen Lebens, vielmehr als Vorgang unhaltsamen Verfalls sich aus. Damit bekennt die Allegorie sich jenseits von Schönheit. Allegorien sind im Reiche der Gedanken was Ruinen im Reiche der Dinge. (353–54)

(When, as is the case in the *Trauerspiel*, history becomes part of the setting, it does so as script. The word "history" stands written on the countenance of nature in the characters of transience. The allegorical physiognomy of the nature-history, which is put on stage in the *Trauerspiel*, is present in reality in the form of the ruin. In the ruin history has physically merged into the setting. And in this guise history does not assume the form of the process of an eternal life so much as that of irresistible decay. Allegory thereby declares itself to be beyond beauty. Allegories are, in the realm of thoughts, what ruins are in the realm of things. [177–78])

The mention of ruins corresponds to the overwhelming emphasis of the *Trauerspiel* on mortal suffering and material decline, which, in Benjamin's view, hides within it the hope of redemption. The ruins point to the absence of the formerly magnificent building in the same way that the formal features of *Trauerspiel* point to Tragedy. Benjamin's concepts of "ruin" and "nature-history" are to *Trauerspiel* what Ortega y Gassett's "present" and "uninteresting" are to the novel. Allegory is to ruin as symbol is to building, so that once again the oppositional principle is tacitly at work. Yet recursivity operates here as well, since the archaeological eye can see the building (tragedy) in its ruins (*Trauerspiel*). The problem with Ortega y Gassett's view, however, is that of explaining the presence of several genres in the same time period. Not a single genre, but rather the specific configurations of the generic system—including the instabilities it produces—are revelatory of ideology. According to Richard Wolin, allegory constitutes the core of *Trauerspiel*'s use-value, since the baroque's "Counter-Reformation world view was polemically directed against the self-confident, this-worldly orientation of the Renaissance, whose reintroduction of pagan (Greek) figures and humanist themes was perceived as a direct threat to authentic Christian values. The popularity of allegory in medieval art proceeds from a similar impulse: the desire to divert men's minds from the temptations of profane life, symbolized by the pagan values of the Greco-Roman world, and to turn them instead toward the contemplation of other-worldly beliefs."[38] Thus, allegory enters *Trauer-spiel* neither as a set of formal features nor as an "essence." It enters as a use-value, and one whose importance lies in its opposition to the use-values of other genres.

Rather than follow Ortega y Gassett in claiming that a genre represents the weltanschauung of a particular epoch, let us apply *fondo* in a different way, uniting it with Galan's analysis of form and effect. The identification of a genre lies not in its features, but in the use it puts them to. It is this use, rather than the use of the critic as Rosmarin insists, which constitutes the pragmatics of genre. Typing the word "value" as a subject heading into the on-line library catalog at my university, I receive 124 citations. *All* of these citations refer to books on economic theories of value. That economics, the science of scarce resources, should feel most compelled to specify its concept of value should come as no surprise. My theory of genre implies that generic systems constitute a kind of (nonquantitative) economics of discourse. However, the science of economics has usually defined and analyzed value quantitatively. Value as a qualitative concept came under scrutiny only relatively recently, as a substitute for philosophical discussions of "the good." Among the first generalized theories of qualitative value were those developed by Christian von Ehrenfels and Nicolai Hartmann.[39] These thinkers developed further the Marxian concept that use-value was the primordial form of value, on which exchange and other sorts of value are built. American philosophers John Dewey and C. S. Peirce incorporated such ideas into the philosophy known as pragmatism. Peirce in particular investigated the concept of aesthetic value; unfortunately, he did not publish this work.[40]

Turning to other fields of inquiry, we find that both modern linguistics and the philosophy of language have increasingly substituted the notion of "value" for that of "meaning." Saussure himself, as an inevitable result of his insistence on language as a system of oppositions, was led to posit the

38. Richard Wolin, *Walter Benjamin: An Aesthetic of Redemption* (New York: Columbia University Press, 1982), 76.
39. Christian von Ehrenfels, *Werttheorie*, ed. Reinhard Fabian (Munich: Philosophia, 1982); Nicolai Hartmann, *Ethik* (Berlin: De Gruyter, 1926).
40. "What Peirce sought [in Aesthetics] was not Beauty, but a method of value-making, freely chosen as an impulsion toward ideal goals." Roberta Kevelson, *Peirce, Paradox, Praxis*, Approaches to Semiotics 94 (New York: Mouton de Gruyter, 1990), 332. See also John Dewey, "Some Questions About Value," *Journal of Philosophy* 41 (1944): 449–55.

concept of linguistic value as the part each term plays in that system. Saussure never defined this principle of value. Instead, he gave examples and analogies, such as the following from chess:

> Take a knight, for instance. By itself is it an element in the game? Certainly not, for by its material make-up—outside its square and the other conditions of the game—it means nothing to the player; it becomes a real, concrete element only when endowed with value and wedded to it [*revêté de sa valeur et faisant corps avec elle*]. Suppose that the piece happens to be destroyed or lost during a game. Can it be replaced by an equivalent piece? Certainly. Not only another knight but even a figure shorn of any resemblance to a knight can be declared identical provided the same value is attributed to it.[41]

The kind of value of which Saussure speaks could be described as exchange value (the knight should not be exchanged for a pawn, can be exchanged for a bishop, should be exchanged for a queen whenever possible), but it is clear that the knight's *use-value* in the game of chess, that is, how it moves and what it can do in comparison to and in coordination with the other pieces, determines this exchange value. Furthermore, it seems clear that a real knowledge of that use-value, available only to the experienced player of chess, cannot be paraphrased or reduced to a set of essential features, though language can give useful orientations for it.

In the above, Saussure seems to approach Ludwig Wittgenstein's view of language. His selection of the game of chess as a model for the idea of linguistic value brings to mind Wittgenstein's notion of "language-game." Wittgenstein maintained that rather than attempt to understand language in its paradigmatic axis (that is, to investigate the meaning of a word by substituting synonyms or definitions for it) we should look instead to the syntagmatic axis (for example, by examining sentences in which that word can be used). The meanings of words cannot be separated from the systems within which they are located. "Brick" may point to an object in the world, or it may mean "hand me a brick," depending on the game being played. The value of "brick" within a game is more informative than the word's "meaning" in the dictionary sense. Wittgenstein's version of the Saussurean chess knight is the number five or a negative, as in the following examples:

41. Saussure, *Cours*, 153–54; Baskin, trans., *Course*, 110.

We can easily imagine human beings with a "more primitive" logic, in which something corresponding to our negation is applied only to certain sorts of sentence; perhaps to such as do not themselves contain any negation. It would be possible to negate the proposition "He is going into the house," but a negation of the negative proposition would be meaningless, or would count only as a repetition of the negation. . . .

The question whether negation had the same meaning to these people as to us would be analogous to the question whether the figure "5" meant the same to people whose numbers ended at 5 as to us.[42]

Roy Harris suggests that Saussure might have dealt with this example by saying that "5" or negation had the same *meaning* but not the same *value* in the two instances.[43] The number five is given value by its position within the number system. That value changes if five is the upper limit for that system rather than something in between. Thus, value does not inhere in the dictionary meaning of a word (what dictionary could describe the number system or the rules of negation in a language?), but only in its concrete usages. But usages are not all reconcilable with each other in general, since each is comprehensible only at the level of the language-game within which they are deployed—think of the various meanings of "to get," for example.

Like Wittgenstein, Mikhail Bakhtin argued that meaning is completely contextual: context can give the interjection "Well!" a meaning as extensive as "we had a lousy summer and now look how it's already snowing outside." In one of the clearest examples of what he means by a "speech genre" Bakhtin describes a situation very much like Wittgenstein's language-game from a different viewpoint, that of the players:

Many people who have an excellent command of a language often feel quite helpless in certain spheres of communication precisely because they do not have a practical command of the generic forms used in the given spheres. Frequently a person who has an excellent command of speech in some areas of cultural communication, who is able to read a scholarly paper or engage in a

42. Ludwig Wittgenstein, *Philosophical Investigations*, 2d ed., ed. G. E. M. Anscombe and R. Rhees (Oxford: Oxford University Press, 1958), 554–55.

43. Roy Harris, *Language, Saussure and Wittgenstein* (London: Routledge, 1988), 37–45.

scholarly discussion, who speaks very well on social questions, is silent or very awkward in social conversation. Here it is not a matter of an impoverished vocabulary or of style, taken abstractly: This is entirely a matter of the inability to command a repertoire of genres of social conversation, the lack of a sufficient supply of those ideas about the whole of the utterance that help to cast one's speech quickly and naturally in certain compositional and stylistic forms, the inability to grasp a word promptly, to begin and end correctly (composition is very uncomplicated in these genres).[44]

The genre of "dinner-table conversation" alluded to here is defined by whatever you have to do to play it. Meaning here, as in the linguistics of M. A. K. Halliday, is not considered in the abstract, but as "a form of behaviour potential . . . what the speaker can do. . . . 'Can mean' is 'can do' when translated into language."[45] Halliday's work attempts to describe the network of options available to speakers which limit what they can mean. In disciplining children, for example, a parent can appeal to authority or to reason, can invoke the general rule or the particular example, can be subject-oriented or person-oriented. The relation between these options and the grammatico-lexical form which the sentence takes is not one-to-one, but will nevertheless "be realized somewhere in the linguistic system."[46] Thus, the use-value of language is the ultimate determiner of its form.

Genre is form, then, only in the way the 6:00 P.M. train is not substance (for everything can be changed about it) but the form of its use. Or, as Fredric Jameson puts it, "Genres are *institutions,* or social contracts between a writer and a specific public, whose function it is to specify the proper use of a particular cultural artifact."[47] Genre is a writing (talking) lesson. Genre is getting your song played on the country music station — or not.

IV

Genre can thus be described as a secondary modeling operation carried out on the brute "facts" of discourse, a channeling of language into the

44. Bakhtin, "Speech Genres," 80.

45. M. A. K. Halliday, "Language in a Social Perspective," *Educational Review* 23 (June 1971): 168.

46. Ibid., 176.

47. Fredric Jameson, *The Political Unconscious: Narrative as a Socially Symbolic Act,* 106.

possibilities of its usage. This passage is, as Philippe Gardy has argued, from a denotative to a connotative system, the latter system being ideological:

> At the level of text linguistics, genre can be defined first of all as an actualizer. . . .
>
> If we make the hypothesis that discourse operates through two grand systems, one denotative (that of brute information) and the other connotative (that of ideological information), then the function of genre is precisely that of permitting the passage from one of these systems to the other in a permanent and reciprocal movement of actualization. At the same time, genre makes possible an ideological communication which brute information necessarily omits.[48]

"Brute information" (an oxymoron) has no more use-value than brute iron ore. Though certain Marxists have argued for a view of the ideological unit as the proper object of literary production (as opposed to "reality" or "history"), such a notion ignores the problem of reading and the problem of genre. The "reality" of a text lies in its use-value, commonly known as its genre. The relation of the text to the "real" is in fact established by our willingness to place it generically, which amounts to our willingness to ideologically appropriate its brute information. Yet, as we have seen in our examples, this ideological actualization of the text is itself split.

For, what happens when primary genres become secondary ones, when a dinner-table conversation is placed in a film, for example? Jacques Derrida begins his essay "The Law of Genre" with just such an invocation of the instability of generic use-value. His opening sentences seem to stand out from the page in the absence of all context for their interpretation, which here amounts to their generic placement: "Genres are not to be mixed. I will not mix genres. I repeat: genres are not to be mixed. I will not mix them." Derrida goes on to analyze the unstable generic status of his own sentences: "As long as I release these utterances (which others might call speech acts) in a form yet scarcely determined, given the open context out of which I have just let them be grasped from 'my' language — as long as I do this, you may find it difficult to choose among several interpretive options."[49] These options do not array themselves around

48. Philippe Gardy, "Le Genre comme structuration idéologique du text formalisé," in *Théorie des genres et communication*, ed. Jean-Claude Barat et al. (Bordeaux: Maison des Sciences, 1978), 74.

49. Jacques Derrida, "The Law of Genre," 55.

different meanings of the sentence "genres are not to be mixed," but rather around different use-values of the same meaning. The two most obvious designations for the sentences as a speech act (Derrida claims there are innumerable possibilities) are constative (that is, explanatory, where genre is being defined as sorting, as the "not-to-be-mixedness" of discourse) and illocutionary (that is, imperative, trying to turn the audience away from its inevitable propensity toward generic miscegenation). Our inability to decide which use-value predominates defines the generic, and hence interpretive, instability of the sentence, that very mixing of genres which the sentence prohibits: "As soon as the word 'genre' is sounded, as soon as it is heard, as soon as one attempts to conceive it, a limit is drawn. And when a limit is established, norms and interdictions are not far behind: 'Do,' 'Do Not' says 'genre,' the word 'genre,' the figure, the voice, or the law of genre."[50] Thus, the term "genre" implies a separation always already denied by its linguistic formulation as a speech act. Like Wittgenstein's "brick," "genre" can be either command or deixis.

Thus, when I define something according to its use-value my definition cannot be paraphrased for three interrelated reasons: first, because use-value implies instrumentality in a certain type of action, rather than an equation with some other thing or with an abstract notion of value; second, because use-values are shifting rather than fixed—which is why generic systems are shifting, rather than fixed; third, because ideology, the political unconscious, lies beyond the limits of discourse. The ideological components of our generic distinctions are no more open to paraphrase than they are to naming. That is perhaps why philosophical attempts to come to grips with genre, such as Ortega y Gasset's or Benjamin's or Derrida's, end up as tautologies or metaphors or paradoxes.

Occasionally, the use-values of different genres become available for ready inspection. Perhaps the most notable example is Aristotle's identification of the genre of tragedy with catharsis. As interpreted and developed by Western theory, catharsis became the use-value of tragedy, particularly in eighteenth-century interpretations of the term as a refinement of the spectator's moral sensibilities. But even the cruder idea of catharsis as emotional release, which allows it to be transferred to sporting events and the like, is clearly a use-value. Similarly, Western theory has taken it for granted that catharsis was the dividing line between tragedy and comedy, that if the lost book of Aristotle's *Poetics*, in which he treats comedy, were

50. Ibid., 55–56.

ever to be found, the chief difference would be the replacement of catharsis by another use-value, such as the idea of ridicule found in Eco's *Rose.*

John D. Dorst, however, locates generic confrontation between folk genres in the realm of the unsaid: "Unlike open polemical confrontation, where contending points of view occur as explicitly stated positions, genre dialogues are nondiscursive. Their effects will be felt not as open argument, but as subterranean conflict over those aspects of reality that the generic participants conceptualize and fix differently. . . . The influence of one genre on another in such interactions is like the effect of an unseen planet on its neighbors."[51] Dorst devotes his attention to one example of this process, the neck-riddle as a "riddle/folktale deflecting and deflected by folktale/riddle."[52] The stakes in such a confrontation are very much like those I analyzed in the influence of litany on ballad in Bob Dylan's "Hard Rain." The riddle is essentially atemporal, not given to narrative. What happens, then, when it comes under the gravitational attraction, so to speak, of the folktale? One example Dorst gives is clear enough, if not particularly encouraging for riddle fans: "I killed no one and yet killed twelve." The answer to this riddle is that a man poisoned a chicken and fed it to twelve people, who all died. The riddle is solved not by the revelation of metaphoric relations or hidden conditions, but by rewriting it as a narrative.[53]

Benjamin's understanding of this "gravitational" relation between genre and ideology, and of genre's unsayability is expressed in his concept of *Ursprung.* Benjamin, always with the Goethean concepts of *Urbild* and *Urphänomen* in mind, emphasizes the word's literal meaning, that of an original or archetypal leap.[54] A work literally "springs out" of its historical period. Genre is discovered in this "extreme" confrontation between historical ambience and literary form:

> Ursprung, wiewohl durchaus historische Kategorie, hat mit Ent-
> stehung dennoch nichts gemein. Im Ursprung wird kein Werden
> des Entsprungenen, vielmehr dem Werden und Vergehen Ent-

51. John D. Dorst, "Neck-Riddle as a Dialogue of Genres," *Journal of American Folklore* 96 (October–December 1983): 421–22.

52. Ibid., 422.

53. Ibid., 425. Dorst calls at the end of his essay for a "*dialectics* that considers the relationship between genres and the larger social forces at work in concrete historical circumstances." This book begins one such elaboration.

54. On the link between Benjamin's *Ursprung* and the Goethean conceptions, see John Pizer, "Goethe's 'Urphänomen' and Benjamin's 'Ursprung': A Reconsideration," *Seminar: A Journal of Germanic Studies* 25 (September 1989): 205–22.

springendes gemeint. Der Ursprung steht im Fluß des Werdens als Strudel und reißt in seine Rhythmik das Entstehungsmaterial hinein. Im nackten offenkundigen Bestand des Faktischen gibt das Ursprüngliche sich niemals zu erkennen, und einzig einer Doppeleinsicht steht seine Rhythmik offen. Sie will als Restauration, als Wiederherstellung einerseits, als eben darin Unvollendetes, Unabgeschlossenes andererseits erkannt sein. In jedem Ursprungsphänomen bestimmt sich die Gestalt, unter welcher immer wieder eine Idee mit der geschichtlichen Welt sich auseinandersetzt, bis sie in der Totalität ihrer Geschichte vollendet daliegt. Also hebt sich der Ursprung aus dem tatsächlichen Befunde nicht heraus, sondern er betrifft dessen Vor- und Nachgeschichte. (267)

(The term origin is not intended to describe the process by which the existent came into being, but rather to describe that which emerges from the process of becoming and disappearance. Origin is an eddy in the stream of becoming, and in its current it swallows the material involved in the process of genesis. That which is original is never revealed in the naked and manifest existence of the factual; its rhythm is apparent only to a dual insight. On the one hand it needs to be recognized as a process of restoration and re-establishment, but, on the other hand, and precisely because of this, as something imperfect and incomplete. There takes place in every original phenomenon a determination of the form in which an idea will constantly confront the historical world, until it is revealed fulfilled, in the totality of its history. Origin is not, therefore, discovered by the examination of actual findings, but it is related to their history and their subsequent development. [45–47])

Much of Benjamin's meaning here lies in the difference—apparent enough in German but obscured by the English translation—between "ent*stehen*" and "ent*springen*." The first verb stem indicates a standing still, the other an abrupt movement. Their shared prefix *ent* indicates "out of." But the two common meanings of *entspringen* create a dialectic between coming into being (compare English "Spring" as a season of growth) and escaping from something. Therefore, when Benjamin writes "dem Werden und Vergehen Entspringendes" ("that which emerges from the process of becoming and disappearance") he is referring to origin as an absence, to the inevitable "escape" of the literary work from a system lacking positive terms.

One clear example of such a system is provided by the constellations we use to sort the firmament. One of Benjamin's most cogent metaphors describes things (here, texts) as stars, and ideas (here, genres) as their constellations: "Die Ideen verhalten sich zu den Dingen wie die Stern-bilder zu den Sternen" (214; "Ideas are to objects as constellations are to stars" [34]). Many peoples have observed the night sky as an interaction of ideas—one thinks of the origins of Greek myth, of the Mayan *Popol Vuh*, or of the "Southern Cross" in the fervent hopes of Magellan's sailors. The star-images (the German composite *Stern-bild* conveys the idea of an image written in the sky) divide up the night sky, including all the (visible) stars so that none survives on its own without a structure to distinguish it from the rest. This division is arbitrary in the Saussurean sense; the important thing is that the constellations be distinguishable from one another so that each can represent its idea. The constellation is grasped as a form rather than as a collection of features or a positioning. It is not a list of features by which stars can be grouped, but a central symbol (bull, archer, dragon, goat) of their relationship, a first attempt at interpreting their existence.

Years later, Roland Barthes would use a similar metaphor to describe the reading process:

> Le texte, dans sa masse, est comparable à un ciel, plat et profond à la fois, lisse, sans bords et sans repères; tel l'augure y découpant du bout de son bâton un rectangle fictif pour y interroger selon certains principes le vol des oiseaux, le commentateur trace le long du texte des zones de lecture, afin d'y observer la migration des sens.

> (The text, in its mass, is comparable to a sky, at once flat and smooth, deep, without edges and without landmarks; like the soothsayer drawing on it with the tip of his staff an imaginary rectangle wherein to consult, according to certain principles, the flight of birds, the commentator traces through the text certain zones of reading, in order to observe therein the migration of meanings.)[55]

55. Roland Barthes, *S/Z* (Paris: Seuil, 1970), 20; translated by Richard Miller, under the title *S/Z* (New York: Hill & Wang, 1974), 14.

One need only replace "text" with "discourse" to make this an analogy of genre as the "actualizer" of reading and writing. Discourses relate to their genres as constellations relate to their stars. Constellations are an imaginary way of representing real relationships between stars. Generic distinctions are imaginary in a similar way. Though the way we constellate texts changes as a function of history through the perspective of individual critics, genres designate relations between texts that are as real as the critical language we have developed and which we can scarcely avoid using in order to describe and understand the effects texts have on us. If there is something similar between *Tristes tropiques* and *Oroonoko*, between Dylan and Degenhardt, between *Die Elephantenuhr* and *Il nome della rosa*, that "something" belongs to the transient, unstable constellations I have drawn between these texts.

Bibliography of Genre Theory and Criticism

This by no means exhaustive bibliography contains works of genre theory as well as studies of specific genres with general theoretical interest.

Alter, Robert. *Partial Magic: The Novel as a Self-Conscious Genre.* Berkeley and Los Angeles: University of California Press, 1975.

Aristotle. *Poetiké.* Translated by Leon Golden, under the title *Aristotle's Poetics.* Englewood Cliffs, N.J.: Prentice-Hall, 1968.

Bakhtin, Mikhail. "Discourse in the Novel." In *The Dialogic Imagination: Four Essays,* translated by Caryl Emerson and Michael Holquist, ed. Michael Holquist, 259–422. Austin: University of Texas Press, 1981.

———. "Problema rechevyx zhanrov." In *Estetika slovesnogo tvorchestva,* 2d ed., 250–96. Moscow: Iskysstvo, 1986. Translated by Vern W. McGee, under the title "The Problem of Speech Genres." In *Mikhail Bakhtin, "Speech Genres" and Other Late Essays,* ed. Caryl Emerson and Michael Holquist, 34–72. Austin: University of Texas Press, 1986.

Barat, Jean-Claude, Pierre Orecchioni, and Alain Ricard, eds. *Théorie des genres et communication.* Bordeaux: Maison des Sciences, 1978.

Behrens, Irene. *Die Lehre von der Einteilung der Dichtkunst, vornehmlich vom 16. bis 19. Jahrhundert. Studien zur Geschichte der poetischen Gattungen.* Halle: M. Niemeyer, 1940.

Ben-Amos, Dan, ed. *Folklore Genres.* Austin: University of Texas Press, 1976.

Benjamin, Walter. "Der Erzähler. Betrachtungen zum Werk Nikolai Lesskows." In *Über Literatur,* 33–61. Frankfurt am Main: Suhrkamp, 1969.

———. *Der Ursprung des deutschen Trauerspiels.* In *Gesammelte Schriften* I.1, ed. Rolf Tiedemann. Frankfurt am Main: Suhrkamp, 1974. Translated by John Osborne, under the title *The Origin of German Tragic Drama.* London: New Left Books, 1977.

Benstock, Shari. *Textualizing the Feminine: On the Limits of Genre.* Norman: University of Oklahoma Press, 1991.

Bickmann, Claudia. *Der Gattungsbegriff im Spannungsfeld zwischen historischer Betrachtung und Systementwurf.* Marburger Germanistische Studien 2. Frankfurt and Bern: Peter Lang, 1984.

Boileau-Despréaux, Nicolas. *L'Art poétique.* Paris, 1674.

Bovet, Ernest. *Lyrisme, épopée, drame: Une loi de l'histoire littéraire expliquée par l'évolution générale.* Paris: A. Colin, 1911.

Briganti, Alessandra. "Sulla teoria dei generi letterari nel Novecento." *Cultura e Scuola* 24 (January–March 1985): 37–45.

Broeck, Raymond van den. "Generic Shifts in Translated Literary Texts." *New Comparison* 1 (Summer 1986): 104–16.

Brunecker, Jürgen. "Allgemeingültigkeit oder historische Bedingtheit der poetischen

Gattungen. Ein Hauptproblem der modernen Poetik. Herausgearbeitet an Dilthey, Unger und Staiger." Ph.D. diss., University of Kiel, 1954.

Brunetière, Ferdinand. *L'Évolution des genres dans l'histoire de la littérature*. Paris: Hachette, 1898.

Burke, Kenneth. *The Philosophy of Literary Form: Studies in Symbolic Action*. Baton Rouge: Louisiana State University Press, 1941. Reprint, New York: Vintage, 1957.

Cairns, Francis. *Generic Composition in Greek and Roman Poetry*. Edinburgh: Edinburgh University Press, 1972.

Caussade, François de. *Rhétorique et genres littéraires*. Paris: Masson, 1888.

Champigny, Robert. "For and Against Genre Labels." *Poetics* 10 (1981): 145–74.

Cilliers, Louise. "Genresisteme in die Klassieke Letterkunde en die nawerking daarvan die Westerse letterkunde." *Tydskrif vir Geesteswetenskappe* 28 (March 1988): 95–111.

Cobley, Evelyn. "Mikhail Bakhtin's Place in Genre Theory." *Genre* 21 (Fall 1988): 321–38.

Cohen, Ralph. "Do Postmodern Genres Exist?" *Genre* 20 (Fall–Winter 1987): 241–57.

———. "History and Genre." *New Literary History* 17 (1986): 203–18.

Colie, Rosalie L. *The Resources of Kind: Genre-Theory in the Renaissance*. Berkeley and Los Angeles: University of California Press, 1973.

Croce, Benedetto. "I 'generi letterari' a Congresso." *Critica* 37 (1939): 396–97.

Cysarz, Hans. "Die gattungsmäßigen Form-Möglichkeiten der heutigen Prosa." *Helicon* 2 (1940): 169–80.

Davis, Lennard J. *Resisting Novels: Ideology and Fiction*. New York: Columbia University Press, 1987.

Demerson, Guy, ed. *La Notion de genre à la Renaissance*. Geneva: Slatkine, 1984.

Derrida, Jacques. "The Law of Genre." Translated by Avital Ronell. *Critical Inquiry* 7 (Autumn 1980): 55–81.

Díaz-Plaja, Guillermo. *Teoría y historia de los géneros literarios*. Barcelona: La Espiga, 1940.

Donohue, James J. *The Theory of Literary Kinds*. 2 vols. Dubuque, Iowa: Loras College Press, 1943–49.

Dubrow, Heather. *Genre*. New York: Methuen, 1982.

Ehrenpreis, Irvin. *The "Types Approach" to Literature*. New York: King Crown Press, 1945.

Esin, A. B. "Tipologicheskie sootnosenija soderzhanija i formy." *Filologicheskie Nauki* 5 (1986): 37–42.

Étiemble, René. "Histoire des genres et littérature comparée." *Acta litteraria* 5 (1962): 203–7.

Fishelov, David. "Theories of Literary Genres: Metaphors and Reality." Ph.D. diss., University of California, Berkeley, 1987.

Flemming, Willi. "Das Problem von Dichtungsgattung und -art." *Studium Generale* 12 (1959): 38–60.

Fohrmann, Jürgen. "Remarks Towards a Theory of Literary Genres." *Poetics* 17 (June 1988): 273–85.

Fowler, Alastair. *Kinds of Literature: An Introduction to the Theory of Genres and Modes*. Cambridge: Harvard University Press, 1982.

———. "The Life and Death of Literary Forms." *New Literary History* 2 (1970): 199–216.

Freedman, Diane P. *An Alchemy of Genres: Cross-Genre Writing by American Feminist Poet-Critics*. Charlottesville: University Press of Virginia, 1992.

Frye, Northrop. "Rhetorical Criticism: Theory of Genres." In *Anatomy of Criticism*, 243–337. Princeton: Princeton University Press, 1971.

Fubini, Mario. "Genesi e storia dei generi letterari." In *Critica e poesia. Saggi e discorsi di teoria letteraria*, 2d ed., 127–257. Bari: Laterza, 1956.

Garasa, Delfín Leocadio. *Los géneros literarios*. Buenos Aires: Nuevos Esquemas, 1969.

Geertz, Clifford. "Blurred Genres: The Refiguration of Social Thought." In *Critical Theory Since 1965*, ed. Hazard Adams and Leroy Searle, 514–23. Tallahassee: Florida State University Press, 1986.

Genette, Gérard. *Introduction à l'architexte*. Paris: Seuil, 1979. Translated by Jane E. Lewin, under the title *The Architext: An Introduction*. Berkeley and Los Angeles: University of California Press, 1992.

Genette, Gérard, and Tzvetan Todorov, eds. *Théorie des genres*. Paris: Seuil, 1986.

"Genres." Special issue of *Poétique* 32 (November 1977).

Ghiano, Juan C. *Los géneros literarios. Principios griegos de su problemática*. 2d ed. Buenos Aires: Editorial Nova, 1961.

Green, Martin Burgess. *Seven Types of Adventure Tale: An Etiology of a Major Genre*. University Park: The Pennsylvania State University Press, 1991.

Guillén, Claudio. "Genere, contro-genere, sistema." In *Critica e storia letteraria. Studi offerti a Mario Fubini*, 2 vols., 1:153–74. Padua: Liviana, 1970.

———. *Literature as System: Essays Toward the Theory of Literary History*. Princeton: Princeton University Press, 1971.

———. "Poetics as System." *Comparative Literature* 22 (1970): 193–222.

Habermas, Jürgen. "Exkurs zur Einebnung des Gattungsunterschiedes zwischen Philosophie und Literatur." In *Der philosophische Diskurs der Moderne*, 219–47. Frankfurt am Main: Suhrkamp, 1985.

Hack, R. K. "The Doctrine of the Literary Forms." *Harvard Studies in Classical Philology* 27 (1916): 1–65.

Hair, Donald S. *Browning's Experiments with Genre*. Toronto: University of Toronto Press, 1972.

Hamburger, Käthe. *Die Logik der Dichtung*. 2d ed. Stuttgart: Klett, 1968.

Hartl, Robert. *Versuch einer psychologischen Grundlegung der Dichtungsgattungen*. Vienna: Österreichischer Schulbücherverlag, 1924.

Hempfer, Klaus W. *Gattungstheorie: Information und Synthese*. Munich: Wilhelm Fink, 1973.

Hermand, Jost. "Probleme der heutigen Gattungsgeschichte." *Jahrbuch für Internationale Germanistik* 2 (1970): 85–94.

Hernadi, Paul. *Beyond Genre: New Directions in Literary Classification*. Ithaca: Cornell University Press, 1972.

———. "Entertaining Commitments: A Reception Theory of Literary Genres." *Poetics* 10 (1981): 195–211.

Hirsch, E. D. *Validity in Interpretation*. New Haven: Yale University Press, 1965.

Hirt, Ernst. *Das Formgesetz der epischen, dramatischen und lyrischen Dichtung*. Leipzig and Berlin: B. G. Teubner, 1923.

Horace. *Ars poetica*. Ed. Augustus S. Wilkins. New York: St. Martin's Press, 1960.

Hutcheon, Linda. *A Theory of Parody: The Teachings of 20th-Century Art Forms*. New York: Methuen, 1985.

Jameson, Fredric. *The Political Unconscious: Narrative as a Socially Symbolic Act*. Ithaca: Cornell University Press, 1981.

Jauß, Hans-Robert. "Theorie der Gattungen und Literatur des Mittelalters." In

Grundriß der romanischen Literaturen des Mittelalters, 3 vols., ed. H.-R. Jauß and E. Köhler, 1:107–38. Heidelberg: Carl Winter, 1972.

Johnson, Barbara. *Défigurations du langage poétique: La Seconde Révolution Baudelairienne.* Paris: Flammarion, 1979.

Jolles, André. *Einfache Formen: Legende, Sage, Mythe, Rätsel, Spruch, Kasus, Memorabile, Märchen, Witz.* 2d ed. Halle: M. Niemeyer, 1956.

Kambobureli, Smaro. *On the Edge of Genre: The Contemporary Canadian Long Poem.* Toronto: University of Toronto Press, 1991.

Kent, Thomas. "The Classification of Genres." *Genre* 16 (Spring 1983): 1–20.

Kiefer, Barbara, ed. *Renaissance Genres: Essays on Theory, History, and Interpretation.* Cambridge: Harvard University Press, 1986.

Kleiner, Juliusz. "The Role of Time in Literary Genres." *Zagadnienia Rodzajów Literackich* 2 (1959): 5–12.

Kohler, Pierre. "Contribution à une philosophie des genres." *Helicon* 1 (1939): 233–44; 2 (1940): 96–147.

Kristeva, Julia. *La Révolution du langage poétique.* Paris: Seuil, 1974.

Langbaum, Robert. *The Poetry of Experience: The Dramatic Monologue in Modern Literary Tradition.* New York: W. W. Norton, 1957.

Layoun, Mary N. *Travels of a Genre: The Modern Novel and Ideology.* Princeton: Princeton University Press, 1990.

Lefevere, André. "Systems in Evolution: Historical Relativism and the Study of Genre." *Poetics Today* 6 (1985): 665–79.

LeJeune, Philippe. *Le Pacte autobiographique.* Paris: Seuil, 1975. Translated by Katherine M. Leary, under the title *On Autobiography.* Minneapolis: University of Minnesota Press, 1988.

Lerner, Lawrence. *Frontiers of Literature.* Oxford: Oxford University Press, 1988.

Letourneau, Charles. "Origins of Literary Forms." *Popular Science Monthly* 43 (May–October 1893): 673–82.

Lewalski, Barbara Kiefer, ed. *Renaissance Genres: Essays on Theory, History, and Interpretation.* Cambridge: Harvard University Press, 1986.

Lotman, Jurij M. "Problems in the Typology of Texts." In *Soviet Semiotics: An Anthology,* ed. and trans. Daniel P. Lucid, 119–24. Baltimore: Johns Hopkins University Press, 1977.

Lukács, Georg. *Probleme des Realismus III. Der historische Roman.* Berlin: Luchterhand, 1965.

———. *Theorie des Romans. Ein geschichtsphilosophischer Versuch über die Formen der großen Epik.* Berlin: Cassirer, 1920. Translated by Anna Bostock, under the title *The Theory of the Novel.* Cambridge: MIT Press, 1973.

Manly, J. M. "Literary Form and the Origin of Species." *Modern Philology* 4 (April 1907): 577–95.

Mantz, Harold Elmer. "Types in Literature." *Modern Language Review* 12 (1917): 469–79.

Marias, Julian. "Les Genres littéraires en philosophie." *Revue internationale de philosophie* 23 (1969): 495–508.

Matthes, Lothar. "Transgressions littéraires de frontières linguistiques et culturelles: A propos de l'importation de genres littéraires d'origine anglo-saxonne en France." *Textes et Langages* 12 (1986): 105–14.

Meyer, Bernard. "Synecdoques du genre." *Poétique* 14 (February 1984): 37–52.

Miner, Earl. *Comparative Poetics: An Intercultural Essay on Theories of Literature.* Princeton: Princeton University Press, 1990.

Morson, Gary Saul. *The Boundaries of Genre: Dostoevsky's "Diary of a Writer" and the Traditions of Literary Utopia.* Austin: University of Texas Press, 1981.

Moseley, E. M. "Religion and the Literary Genres." *Comparative Literature Studies* 2 (1965): 335–48.

Mücke, Dorothea E. von. *Virtue and the Veil of Illusion: Generic Innovation and the Pedagogical Project in Eighteenth-Century Literature.* Stanford: Stanford University Press, 1991.

Müller, Günther. "Bemerkungen zur Gattungspoetik." *Philosophischer Anzeiger* 3 (1928): 129–47.

Ortega y Gassett, José. "Meditación primera." In *Meditaciones del Quijote.* 2d ed., 127–94. Madrid: Calpe, 1921. Translated by Evelyn Rugg and Diego Marín, under the title "First Meditation. A Short Treatise on the Novel." In *Meditations on Quixote,* 111–65. New York: W. W. Norton, 1963.

Peavler, Terry J. *Individuations: The Novel as Dissent.* Lanham, Md.: University Press of America, 1988.

Perez-Firmat, Gustavo. "The Novel as Genres." *Genre* 12 (1979): 269–92.

Perloff, Marjorie. "Barthes and the Zero Degree of Genre." *World Literature Today* 59 (Autumn 1985): 510–16.

Pratt, Mary Louise. *Toward a Speech-Act Theory of Literary Discourse.* Bloomington: Indiana University Press, 1977.

Propp, Vladimir. *Morphology of the Folktale.* Translated by Lawrence Scott. 2d ed. Austin: University of Texas Press, 1968.

Radway, Janice. *Reading the Romance: Women, Patriarchy, and Popular Literature.* Chapel Hill: University of North Carolina Press, 1984.

Reichert, J. F. " 'Organizing Principles' and Genre Theory." *Genre* 1 (1968): 1–12.

Reid, Ian. "Genre and Framing: The Case of Epitaphs." *Poetics* 17 (April 1988): 25–35.

———. *The Place of Genre in Learning: Current Debates.* Geelong, Victoria: Centre for Studies in Literary Education, Deakin University, 1987.

Rich, Mabel Irene. *A Study of the Types of Literature.* 2d ed. New York: Appleton-Century, 1937.

Rodway, Allan. "Generic Criticism: The Approach through Type, Mode and Kind." In *Contemporary Criticism.* Stratford upon Avon Studies 12. New York: St. Martin's Press, 1970.

Rosmarin, Adena. *The Power of Genre.* Minneapolis: University of Minnesota Press, 1985.

Ruiz Soto, Alfonso. "Una teoría dinámica de los géneros literarios y no literarios." In *Teoría semiótica: Lenguajes y textos hispánicos,* ed. Garrido Gallardo and Miguel Angel, 593–99. Madrid: Consejo Superior de Investigaciones Científicas, 1985.

Ruttkowski, W. V. *Die literarischen Gattungen. Reflexionen über eine modifizierte Fundamentalpoetik.* Bern and Munich: Francke, 1968.

Ryan, Marie-Laure. "Introduction: On the Why, What and How of Generic Taxonomy." *Poetics* 10 (1981): 109–26.

Sacks, Sheldon. "Toward a Grammar of the Types of Fiction." In *Fiction and the Shape of Belief: A Study of Henry Fielding with Glances at Swift, Johnson, and Richardson,* 1–69. Chicago: University of Chicago Press, 1980.

Samson, John. *White Lies: Melville's Narratives of Facts.* Ithaca: Cornell University Press, 1989.

Scherpe, Klaus R. *Gattungspoetik im 18. Jahrhundert. Historische Entwicklung von Gottsched bis Herder.* Stuttgart: Metzler, 1968.

Schlegel, Friedrich. "Gespräch über die Poesie." In *Charakteristiken und Kritiken I*, ed. Hans Eichner, 284–362. Vol. 2, part 1, of the *Kritische Friedrich-Schlegel-Ausgabe.* Zurich: Ferdinand Schöningh, 1967. Translated by Ernst Behler and Roman Struč, under the title "Dialogue on Poetry." In *Dialogue on Poetry and Literary Aphorisms*, 53–105. University Park: The Pennsylvania State University Press, 1968.

Sengle, Friedrich. *Die literarische Formenlehre. Vorschläge zu ihrer Reform.* 2d ed. Stuttgart: Metzler, 1967.

Shaeffer, Jean-Marie. "Du texte au genre: Notes sur la problématique génératique." *Poétique* 12 (February 1983): 3–18.

Skwarczynska, Stefanie. "Un Cas particulier d'orchestration générique de l'œuvre littéraire." In *To Honor Roman Jakobson*, 3 vols., 3:1832–56. Janua Linguarum, series maior, 31–33. The Hague: Mouton, 1967.

Smith, Barbara Herrnstein. *On the Margins of Discourse.* Chicago: University of Chicago Press, 1978.

Snyder, John. *Prospects of Power: Tragedy, Satire, the Essay, and the Theory of Genre.* Lexington: University Press of Kentucky, 1991.

Stewart, Susan. *Nonsense: Aspects of Intertextuality in Folklore and Literature.* Baltimore: Johns Hopkins University Press, 1979.

Strelka, Joseph P., ed. *Theories of Literary Genre.* University Park: Pennsylvania State University Press, 1978.

Stutterheim, C. F. P. "De theorie der literaire genres." In *Feestbundel angeboden door vrienden en leerlingen aan Prof. Dr. H. J. Pos*, 128–41. Amsterdam: N. V. Noordhollandsche Uitgevers Maaschappij, 1948.

Szili, Jóseph. "Genres in Literature and Non-Literature." *Neohelicon* 13, no. 1 (1986): 37–56.

Szondi, Peter. "Historische Ästhetik und Gattungspoetik." In *Theorie des modernen Dramas*, 4th ed., 9–13. Frankfurt: Suhrkamp, 1967.

————. "La Théorie des genres poétiques chez Friedrich Schlegel." *Critique* 225 (1968): 264–92.

Takei, Ferenc. *Genre Theory in China in the 3rd–6th Centuries (Liu Hsieh's Theory on Poetic Genres).* Budapest: Akademiai Kiado, 1971.

Tarot, Rolf. "Mimesis und Imitatio. Grundlagen einer neuen Gattungspoetik." *Euphorion* 64 (1970): 125–42.

Tieghem, Paul van. "La Question des genres littéraires." *Helicon* 1 (1939): 95–101.

Todorov, Tzvetan. *Les Genres du discours.* Paris: Seuil, 1978. Translated by Catherine Porter, under the title *Genres in Discourse.* Cambridge: Cambridge University Press, 1990.

————. *Introduction à la littérature fantastique.* Paris: Seuil, 1970. Translated by Richard Howard, under the title *The Fantastic: A Structural Approach to a Literary Genre.* Cleveland: Press of Case Western Reserve University, 1973.

————. "The Origin of Genres." *New Literary History* 8 (Autumn 1976): 159–70.

————. "A Typology of Detective Fiction." In *The Poetics of Prose*, translated by Richard Howard, 42–52. Ithaca: Cornell University Press, 1977.

Tomashevski, Boris. *Teorija literatury.* 4th ed. Moscow and Leningrad: State Publishing House, 1925.

Trzynadlowski, Jan. "Information Theory and Literary Genres" (in Polish). *Zagadnienia Rodzajów Literackich* 4, no. 1 (1961): 27–45.

Van Vliet, Lucille W. *Approaches to Literature Through Genre.* Phoenix: Oryx Press, 1992.

Viëtor, Karl. "Die Geschichte der literarischen Gattungen." In *Geist und Form. Aufsätze zur deutschen Literaturgeschichte,* 292–309. Bern: Francke, 1952.

———. "Probleme der literarischen Gattungsgeschichte." *Deutsche Vierteljahresschrift für Literaturwissenschaft und Geistesgeschichte* 9 (1931): 425–47.

Vincent, Claude. *Théorie des genres littéraires.* Paris: C. Poussielgue, 1902.

Vivas, Eliseo. "Literary Classes. Some Problems." *Genre* 1 (1968): 97–105.

Watt, Ian. *The Rise of the Novel: Studies in Defoe, Richardson, and Fielding.* Berkeley and Los Angeles: University of California Press, 1967.

Weissenberger, Klaus, ed. *Prosakunst ohne Erzählen: Die Gattungen der nicht-fiktionalen Kunstprosa.* Tübingen: Niemeyer, 1985.

Wellek, René. "Genre Theory, the Lyric and 'Erlebnis.' " In *Discriminations,* 225–52. New Haven: Yale University Press, 1970.

Whitmore, Charles E. "The Validity of Literary Definitions." *PMLA* 39 (1924): 722–36.

Wicke, Jennifer. *Advertising Fictions: Literature, Advertisement, and Social Reading.* New York: Columbia University Press, 1988.

Yaari, Monique. "Questions de mode et de genre." In *Ironie paradoxale et ironie poétique: Vers une théorie de l'ironie moderne sur les traces de Gide dans "Paludes,"* 69–94. Birmingham, Ala.: Summa, 1988.

Zéraffa, Michel. "Le Genre et sa crise." *Degrés* 12 (Autumn–Winter 1984): 1–19.

Zutski, Margot. *Literary Theory in Germany: A Study of Genre and Evaluation Theories, 1945–1965.* Las Vegas: Lang, 1981.

Index

Works are listed under authors' names; cities (other than U.S. cities) are listed under country names. Individual genres and genre topics are listed as subheadings of the section "genre(s)," while theorists of genre are listed under "genre theory."

Höllerer, Walter, (cont'd)
  Gustaf Lorch, 222–24, 228, 240
  plot of, 218–19
  semiology exhibit, 227
Holmes, Sherlock, 231–33
Homer, 11
  Iliad, 24 n. 42, 266 n. 26
  Odyssey, 24 n. 42
Horace, 246. *See also* genre theory:
    Horace's
Hornbeak, Katherine, 70, 71
Houssaye, Arsène, 128
Howard, Richard, 117, 156 n. 13
Hugh of Saint Victor, 217
Hugo, Victor, 147
  Hernani (drama), 147
Hunt, Lynn, 86

ideology, 15–19 passim, 31–32, 71 n. 7, 83,
    86, 90 n. 27, 91, 99, 107–9, 111, 116,
    121, 175, 190, 233, 278. *See also*
    genre(s): ideology of
internats, 79–111 passim
  Écouen, 84, 102–4
  Maisons impériales, 102
  Saint-Cyr, 93–94, 102
  Saint-Denis, 84
  Saint-Germain, 102
  Saint-Louis, 102
Italy, 225, 234
  Bari, 227–28, 244
  Bologna, 227
  Montecassino, 248
  Rome, 221, 241–42
    Roman Empire, 221
    Testaccio Hill, 221, 227, 247
Ives, Burl, 179

Janin, Jules, 79
Japan, 113–16, 147, 219, 242
  absence of signified in, 117–21
  anti-Christian practices of, 115 n. 3
  art of, 113–14, 143–44, 146
  Barthes's view of, 117–25
  isolationism, 115
  novel in, 125 n. 16
  Tokyo, 119, 121, 244
  as Western invention, 113, 115–16, 118,
    141–42
japanery. *See* genre(s): prose poem
Jean-Paul. *See* Richter, Jean-Paul

Jerusalem, 208
Johnson, Barbara, 130, 135, 137
Joyce, James, 230

Kafka, Franz, 172, 174
  "Before the Law" (short story), 175
Kalevala (epic), 24 n. 42
Kant, Immanuel, 28, 150
Kauffman, Linda, 110
Kevelson, Roberta, 153
Kissinger, Henry, 6, 14
Knight, Charles, 159, 168
Kristeva, Julia, 269 n. 31

Lacan, Jacques, 15, 16 n. 30
Laclos, Choderlos de, *Les Liaisons danger-
    euses* (novel), 67–68, 71, 92–93
law. *See* genre(s): legal discourse
sLeach, Edmund, 35
Léry, Jean de, 33
Lesage, Alain René, 79
Les Lettres Françaises (journal), 127
Levant, 115
Lévi-Strauss, Claude, 15, 28
  and Brazil, 32, 35, 39
  Dina Dreyfus (wife) and, 32, 47–48
  Elementary Structures of Kinship Relations,
    64–65
  Jewish background, 64–66
  on Martinique, 32, 40, 54, 226
  membership in Académie Française, 33
  The Raw and the Cooked, 44
  The Savage Mind, 59 n. 39
  theories of
    bricolage, 40, 43–44, 113, 244, 246, 255
    bricoleur, 40
    myth, 40, 45, 47
    nature vs. culture, 46–47
    structuralism, 40–41, 43, 55 n. 33, 64–
      65
    writing, 34, 53–54, 87–88
  travels of, 32–33
  Tristes tropiques, 11, 31–66 passim, 117,
    174, 254, 264, 283
    chapters of: "L'Apothéose d'Auguste"
      (The apotheosis of Augustus) 41–
      48; "Caduveo" (A native society
      and its style), 40; "La Fin des
      voyages" (An end to traveling),
      39; "La Leçon d'écriture" (The
      writing lesson), 54–56, 87–88;